THE EUROPEAN
EQUITY MARKETS

The **European Capital Markets Institute** was founded in 1993 as an independent non-profit organization aiming to serve as a central forum for practitioners and academics. The principal objective of the Institute is to initiate projects, programmes, and conferences related to the functioning and growth of the European capital markets, and to the development of cross-border trading and investment.

The Institute's founding members are the European Federation of Financial Analysts' Societies (EFFAS), the Federation of European Stock Exchanges (FESE), and the International Securities Market Association (ISMA). Ordinary membership is open to European companies, institutions, associations in the financial sector and industry, and business-oriented universities and business schools.

Enquiries should be directed to the *European Capital Markets Institute, c/o Copenhagen Stock Exchange, 6 Nikolaj Plads, Box 1040, 1007 Copenhagen K, Denmark, telephone +45 3393 3366, fax +45 3312 8613.*

THE EUROPEAN EQUITY MARKETS

The State of the Union and an Agenda for the Millennium

BENN STEIL

with Erik Berglöf, Frederick D.S. Choi, Richard Dale, E. Philip Davis, Jeffrey A. Frankel, Ian Giddy, Richard M. Levich, Marco Pagano, Anthony Saunders, Robert A. Schwartz, Ingo Walter, and Simon Wolfe

ECMI

RIIA

First published in Great Britain in 1996 by
Royal Institute of International Affairs, 10 St James's Square, London SW1Y 4LE
(Charity Registration No. 208 223) and the European Capital Markets Institute,
c/o Copenhagen Stock Exchange, 6 Nikolaj Plads, Box 1040,
1007 Copenhagen K, Denmark

Distributed worldwide by
The Brookings Institution, 1775 Massachusetts Avenue NW,
Washington DC 20036-2188, USA

British Library Cataloguing in Publication Data
A CIP catalogue record for this book is available from the British Library.

Hardback: ISBN 1 899658 10 6
Paperback: ISBN 1 899658 11 4

Printed and bound in Great Britain by Redwood Books Ltd, Trowbridge, Wilts.
Cover design by Robert Steil.

CONTENTS

ABOUT THE AUTHORS

PROJECT DIRECTOR AND EDITOR

Benn Steil is Head of the International Economics Programme at the Royal Institute of International Affairs in London. He is also an Associate Fellow of the Financial Options Research Centre at Warwick Business School, and a member of the Advisory Board of the European Capital Markets Institute. Previously, he held a Lloyd's of London Tercentenary Research Fellowship at Nuffield College, Oxford. Dr Steil has written and spoken widely in the area of international financial market regulation, his previous book being an edited volume of this title for John Wiley Publishers. His other areas of published research include derivatives, risk management, and decision theory. Dr Steil has also worked for investment banks in New York and London, both in systems analysis and foreign exchange.

CHAPTER 1

Equity Trading I: The Evolution of European Trading Systems

MARCO PAGANO AND BENN STEIL

Marco Pagano is Associate Professor of Economics at Università degli Studi di Napoli Federico II, Naples, and Research Fellow at the Centre for Economic Policy Research, London. His research interests are in the fields of finance and macroeconomics. His early research in finance centred on the relationship between trading volume, price volatility, and liquidity in security markets. More recently, Professor Pagano's contributions (joint with Dr Ailsa Röell of the London School of Economics) have analysed the relationship between market transparency and liquidity, and the relative merits of dealer and auction markets, drawing on evidence about dually-traded European equities.

CHAPTER 2

Equity Trading II: Integration, Fragmentation, and the Quality of Markets

ROBERT A. SCHWARTZ

Robert A. Schwartz is Professor of Finance and Economics and Yamaichi Faculty Fellow at New York University's Leonard N. Stern School of Business, where he has been a member of the faculty since 1965. His recent research is in the area of financial economics, with a primary focus on the microstructure and architecture of securities markets. His publications have appeared in such journals as the *Journal of Finance, Journal of Financial Economics, Journal of Financial and Quantitative Analysis, Journal of Political Economy,* and the *Journal of Portfolio Management.* He is author of *Reshaping the Equity Markets: A Guide for the 1990s,* Harper Business (1991, reissued by Business One Irwin, 1993), *Equity Markets: Structure, Trading and Performance,* Harper and Row (1988), and co-author of *The Microstructure of Securities Markets,* Prentice-Hall (1986). Professor Schwartz has been a consultant to various market centres, including the New York Stock Exchange, the American Stock Exchange, the National Association of Securities Dealers, Instinet, the Arizona Stock Exchange, Deutsche Börse, and the Bolsa Mexicana. From April 1983 to April 1988, Professor Schwartz was an associate editor of *The Journal of Finance.*

CHAPTER 3

Equity Trading III: Institutional Investor Trading Practices and Preferences

ROBERT A. SCHWARTZ AND BENN STEIL

CHAPTER 4

Equity Trading IV: The ISD and the Regulation of European Market Structure

BENN STEIL

CHAPTER 5

Corporate Governance

ERIK BERGLÖF

Erik Berglöf is Assistant Professor at the European Centre for Advanced Research in Economics (ECARE) in Brussels and is currently visiting Stanford University. He is a Research Fellow at the Centre for Economic Policy Research and serves on the academic panel set up by the European Commission to review the Internal Market Programme. Dr Berglöf has written widely on the topic of corporate governance, including publications in the *Quarterly Journal of Economics, Journal of Financial Economics,* and the *Journal of Law, Economics and Organization.* He has also contributed to books such as *Institutional Investors and Corporate Governance* (editors: Baums and Buxbaum), and *The Firm as a Nexus of Treaties* (editors: Aoki, Gustafson, and Williamson).

CHAPTER 6

Pension Fund Investments

E. PHILIP DAVIS

E. Philip Davis has worked at the Bank of England since leaving Oxford University in 1980, except for two spells on secondment: to the Bank for International Settlements in 1985–87, and, currently, to the European Monetary Institute. He is also a research associate of the Financial Markets Group at the London School of Economics. He has published widely in the fields of institutional investment, euromarkets, banking, corporate finance, financial regulation, and financial stability. His major projects include books published by Oxford University Press entitled *Debt, Financial Fragility and Systemic Risk* (1992, revised edition 1995) and *Pension Funds, Retirement Income Security and Capital Markets* (1995).

CHAPTER 7

Capital Standards

RICHARD DALE AND SIMON WOLFE

Richard Dale took his first degree in Economics at the London School of Economics. Subsequently he qualified as a barrister and was awarded a PhD in law and economics. Prior to becoming an academic Professor Dale worked for merchant bankers N.M. Rothschild and Sons. Professor Dale has written extensively on the subject of financial regulation and recently completed a fellowship at the Bank of England, undertaking research on the regulation of European securities markets. He has also testified before US Congressional Committees, acted as an advisor to UK parliamentary committees, and undertaken consultancy work for the UK Treasury. Professor Dale is author of *International Banking Regulation* (Woodhead-Faulkener 1980) and *International Banking Deregulation* (Blackwell 1992), and co-author of *Banks and Bad Debts* (John Wiley 1995).

Simon Wolfe is a Lecturer in Finance at the University of Southampton. He worked in industry for a number of years before becoming an academic. His current research focus is on the financial implications of environmental legislation for the UK banking industry. Other areas of research include market value accounting, financial regulation, and the Japanese financial system.

CHAPTER 8

Accounting Diversity

FREDERICK D.S. CHOI AND RICHARD M. LEVICH

Frederick D.S. Choi is Research Professor of Accounting and International Business at New York University's Leonard N. Stern School of Business. He served as Chairman of NYU's Department of Accounting Taxation and Business Law from 1983–86, and is former Director of the Vincent C. Ross Institute of Accounting Research. His current research focus is on the information content of foreign accounting numbers, the capital market effects of accounting diversity, and issues associated with international statement analysis. Professor Choi is currently serving as Editor of *The Journal of International Financial Management and Accounting* and is a member of the ALCPA's International Accounting Standards Advisory Committee.

Richard M. Levich is Professor of Finance and International Business at New York University's Leonard N. Stern School of Business. From 1984–88 he served as the Chairman of Stern's International Business Program. He is also a Research Associate with the National Bureau of Economic Research in Cambridge, Massachusetts, and he currently serves as Editor of *The Journal of International Financial Management and Accounting*. Professor Levich has been a visiting faculty member at the University of Chicago, Yale University, the University of New South Wales (Australia), and City University Business School (London), and a visiting scholar at the Board of Governors of the Federal Reserve System and the International Monetary Fund. He has lectured on international economic issues at many institutions in the United States and overseas. Professor Levich is now writing his next book, *International Financial Markets: Prices and Policies* (Irwin Publishing, 1996 forthcoming).

CHAPTER 9

Clearance and Settlement

IAN GIDDY, ANTHONY SAUNDERS, AND INGO WALTER

Ian Giddy is on the faculty of the Stern School of Business at New York University. In the past he has been Director of the International Product Group at Drexel Burnham Lambert. He has also held appointments at the Wharton School of the University of Pennsylvania, Columbia University, the University of Michigan, the University of Chicago, and Georgetown University. He has served in the US Government at the Comptroller of the Currency and at the Board of Governors of the Federal Reserve System. Dr Giddy has served as a consultant to a number of multinational corporations and financial institutions, including Credit Suisse, Yamaichi Securities, Banca Commerciale Italiana, Barclays, Deutsche Bank, First Boston, Morgan Stanley, and Citibank. He is co-author of *The International Money Market* and *Cases in International Finance,* and co-editor of the two-volume *International Finance Handbook.* His latest book, *Global Financial Markets,* will be published this year.

Anthony Saunders is the John M. Schiff Professor at the Stern School of Business at New York University. Professor Saunders specializes in financial institutions and international banking. He is currently on the Executive Committee of the Salomon Brothers Center for the Study of Financial Institutions, as well as on the Board of Academic Consultants of the Federal Reserve Board of Governors and the Council of Research Advisors for the Federal National Mortgage Association. His research has been published in all of the major money and banking journals and in several books. He is the editor of *The Journal of Financial Markets, Instruments and Institutions.*

Ingo Walter is the Charles Simon Professor of Applied Financial Economics at the Stern School of Business, New York University, and also serves as Director of the New York University Salomon Center. He also holds a joint appointment as the Swiss Bank Corporation Professor of International Management, INSEAD, Fontainebleau, France. Professor Walter's principal areas of academic and consulting activity include international trade policy, international banking, environmental economics, and the economics of multinational corporate operations. His most recent book is *Global Financial Services*, published by Harper Collins in 1990 and co-authored with Professor Roy C. Smith. At present, his interests focus on competitive structure, conduct, and performance in the international banking and financial services industry, as well as international trade and investment issues.

CHAPTER 10

Exchange Rates and the Single Currency

JEFFREY A. FRANKEL

Jeffrey A. Frankel is a Senior Fellow at the Institute for International Economics in Washington, DC, and Professor of Economics at the University of California, Berkeley, where he is also Director of the Center for International and Development Economics Research. Currently he is a member of the Presidential Economic Policy Advisory Board, Council of Economic Advisers, Washington, DC. Professor Frankel is a specialist in international economics, finance, and macroeconomics. His research interests include targets and indicators for monetary policy, international macroeconomic policy coordination, the workings of the foreign exchange market, the globalization of financial markets, financial and trade issues in Japan and the Pacific, and regional economic blocs. Papers published in 1994 include 'The Constrained Asset Share Estimation (CASE) Method: Testing Mean-Variance Efficiency of the US Stock Market', *Journal of Empirical Finance,* and 'An Indicator of Future Inflation Extracted from the Steepness of the Interest Rate Yield Curve Along its Entire Length', *Quarterly Journal of Economics* (both with co-authors).

PREFACE

This study, the first major research effort sponsored by the European Capital Markets Institute, was motivated by a strong consensus in the ECMI Board and Advisory Board on the need for a comprehensive and independent investigation into the barriers to European equity market integration which would remain after implementation of the Investment Services Directive in 1996. As is well documented in the study, these barriers are still many and substantial, although in some cases the forces of competition and technological advance are already making considerable progress in overcoming them.

In preparing this material, the authors have benefited enormously from the contributions of well over a thousand market participants and government officials from across Europe. In addition to our personal interviews, we conducted three major questionnaire-based studies involving 800 institutional investors and 500 corporate issuers. All of the authors wish to express their gratitude for the extraordinary level of cooperation and support we received.

I would also like to acknowledge gratefully the additional financial and data processing support of *Institutional Investor* magazine for the investor trading survey discussed in Chapter 3, as well as financial support from The Leverhulme Trust for the specific research on European financial market regulation.

In preparing the text for publication, I had the benefit of truly extraordinary support from Hannah Doe and Margaret May of the Royal Institute of International Affairs. They are the epitome of dedication and professionalism, and I could not have picked more suitable colleagues to share my suffering.

Finally, I would like to express my personal gratitude to the ECMI Secretary General, Poul Erik Skaanning-Jørgensen, and to the members of ECMI who have provided invaluable support and personal assistance throughout the project. I hope and expect that the Institute will continue to grow and prosper, as it represents a unique vehicle for promoting interest in and the development of the European capital markets.

Of course, responsibility for the content of the report and for the views expressed lies wholly with the authors, and not with the Board or members of ECMI or with any institutions with which the authors are associated.

I trust there will be no shortage of alternative views in the market.

December 1995 Benn Steil

EXECUTIVE SUMMARY

This study investigates the barriers to European equity market integration which will remain after implementation of the Investment Services Directive (ISD) in 1996, and puts forward market-oriented proposals for eliminating them. The premise underlying our proposals is that the ultimate structure of the European equity markets should, to the greatest degree possible, be determined by market forces rather than political edict. On the demand side of the markets, we wish to see firms able to raise capital more cheaply and efficiently by facilitating access to equity-trading and trade-processing systems on a pan-European basis. On the supply side, we wish to see greater scope for investors to improve their risk-return profiles through expanded and more efficient access to pan-European equity investment opportunities. Within the confines of a sensible European competition policy, we wish to see market service providers afforded expanded opportunities for both collaborative and competitive initiatives across Europe.

EQUITY TRADING

The past decade has been one of remarkable change for European stock exchanges. Trading structures, systems, and rules have been completely revamped, largely in response to the early competitive success of the London dealer market. Since 1991, the trading structure through which London dealers made their markets in continental equities – the London Stock Exchange's SEAQ International – has been crumbling, owing to increasing competition from new continental electronic auction markets and the declining profitability of 'all weather' market making in London. While the London Stock Exchange, as distinct from its members, has effectively ceased playing any material role in continental equity trading, London-based trading houses continue to be a major force shaping the development of European trading. Gradually, the European dealer market which developed under the structure of SEAQ International is becoming a pan-European telephone and proprietary data screen network. This network operates in tandem with the electronic auction systems of the national exchanges, and while the two layers compete for customer order flow, they are also each dependent on the liquidity supplied by the other. In the absence of government intervention, we can expect market forces to generate a mix of auction and dealer trading services appropriate to the diverse needs of retail and institutional investors.

Increasingly, we expect that these services will be offered by private companies owned outside the primary national exchanges. Proprietary electronic trading, brokerage, order routing, price dissemination, and post-trade support systems will further drive down trading costs through improved technology, lower overheads, and bypassing oligopolistic intermediaries. This competitive pressure may be further increased through the cross-border expansion of exchange trading systems via remote membership. As the market for trading services becomes increasingly contestable, European exchanges will be forced to react by widening access, reducing fees, hiving off ancillary services, expanding their product range, and instituting new and cheaper modes of transacting. In order to do this, they may first have to undergo painful organizational restructuring, generally involving the dilution of member-firm control and increasing the direct influence of issuers and investors.

The most critical factor in determining the European market structure of the future will be the growth of trading by institutional investors. As institutions increase the size of their portfolios of stock and liquid instruments, their trading desks will increasingly dictate modes of trading to exchanges and intermediaries. Our survey of the trading practices and preferences of European institutional investors revealed the following findings:

- European investors are becoming aware of and concerned about the costs of trade intermediation and immediate execution, and would be willing to make considerable use of alternative electronic trading vehicles which provide less immediacy but lower transaction costs.
- Sixty-nine percent of respondents expected over 1 in 10 European equity trades to be transacted through new proprietary trading systems (PTSs) by the end of the decade.
- PTSs are expected to outperform SEAQ on 9 of 11 major trading system features; in particular, transaction costs and anonymity.
- Many of the market structure provisions of the ISD are not conducive to investor interests. In particular, the concentration provisions (Article 14.3) are a potential barrier to the expansion of PTS and dealer trading of exchange-listed stocks, both of which are widely favoured by investors. As the concentration provisions are optional for Member States, we urge that they not be applied. Additionally, over three-quarters of respondents rejected the need for minimum transparency requirements to be set at the European level, and over half indicated that they should be set by the individual stock exchanges themselves.

Our analysis of the history of the ISD reveals that the redrafting of the text in the Council of Ministers resulted in a considerable dilution of its liberalizing potential. In particular, the introduction of the legal concept of a 'regulated market', defined wholly in terms of listing and transparency requirements, gives rise to considerable scope for *new* protectionism on behalf of national stock exchanges. We therefore conclude that the effective liberalization of European equity trading lies not with EU directives, but rather with the enlightened self-interest of the Member State governments, and particularly with the pressure generated by market participants aggressively pursuing cross-border commercial opportunities.

Current thinking about public policy towards the markets will have to undergo a radical change. The equity market remains one of the few segments of the economy where the regulatory principles derived from industrial economics are largely ignored. Current public policy aimed at controlling modes of transaction and the dissemination of information is a dysfunctional remnant of a bygone era of natural monopoly exchanges. Rapid advances in computerization over the past twenty years have fundamentally reshaped the structure of the equity markets. These markets are now contestable, if not yet fully competitive. As competition comes into the sector, the proper scope for government intervention and market structure regulation is correspondingly reduced.

CORPORATE GOVERNANCE

Existing corporate governance arrangements in Europe impede the development of more uniform, and more liquid, secondary equity markets. There are substantial differences in concentration of ownership and liquidity of secondary equity markets across Europe, with countries such as Germany, on the one hand, where ownership is concentrated and markets relatively illiquid, and the United Kingdom on the other, characterized by dispersed shareholdings and high market liquidity. Not only are certain corporate governance arrangements anathema to the development of active markets, but large differences *per se* can impose substantial costs on investors.

The observed correlation between concentration of ownership and liquidity reflects a fundamental trade-off. Concentration reduces liquidity by limiting the number of traders in the market. Issuers can escape this trade-off through various mechanisms – such as dual-class shares, pyramiding, and proxy votes – but only at the cost of worsening incentives for controlling owners. Similarly, forbidding the use of arrangements such as dual-class shares in order better to motivate investors will most likely make the stock less liquid. But, despite frequent claims to the contrary, improvements in liquidity do not necessarily come at the expense of effective corporate governance.

Restrictions on ownership concentration or the exercise of control are likely to be costly ways of improving liquidity. In general, corporate governance reform is a risky means of improving liquidity, and liquidity should therefore be addressed directly, rather than through restricting ownership concentration. In fact, the improved liquidity which can be expected to derive from eliminating barriers to cross-border trading integration should facilitate the accumulation of controlling blocks in secondary markets.

Efforts to harmonize the structure and control of corporations at the EU level are unlikely to succeed. There is a strong persistence in corporate governance arrangements. Reform, if undertaken, would most likely have to extend beyond issues of finance to the functioning of labour markets and company organization. Regulators also cannot rely on competition between regulatory systems to harmonize corporate governance patterns. Indeed, experience shows that increased competition can serve to reinforce existing traits rather than lead to convergence.

The subsidiarity principle should have a strong bite when it comes to corporate governance regulation. Yet the market might benefit considerably if EU corporations were merely obliged to disclose their governance practices. Annual reports should contain information on such matters as the composition of the board (executive versus non-executive directors, relationship to major shareholders etc.), existence and role of additional committees, procedures for appointment of directors, managerial compensation schemes, and internal and external control practices. Increased corporate transparency brings down barriers to integration, and thus improves liquidity.

PENSION FUND INVESTMENTS

Equity holdings of EU pension funds, both domestic and cross-border, are strongly influenced by regulations such as those relating to minimum funding and portfolio composition, as well as factors such as taxation, accounting standards, risk aversion of fund members, and the competitiveness of the domestic fund management industry. These often act to prevent funds from reaching an optimal tradeoff between risk and return. We suggest that streamlining of regulations so as to allow 'prudent man' rules and flexible funding limits may serve not only to boost equity market activity and integration, but also to increase coverage of private pensions by raising their attractiveness to the sponsor or member (or, in the case of compulsory provision, reduce the cost of providing a given level of private pensions).

Development of externally invested, privately funded pension schemes is held back in a number of countries by factors such as the generosity of social security, taxation provisions, incentives to reserve-funding, or even outright banning of company-based schemes. Reform of these regulations is urgently required to resolve the future demographic difficulties which EU Member States are likely to face. As a significant side-effect, appropriate reforms would also boost the demand for equities.

One possible avenue for eliminating barriers to pension fund development is action at the EU level. The Commission has shown increasing interest in retirement income provision, an area where free competition among fund managers is often limited by requirements to employ local managers, free movement of capital is limited by investment restrictions, and mobility of labour is limited by restrictions on cross-border pension fund membership. However, the proposed directive to liberalize pension fund investments has been shelved, owing to significant Member State resistance. The current approach of the Commission is based on applying the Capital Movements Directive to address barriers to cross-border investment, and attacking existing regimes in the more restrictive Member States for not constituting 'reasonable prudential restrictions', as defined in the Directive. Progress along these lines may be politically difficult, but should nonetheless be pursued vigorously.

The EU may not, however, be the only international forum through which restrictions on equity investments may be challenged. The OECD has a Code on the Liberalization of International Capital Movements, to which all members are obliged to subscribe. Deviations from the principle of free movement of capital are required to be justified. Autonomous pressure on governments is also likely; on the one hand from the demographic pressures on their pay-as-you-go pension systems, which should lead them increasingly to adopt initiatives to expand funding, and on the other from their own companies, which will seek minimum-cost methods of providing privately funded pensions. Abolition of limits on equity and international investment are demonstrably efficient means of reducing the costs of provision.

Once regulations are liberalized, the benefits to pension funds will spread to the equity markets more generally. Established issuers should face a reduced cost of equity finance, and access to such finance should extend to a wider range of companies. Privatizations would also be facilitated. Increased financing activity by pension funds may also contribute to better corporate governance, as the funds obtain greater leverage to put pressure on underperforming managers and firms. Intermediaries such as broker-dealers will benefit from increased market capitalization (as more equity is issued) and increased turnover, which will further benefit the corporate sector via lower liquidity premia on equity. Fund managers generally will benefit from a greater volume of business available on competitive terms, although those accustomed to the competitive tranquillity of protected domestic environments will have to develop stronger technical abilities in equity and international investment to survive liberalization.

CAPITAL STANDARDS

The Capital Adequacy Directive (CAD) has two underlying aims: to ensure that securities business is conducted prudently in the interests of both financial stability and investor protection, and to establish a 'level playing field' for EU institutions undertaking securities activities. Our analysis of the Directive indicates that it will not serve to promote either of these aims.

The CAD regulatory regime suffers from a number of material defects, in particular the following:

- the imposition of different capital standards for the trading book and the banking book makes no sense on prudential grounds, since the risks incurred on each book are not segregated;
- the ability of banks to fund their securities trading with cheap, protected bank deposits may distort competition while also posing significant moral hazard problems;
- the CAD's 'building block' methodology provides a poor representation of the actual equity position risk being borne, as it fails to take proper account of portfolio diversification, and thereby provides perverse incentives for securities businesses.

Most fundamentally, common capital standards cannot of themselves ensure a level playing field, as an institution's *cost* of capital depends on a range of highly influential factors, such as taxation arrangements and the extent of the official financial 'safety net'.

Through an examination of the UK experience, we further demonstrate that significant competitive distortions may arise in the implementation of the Directive. CAD implementation in the UK has resulted in UK rules being more stringent than the CAD minimum requirements, particularly in the application of target and trigger capital ratios and the treatment of equity position risk for non-qualifying countries. Such rules may encourage UK-based institutions to conduct equity business through continental European subsidiaries governed by the CAD minimum requirements, or through wholly exempt non-EU subsidiaries.

Finally, the CAD will have to be brought into line with the Basle rules for regulating market risks, particularly in the area of internal risk models. The need to update the CAD before it had even been implemented underscores the damaging inflexibility of a European regulatory regime which relies on primary legislation for detailed rule-making.

ACCOUNTING DIVERSITY

Owing to the diversity in accounting practices across Europe, a company can report vastly different profit and loss figures depending on the accident or choice of where the firm is headquartered and what accounting principles are used there. This licence for accounting diversity creates a *potential* barrier to international equity investments. However, an externally imposed accounting system which fails to communicate material cross-country differences in the underlying economic environment would be unlikely to facilitate market integration. Accounting diversity is often just a logical reflection of differences in the legal, tax, and social environments in which firms happen to be based. As we demonstrate, accounting harmonization in Europe – whether towards IASC, US GAAP, or new EU standards – is only likely to improve cross-border investment flows if important components of each of these environments are sufficiently harmonized first.

There is no doubt that accounting diversity (or the diversity in the operational environment underlying it) can create difficulties for European investors seeking to invest cross-border. Our survey of European institutional investors confirmed that accounting information is generally important to their investment analysis, and that they do endeavour to make cross-country investment comparisons of individual firms. Forty-five percent of respondents indicated that they assign a higher risk rating to companies which disclose insufficient information, 35 percent avoid investing in such companies altogether, and 26 percent require higher returns from them. Fifty-six percent indicated that they would be more likely to invest in a foreign company if it prepared its accounts according to their own domestic accounting standards, 57 percent would be more likely to invest if the foreign company provided accounts prepared according to International Accounting Standards, and 44 percent would be more likely to invest if the company reported in accordance with US GAAP. However, investors apply a range of reasonably effective coping strategies when the preferred form or amount of disclosure is not available. Furthermore, they indicate that accounting barriers to cross-border investment are relatively insignificant in comparison with those deriving from such factors as liquidity and currency risks.

While investors would, understandably, like more accounting information as well as restatements according to more familiar principles, there is a clear cost to issuers in obliging them to produce this. Our survey of European corporate issuers revealed that they were highly reluctant to supply additional accounting information prepared according to *different accounting principles*, although they were somewhat less reluctant to supply *additional accounting disclosures*. Given that issuers have a strong incentive to provide accounting information which attracts foreign investors, and that both issuers and investors have developed a range of routine mechanisms to facilitate communication, the cost to issuers of authorities *imposing* an additional layer of accounting requirements is likely to outweigh the benefits to the wider market. Imposed accounting *harmonization* should also be pursued with caution, as it would not be advisable to eliminate existing national accounting practices which may be effective in communicating material idiosyncrasies of the home-state operating environment.

CLEARANCE AND SETTLEMENT

Continued growth in cross-border trading is very much dependent on the degree to which the associated transaction costs can be reduced. The costs of clearing and settling cross-border trades can be a significant subset of the total transaction costs. This makes it imperative to examine the barriers which exist to the development of more efficient structures for processing trades.

There are five different mechanisms for effecting cross-border European trades: (1) direct access to the home-country central securities depository (CSD); (2) indirect access through local members of the home-country CSD; (3) indirect access through global custodians; (4) through international CSDs (ICSDs) such as Euroclear and Cedel (which are in turn linked to local CSDs); and (5) through local-CSD-to-local-CSD links. Currently, the second and third mechanisms are the most widely used.

We demonstrate that the economics of the clearance and settlement industry support the case for greater centralization of CSD services through the development of a so-called 'Euro-hub', along the lines of model 4 above. This derives from such factors as the considerable 'positive externalities' emanating from the creation of a large CSD network, more efficient use of member collateral, and the existence of economies of scope and scale in CSD service provision. This raises the critical question as to why market forces have not generated a more substantial movement in the direction of greater centralization.

We argue that the power of national CSDs to prevent the emergence of a Euro-hub is not nearly as great as has sometimes been suggested, and will decline further with the growth of new competitive trading platforms. However, we demonstrate that direct and indirect transaction costs associated with the existence of very different clearance and settlement standards and procedures across Europe have created an economic environment in which the advantages to further centralization are currently relatively small. These include such factors as different settlement cycles, taxation, forms of securities, and payment systems operations and access. We propose a number of recommendations for removing these barriers, and suggest that the growth in competition from global custodians is highly welcome – both in terms of directly expanding trade support services for institutional investors, and by indirectly encouraging the removal of existing barriers to greater harmonization of clearance and settlement systems in Europe.

EXCHANGE RATES AND THE SINGLE CURRENCY

The existence of fluctuating exchange rates need not be as large an obstacle to regional equity market integration as it may at first appear. Investors have access to forward and futures markets to hedge exchange risk at relatively low cost. Nevertheless, the extreme neutrality view held by some finance theorists – that exchange-rate regimes are irrelevant to equity markets – does not accord with the evidence. We document evidence of 'currency myopia' and related institutional rigidities, in the form of examples such as the home-country investment bias puzzle, reactions to accounting rule changes affecting currency translation, and the effect of exchange-rate changes on country-fund discounts and premia.

We further document evidence that return differentials between different national equity markets appear to be correlated with bilateral exchange-rate variability. But we cannot, on this basis, infer a causal relationship between exchange rates and equity prices: both may be affected by a third factor. For this reason, it is important to identify a test which can isolate an exogenous component of exchange-rate variability. We therefore examined statistically the patterns of cross-border equity market correlations under different exchange-rate regimes. Ireland provided the cleanest experiment, having experienced a number of clear-cut changes in exchange-rate regime *vis-à-vis* major currencies. The most convincing evidence was offered by Ireland's switch from a British pound peg to the European Exchange Rate Mechanism. In this case the increase in punt/pound variability and decrease in punt/DM variability were exogenous, yet Irish equity prices became demonstrably more closely linked with German equity prices. In short, currency regimes do matter.

In terms of the further integration of the European equity markets, the implication is that stabilizing bilateral exchange rates would be beneficial, and adopting a single currency would be more so. In the absence of such steps, the volume and pattern of cross-border equity investment in Europe may be further from the optimum than it need be.

Finally, we point out that the move to a single currency can be expected to have a significant effect on the structure of equity market trading in Europe. The primary continental trading systems are basically variations on the same theme: continuous electronic auctions. With currency costs and risks removed, and government-imposed currency matching requirements on pension funds rendered meaningless, the positive network externalities and economies of scale in trading service provision should swamp any remaining benefits to, or barriers supporting, trading fragmentation along national lines. Thus, the forces for concentrating trading – at least within different market architectures (e.g. continuous auction, call auction, and dealer market) – will be very strong. Some exchanges can be expected to merge, while others will simply disband. Monetary union may therefore act as a far more powerful force for liberalizing European market structure than any directive ever could.

ABBREVIATIONS

ABO	accumulated-benefit obligation
ADR	American Depository Receipt
ADTV	average daily trading volume
AIDA	Automatic Interprofessional Dealing System Amsterdam
AIM	Amsterdam Interprofessional Market/Alternative Investment Market (London)
ASE	Amsterdam Stock Exchange
ASSET	Amsterdam Stock Exchange Trading System
AZX	Arizona Stock Exchange (parent company)
BBA	British Bankers' Association
BSRD	Bank Solvency Ratio Directive
CAC	*Cotation Assistée en Continu* (Paris trading system)
CAD	Capital Adequacy Directive
CAPM	Capital Asset Pricing Model
CHX	Chicago Stock Exchange
CLOB	consolidated limit order book
COB	*Commission des Opérations de Bourse*
CQS	Consolidated Quotation System
CSD	central securities depository
CTA	Consolidated Tape Association
DTB	Deutsche Terminbörse
DVP	delivery versus payment
EASDAQ	European Association of Securities Dealers Automated Quotation System
EDI	electronic data interchange
EMS	European Monetary System
EMU	Economic and Monetary Union
EOE	European Options Exchange
ERM	Exchange Rate Mechanism
FAS	Financial Accounting Standard
FASB	Financial Accounting Standards Board
FESE	Federation of European Stock Exchanges
GAAP	Generally Accepted Accounting Principles
GDP	Gross Domestic Product
GMP	guaranteed minimum pension
IASC	International Accounting Standards Committee

IBIS	*Integriertes Börsenhandels- und Informationssystem* (German trading system)
IBO	indexed-benefit obligation
ICSD	international central securities depository
IPD	international portfolio diversification
IPO	initial public offering
ISC	Investment Services Directive
ITS	Intermarket Trading System
LIBA	London Investment Banking Association
LIFFE	London International Financial Futures and Options Exchange
LSE	London Stock Exchange
MPC	multiple principles capability
NASDAQ	National Association of Securities Dealers Automated Quotation System
NBS	Normal Block Size
NMS	Normal Market Size/National Market System
NYSE	New York Stock Exchange
OFD	Own Funds Directive
PBO	projected-benefit obligation
PTS	proprietary trading system
RAP	Regulatory Accounting Principles
REV	Regulated Environment View
RTGS	real-time gross settlement
SEAQ-I	Stock Exchange Automated Quotation System – International
SEC	Securities and Exchange Commission
SIB	Securities and Investments Board
SFA	Securities and Futures Authority
TAP	Tax Accounting Principles
TSV	Trading System View
VAR	value at risk
2BCD	Second Banking Coordination Directive

Chapter 1

EQUITY TRADING I: THE EVOLUTION OF EUROPEAN TRADING SYSTEMS

1. INTRODUCTION

This chapter aims to illuminate the economic forces which have been driving the evolution of European trading systems over the past decade, and to identify those which will be critical in the coming years. This will serve to lay the foundations for the analysis in the next three chapters, and in particular will guide our critique of European public policy towards the markets, which we develop in Chapter 4.

We begin in section 2 by presenting a brief statistical overview of the European equity markets. Section 3 details the development of the major European market centres over the past decade, emphasizing the critical role which London-based competition has played in driving continental reforms. Section 4 provides a more general discussion of the performance of different market trading structures, drawing particular attention to how such structures develop in parallel. We focus in large measure on two critical aspects of market structure, transaction costs and transparency, examining both theoretical arguments and empirical evidence. Section 5 analyses the forces which will drive the evolution of European market structure in the future, referring to current developments to illustrate our arguments. Finally, section 6 provides a summary and conclusions.

2. A SNAPSHOT OF THE EUROPEAN EQUITY MARKETS

Table 1 provides market capitalization and turnover data for the major exchanges in the 15 EU Member States. US and Japanese data are provided for comparison. Figures 1 and 2 reproduce the more important data in graphical form for the largest markets.

For reasons which we explain in some detail in Appendix 1, turnover data must be treated with considerable caution. In particular, London foreign equity turnover is inflated by double-counting of trades which are actually executed through the domestic market trading systems, and German domestic turnover is artificially boosted by such factors as the commission arrangements on floor trading, which encourage multiple intermediation of trades.

Table 1. EU Equity Markets versus US and Japan, end-1994

					Annual turnover						
	Listed companies[a]		Domestic market capitalization		In millions of ECUs			as % of EU total			as % of GDP
Market	Domestic	Foreign	in millions of ECUs	as % of GDP	Domestic	Foreign	Total	Domestic	Foreign	Total	Domestic
Amsterdam	317	215	182,492	68.10	72,251	158	72,409	5.04	0.03	3.48	26.96
Athens	165	0	11,678	18.45	4,293	0	4,293	0.30	0.00	0.21	6.78
Brussels	155	141	68,583	37.09	10,477	3,130	13,608	0.73	0.65	0.65	5.67
Copenhagen	243	10	38,343	31.89	24,082	488	24,570	1.68	0.10	1.18	20.03
Dublin	56	9	16,003	37.87	3,945	0	3,945	0.28	0.00	0.19	9.34
Germany	423	227	388,024	23.30	509,408	14,833	524,240	35.57	3.06	25.21	30.59
Helsinki	65	0	33,936	43.38	11,194	2	11,196	0.78	0.00	0.54	14.31
Lisbon	83	0	11,890	16.66	3,195	0	3,195	0.22	0.00	0.15	4.48
London	1,747	462	932,018	112.72	391,635	463,063	854,698	27.34	95.42	41.11	47.37
Luxembourg	55	217	23,127	208.47	862	19	881	0.06	0.00	0.04	7.77
Madrid	375	4	126,401	32.26	43,631	14	43,645	3.05	0.00	2.10	11.14
Milan	219	4	147,511	17.73	121,835	53	121,888	8.51	0.01	5.86	14.64
Paris	459	195	367,939	34.20	161,662	3,228	164,890	11.29	0.67	15.71	15.03
Stockholm	106	8	97,106	61.14	66,733	58	66,791	4.66	0.01	3.21	42.02
Vienna	94	41	23,521	14.74	7,065	251	7,316	0.49	0.05	0.35	4.43
EU major markets	**4,562**	**1,533**	**2,468,572**	**41.49**	**1,432,268**	**485,297**	**1,917,566**	**100.00**	**100.00**	**100.00**	**24.07**
New York	1,689	216	3,460,354	63.90	1,884,429	202,511	2,086,940	n/a	n/a	n/a	34.80
Nasdaq	4,577	325[b]	644,661[c]	11.90	1,115,319	63,784	1,179,103	n/a	n/a	n/a	20.60
Tokyo	1,651	110	2,926,215	77.13	713,244	614	713,857	n/a	n/a	n/a	18.80

Notes: [a] Main market only. [b] Includes 221 listed companies and 104 ADRs. [c] Includes foreign companies.
Source: *London Stock Exchange Quality of Markets Review* (Summer 1995); *European Stock Exchange Statistics*, FESE (1994 Annual Report); Datastream; Nasdaq.

Figure 1. Market Turnover, 1994

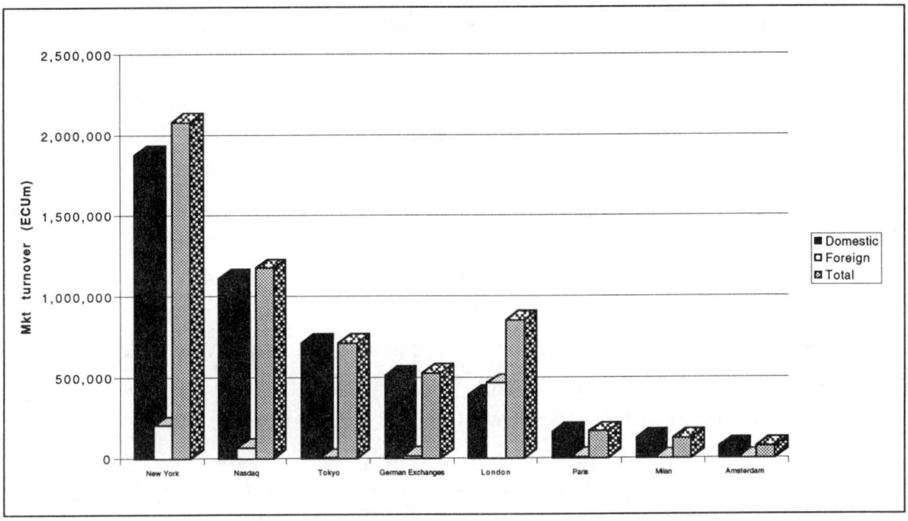

Figure 2. Market Capitalization, 1994

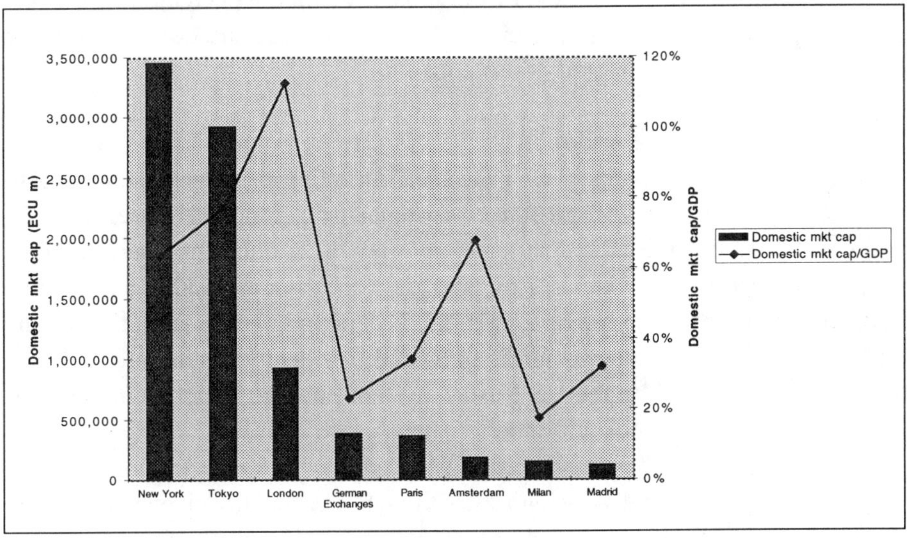

The table in Appendix 2 widens the perspective to the world's 20 largest markets, indicating the percentage of world market capitalization represented by each between 1982 and 1994. The accompanying figures show such data by region in graphical form, for 1985 and 1994. Europe's share of world market capitalization has declined very slightly, while that accounted for by the 'Asian Tiger' economies has risen considerably, largely at the expense of North America.

3. THE EUROPEAN STOCK EXCHANGES: A DECADE OF REFORMS

Trading systems in the European equity markets have undergone very substantial reforms since the mid-1980s. This decade of rapid change stands in stark contrast to the uneventful history of previous decades. Until 1985, European stock exchanges still worked largely according to a blueprint laid out in the nineteenth century. Most of continental Europe featured open outcry call auction markets, where publicly licensed single-capacity[1] intermediaries conveyed the orders of their customers and were compensated via statutorily fixed commissions. In London, stock trading was managed by dealers, called 'jobbers', who received customer orders via single-capacity brokers, and commissions were fixed by the members of the exchange. In all countries, the stock exchange was a closed membership organization, with high barriers to potential entrants. Each exchange operated in isolation from the others, well sheltered from competition by national regulations, barriers to capital mobility, and high costs of telecommunications.

These obstacles to European equity market integration began to crumble in the mid-1980s. External capital controls were removed; advances in computers and telecommunications spurred the creation of new vehicles for trading and drove down transaction costs; and institutional investors stepped up their participation in the equity markets, exploiting the growing ease and declining cost of cross-border trading to diversify their portfolios.

3.1. The First Mover: London

The London Stock Exchange (LSE) was the first in Europe to launch a full-scale restructuring, albeit not without fierce resistance from many of its members. In 1986, the LSE embarked on a series of reforms of its domestic equity market nicknamed 'Big Bang'. The reforms involved scrapping the traditional distinction between jobbers and brokers; opening dealership to banks and other financial institutions; liberalizing commissions; and introducing a screen-based system, SEAQ, modelled on the US Nasdaq system, through which dual-capacity dealers could disseminate their quotes.

However, London retained one basic feature of its former trading system – i.e. its dealership structure. Although some thought was initially given to the possibility of introducing an automated order-matching system, it was feared that, for most stocks, the order flow on the London market would be insufficient to sustain it. Few stocks were actively traded, and therefore the 'private liquidity' of dealers was thought necessary to provide price continuity and timely execution.[2] Indeed,

[1] A single-capacity intermediary acts only as agent (on behalf of the client) or as principal (on own account). A dual-capacity intermediary acts in both roles.

[2] Kregel (1990).

London domestic equity turnover as a percentage of market capitalization was low in comparison with other market centres.[3]

3.1.1. The Rise of SEAQ International . . .

These changes were extended to the London market for non-UK stocks through the establishment of a similar screen-based system, SEAQ International (SEAQ-I). For each stock traded on SEAQ-I, designated market makers are charged with posting firm bid and ask quotes during the relevant 'mandatory quote period' for trades of at least 'minimum marketable quantity' – the specified 'Normal Market Size' (NMS). To further increase the competitiveness of the London market, 'stamp duty' (turnover tax) on UK equity trades was halved, and no stamp duty was levied on non-UK equity trades.

These reforms were, on balance, very successful. They helped the City of London to capitalize on the traditional and growing presence of a large number of international intermediaries and investors, in particular US banks and investment funds, and to become the natural port of access to the continental European equity markets. This is because the new trading system catered to the needs of market participants far better than the continental exchanges. First, being continuously available on the phone throughout the trading day, London market makers provided a far greater degree of immediacy than the call auction markets on the continent (where trading outside the call auction, if allowed, was invariably for very small amounts). Secondly, London market makers committed substantial capital to providing a deep market, standing ready to trade very large blocks of stock. Thirdly, the absence of any transaction tax on non-UK stocks provided London with an explicit trading cost advantage.

A measure of the success of SEAQ-I in the late 1980s is provided by its increasing share of turnover in continental European equities. The figures in Pagano and Röell (1991 and 1993a), provided in Panel A of Table 2, show that the ratio of SEAQ-I trading volume to domestic volume in French, German, and Spanish stocks rose substantially between 1988 and 1989, and the same occurred for Italian stocks between 1989 and 1990 (Italian stocks started trading on SEAQ-I only in 1989).[4] Panel B of Table 2, drawing figures from Worthington (1991),

[3] Data from Touche-Ross, cited by Kregel (1990), show that London domestic equity turnover as a percentage of market capitalization was 28.3 percent in 1986 and 53.2 percent in 1987 (an exceptional year for turnover). This compares with 37.4 percent (1986) and 56.2 percent (1987) for Paris, 81 percent and 105 percent for Germany, 40.5 percent and 102.9 percent for Amsterdam, and 64.6 percent and 88 percent for the New York Stock Exchange (NYSE). The precise figures should be treated with caution because of differences in market structure and calculation, as explained in Appendix 1.

[4] Since SEAQ International and the German exchanges count both purchases and sales, their turnover figures are divided by two.

Table 2. Trading of Continental European Stocks Effected by Members of the London Stock Exchange, as Percentage of Stock Trading on 'Home-Country' Exchange

Panel A (from Pagano and Röell, 1991 and 1993a)

Nationality of stock	1988	1989 (Jan.-June)	1989 (June-Dec.)
German	12.65	16.21	
French	13.72	25.08	
Italian		6.50	11.20
Spanish	0.53	6.15	

Panel B (from Worthington, 1991)

Nationality of stock	1990 Q1	1990 Q2	1990 Q3	1990 Q4	1991 Q1
German	12.5	12.2	11.3	12.8	10.3
French	26.9	26.8	25.3	26.3	29.5
Italian	23.1	18.1	19.1	27.1	24.7
Spanish	14.3	15.9	25.5	18.4	18.4
Dutch	38.3	49.8	63.0	54.2	52.9
Swiss	-- .-	29.2	25.5	33.5	35.5
Swedish	39.5	64.9	62.4	50.0	45.0

reports the same measures for 1990–91 and a larger set of countries.[5] For German and French stocks, the turnover ratio approximately stabilized between 1990 and the first quarter of 1991, whereas it kept growing for Italian and Spanish stocks, and even more so for Dutch, Swiss, and Swedish equities. The table also shows that, as of the beginning of 1991, London had managed to attract a relatively large share of overall trading in continental European equities.

But these figures should be interpreted with some caution. First, they are vitiated by significant statistical problems.[6] Reported trading volume in a dealership (quote-driven) market is not directly comparable with turnover in an auction (order-driven) market. A direct customer trade with an LSE dealer tends to generate a series of inter-dealer transactions, by which the first dealer rebalances his inventories – an effect not present in an auction market where two customers' orders are merely crossed. In addition, trades effected on continental bourses by London-based dealers are often also reported in London.

[5] The figures in this table are not directly comparable with those reported by Pagano and Röell (1991, 1993a): since February 1990, LSE turnover data are more complete and reliable.

[6] See Appendix 1.

Secondly, and more importantly, one must avoid mistaking all London trading in non-UK stocks for trade *diverted* away from the respective domestic exchanges. A portion of it is trading volume *created* by the availability of SEAQ-I dealers. Many institutional investors, particularly US-based funds, began diversifying into European stocks in the late 1980s. This new investment was significantly aided by the growth of the London dealer market, which provided the liquidity in size that was not generally available in the unfamiliar, slow-paced, and thin auction markets on the continent.

At least for the Italian and Belgian cases, the available evidence actually indicates that the inception of trading on SEAQ-I did not reduce trading volume on the domestic exchanges. Pagano and Röell (1991) and Impenna, Maggio, and Panetta (1995) document that for several Italian stocks the inception of SEAQ-I trading *increased* trading volume on the Milan stock exchange.[7] Trade diversion appears to have been large and statistically significant only for a few high-volume stocks. Pagano and Röell report that the inception of SEAQ-I trading had no effect on *overall* Milan turnover at conventional significance levels.[8] In a similar study of Belgian cross-listed stocks, Anderson and Tychon (1993) conclude that London trading on balance has stimulated greater trading in Brussels. These results are reasonable, considering that London dealers routinely use continental exchanges to unload part of their excess positions, so that flurries of trading activity in London also raise trading in the respective continental markets.

3.1.2. . . . and the Fall of SEAQ International

As a disciplined trading structure, SEAQ-I began slowly to crumble around 1991. Quoted spreads roughly doubled between 1990 and early 1994. For French cross-listed stocks, the spread between the lowest ask and the highest bid quoted on SEAQ-I (known in London as the market 'touch', and elsewhere as the 'inside spread') increased from an average value of 1.52 percent in July 1990 to 2.66 percent in 1993 and 3.37 percent in the first half of 1994.[9] Similarly, for Italian cross-listed stocks the market touch was on average 1.7 percent at the

[7] Both studies estimate volume regressions in which the explanatory variables are a constant: the trading volume for the entire market, the average monthly return on the relevant stock and its estimated monthly volatility, and a dummy for the inception of SEAQ-I trading (or the actual volume of SEAQ-I trading since inception). Pagano and Röell (1991) employ monthly data over the 1982-90 interval for 12 stocks. Impenna, Maggio, and Panetta (1995) employ monthly data for the 1985-93 interval for 23 stocks.

[8] This statement has to be taken cautiously, because of several limitations of the data. The Italian turnover data omit the large off-exchange turnover that occurred at the time to which the data refer (1982-90): off-exchange trading volume could have been diverted to London, and the data would not reveal it. In addition, the inception of trading on SEAQ-I may be unrepresentative, because several Italian stocks were unofficially traded in London before being assigned to a SEAQ-I market maker.

[9] The figure for 1990 is drawn from Pagano and Röell (1993a), and those for 1993 and 1994 from the *Quality of Markets Review* (Summer 1994).

end of 1990 and in the first half of 1992, but rose to 2.53 percent in the second half of 1992 and 3.5 percent in 1993.[10] Spreads continued to expand to such an embarrassing width that in October 1995 the Exchange found it necessary to impose new maximum quoted spread limits. Essentially, dealers have abandoned their market making commitments to the system: *pro forma* quotes are posted merely to keep within Exchange rules and to advertise a dealer's availability. Many London trading houses continue to commit significant capital to European equity dealing, but competitive prices will now generally be made only over the phone.

There are a number of reasons for the system's decline:

- Most significantly, the introduction of new transparent electronic continuous auction systems on the continent – particularly CAC in Paris and IBIS in Frankfurt – drew liquidity into the home markets (see section 3.3). London dealers therefore began working customer orders through these trading systems, rather than taking these orders on their own books. Many also became members of the continental exchanges.
- A number of London houses lost considerable sums on continental equity dealing in the early 1990s, and consequently some decided to pull back from their market making commitments on SEAQ-I.
- The growing number of new (particularly foreign) players in the London market served to undermine the 'collegiate' environment in which business had previously been done. Unwritten codes of practice among dealers (such as not hitting stale quotes) began breaking down, and a number of dealers subsequently became unwilling to commit themselves to prices on-screen. Many simply widened their spreads to avoid having to monitor the markets, ensuring that they would not be hit when the markets moved.

Figures 3–5 below illustrate the historical trend in reported SEAQ-I turnover in German, Italian, and French stocks as a percentage of home market turnover in these same stocks. For reasons which we have already detailed, the data must be interpreted with considerable caution. The actual percentages are not necessarily meaningful, nor are they directly comparable across countries,

[10] The figure for 1990 refers to trading days between 25 October and 7 November, and is drawn from Pagano and Röell (1991). The 1992 figures are from Impenna, Maggio, and Panetta (1995), and those for 1993 are from the *Stock Exchange Quarterly* (Summer 1994).

3.1.3. The Development of a UK Auction Market

It is not only in continental equities that the London dealer market is under competitive challenge. A new London exchange, Tradepoint, began offering its trading services in UK equities in September 1995.[13] Run as a proprietary trading system (PTS)[14] – i.e. as a company selling trading services, rather than a membership-based exchange – the new exchange allows both 'buy-side' (institutional investor) and 'sell-side' (broker-dealer) firms[15] to trade directly and anonymously. More liquid stocks will be traded through a continuous electronic auction system similar to those operated by the continental exchanges. Initially, the largest 400 UK stocks are to be continuously traded, but non-UK stocks may be added in the future. Less liquid UK stocks are to be traded in an electronic single-price call auction (see the Appendix to Chapter 2). At the time of writing, Tradepoint trading volume is still extremely low.

SEAQ is scheduled to be replaced by a new electronic trading platform, Sequence VI, in mid-1996. Much of the Sequence project represents little more than an overhaul of SEAQ's electronic 'plumbing', but the new infrastructure will have order-matching capability. The extent to which this capability will actually be made operational depends on the results of discussions between the Exchange board and the members, which should be made known in early 1996. While the board is under pressure to react to the competitive challenge posed by alternative trading platforms, such as Tradepoint, the major market makers are actively resisting the introduction of an order-driven segment into the Exchange's trading system, which may serve to reduce returns on their commitment of dealer capital. It is expected that automatic order-matching will be made available to members from August 1996, although a compromise may be agreed to exclude the largest (FTSE 100) stocks. Paradoxically, this segment of the market would benefit most from order-matching, as the high level of 'public liquidity' mitigates the need for intermediation through private dealer capital. Furthermore, it is important to recognize that direct participation in the new system will still be limited to Exchange members, while institutional investors will continue to have direct access to Tradepoint.[16]

[13] Tradepoint was created by former LSE executives who tried unsuccessfully to introduce an order-driven component into that market. The company aims to compete on the basis of the lower trading costs implied by disintermediation.

[14] See section 5.4 on proprietary trading systems.

[15] The term 'buy-side' refers to the customers of the trading service industry, and 'sell-side' refers to the intermediaries who service their orders.

[16] See section 5.3 on exchange governance.

3.2. The Competitive Response of the Continental Exchanges

Following the successful introduction of SEAQ-I, the danger of losing an ever-increasing volume of equity trading to London pushed continental exchanges and their regulatory authorities to embark on a complete overhaul of traditional trading structures, systems, and regulations; an overhaul specifically designed to recapture and increase domestic equity order flow.[17] The Paris Bourse was the first to respond to London's challenge: in the words of Bourse chairman and chief executive Jean-François Théodore, SEAQ-I 'has been quite an incentive for the modernisation of the Paris market'.[18] The Paris model was closely emulated by Madrid, Brussels, and Milan. The Frankfurt and Amsterdam markets were also substantially reorganized in the early 1990s, but along somewhat different lines.

3.2.1. Paris

Since 1986, the Paris Bourse has implemented four key reforms:

- the introduction of a continuous order-driven screen-based trading system (1986);
- the replacement of publicly appointed brokers with corporate dual-capacity intermediaries (1988);
- the liberalization of trading commissions (1989);
- the partial abandonment of the principle that trading should be concentrated on one central trading system (1994).

CAC

In July 1986, a continuous electronic auction with automatic clearing replaced the traditional Paris trading system of periodic call auctions with open outcry dealing. Incoming market orders, or executable limit orders, are automatically and instantaneously executed against outstanding limit orders according to price and time priority. This computerized trading system – CAC (*Cotation Assistée en Continu*) – was extended to the securities traded on the six floor-based regional exchanges[19] in January 1991, thereby concentrating virtually all domestic equity trading in Paris. For the more liquid stocks, a (fully electronic) call auction remains only to open the market at 10.00, after which trading is continuous until the close at 17.00. The opening call auction reportedly executes about 10 percent

[17] These struggles are frequently mirrored in proxy battles among national treasury officials, which openly manifest themselves within a number of international fora, most notably the European Council of Ministers (see Chapter 4).

[18] Cited in Cohen (1994).

[19] Bordeaux, Lille, Lyon, Marseille, Nancy, and Nantes.

of daily executed orders, although this accounts for no more than about 5 percent of total trading volume by value.

An important feature of the CAC system, which is often referred to when comparing it with the London SEAQ-I dealer market, is its relatively high degree of transparency. The full breakdown of the central order book is visible to all Bourse members, including the codes identifying the member firms which have placed each order. However, this 'pre-trade transparency' is diminished by the use of 'hidden orders'; i.e. the undisclosed portions of orders which only become visible as the disclosed portions are executed. Hidden orders represent a significant proportion of limit orders: estimates go as high as 50 percent.[20] As for non-members, they may have access through private data vendors to a more limited range of information; such as the inside spread with volume, the number of orders, total shares bid and offered, and past transaction prices. 'Post-trade transparency' in Paris used to be complete and immediate, but this has been diminished recently at the behest of large member firms for whom such transparency inhibits their willingness to trade as principal. Member codes of the broker-dealers involved in a trade are now suppressed when transaction details are published (over the objections of smaller member firms, who do little or no trading as principal, and who would benefit from seeing the direct counterparties). More significantly, trade publication is now delayed for large transactions carried out by member firms acting as principal (see 'block trading' below).

Sociétés de Bourse

In January 1988, the old *agents de change*, publicly appointed single-capacity brokers, lost their legal monopoly in equity trading. They were replaced by new corporate intermediaries called *sociétés de bourse*, who may act as dual-capacity broker-dealers. Banks and securities firms became eligible to own *sociétés de bourse* as separately capitalized subsidiaries, and by the end of 1989 about two-thirds of *sociétés de bourse* were at least partially owned by such institutions, including many foreign ones. The aim of this reform was to increase market liquidity by attracting better capitalized intermediaries, who would supplement brokerage activities through significant trading on own-account.

Elimination of Fixed Commissions

In order to increase the price competitiveness of the French market, fixed trading commissions were eliminated in July 1989. They have since been fully negotiable between member firms and clients. More recently, trading costs were further

[20] London Stock Exchange Quarterly (Summer 1992:21). A more recent, unpublished, estimate from a Paris Bourse official put the volume of hidden orders at between 20 and 40 percent of disclosed orders.

reduced by fixing a FFr 4000 ceiling on stamp duty (from July 1993), and by exempting non-residents altogether (from January 1994).

Block Trading Rules

In 1989, following the creation of the dual-capacity *sociétés de bourse*, new rules were instituted to allow large block trading by designated members acting as principal outside the central CAC system. For only the most liquid shares, trades above a set minimum volume could be effected at a price outside the *fourchette*, or the CAC inside spread, on the condition that the member firm acting as principal satisfied all CAC buy orders with higher price limits, and sell orders with lower limits, within five minutes. The requirement to place such orders severely limited the attractions of block trading in Paris, and therefore reinforced the growth in French share trading through London's SEAQ-I. Paris was therefore forced to respond by instituting a more liberal block trading regime, which came into force in September 1994. This reform represented the effective abandonment of the position, long held by both the Bourse and French Treasury, that all trading in French equities should be concentrated on one central trading system.

Under the new rules, member firm principal trades in the top 53 stocks exceeding 'normal block size' (NBS)[21] may be effected within the *fourchette moyenne ponderée* – the 'weighted average' CAC spread – rather than the narrower *fourchette*, without any requirement to satisfy orders in the central CAC order book. Furthermore, trade publication is delayed for two hours for trades between one and five times NBS, and until the following morning for trades exceeding five times NBS. Roughly five block trades a day are reported to the Bourse under the new rules.[22]

It would appear that relatively few block trades which would previously have been 'traded in London' (i.e. reported only to London) are now 'traded in Paris' in response to this rule change. Prior to 1996, block trading restrictions were still considerably greater in Paris than in London,[23] meaning that the largest block traders, who are also members of the London Stock Exchange, had a strong incentive to continue executing French block trades in London. While the Paris Bourse requires all domestic trades to be reported to its authorities, it is well known that this does not occur for certain members taking particularly large pro-

[21] NBS is roughly 2.5 percent of average daily trading volume in a given stock over the preceding three months, but is never less than FFr 1m.

[22] Indications are that Bourse officials would like a more liberal block trading regime, but that the *Commission des Opérations de Bourse* (COB) has not been prepared to assent to a system which further disconnects upstairs trading from the central CAC order book.

[23] Post-trade transparency requirements on the LSE were significantly tightened as of 1 January 1996 (see section 4.3.4).

prietary positions. One member indicated that approximately four out of every five of its French block transactions were reported only to London, thereby avoiding the weighted average spread rule and the publication requirement. Others reported a lower figure to us, but their explanations indicate that this is only because their average block sizes are smaller.

3.2.2. Madrid, Brussels, and Milan

These three markets, formerly designed on the French model of an open outcry call auction, have closely followed the French example in responding to the competition posed by London-based market makers.

In 1989, the Bolsa de Valores in Madrid adopted an automated continuous trading system, and replaced the *agentes de cambio* with *sociedades de bolsa* which can trade on own-account and can be owned by domestic or foreign banks, insurance companies, or securities firms. Commissions were deregulated, and a special facility for block trading was introduced. To cope with increasing volumes and demands from users for an expanded range of trading features, the Bolsa introduced a new electronic system, SIBE (*Sistema de Interconexión de las Bolsas Españolas*), in September 1995. SIBE links four Spanish exchanges, producing a single price for each asset. The system is used for bonds and derivatives as well as equities.

Similar reforms were undertaken in Brussels. The Brussels Stock Exchange introduced an automated auction system in 1989. In December 1990, a new law replaced the Belgian *agents de change* with French-style *sociétés de bourse*, imposed a ceiling on stock transactions taxes, and allowed off-exchange trades, provided their prices did not deviate by more than 2.5 percent from the previous on-exchange trade.

The Borsa Valori in Milan went through the same exercise in 1991. Italian stocks were gradually transferred from the open outcry call auction to an automated continuous auction, the *agenti di cambio* were replaced by *Società di Intermediazione Mobiliare* (SIM), commissions were liberalized, and all trade was concentrated on the official exchange. The latter step was a major change for the Italian equity market, which had previously been characterized by a very large off-exchange trading volume – in some years estimated to be over three times as large as on-exchange trading volume.[24] At present, trading opens with

[24] This extraordinary segmentation of the Italian equity market before 1991 was mainly due to the existence of statutorily fixed commissions on the exchange. To avoid paying the 0.7 percent commission to an *agente di cambio*, a bank receiving a client's order would trade with another bank off the exchange (so that it could retain a 0.35 percent commission) or, even better, cross the trade in-house (in which case it would appropriate the entire 0.7 percent commission from the two clients). The concentration rule was accepted by Italian banks because it was introduced together with the liberalization of commissions and the elimination of the *agenti di cambio*'s monopoly.

an electronic call auction at 9:30. A block trading facility is available, allowing a one-hour publication delay for large proprietary trades, although this is not currently of great value to Italian SIMs, which rarely commit capital as dealers.

3.2.3. Germany

German domestic company market capitalization is less than half that of the UK, and is very low relative to the size of the German economy (see Table 1). Moreover, relatively few German companies are publicly listed, and even fewer are actively traded: of the 810 listed domestic companies, roughly 100 are 95 percent owned by one party, and 400 may be classified as 'illiquid', with annual turnover under DM 15m.[25] Three stocks – Deutsche Bank, Daimler-Benz, and Siemens – accounted for about one-third of turnover in 1994, while the top six stocks accounted for just under half.

The absence of a liquid domestic equity market is widely ascribed to the lack of an 'equity culture' in Germany. Indeed, only just over 5 percent of German households own stocks in public companies, compared with over 20 percent in the US and the UK. Yet the lack of a developed equity market also derives from a wide range of other interrelated factors, including the traditional role of large universal banks in company financing, corporate governance arrangements, and the structure of private pension plans.

Against this backdrop is an equity market trading structure in a state of considerable flux. The recent evolution of the market, particularly the advent of electronic trading, owes much to market pressures being generated by substantial foreign interest in German stocks – foreigners accounting for nearly half of all purchases in recent years.

The present trading structure may be broadly described as an auction market, although with a number of distinctive features:

- First, floor trading is fragmented across eight regional stock exchanges: in order of trading volume, Frankfurt (75 percent), Düsseldorf (10 percent), Munich (5 percent), Hamburg, Stuttgart, Berlin, Bremen, and Hanover. Many stocks are cross-listed on multiple exchanges, and prices can and do often vary across them. Wide access to a cross-exchange electronic trading system should eliminate pricing discrepancies, but Deutsche Börse AG,[26] the holding company for the Frankfurt Stock

[25] Source: Schroeder Münchmeyer Hengst Research GmbH.

[26] Deutsche Börse AG is organized as a joint-stock corporation, whose primary shareholders are the bank members (the biggest being Deutsche Bank, Commerzbank, and Dresdner Bank). The remaining shareholders are the regional exchanges (10 percent), the *Freimaklers* (6 percent), and the *Kursmaklers* (5 percent).

Exchange and the Deutsche Terminbörse (DTB) derivatives exchange, documents that this is often not the case.[27] Certainly, it must be open to serious doubt whether fragmentation of trading across *identical trading structures* could, on balance, benefit the liquidity of German stocks, and the apparent occurrence of significant pricing discrepancies would indicate that effective arbitrage is not possible under the existing structure. In May 1995, the three largest exchanges – Frankfurt, Düsseldorf, and Munich – signed a (tentative) cooperation agreement which could, in time, lead to a full merger. In the first instance, a coordination arrangement would be put in place to achieve unitary pricing on DAX 100 stocks, while smaller stocks would thereafter be traded on only one of the three exchanges.

- Secondly, German floor trading features a limit order book for each stock, providing an auction market base, although 'specialist' broker-dealers (*Kursmaklers*)[28] manage these books while trading for their own account, thus adding a significant dealer component. Each stock is assigned to only one *Kursmakler*, although each *Kursmakler* can be responsible for multiple stocks. Orders may be routed to the *Kursmaklers* during floor trading hours (10:30-13:30) either directly on the floor, or from remote locations through the BOSS electronic order routing system.

  The limit order books are open only to the *Kursmaklers*; this informational advantage allowing them to quote more narrowly for their own account than other dealers. *Kursmaklers* also receive a '*courtage*', or floor commission, of 0.04 percent (for DAX 30 stocks) or 0.08 percent, for trades executed against their limit order books as well as for their brokered or own-account trades[29] on the electronic IBIS system (see below).[30] While *Kursmakler* privileges may or may not provide a net benefit to the wider market in terms of added liquidity and price stability, it is important to recognize that they do not have the affirmative trading obligations of New York Stock Exchange specialists, and are therefore more accurately described as privileged market makers than as specialists.

[27] Examining trading over the period 7 June–6 July 1995, Deutsche Börse concluded that approximately 20 percent of prices set on the Frankfurt floor were outside the concurrent IBIS spread. Using a different methodology, Schmidt, Oesterhelweg, and Treske (1995) conclude that 9 percent is a more accurate figure.

[28] We 'anglicize' the German plural to make the text easier to read in English.

[29] For brokered trades through IBIS, the *Kursmakler* will receive a *courtage* from both buyer and seller.

[30] During floor hours, *Kursmaklers* may only quote their assigned stocks on IBIS. After hours, they may quote freely on a proprietary basis.

Stock exchange members route orders to floor brokers, who are either employees of the member firms (*Händlers*) or independent brokers (*Freimaklers*). *Freimaklers* also take proprietary positions, and therefore compete directly against the order books of the *Kursmaklers*. The traditional *Freimakler* role is growing increasingly untenable, owing both to exchange restrictions limiting the provision of their services to exchange members only (i.e. the banks, and not private clients) and to the growth of direct inter-bank electronic trading (see below).

- Thirdly, an anonymous electronic trading system called IBIS (*Integriertes Börsenhandels- und Informationssystem*) operates in tandem with the floor, although over considerably longer trading hours (8:30-17:30). Introduced by the banks in 1991, IBIS subsequently became a major segment of the German exchanges. Its share of DAX 30 share trading has risen dramatically, from 15.7 percent at the end of 1991 to nearly 40 percent today. Some of the larger banks execute a considerably higher percentage of their trades through IBIS (on the order of 60 percent). Non-DAX stocks, however, still trade overwhelmingly on the floor. Bank traders often split larger orders, combining IBIS and floor trading strategically to obtain a better average price.

  As participants can only enter one-way quotes in IBIS, the system should formally be characterized as order-driven rather than quote-driven. However, proprietary trading by competing bank traders, *Freimaklers*, and *Kursmaklers* gives the system some of the features of a dealer market (although quotes are not mandatory, as on SEAQ or Nasdaq). Unlike the Paris CAC, IBIS does not have the capacity to execute matched orders automatically, and participants must therefore actively intervene to 'hit' orders in the book
- Finally, trades arranged by phone are formally 'off-exchange', and are therefore not published. Floor trades not involving a *Kursmakler* (as principal or agent) are also considered not to be 'official' trades, and are therefore not subject to any publication requirements. The 'off-exchange' telephone market trading (not including SEAQ-I) is very substantial, representing approximately 30 percent of total European trading volume in German shares.

The main components of the present hybrid structure – multiple regional exchanges, floor trading, and IBIS – are unlikely to survive for more than a few years. Deutsche Börse announced in May 1995 that it intended to develop a fully electronic trading system for both equities and bonds, which would eliminate pricing discrepancies and improve transparency. Plans are also being considered to supplement continuous trading with three daily electronic call auctions. This system, whatever its final form, would obviate the need for trading floors and floor brokers.

3.2.4. Amsterdam

Of the major European markets, the Amsterdam market has been under the greatest international pressure to adapt its trading structures. Because of the small size of the domestic market and the large international interest in Dutch equities, the long-term survival of the Amsterdam Stock Exchange (ASE) depends critically on its implementing an appropriate strategy.

In terms of domestic company market capitalization, the Dutch equity market is the fourth largest in the EU, yet it is second only to London in relation to the size of its domestic economy (GDP). The Dutch equity market is particularly vulnerable to international competition, being highly dependent on trading in about 25 international stocks of Dutch origin (representing 85 percent of Amsterdam volume) which are actively traded around the world.

The trading system of the Amsterdam Stock Exchange has long been a hybrid. When the Exchange introduced a computer assisted trading system in 1988, it maintained the traditional floor trading and created a mixed quote-/order-driven market. Banks and brokers could operate dual-capacity, but were not permitted to deal directly. Orders had to be routed (electronically) to a jobber (the *hoekman*) on the trading floor, where limit orders could be matched and executed automatically, or where market orders would be submitted to a competitive bidding process involving all jobbers dealing in the particular stock. Banks and brokers did not have access to *hoekman* firms' screens, but could observe their bidding activities on the floor. Exceptions to these procedures were made for transactions in excess of Dfl 1m, which were subject to the rules of the Amsterdam Interprofessional Market (AIM). Provided that prices did not deviate beyond a specified limit from the current *hoekman* quotation, banks and brokers were permitted to negotiate prices 'upstairs' on behalf of their clients, free of commissions (i.e. on a 'net basis'). These trades were then simply reported to the *hoekman*.[31]

For a number of reasons, this arrangement was not effective in concentrating Dutch equity trading on the ASE. Certain internal factors were clearly not conducive to the growth of the domestic market, such as turnover tax (eliminated in 1990) and restrictions on price movements and direct inter-bank trading, but these were not determinant. The roots of the ASE's problems were outside the

[31] For further details, see Kregel (1990).

Netherlands, and largely beyond the Exchange's control. Two factors were particularly significant:

- **Competition from non-Dutch intermediaries**. The world's largest international securities houses – all members of the London Stock Exchange (SEAQ-I) – bid aggressively for institutional trading business in Dutch equities across Europe and North America. The major US and UK houses even made major inroads into Netherlands-based institutional business, offering better research and lower fees than Dutch banks. Rather than lay off their positions on the ASE, these non-Dutch houses overwhelmingly opted to manage their Dutch inventory internally through their sales networks (approximately 75 percent of their trading flows), and to rebalance most of the remainder through trading among themselves in London.[32]
- **Growth in foreign holdings of Dutch equities**. This factor is strongly linked with the previous one. Foreign investors generate roughly two-thirds of trading volume in Dutch equities – very high by European standards – and their *entrée* into this market was naturally through more aggressive US and UK intermediaries. The dominance of foreign investors is reinforced by the fact that Dutch institutions' portfolio turnover is far lower than that of their Anglo-American counterparts.

Between 1988 and 1991, the ASE's market share in Dutch equity trading declined from about 80 percent to 60 percent – most of this decline accounted for by the steep rise in trading over the London Stock Exchange. ASE market share in block trading (above Dfl 1m) was particularly hard hit, falling from 68 percent to 33 percent, although smaller size trading was also affected (82 percent to 66 percent). Over these three years, the London Stock Exchange significantly increased its market making commitment in Dutch equities; the number of traded stocks rising from 13 to 30. In tandem, Dutch intermediaries saw their share in domestic equity trading by Dutch investors decline from 84 percent to 58 percent, and by foreign investors from 95 percent to 80 percent.[33]

Against such a backdrop, the ASE was forced to respond vigorously or to accept a terminal decline in its trading role. An overhaul of the Exchange's trading structure was launched.

[32] McKinsey & Co. (1992).
[33] McKinsey & Co. (1992).

Recent Reforms

The present trading system was introduced in October 1994, and is scheduled for a major review in mid-1997. Even more than in Germany, the overall trading system is a multi-faceted hybrid: it combines features of the Paris CAC, the Frankfurt IBIS, the London SEAQ-I, and the New York specialist. It is unlikely that any one mind would construct such an eclectic system starting *de novo*; the outcome clearly represents a compromise among the pre-existing players in the Dutch market; i.e. the banks, the non-bank brokers,[34] and the *hoekman* member firms. The system does, however, address trading requirements specific to both the 'wholesale' and 'retail' market segments, as well as the domestic and foreign client base.

The 'Wholesale' Segment

The reforms in the wholesale segment are the most critical in terms of attracting international trading in Dutch equities into Amsterdam. It is not surprising, therefore, that the wholesale end of the equity market was transformed into a Dutch version of SEAQ-I. The public face of this international dealer market is an electronic quotation and advertisement system called ASSET (Amsterdam Stock Exchange Trading System). Dealers advertise quotes in approximately 25 major Dutch stocks, although such quotes are, formally, only binding to the *hoekmannen*, who are charged with 'integrating' the retail and wholesale segments through arbitrage trading.

The electronic billboard itself is not a significant development; rather, it is the rulebook changes accompanying it which made ASE block trading more attractive. Wholesale prices are now fully negotiable: they are no longer tied to prices made for much smaller trade sizes on the floor. Furthermore, prior to implementation of the Investment Services Directive (ISD) there was no *individual transaction* price or volume publication; only cumulative turnover and total transactions were published (in real time for transactions below a certain size). By minimizing the post-trade transparency requirements, the Exchange expected that dealers would be more willing to commit capital to market making *from Amsterdam*. The very deliberate design strategy was to ensure that trading through ASSET was, at the very least, no less favourable to dealers than trading through SEAQ-I. The (stricter) post-ISD transparency rules are summarized in section 4.3.4.

Also featured in the wholesale segment of the market is an inter-dealer broker (IDB) system called AIDA (Automatic Interprofessional Dealing System Amsterdam), an electronic order-driven system resembling Frankfurt's IBIS sys-

[34] Brokers can be owned by banks, but they represent a separate category of intermediary.

tem. Orders above a certain size ('wholesale orders') can be traded anonymously by ASE members, including *hoekmannen*.

The 'Retail' Segment

Orders below a given size (roughly Dfl 100,000 to Dfl 2m, depending on the stock) *must* go through the 'retail' order book. This comprises an electronic order-driven system, resembling the Paris CAC, with *hoekman* intermediation. The *hoekman* in this new system operates as a monopolist market maker, whose presence is intended to provide supplementary liquidity for a given set of stocks in the central market.

The new *hoekmannen* are often referred to in Amsterdam as 'specialists', although they, like their German *Kursmakler* counterparts, have none of the affirmative trading obligations of New York Stock Exchange specialists, and actively compete with customer orders. *Hoekmannen* are obliged to provide continuous two-way prices for a size at least as large as the relevant wholesale threshold (which varies by stock). Bank and broker trades with *hoekmannen* in the wholesale segment are fully negotiable, although commissions are fixed in the retail segment: 0.016 percent for executed trades in which the *hoekmannen* do not participate, and five times as much for executed trades in which they are a counterparty. This higher (0.08 percent) commission encourages them to improve spreads in the order book and increase executions. Commissions being relatively low, *hoekmannen* are expected to supplement their incomes through proprietary trading, particularly keeping the retail and wholesale prices in line through arbitrage against AIDA and ASSET quotes. *Hoekman* screens are visible to all member firms, with the exception of the member ID codes.

The Exchange estimates that the value of trading going through the central order book is roughly 50 percent of total Amsterdam volume, down somewhat from the pre-reform era. While the *hoekman*'s order book is officially referred to as the 'retail' market, this is somewhat misleading, since a significant portion of the transactions is the result of dealers working off their positions.

Views of the Intermediaries

At the polar extremes in this new trading system are the dealers representing the big banks in the wholesale segment, and the *hoekmannen* operating in the retail segment. While the two segments are formally 'integrated', through online quotes and cross-system trading, the markedly different trading structures defining each segment ensure that there is always a degree of tension implicit in operating them in tandem under a single institutional rulebook. Traders in each segment naturally have very different perspectives on who 'makes the market', and how the ASE trading structure could be better adapted accordingly.

Wholesale dealers tend to be sceptical about the remaining usefulness of the *hoekman* role, complaining about both explicit costs (e.g. commissions) and implicit costs (e.g. alleged frontrunning by *hoekmannen*)[35] in the retail market. Some would advocate replacing the *hoekman* with a non-intermediated CAC-type order-driven trading system, at least for the more liquid shares. They point to the alleged large migration of trading volume away from the order-driven system after the 1994 reforms in support of their claims.

The *hoekmannen* see things much differently. Many prefer the old open-outcry market (claiming spreads were narrower then), but insist that the present specialist system is highly preferable to what they see as the most likely alternative – a fragmented, bank-run 'telephone market', with most business migrating abroad. *Hoekmannen* insist that the additional liquidity which they bring to the order-driven segment of the market is vital to the Exchange, and blame the AIDA IDB system for reducing depth and liquidity of their order book.

Future Reforms

As with the *Kursmaklers* in Germany, the *hoekmannen* in Amsterdam are unlikely to survive the turn of the millennium. The trading privileges accorded to *hoekmannen*, which are arguably necessary to maintain the viability of their role, are likely to be increasingly questioned by both the banks and institutions, particularly given the strong doubts expressed over the significance of the supplemental liquidity they provide. Still, under the structure of the ASE in place at the time of writing, the *hoekmannen* together with the non-bank brokers, who generally share their interests, control six of the ten seats on the Exchange board. As long as this structure remains unchanged, piecemeal rather than radical reforms are likely.

However, under proposals scheduled to be submitted for member approval in December 1995, the ASE would be merged with the Amsterdam-based European Options Exchange (EOE), resulting in an entirely new corporate structure. The new holding company, Amsterdamse Beursholding (ABH), would have the primary say on rules governing trading. Only half the shares of the new ABH would be held by ASE Association members, with the other half split between listed companies and institutional investors. Shares would become freely tradable after five years.[36] In preparation for the merger, the ASE intends to change its legal status from an association (*Vereniging*) to a limited liability company

[35] Specifically, the charge is that *hoekmannen* receive orders over the phone, and execute proprietary trades against AIDA or ASSET quotes (which are only firm to *hoekmannen*) before entering or executing the customer order.

[36] During the first five years, only existing shareholders will be permitted to trade the shares. After this period, the trading restrictions will be lifted, but no shareholder will be permitted to control more than 20 percent of the shares (*Financial Times*, 10 October 1995).

(*besloten vennootschap met beperkte aansprakelijkheid*). Not surprisingly, the large bank members strongly support the merger, while the *hoekmannen* and brokers had voted against the proposal in June 1994. Should this radical restructuring actually go forward, swift and sweeping reforms of the retail segment of the equity market will become far more likely.[37]

3.3. Effects of the Continental Trading System Reforms

How effective has the response of the continental exchanges been to the competitive pressure of SEAQ-I? The immediate impact of the reforms was to offer a competitive market for retail-sized orders, but no apparent increase in trading volume relative to SEAQ-I. But more recently liquidity has been flowing back towards the home bourses.

Initially, markets appeared to specialize according to trade size. As we document in section 4.2, there is solid and consistent evidence that the automated auctions of the continental exchanges had a comparative trading cost advantage in the retail segment of the market. But initially the continental exchanges did not recover market share relative to SEAQ-I. On the contrary, Pagano and Röell (1993a) find that, at least initially, the switch to the computerized auction was associated with a fall in the trading volume of the Paris Bourse: as stocks were moved to the new system, their turnover fell by about 20 percent relative to the market as a whole. Urrutia (1990) finds the same result for the Madrid Stock Exchange. Murgia (1993) and Impenna, Maggio, and Panetta (1995) find the opposite for Milan, but their result may reflect the concomitant introduction of the obligation to concentrate trade on the official exchange, rather than the switch to continuous trading. A possible explanation for the early fall in volume in Paris and Madrid is the initial lack of experience with the new trading system. But another reasonable explanation is that the new automated systems of the continental bourses were assisting SEAQ-I dealers in making a more liquid market in London, allowing them to take advantage of the greater transparency and faster information dissemination produced by these systems.

Over the past few years, however, trading volume has been migrating back towards the continental bourses.[38] Although official exchange turnover

[37] See section 5.3 on exchange governance.

[38] This process is now publicly recognized by leading UK market makers. For example, Natwest Securities recently announced that it will 'conduct far more of its business on continental bourses than on London's SEAQ International system'. Managing Director and Head of Equities Joe Lafferty explained this shift as follows: 'Although London remains the most active centre in the world for European equities, we believe that our clients can benefit significantly from the growing sophistication and transparency of local dealing systems in Europe.' In his view, SEAQ-I provided 'a very useful service' when continental bourses were inefficient, but continental exchanges currently offer 'greater efficiency in both cost and execution' (*Financial Times*, 26 October 1995).

statistics are notoriously unreliable, for reasons detailed previously, there would appear to be a rough market consensus that London's proportion of total French share trading, for example, has declined from about 25-30 percent in 1990-91 to about 5-15 percent today. This latter estimate is also consistent with a recent study by Jacquillat (1995), which produced an estimate of 8.35 percent for 1993. French equity trades actually executed through the London Stock Exchange are now primarily large block and program trades, which require the services of a dealer market.

It must be recognized that it is difficult to disentangle the effects of trading system changes from those of wider market developments. In particular, many large dealers throughout Europe emphasize the substantial effect which ebbs and flows in US institutional orders can have on European trading volumes, and on which exchange(s) trading volume officially appears. London-based US and UK trading houses were the natural first port of call for US fund money moving into Europe. During the heyday of SEAQ-I, 1988-91, London-based dealers were also committing substantial capital to market making in continental equities. Some accumulated substantial losses from such dealing in the early 1990s, and subsequently withdrew capital from this area of business. Thereafter, liquidity was increasingly to be found primarily on the local exchanges.

The increased liquidity of the continental bourses would therefore appear to be a function both of the execution cost advantages for smaller trades inherent in the new continental electronic auction markets, and the declining willingness of London dealers to commit capital to 'all weather' market making in continental stocks. Therefore, buy-side traders are now both increasingly *willing* to forgo immediacy on block trades, in favour of splitting orders and working them through the continental auction markets, and at the same time increasingly *obliged* to forego immediacy because of a deterioration in the market making commitment of London dealers. Correspondingly, London broker-dealers are now doing considerably less *dealing* in continental equities for their customers, and considerably more *broking* through the continental bourses. This serves to reinforce the liquidity of these local markets.

4. THE EVOLUTION OF PARALLEL TRADING UNDER DIFFERENT MARKET STRUCTURES

4.1. Competition and Interdependence

Continental auction markets and SEAQ-I dealers compete for order flow, but at the same time are interdependent. SEAQ-I market makers set their quotes utilizing the real-time price and order flow information disseminated by the auction market screens, and use those markets to unwind their excess positions. But the continental auction markets also benefit from the additional liquidity that London dealers provide by placing orders in their limit order books. This mixture of competition and interdependence between the markets is witnessed by at least two pieces of evidence: the effect of trading activity on the continental bourses on the SEAQ-I spread, and the continuous arbitrage between these trading systems.

4.1.1. Impact of Continental Auction Trading on SEAQ-I Spreads

Pagano and Röell (1990, 1993a) report that the London market touch for cross-listed French stocks falls from 3 percent to 1.5 percent when the Paris Bourse opens at 9.00 (UK time), stays approximately constant at that level until the Bourse closes at 16:00, and then shoots back up to almost 3 percent after the Paris close. This doubling of the spread size far exceeds the corresponding increase for British stocks in the London market.[39] A similar pattern also emerges for German stocks between both IBIS and SEAQ-I, on the one side, and the Frankfurt Stock Exchange on the other: just prior to the opening of the FSE at 9:30, spreads in both IBIS and SEAQ-I widen and both markets become less deep.[40]

There are two possible interpretations of these intra-daily swings of the market touch for cross-listed stocks, and they are not mutually exclusive. The first is that when the continental bourses are open, they exert a competitive discipline on London market makers who post prices for the same stocks. This 'discipline' hypothesis is consistent with most of the available evidence on the effects of inter-market competition in the United States. The second explanation relies on the presence of informed traders. When continental bourses are open, London market makers count on their prices as a guide to set their quotes, and thus feel less exposed to traders using privileged information. As a result, they tighten their spreads.

A related finding is reported by Impenna, Maggio, and Panetta (1995), who compare the SEAQ-I bid-ask spread on Italian cross-listed stocks which

[39] Using evidence reported by Lee (1989), one can estimate by how much the market touch for British stocks rises outside the 'mandatory quote period' (from 9:00 to 17:00): in the early morning and in the evening the average touch is 14.3 percent higher for the most heavily traded stocks (at the time called 'Alpha' stocks), and between 9.9 percent and 8.2 percent for less heavily traded stocks (called 'Beta' and 'Gamma', respectively).

[40] Brown (1994). A similar result was also found for Italian cross-listed stocks in 1990, before the transition of the Milan Stock Exchange to a continuous automated auction, but the increase of the London spread after the Milan close was considerably smaller. Pagano and Röell (1991) report that the average market touch on Italian stocks in London started at 1.75 percent at 10:30, decreased to 1.53 percent at 12:00, then climbed to 1.62 percent at 13:30, and finally reached its highest value after the Milan close, being 1.86 percent at 15:00 (at the time the Milan Stock Exchange closed at 14:00 on a normal trading day). Similar figures are also found by Panetta (1991). The fact that the effect is much weaker than for the French cross-listed stocks may be due to the fact that in 1990 the Milan Stock Exchange was not yet an automated exchange, and thus did not provide the same type of real-time information on prices and order flow as the Paris Bourse.

were shifted to the continuous auction in Milan, on the one hand, with the bid-ask spreads of the stocks which kept trading in the Milan call auction on the other. In 1992, as the stocks of the first group made the transition to continuous electronic trading, their average bid-ask spread on SEAQ-I declined 35 basis points below that of the second group of stocks. So the effect of home-country trading on the SEAQ-I spread appears to be specifically linked to the fact that this trading activity occurs on the continuous automated auction. This is not surprising if one considers that – in contrast with the pre-existing auction system – the automated auction features very fast dissemination of price and order flow data, and allows very rapid order placement.

These empirical findings suggest that – at least since the introduction of the electronic continuous auction – the trading activity of the continental bourses also benefits the users of the London market, making it more liquid than it would otherwise be.

4.1.2. Continuous Arbitrage and Cross-Border Trading

The rapid and widespread dissemination of trading information made possible by screen-based quotation and auction market systems allows arbitrageurs to keep the two types of markets strictly in line with each other. Pagano and Röell (1993a) find that SEAQ-I and the Paris Bourse are perfectly arbitraged: in a sample of 380 perfectly time-matched observations for 16 different stocks taken in July 1989, they do not find a single unexploited arbitrage opportunity. By way of comparison, arbitrage in Italian stocks was less than perfect before the transition to automated trading: Pagano and Röell (1991) and Panetta (1991) find that some transaction prices struck in Milan in the '*durante*' session (the bilateral trading session before or after the call auction) fell outside the contemporaneous best bid and ask quotes of SEAQ-I dealers. It should be mentioned that these trades generally involved rather small amounts and were not very visible to the generality of market professionals.

This suggests that the visibility and the speed of transmission of price information featured by the continuous auction increased the integration between the London market and the continental bourses. This process of integration has also been assisted by the fact that some of the most important London market makers in continental equities are major continental banks (such as France's Paribas, Germany's Deutsche Bank, and Italy's IMI) which have simultaneous access to SEAQ-I screens and screens from their own domestic markets. Likewise, the larger UK-based European equity dealers, such as SBC Warburg, have become major players on the local markets.

But the two markets are linked not only by arbitrageurs. As already mentioned, the continental auction markets are used by London market makers to close out their excess positions.[41] Moreover, dealers increasingly operate on the continental auction markets without taking the client orders on their books at a preset price, but rather by working the orders gradually into the continuous auction at a price very close to the bounds of the spread, or even within the spread.[42] On the Paris Bourse, one major *société de bourse* claims to execute three-quarters of its block orders in this fashion; whereas in 1987 three-quarters of its block orders were handled 'upstairs', outside the central market.

A common strategy to 'work' a block order involves placing a sequence of limit orders which equal or improve the best market quotes, rather than market orders. In their detailed analysis of the order flow and limit order book in Paris, Biais, Hillion, and Spatt (1992) find that 65 percent of order placements equal or improve on the current best quote. In fact, quote improvement is a very common strategy used deliberately to gain execution priority over existing orders. The Bourse's rules actually encourage the use of such aggressive limit orders, rather than market orders: if one places a market order, any excess that cannot be executed at the best price on the opposite side of the limit order book is converted into a limit order at the best quote.[43] So the architecture of the trading system implies that a dealer who wants to 'work a block' into the continuous auction quickly must 'provide liquidity' to the opposite side of the market by placing limit orders, rather than 'consume liquidity' by placing a single large market order. This trading activity of the dealers is likely to contribute to the liquidity of the continuous auction. In this sense, the auction and the dealer market are truly interdependent.

4.2. Transaction Costs and Market Structure

One of the most consistent empirical findings regarding the relative efficiency of auction and dealer markets is that auction markets offer lower transaction costs. However, auction markets are generally unable to provide immediate execution of large orders without substantial 'price erosion', or market impact. In other words, auction markets offer cheap execution, but can provide immediacy only for retail-sized orders: a trader who wishes immediate execution of a large order can only obtain it cost-effectively on a dealer market.

[41] In fact, Pagano and Röell (1991) find that, even though most of the time the Milan prices appear to lead those in London, in some instances the reverse occurs. This may reflect the price impact of large order imbalances created by London market makers offloading positions in Milan.

[42] On the Paris Bourse, member firms can execute pre-arranged trades at a price within the *fourchette* via a procedure known as *application*.

[43] In other words, one cannot execute a single large market order sweeping away, in one shot, many limit orders on the opposite side of the market. This implies, paradoxically, that an impatient trader is forced to place a sequence of limit orders *within* the *fourchette*, whereas a patient one is more likely to place a market order, have part of it converted automatically into a limit order *at* the best bid or ask quote, and wait until the latter executes.

One can use several methods to compare the liquidity of a dealer and an auction market. The simplest one involves comparing the difference between the lowest ask and the highest bid quoted by the competing dealers (in London, the so-called market 'touch') with the difference between the best buy and sell limit orders outstanding in the auction market (in Paris, the so-called '*fourchette*'). A first problem with this measure, however, is that the two best limit order prices in an auction market generally apply to smaller transactions than those for which dealers commit to quote firm prices. In other words, the *fourchette* applies to smaller trades than the market touch. But this problem can be overcome by computing the hypothetical average price that one could obtain in the auction for a given order size, provided it does not exceed the entire limit order book. So one can compute a weighted-average market spread in the auction market (*fourchette moyenne ponderée*) for the order size for which market makers post firm quotes, and compare this spread with the market touch.

This approach has been applied in a variety of studies, which have invariably concluded that SEAQ-I quotes are wider than domestic auction spreads in Paris,[44] Brussels,[45] Milan,[46] and Germany.[47] However, a serious methodological criticism may be levelled at these studies: by looking at *quoted* spreads they will overestimate trading costs in dealer markets, where trades often take place within the market makers' quotes, especially for medium and large transactions.[48]

[44] Pagano and Röell (1990, 1993a) use two weeks of perfectly time-matched data from SEAQ-I and the Paris Bourse recorded in July 1989 for 16 cross-listed French stocks, and find that the SEAQ-I average touch for these stocks was 1.52 percent, compared with a *fourchette* of 0.41 percent. The results do not change much when the market touch is compared with the *fourchette moyenne ponderée* (weighted-average spread) computed for order sizes ranging from half to twice the SEAQ 'normal market size'.

[45] Andersen and Tychon (1993) analyse a group of 12 cross-listed Belgian common stocks, accounting for more than half the total Brussels volume in 1992. They find that the typical market touch on SEAQ-I was 1.9 percent, compared with a *fourchette* of about 0.4 percent and a *fourchette moyenne ponderée* of 0.6 percent for deals of 1.3 million francs (the SEAQ 'normal market size') in Brussels.

[46] Impenna, Maggio, and Panetta (1995) analyse the Italian cross-listed shares in 1992 and report a market touch of 1.69 percent on SEAQ-I and a *fourchette* of 0.41 percent in Milan.

[47] Schmidt and Iversen (1992) report comparative spreads on IBIS and SEAQ-I over the first and second quarters of 1991 and find that average quoted spreads are 0.76 percent on IBIS and 1.25 percent on SEAQ-I, and that the inside spread for SEAQ-I (6 stocks only) is 0.64 percent. Davis (1993), using June-November 1993 data, shows that a large proportion of SEAQ-I trades occurs at prices within 0.5 percent of the quote mid-point. Brown (1994) performs a detailed analysis of data between October 1991 and March 1992. He confirms that IBIS offers a narrower spread than SEAQ-I if one considers quoted spreads.

[48] For the London Stock Exchange, this is documented by the figures reported in the *Stock Exchange Quarterly* (April-June 1992 and October-December 1993). Clemons and Weber (1989) report that 45 percent of all trades on the London Stock Exchange are done at a price within the market touch. Reiss and Werner (1994) show that the most common form of competition among market makers is not publicly undercutting other quotes, but rather offering price improvement over the phone, especially for intermediate trade sizes. Röell (1992) reports similar results also for SEAQ-I, where the difference between realized transaction prices at which dealers sell and buy French stocks is about half the quoted bid-ask spread for the 'normal market size'.

But a more recent study is immune from this particular criticism, being based on transaction prices rather than on quoted prices. This study – by de Jong, Nijman, and Röell (1995) – presents a considerably more subtle picture.[49] Again, looking only at average *quoted* inside spreads, they find that transaction costs for small trades are lower in Paris than in London. For larger sizes, however, the Paris limit order book is too shallow and the average quoted spread rises steeply. The London dealer market provides more liquidity at larger trade sizes. Looking instead at the average *realized* spreads, based on actual transactions, Paris fares somewhat better. This reflects the inclusion of crossed trades: trades matched outside the CAC system, and therefore of larger size, but priced within the quoted spread. Paris trades now look cheaper even at larger sizes: the authors find an *implicit* transaction cost advantage (i.e. excluding taxes and commissions) even at trade sizes of twice normal market size (roughly twice median transaction size, or about 5 percent of average daily trading volume).

However, this study also points to several very important caveats. First, Paris trades are, on average, much smaller than London trades. There are few Paris transactions exceeding NMS, while roughly half of all London transactions exceed NMS. In terms of trade size, the 99th percentile in Paris is just around NMS, whereas the 90th percentile in London is already around five times NMS. Second, large Paris trades are almost exclusively crosses, outside the CAC system, which do not provide the immediacy available from a London dealer. Third, *explicit* transaction costs (i.e. taxes and commissions) are considerably lower in London for large transactions (roughly 0.14 percent of transaction value for a FFr 7m trade, compared with 0.5 percent in Paris). This is because many large London deals are done on a 'net' basis, with commissions 'included' in the price. This explicit transaction cost advantage tends to compensate for London's wider spreads.

This study confirms what one would expect in comparing trading costs in continuous auction and dealer markets. If the order is small, it can generally be handled more cheaply by bypassing the dealer intermediary and submitting it directly to the 'public liquidity' of an auction market. If the order is large, the choice will depend on the trader's demand for immediacy. Those who want the order traded quickly *en bloc* will generally find a cheaper execution in a dealer

[49] Another study (Brown 1994) finds that SEAQ-I provides transaction prices comparable with those provided by IBIS for trades executed with market makers.

One could suggest that even these comparisons are unfair because they do not allow for home-country informational advantage: if information reaches the domestic exchange before the foreign dealers, the domestic bid-ask spread may be tighter than the foreign one for reasons unrelated to the intrinsic functioning of the two markets. But the home-country informational lead is not sufficient to explain these differences, as shown by Booth, Iversen, Sarkar, Schmidt, and Young (1994) in a study of a matched sample of American stocks traded on Nasdaq and German stocks traded on IBIS.

market. Immediacy is important to many traders as insurance against *execution risk*: i.e. the danger of adverse price changes while the order is being filled.[50] Those who are willing to forego such insurance, and wait patiently for the arrival of counterparties, are likely to find the auction market less expensive.

4.3. Transparency and Market Structure

Market transparency refers to the ability of market participants to observe the information in the trading process. This definition, though simple to state, masks an enormous amount of complexity. Transparency is one of the most hotly debated issues in the design and regulation of equity markets, in Europe as elsewhere. It is a contentious issue both domestically in the UK, where the relevant rules have been repeatedly changed and are still passionately debated by academics and policy-makers, and in the European Union, where the regulation of last trade publication was a major source of conflict between the UK and France in the drafting of the Investment Services Directive (see Chapter 4).

Transparency has two different aspects, which are sometimes conflated. *Pre-trade* transparency refers to the availability of data about the order flow impending on the market and the prices at which incoming orders are likely to be executed. *Post-trade* transparency refers instead to the availability of information about the last executed trades, and depends on the publication rules of the exchange.[51]

4.3.1. Pre-Trade Transparency

Pre-trade transparency varies widely in different markets. The minimum level of pre-trade transparency is that achieved in a pure telephone market, where not even the quotes of competing market markers are visible to the investing public (e.g. the foreign exchange market). The maximum level of pre-trade transparency in a dealer market is achieved with publicly visible firm two-way quotes in large size. However, no one can see the consolidated order flow which impacts the market at each moment, because each dealer observes only the orders placed with him, and can at best try to infer some information on the orders received by other dealers by observing their quote revisions and by trading with them.

In practice, even when market makers are required to post firm two-way quotes, the information reflected in these quotes can be very limited. Trades be-

[50] Pagano and Röell (1993b) provide a model where agents who are more averse to execution risk may prefer the implicit insurance offered by a dealer to the lower expected trading costs of the auction market.

[51] It should always be kept in mind that trade reporting differs from trade *publication*: even if stock exchange members are required to report their trades immediately to stock exchange authorities, the latter may publish these data with some delay, and it is this that matters for the working of the market.

yond the quoted size must be negotiated privately over the phone. More importantly, quoted prices may not be an accurate guide to the transaction prices that can actually be obtained. Clemons and Weber (1989) found that 20 percent of trades, accounting for 45 percent by value, are executed at prices within the touch. A published estimate for SEAQ-I was 'up to 80 percent' of trades in 1992,[52] and this figure is probably higher today. SEAQ-I continental equity quotes are currently so wide that they serve merely as public advertisements for dealer services – services which can only be obtained at reasonable cost over the phone.

In an auction market, the degree of pre-trade transparency can range from a minimum of publishing no information about impending orders to a maximum of communicating details about all the orders to be executed in the market: in other words, the full supply and demand curves for each stock at each instant, together with the identities of those placing the orders. Naturally, most continuous auction markets adopt intermediate positions between these two extremes. In most European auction markets, the full limit order book is accessible to member firms in real time, although certain orders may be 'hidden' and broker-dealer IDs are often suppressed. At a minimum, the two best outstanding bid and ask limit orders are generally available publicly through data vendors.

4.3.2. Post-Trade Transparency

Post-trade transparency tends to be considerably higher in auction markets than in dealer markets. Continuous electronic auction markets generally publish executed trades automatically and immediately. In dealer markets, trades must be manually reported to the exchange within a set time limit, after which they *may* be published, perhaps with a time delay, according to the rules of the exchange. At a minimum, exchanges generally publish consolidated trading volume data in each security. Maximal post-trade transparency would comprise immediate publication of price and volume data for each transaction, as well as the identifications of the transacting member firms.

4.3.3. Transparency in Continuous Auction and Dealer Markets

Central electronic auction markets cannot function without a relatively high degree of pre- and post-trade transparency, because of the absence of dealer intermediation. Since the investing public are obliged to interact directly (perhaps through brokers, but not via dealers' books), some portion of the consolidated limit order book (*at least* the best bid and ask) must be publicly visible (*at least* to member firms). Since these visible orders are usually from traders wishing to

[52] *Stock Exchange Quarterly* (Summer 1992).

take on or dispose of a specific position – unlike market maker quotes, which are offers to facilitate an inter-temporal *transfer* of positions – transacting parties are generally not put at risk by public revelation of trade price and volume information. Thus when orders are matched, electronic auction markets have no compelling incentive to suppress trade publication. Indeed, such markets have a strong *positive* incentive to ensure that post-trade price and volume information is quickly and widely disseminated, since this information attracts the interest, and limit orders, of other traders.[53]

The scenario is wholly different in a dealer market. Market makers commit capital to provide immediate 'private liquidity' for investors looking to buy or sell at a specific point in time, regardless of whether there happens to be a natural counterparty at that point in time. Market makers are naturally reluctant to reveal their trades to the market, particularly very large trades, because they, unlike auction market traders, generally do not wish to hold the positions they take from customers. Market makers absorb large positions in their capacity as liquidity providers, and will subsequently have to rebalance their inventories in the market.

Forcing a *market maker* to publish a block trade immediately, therefore, is generally the equivalent of forcing him to reveal his immediate trading intentions. No trader in *any* market reveals his intentions if it is not in his interests to do so: market makers are not exceptional in this regard. Any trader, buy-side or sell-side, who slices up a block order and feeds pieces through the market over time is deliberately withholding valuable price-relevant information from the market (i.e. the full size of the order), and is therefore attenuating the market's transparency. But this allows him to lower his trading costs, and thus affords him an incentive to trade actively. This explains why the Paris CAC system actively assists traders in shielding their full trading intentions: traders may submit 'hidden orders' into the system, and the Bourse allows them to do this because it is believed to be worthwhile sacrificing some measure of transparency in order to attract more turnover.

Dealers' incentives to conceal information about their recent trades are so strong that even when immediate trade publication is mandated it tends to generate a variety of avoidance responses. These may, in fact, limit considerably the impact of mandatory trade publication on market transparency. The three most common avoidance responses are the following:

[53] Many electronic auction exchanges, such as Stockholm and London's Tradepoint, emphasize publicly the transparency of their systems as a means of attracting order flow from the dealer markets: that is, they see transparency in their auctions as a *source of competitive advantage*. See, for example, *The Wall Street Journal Europe* (22 June 1995:12).

1. The dealer *crosses* the trade with one or more counterparties, rather than taking the position into his personal inventory. This is the general response of US Nasdaq dealers who, faced with immediate publication requirements, will not generally provide the immediate execution which their UK SEAQ counterparts will.[54] SEAQ dealers also circumvent publication requirements through the use of 'protected trades'.[55] During the period in which the dealer searches for counterparties, he is in possession of price-relevant information which is not being revealed to the market. The party placing the order therefore loses the possibility of achieving immediate execution at a fixed price, with no net benefit to the wider market in terms of earlier information dissemination.
2. The dealer agrees with the party initiating the trade to report it later in the day, in violation of the rules of the exchange.
3. The dealer executes the trade in a foreign market without immediate publication, or 'off-exchange'.

If the dealer should offer a less attractive price because of the publication requirement, the party wishing to trade may choose to execute his order directly in an auction market. In this case, he, like a dealer, does not disclose his true inventory to the market, but instead trickles small orders through the market over time. Essentially, he behaves *exactly* as the dealer would have, had the dealer been willing and able to take his position. The basic effect on the market is identical. There will be a market impact from the large size of the position as it is being worked off, and the earlier counterparties lose relative to the later because of their lack of awareness of the future orders. Under the reasonable assumption that the trader is less skilled than the dealer in working the order, the market impact will be quicker, larger, or both. When a trader offloads a block position onto a dealer, then, he is often buying a 'market impact management service'. This service will generally be either unavailable or more expensive under an immediate publication requirement.

Such common market behaviour suggests that a fully transparent market is a chimera. Regulators cannot compel private agents to reveal their trading intentions, nor can they assume that private agents will provide liquidity to a market irrespective of the transparency regime. However, it is certainly possible

[54] See Franks and Schaefer (1991).

[55] These are trades where the market maker provides a guaranteed price for a particular quantity but tries to execute it at an improved price depending on market conditions, and rebates part of the price improvement back to his customer. As a result, the trade is reported at the time of completion of the trade, rather than at its inception. See Franks and Schaefer (1995).

to *encourage* both order revelation and liquidity provision through *intelligent trading system* design. Examples of this are:

- CAC 'hidden orders', which facilitate a *controlled* revelation of orders to the market, and increase the depth of the limit order book.
- Tradepoint continuous auction commission pricing: only market orders (which demand liquidity) pay an execution fee; limit orders (which supply liquidity) are free.
- AZX call auction[56] pricing: visible orders submitted early to the market (which contribute more to price discovery) pay a lower execution fee than orders submitted later.

4.3.4. The Current State of Transparency Rules in European Dealer Markets

On the London Stock Exchange, post-trade transparency rules have undergone considerable change since 1986.[57] The most recent changes agreed between the Exchange and the Securities and Investments Board (SIB) will increase the speed of large trade publication. The goal is to ensure that 75 percent of liquid domestic equity trades by value are published immediately, and 95 percent within one hour. From 1 January 1996, all trades up to 6 times NMS will be published immediately, trades from 6 to 75 times NMS within one hour, and trades above 75 times NMS within five days. Under legal advice which the LSE is said to have taken regarding the requirements of the ISD, these rules will be extended to EU stocks quoted on SEAQ-I.

[56] AZX is the parent company of the Arizona Stock Exchange, a US proprietary trading system. See the appendix to Chapter 2 on call auctions.

[57] There have been four different regimes so far. From 1986 to 1989, immediate publication was mandated for trade sizes and prices for Alpha stocks: that is, the most actively traded stocks (78 percent of the trades by value). This still left a gap of 3 to 5 minutes between trade and publication to allow reporting by member firms.

After a price war which reduced the profitability of many market makers and caused a surge in off-exchange dealing, in February 1989 the Exchange reversed its position and allowed a 24-hour delay in publication for large trades (the prices of all trades in Alpha stocks over £100,000 were published after 24 hours, although the size of each trade was still published immediately). This implied that only 30 percent of the transaction prices of Alpha stocks, and as little as 6 percent of the total value of trades, were immediately reported. This change in regulation was motivated by the argument that immediate last-trade publication exposed market makers to the reaction of competitors, who would move their quotes in line with the last reported trade prices.

Later on, the classification of stocks in terms of Alpha, Beta, and Gamma was abandoned, and each stock was ranked according to its normal market size (NMS) – a measure of its average transaction size. From February 1991 to December 1995, immediate publication was required for almost all trades smaller than 3 times NMS, which meant that approximately 52 percent of trades by value were published immediately. Trades from 3 to 75 times NMS were subject to a maximum 90-minute publication delay. For exceptionally large trades, above 75 times NMS, a maximum delay of five days could be requested from the Exchange.

From 1 January 1996, the publication requirement was tightened, as described in the text.

This rule change so dramatically increases post-trade transparency on SEAQ-I that, inadvertently, *the London Stock Exchange may find itself the most transparent dealer market in Europe* come 1996. The Frankfurt Stock Exchange has stated that telephone trading and floor trading without *Kursmakler* intermediation would remain 'off-exchange', and therefore not subject to any publication requirement. The Amsterdam Stock Exchange will begin immediate publication of transaction volumes and prices for wholesale (AIDA and telephone) trading in 1996, but delayed publication for large proprietary telephone deals will be possible, subject to the discretion of the officer of quotations. Delay will not normally be granted for trades under 5 times 'normal market size'.[58] The Paris Bourse indicated that there would be a modification of its publication rules for the block trading regime, but did not specify what this would be. The existing rules allow a 2-hour delay for proprietary trades from 1 to 5 times NBS (roughly equivalent to London's NMS), and next morning publication on larger trades, making it considerably less transparent than London under its revised rules.

Discussions with London dealers indicate considerable concern over the new SEAQ-I publication rules, which they feel will put them at risk in their proprietary trading. It is entirely possible that trade reporting will therefore be diverted from London onto more opaque continental exchanges, possibly requiring the establishment of new legal entities to avoid requirements directed at LSE member firms. As we explained earlier, such regulatory arbitrage is inevitable.

4.3.5. Transparency and Trading Costs: Theory and Evidence

Theoretical Models

There is a rapidly growing theoretical literature on market microstructure, examining the trading process under alternative trading structures. When analysing the tradeoff between transparency and liquidity in the dealer market, many of these models focus on the implications of having two classes of investors active in the market: the 'informed' and the 'uninformed'. This is clearly an extreme simplification of the trading environment, but it serves to isolate factors which we might expect to be significant.

With delayed trade publication, each dealer knows only the orders submitted to him when he sets his quotes. His order flow information is therefore less complete than in a continuous auction market or in a dealer market with immediate publication. As a result, the dealer is more exposed to the danger of being taken advantage of by an informed trader. Pagano and Röell (1993c) show that for this reason lower transparency may increase the average trading costs of

[58] Normal market size in Amsterdam is roughly 1 percent of average daily trading volume for a large stock like Royal Dutch Petroleum.

uninformed investors, although not necessarily at all trade sizes. Conversely, informed traders can earn larger average profits in the dealer market, where they can better camouflage behind the 'noise' of uninformed traders.

Transparency may also serve to lower trading costs where it makes it easier for customers to monitor the actions of their broker-dealers. Of course, dealers and many of their institutional clients have long insisted that there is an important tradeoff to be acknowledged between transparency and liquidity: that is, dealers required to post firm two-way prices will widen their spreads if forced to reveal their trades instantly to the market. The existence of this tradeoff receives confirmation in the market microstructure literature, but the literature generally concludes, not surprisingly, that the benefits of increased liquidity with decreased transparency are reserved for certain classes of investors, trading with whom is believed to provide dealers with a subsequent advantage in the market. If dealers can gauge the information conveyed by a trade and exploit it later with other traders, they can give better prices to information-intensive orders relative to the rest of the market.

This argument has been formalized by Röell (1990a) and by Naik, Neuberger, and Viswanathan (1994). In these models, delayed reporting allows dealers to profit from trades made with informed traders and with large liquidity traders: they 'learn' information about fundamentals from informed traders and about impending orders from large liquidity traders, and can use this information in their subsequent trading with smaller liquidity traders. Thus they may be willing to make a very liquid market to the large and information-intensive traders, at the expense of small liquidity traders. The same result obtains in Madhavan (1995), which demonstrates how delayed publication may benefit informed traders and large liquidity traders at the expense of small retail traders with no private information.

This effect is not unambiguous, however. Informed traders often cannot be recognized as such, and dealers therefore face an 'adverse selection' problem. To the extent that dealers fear becoming the victims of an informed trade, they will widen their spreads rather than narrow them.

Empirical Evidence

There are two general arguments why market makers will offer better prices on block trades with delayed publication. The first is that delayed publication allows them to rebalance their inventories at lower cost, because the rest of the market is unaware of their full trading requirements. The second is the information argument described immediately above, which asserts that market makers 'learn' from transacting with certain types of traders, and are therefore willing to pay for information through narrower spreads.

The empirical evidence is not extensive, but provides some modest support for the conclusions of the two arguments. Gemmill (1994) uses an event study methodology on UK equity data, analysing the effect of publication speed on UK share prices. Since small trades tend to be executed *at* the market touch, and larger trades *within* the touch, Gemmill measures the relative cost for different trade sizes by the gap between the size of the estimated transactions spread for large trades and the size of the SEAQ touch. He finds that in three of the four years in which publication was delayed, spreads were narrower for large trades, both in absolute size and relative to spreads on small trades, indicating that large trades received 'price improvement' relative to small ones. Although Gemmill finds the evidence statistically inconclusive, the data do on average suggest a relative advantage for large trades under delayed publication. Breedon (1993) also compared a period in the UK's immediate-publication regime with a period in the 90-minute-delay regime, and found that immediate publication increased large trade spreads relative to small. Gemmill's positive results for a period comparable with that which Breedon examined are consistent with Breedon's findings.

It is not clear, however, to what extent these findings should be read as evidence in support of the models just discussed. Small investors may be relatively disadvantaged in a dealer market because of factors wholly unrelated to transparency, such as a relatively high fixed-cost component of trading. De Jong, Nijman, and Röell (1995) do, in fact, find that the cost of trading is decreasing in trade size, indicating that order-processing costs are an important determinant of bid-ask spreads (in contrast with the predictions of most theoretical market microstructure models). Second, and more significantly, dealers themselves believe that true 'information' trades are rare,[59] which throws into question the very relevance of modelling a world in which the critical independent variable is the classification of traders as either 'informed' or 'uninformed'.

5. FORCES SHAPING THE DEVELOPMENT OF EUROPEAN EQUITY TRADING

As we discuss in Chapter 2, modern equity markets are subject to economic forces encouraging both concentration and fragmentation of trading. On the one hand, securities markets feature external economies in the production of liquidity, so that order flow tends naturally to concentrate on a single market-place. On the other hand, technological advance has enabled competition among alternative market architectures, and thus a market-driven segmentation of trading accord-

[59] Franks and Schaefer (1991).

ing to the specific characteristics of different securities, investors, and trading strategies. In this section, we examine how these countervailing tendencies are manifested in the behaviour of market participants.

5.1. Inter-Exchange Collaboration

The European Commission's 1985 White Paper 'Completing the Internal Market' represented the launch pad for the Community's 'Single Market' programme. The White Paper's section on the European securities sector presented the following vision of how the European equity markets would become 'integrated':

> Work currently in hand to create a European securities market system, based on Community stock exchanges, is also relevant to the creation of an internal market. This work is designed to break down barriers between stock exchanges and to create a Community-wide trading system for securities of international interest. The aim is to link stock exchanges electronically, so that their members can execute orders on the stock exchange market offering the best conditions to their clients. Such an interlinking would substantially increase the depth and liquidity of Community stock exchange markets, and would permit them to compete more effectively not only with stock exchanges outside the Community but also with unofficial and unsupervised markets within it (p.29).

In essence, integration was to be seen as a 'networked' version of the national market *status quo*. 'Depth and liquidity' were to be substantially increased through the magic of modern electronics, moulded by grand committee design. This vision was subsequently translated into the 'Euroquote' initiative of the Federation of European Stock Exchanges (FESE) – an initiative which collapsed under the weight of the divergent interests of its members.

A central electronic quotation system for Community stock exchanges has neither a compelling commercial logic, nor a wider economic logic. To the extent that any particular exchange would benefit, it would almost certainly mean that this exchange would be free-riding off the costly and valuable price discovery services of another. In the case of Euroquote, London is likely to have benefited in this manner *vis-à-vis* Frankfurt, for example, which would explain why German reservations were particularly significant in the demise of the project. The present scenario, where independent data vendors (e.g. Reuters and Bloomberg) purchase price feeds from exchanges and sell them to intermediaries and investors, and where proprietary order routing systems (e.g. Cedel's Liberty subsidiary) construct specific network linkages according to actual market demand, would appear to be the only viable arrangement from a commercial perspective. Yet taking a broader market-wide perspective, it is difficult to see why a European market comprised of relatively illiquid national exchanges should itself become liquid – or even in any meaningful sense 'integrated' – on the basis of simple electronic interfacing. Networking mules does not make them into racehorses.

A more modest venture by the four Nordic exchanges, 'Nordquote', did in fact get off the ground in May 1994. Begun as a quote dissemination system for the largest 100 Nordic stocks, it was hoped that it would eventually evolve into a full-scale electronic trading platform. However, as with the Euroquote blueprint, it relied on the mere existence of an electronic billboard to unleash imaginary latent trading interest. The system was wound up in August 1995, having generated no perceptible increase in cross-border activity.

A third such initiative, 'Eurolist', was officially launched by the FESE in September 1995. By paying a single fee to the home exchange, issuers can obtain a 'single passport' for listing on all member exchanges. This liberates them from having to meet the administrative requirements of each individual European exchange. However, trading will undoubtedly continue to concentrate where the shares are already most liquid: i.e. almost invariably on the home exchange trading system and/or through (largely London-based) international dealing banks. Any net addition to the liquidity of the shares – which should be minimal – will probably come from wider public exposure to the cross-listed company, rather than from new trading volume on other European exchanges.

To conclude, collaborative arrangements among European exchanges, of the sort described above, will not in and of themselves achieve any significant increase in the liquidity of European stocks. This will only come with the removal of barriers to competition among market intermediaries. This was never implicit in Euroquote, Nordquote, or Eurolist.[60] To date, removing such barriers has been extremely difficult to achieve because of the vested interest which national exchange members have in restricting competition from new broker-dealers or trading systems. These barriers are now just beginning to fall, however, under the pressure of issuers, foreign intermediaries, and institutional investors, and in some cases supported by deregulation at the national and European Union level.

5.2. Remote Membership

The London Stock Exchange dramatically demonstrated the benefits of competition to European liquidity provision with the launch of SEAQ-I in 1986. Conti-

[60] Under the terms of an October 1995 letter of intent signed by Deutsche Börse, the Paris Bourse operator SBF, the French options exchange Monep, and the French futures exchange Matif, a joint French-German trading platform, involving common membership, could *possibly* emerge after further discussions. A decision is to be reached by 31 March 1996. Such a collaborative arrangement *would* involve expanding direct access to new intermediaries, and therefore has significant potential to expand turnover and liquidity.

nental exchanges, the early victims of this competition, attempted to fight back in a number of ways. One was collaboration, which failed for the reasons described above. The second was to seek government protection. As we explain in Chapter 4, the French Treasury attempted to provide such protection through the transparency and 'concentration' provisions of the Investment Services Directive. This strategy is unlikely to succeed in protecting less competitive exchanges for long, but to the extent that it does it is likely to reduce market liquidity. The third strategy was to compete on the basis of an overhaul of trading structures, systems, and rules, which has clearly shown signs of success. In 1995, the Stockholm Stock Exchange, among the hardest hit by the emigration of liquidity to London, became the first in Europe to introduce a major new component to this third strategy: the establishment of remote foreign membership.

Remote membership allows foreign intermediaries direct electronic access to national screen-based systems without having to establish a physical presence in the home Member State. Without such direct membership, foreign intermediaries are obliged to trade through local member firms, implying higher transaction costs and less access to real-time market information. By expanding direct access, increasing competition, lowering costs, and increasing information flows, remote membership has significant potential for expanding home exchange turnover, and therefore liquidity. It also reduces the attractiveness of the type of inter-exchange collaborative arrangements described above, which explains Stockholm's public indifference to the collapse of Nordquote.

In the pre-ISD era, an exchange was required to secure approval as a 'recognized' foreign investment exchange from each Member State in which it sought to establish remote members. Under Article 15.4 of the Directive, exchanges designated as 'regulated markets' by their home authorities no longer require such approval from foreign authorities. Therefore, it might be expected that 1996 would witness a surge in remote membership.

This may not occur soon for two reasons. The first is that, at the time of writing, it is expected that fewer than one-third of Member States will have fully implemented the ISD on time. Thus regulated markets will be unable to invoke their single passport rights in many Member States for some considerable time beyond 1 January 1996. The second reason is the resistance of many present members of national exchanges to the increased competition implied by the expansion of membership to new non-resident intermediaries. A membership association's incentive is to maximize the value of membership, and this is often achieved by maintaining present member access privileges and by restricting organizational innovations – including those which could increase liquidity and share value.

Currently, Stockholm is the only continental stock exchange actually to have implemented remote membership – having four Danish, one Norwegian, and one UK member – and this cannot be accounted for purely by the pre-ISD administrative inconvenience of pursuing foreign authorization.[61] The members of the Stockholm Stock Exchange are no different from those of other exchanges in having reservations about wider direct access to foreign members; but Stockholm is unique in that it is not effectively controlled by its members. This leads us into the next issue of critical importance for the future development of European trading structures: the governance of exchanges.

5.3. Exchange Governance

Exchanges are almost exclusively membership organizations, although a number of membership exchanges in Europe now also have a corporate structure. Even where an exchange is organized as a company, however, control is almost invariably vested in the member firms, who are brokers or broker-dealers. Particularly where the exchange is a monopolist, this dominance by the intermediaries severely limits the responsiveness of the exchange to the requirements of investors and issuers, and to technological change which facilitates new modes of trading (such as electronic order-driven trading in London, and electronic call market trading more widely).

Swedish legislation transformed the Stockholm Stock Exchange into a limited liability company in 1993, and a new corporate structure was created in which members and issuers each control half the shares. From 1994, these shares became freely transferable, meaning that other institutions (including foreign institutions) may tender for the shares, and even for effective control of the Exchange. The new Exchange also has no legal monopoly in share trading. Following the reorganization, the Exchange moved quickly to reduce membership fees sharply and to institute remote membership – reforms which clearly served the interests of issuers, and which Exchange officials ascribe specifically to issuers' newly won influence.

In the future, we are likely to see exchanges reorganized so as to include not only a measure of issuer control, but investor control as well. Such structures will enable exchanges to react more quickly to the demands of their customers, more closely emulating true private businesses. Such exchanges should, *ceteris paribus*, have a competitive advantage over their broker-dealer-dominated rivals.

Investor participation has been at the root of a fierce debate in Copenhagen over the pending reorganization of that exchange. Under the present working proposal, a 60:40 share split between members and issuers would leave investors

[61] The Amsterdam Treasury Market has 18 remote members based in London, Paris, Frankfurt, and Brussels.

out in the cold. Their annoyance was sufficient to provoke several into discussions with Tradepoint about the possibility of trading Danish equities on this alternative platform.

Under the terms of a proposed reorganization of the Amsterdam market (see section 3.2.4), the stock exchange company which would succeed the ASE would be the first in Europe to offer share ownership (25 percent) to institutional investors. Listed companies would have an equivalent holding. Should the plan go forward, it will undoubtedly provoke a wider European debate about the role of investors in exchange governance.

As exchanges begin to behave more like businesses, we can also expect to see more and more exchange functions hived off to specialized institutions. Particularly in the case of a dealer market (such as the LSE), it is certainly possible to envisage a 'minimalist' exchange, which is little more than a loose self-regulatory association. Information and execution systems can be provided by private electronic vendors (such as Reuters and Bloombergs); clearance, settlement, and custodial services can be provided by banks and specialized institutions (such as Citibank, Euroclear, and Cedel); and even 'listing' services can be provided by private ratings agencies (such as Moody's and Standard & Poor's). In the United States, the move towards subcontracting ancillary services appears already to have begun. In September 1995, the Chicago Stock Exchange announced its intention to shed all its clearance, settlement, and depository services businesses.[62] To the extent that such 'subcontracting' reduces operating costs, exchange members will come increasingly to demand it.

Specialized institutions are also showing signs of wanting to compete aggressively for trading support services. It is understood that a major international data vendor held discussions with LSE member firms aimed at persuading them to post their quotes on its system, rather than on SEAQ. We can expect the future to see the proliferation of electronic trading systems which are not organized as exchanges at all. These non-intermediated systems, known widely as 'proprietary trading systems' (PTSs), are the subject of our next section.

5.4. Proprietary Trading Systems

The traditional stock exchange where traders had to meet face-to-face in order to transact is a remnant of a bygone era, before the advent of computerization. Limitations of space required limitations of access, generally in the form of a fixed number of 'seats' whose market value reflected the profitability of restricted access to broking and dealing activity. Technological barriers to intermediary access

[62] See *Global Investment Technology* (2 October 1995:12).

have now been entirely eliminated, as reflected in the proliferation of screen-based exchanges. Of course, some major exchanges – such as the New York Stock Exchange (NYSE) and London's LIFFE derivatives exchange – still operate effectively with trading floors, but they are now subject to a degree of competition (both actual and potential) which was unimagined twenty years ago. A growing number of these challengers are private companies, PTSs, selling electronic trading services direct to the trading public – currently just institutions, but plans are already in place to extend such services to individual investors.[63]

PTSs already offer a range of market architectures. Some do not provide independent price discovery, and simply cross orders at a reference price drawn from an official exchange. In the United States, ITG's Posit runs a highly successful crossing network, where commissions are roughly one-third of the normal five to six cents brokerage fee on the NYSE. AZX, on the other hand, operates a daily call *auction*, with independent price discovery, after the close of NYSE business.[64]

Reuters' Instinet, operating in a number of major market centres around the globe, runs two electronic systems: a continuous auction with an anonymous online negotiating facility, and a crossing network where traders' orders are matched at the main market's mid-quote. Estimates of its Nasdaq share trading volume range from 13 to 50 percent, indicating how successful order-driven systems can be operating alongside a dealer environment.

In September 1995, Tradepoint began London operations with a continuous electronic auction on the 400 most active UK stocks. The company plans to introduce an electronic call auction for less liquid stocks in due course. As with Instinet in the Nasdaq market, Tradepoint has introduced an order-driven component into a predominantly quote-driven market, and hopes thereby to attract institutional traders through lower transaction costs. However, Tradepoint is also considering adding non-UK stocks to its trading menu, which would put its continuous auction into parallel operation with those on the continent. In this case, it would not have the advantage of an unexploited market structure niche, as it does in London, but rather would have to compete with continental exchanges on the basis of cheaper access. With a staff of 40 (4 percent of the LSE), an annual budget of £5.5m (3 percent of the LSE), and no member firms required to intermediate trades, Tradepoint – and similar systems – may be able to undercut tradi-

[63] ESI intends to offer a 24-hour small-cap continuous auction market in the UK, accessible through home PCs, direct to retail investors.

[64] Owing to current regulatory restrictions limiting AZX to after-hours trading, and relatively low volumes, the system at present effectively operates as a crossing network, since bidders tend to use the NYSE closing price.

tional member exchanges. The commoditization of trading services is under-way, and no European exchange will be immune from its effects.

Even though Tradepoint's continuous auction system is conceptually similar to that operated by Instinet, the two companies are very different legal entities. In contrast to Tradepoint, Instinet functions legally as a *broker* rather than a *trading system.* This has allowed it to set up European operations quickly, by becoming a *member* of each major stock exchange: at the time of writing, London, Paris, Frankfurt, and Zurich. As a result, Instinet and Tradepoint are regulated on an entirely different basis. This leads us into our next area of discussion, 'regulatory arbitrage', a phenomenon which is likely to grow rapidly in significance in the coming years.

5.5. Regulatory Arbitrage

Like a traditional broker, an electronic broker often matches customer orders internally. This, of course, is also precisely what a trading system does. Quite understandably, many exchanges object to having competing trading systems as members, which explains why a number of European exchanges ban automatic electronic internal order matching and routing by members. Yet it is extremely difficult to stop this practice: electronic 'brokers' will generally find some exchange to abet their operations, and they will simply route matched orders forbidden on the home exchange to a more accommodating exchange. London currently plays the role of 'exchange of last resort', attracting forbidden matched trades and large block trades from around Europe and the United States[65] on the basis of pure regulatory arbitrage.

The choice of regulatory classification is itself a form of regulatory arbitrage. As noted above, Instinet was able to expand quickly into Europe, without any ISD 'single passport', because of the relatively light regulatory requirements which apply to brokers, as opposed to trading systems. However, the company is obliged to negotiate its terms of operation with each and every exchange on whose national turf it wishes to operate – unlike Tradepoint which, in theory, can use its 'single passport' to cart its own rulebook around Europe. While brokers can arbitrage some rules across exchanges, others cannot easily be avoided. The LSE has invented a separate member classification for Instinet – a 'closed user-group trading system' – and can impose restrictions on the manner in which other member firms transact through it. Tradepoint faces different problems. For example, it has been argued that US mutual funds could not, under US law, trade directly through Tradepoint (because it is an 'exchange'), although they can do

[65] US trades are often booked in London to avoid the immediate trade publication requirement.

so through Instinet (because it is a 'broker'). Additionally, Article 15.5 of the ISD could be invoked by a Member State authority to prohibit another Member State's 'regulated market' (i.e. an exchange) from placing screens on its territory in order to trade equities already listed on a domestic exchange (see Chapter 4). Again, this provision disadvantages Tradepoint relative to Instinet. In short, regulatory classification can have a significant impact on the ultimate success or failure of a trading service provider.

Regulatory arbitrage will, over time, render ineffective most government efforts to control the development of European market structure. Questions whose answers could previously be dictated by government will increasingly be answered in the market-place:

- *Who* performed the trade? Intermediaries will establish separate legal entities to carry out transactions at the lowest cost and under the most accommodating regulation.
- *What* is the status of the trading system? Is it an *exchange*, a *broker*, a *price display system*, or something else? Intermediaries will seek out the most favourable regulatory classification.
- *When* was the trade performed? Intermediaries will agree the timing of trade reporting with clients to accommodate large block and program trades.
- *Where* was the trade performed? Intermediaries will report trades to the exchange or regulatory body where costs are lowest and, in the case of large proprietary trades, where publication requirements pose the least risk.

5.6. The Role of Dealers

Many market observers appear to confuse the demise of SEAQ-I with the demise of the London dealer market. This is a serious mistake. The SEAQ-I system itself is no longer used to attract trading, but the dealers on the telephones behind the screens continue to commit capital to large block and program trading in continental equities. The latter in particular appears to be growing in importance.

Dealers around Europe tell the same general story. Since the introduction of continuous electronic trading on the continent, the proportion of customer orders which are taken on dealers' books to those which are 'worked' on an agency basis has undoubtedly declined dramatically. One major French *société de bourse* reports that in 1987 approximately 75 percent of its French equity trading was done 'upstairs' (on its own books) and only 25 percent was crossed or worked through CAC; while now 75 percent of its orders are worked through CAC, 5 percent are crossed, and only 20 percent are done on own-account. A major London dealer reports that in 1988-89 approximately 80-90 percent of continental equity orders were taken on the firm's books, while this figure is now down to around 5-10 percent. But whereas fewer customers are demanding the firm's capital now, the firm is actually committing *more* capital to trading to accommodate those customers who do demand immediacy. Increasingly, this is for program trading. A significant segment of the European markets still operates through dealers, and their importance may actually grow as institutions come increasingly to dominate trading.

Institutions differ dramatically in their trading practices, and in their demand for dealer capital (i.e. immediacy). Nationality is certainly one factor, as this determines the trading environment institutions are most accustomed to. The head European equity trader of one major European bank reported that Dutch and UK institutions, for example, were far more likely to demand immediacy than US and French institutions. He estimated that he was asked to commit his capital to servicing approximately 70 percent of Dutch institutional orders and 50 percent of UK orders, but only 20 percent of French and 5 percent of US orders. In the case of French and US institutions, he was generally expected to work the order in the markets over time.

Approximately 35 percent of German equity trading currently takes place over the phone (including London trading), despite a high level of dealer satisfaction with IBIS. Obviously, not all of this is own-account trading, but major trading banks indicate that customer demand for dealer capital is strong and growing.

Traders in Milan indicate that the move to T+5 rolling settlement in February 1996 should lead to an embryonic form of dealer activity in the Italian market. Under the old monthly account system, buyers did not need to put up capital for their purchases until the end of the monthly settlement period (by which time many would have liquidated their positions). Under rolling settlement, large purchases will have to be financed up front, leading to a demand for dealer capital.

While most of the biggest European trading banks have their European trading headquarters in London, it is increasingly meaningless to say that their own-account trades take place 'in London', and certainly misleading to suggest that they take place 'through the London Stock Exchange'. The LSE, as distinct from its members, no longer has any significant role to play in continental equity trading. As for the members themselves, their trading capital is controlled by individuals who, depending on the firm, may sit in London or in the local market: Morgan Stanley's head German equity trader sits in Frankfurt, UBS' head Dutch equity trader sits in London, and Crédit Lyonnais' head French equity trader sits in Paris – where he controls the London SEAQ-I screen. In short, European telephone trading does not meaningfully take place *anywhere* – and certainly not through a stock exchange.

Yet if officially reported LSE continental equity trading declines after 1 January 1996 – when increased transparency is likely to push trade reporting out of the Exchange – this will undoubtedly be heralded as evidence of the success of reformed continental markets. This will be a serious mistake, not simply because it is not accurate, but because it will further blind continental exchange officials to the significance of the dealer market. The size of institutional equity holdings in Europe is set to grow rapidly in the coming years, and institutional orders can often swamp the public liquidity available in a continuous auction market at any given point in time (see Chapter 3). Institutional equity holdings in the United States have risen from 6.1 percent of the total outstanding in 1950 to around 44 percent today, and US market structure has been forced to adapt accordingly. The provision of dealer capital to service European institutional transactions may be critical to increasing the liquidity of the European markets, and exchanges should not be fooled by the fact that these transactions are often not visible into thinking they do not exist. Their existence is a signal that alternative trading structures which cater to the type of trading currently accommodated by dealers (e.g. program trading) should perhaps be made available. We discuss one such alternative, electronic call market trading, in Chapter 2.

5.7. Disintermediation

Institutionalization of European equity trading implies increasing dealer intermediation for some types of trading, but growing *disintermediation* for others. That is, investors – especially institutional investors – will increasingly look to bypass what they consider to be costly and unnecessary intermediation. In the United States, this demand has led to the growth of proprietary trading systems which allow investors to deal directly, anonymously, and on equal terms with other investors or intermediaries. In Europe, the development of semi-open architecture trading platforms, such as CAC, has inadvertently opened up *de facto* (if not *de jure*) direct access for clever institutions. Since it is possible for French broker-dealers to create their own front-end trading interface with CAC, it is likewise possible for their clients to create their own indirect computer interfaces with CAC (i.e. via their broker-dealers' systems). It is understood that a number of smaller (and therefore weaker) French broker-dealers have already provided such (unmonitored) access – in violation of the rules of the Bourse. Bourse officials acknowledge that in the future open and direct access may have to be extended to institutional investors. If exchanges cannot overcome member-firm resistance to such liberalization, an increasing volume of investor order flow is likely to be diverted to proprietary trading platforms.

6. SUMMARY AND CONCLUSIONS

The past decade has been one of remarkable change for European stock exchanges. Trading structures, systems, and rules have been completely revamped, largely in response to the early competitive success of the London dealer market.

Since 1991, the trading structure through which London dealers made their markets in continental equities – the London Stock Exchange's SEAQ International – has been crumbling, owing to increasing competition from new continental continuous electronic auction markets and the declining profitability of 'all weather' market making in London. While the London Stock Exchange, as distinct from its members, has effectively ceased playing any material role in continental equity trading, London-based trading houses continue to be a major force shaping the development of European trading. They remain the primary brokers for the continental equity orders of UK and US institutions, and the primary source of immediate liquidity for large block and program trading.

Gradually, the European dealer market which developed under the structure of London's SEAQ International is becoming a pan-European telephone and proprietary data screen network. This network operates in tandem with the electronic auction systems of the national exchanges, and while the two layers compete for customer order flow, they are also each dependent on the liquidity supplied by the other. Dealers operate to provide 'private liquidity' for customers whose large orders cannot be cost-effectively accommodated in public auction markets, but such private liquidity would be considerably more expensive without public auction markets for dealers to work off their excess positions. Just as the London market spread to continental Europe to provide the dealer component which was missing there, so the missing order-driven component in London is now being offered by new competitors, such as Instinet and Tradepoint.

As we have documented, trading costs tend to be considerably lower in order-driven auction markets than in dealer markets, at least for orders whose size does not overwhelm the public limit order book. Dealer markets, however, generally better serve clients requiring protection from execution risk on large orders. In the absence of government intervention, we can expect market forces to generate a mix of auction and dealer trading appropriate to the diverse needs of retail and institutional investors.

Increasingly, we expect that these services will be offered by private companies owned outside the primary national exchanges. Proprietary electronic trading, brokerage, order routing, price dissemination, and post-trade support systems will further drive down trading costs through improved technology, lower overheads, and bypassing oligopolistic intermediaries. This competitive pressure may be further increased through the cross-listing of stocks on existing exchanges, combined with the cross-border expansion of exchange trading systems through remote membership – a process which is already under way. As the market for trading services becomes increasingly contestable, European exchanges will be forced to react by widening access, reducing fees, hiving off ancillary services, expanding their product range, and instituting new and cheaper modes of transacting. In order to do this, they may first have to undergo painful organizational restructuring, generally involving the dilution of member-firm control and increasing the direct influence of issuers and investors.

Although growing competition among trading systems will make it difficult for national exchanges to concentrate domestic trading within their own structures, the cross-border expansion of intermediary access (through remote membership) and market information (through private electronic data vendors) will ensure that the European equity markets remain well integrated. But whereas national exchanges may be concerned about increasing fragmentation of domestic share trading, some – particularly the smaller ones – may soon be more concerned about forces for international consolidation. We discuss the issue of a possible single European currency in Chapter 10. Should a single European currency actually materialize, this can be expected to have a dramatic effect on European market structure. The primary electronic trading systems currently employed by continental exchanges are fundamentally identical, and once currency costs and risks are eliminated, these systems will be pitted head-to-head against one another with little to differentiate them. The consolidation of regional exchanges *within* European countries should be completed within a few years' time, but a single currency can be expected to impel the consolidation process *across* national borders. Some exchanges can be expected to merge, while others may simply be forced to disband.

On the demand side, the most critical factor in determining the European market structure of the future will be the growth of trading by institutional investors. Funds under institutional management are growing rapidly, and still have enormous unexploited potential in Europe. Such potential could be realized very quickly if governments were to remove barriers to the growth of private pensions and restrictions on pension fund asset allocation (see Chapter 6). As institutions increase the size of their portfolios of stock and liquid instruments, their trading desks will increasingly dictate modes of trading to exchanges and intermediaries. Chapter 3 is devoted entirely to an analysis of their trading practices and preferences, which should allow us to gauge how their growing participation will shape the markets of the future.

On the supply side, a key factor over the next decade will be the growth in privatizations of state-owned companies. While the UK is well advanced with its privatization programme, most continental countries are only at the mid-stage (such as France) or just at the beginning (such as Italy and Spain). Some financial intermediaries are even concerned about possible 'gluts' in the supply of equities deriving from large-scale uncoordinated national privatization schemes, although the expected growth of pension and unit trust funds should go some way towards bridging the gap between supply and demand.

Somewhat worrying for the development of the European equity markets, and the wider European economy, is the anaemic growth in exchange listings for small and medium-sized companies. Success in encouraging such firms to seek a public listing creates its own virtuous cycle: increasing the ease with which new firms can be brought to the market increases the attractiveness of committing private venture capital, which in turn increases the supply of new firms available to the market. The ability of new small company markets – such as AIM in London, Nouveau Marché in Paris, and the pan-European EASDAQ – to attract issuers and investors will be important in determining the future growth and vitality of the wider European capital markets.

Finally, current thinking about public policy towards the markets will have to undergo a radical change. The equity market remains one of the few segments of the economy where the regulatory principles derived from industrial economics are largely ignored. Current public policy aimed at controlling modes of transaction and the dissemination of information is a dysfunctional remnant of a bygone era of natural monopoly exchanges. Rapid advances in computerization over the past twenty years have fundamentally reshaped the structure of the equity markets. These markets are now contestable, if not yet fully competitive. As competition comes into the sector, the proper scope for government intervention and regulation is correspondingly reduced. This will be the focus of our discussion in Chapter 4.

Appendix 1

LIES, DAMNED LIES, AND TURNOVER STATISTICS

European exchanges are engaged in an increasingly fierce competition over turnover figures. Much of this competition is driven by official LSE statistics for foreign equity turnover, which can reflect both real and fictitious deficiencies in the trading systems of the continental bourses. This generates endless public disputes over whether and to what degree trading system reforms on the continent have been successful in repatriating trading volume from London.

London – in common with Amsterdam, Copenhagen, Dublin, Milan, Oslo, Stockholm, and Switzerland – adopts what is known as the 'Regulated Environment View' (REV) in calculating its turnover. This method incorporates all trades over which it has a 'regulatory oversight' into its turnover statistics. To ensure strict compliance, both UK and non-UK members of the LSE tend to report proprietary trades in non-UK equities to the LSE as well as to the local bourse, even where the members' London staff have no role in facilitating the trades. Thus London foreign turnover statistics are artificially inflated, although the degree of inflation depends on the specific foreign stock in question. Exchanges adopting the REV approach will generally produce, *ceteris paribus*, higher turnover statistics than exchanges adopting the 'Trading System View' (TSV), which only count trades passing through their specific trading system. The TSV approach is used by many exchanges operating central order books, such as Athens, Brussels, Helsinki, Lisbon, Luxembourg, Madrid, Paris, and Vienna. Deutsche Börse is recorded by the Federation of European Stock Exchanges as using the REV approach, although officials at Deutsche Börse indicate that they actually use the TSV approach.

One particularly surprising item in the domestic turnover statistics is that for Deutsche Börse, which is, as reported, higher than London's. This is very likely a statistical artefact of the structure of the floor trading environment. 'Courtage arbitrage', for example, encourages trading intermediation through *Freimaklers*, who benefit from a courtage discount when trading with *Kursmaklers*. Thus, what is effectively one trade can wind up producing several official trades.

There is one relatively minor source of distortion in the present turnover statistics which, unlike the others, is highly significant in terms of the future development of the European equity markets. This is what might be termed 'rulebook arbitrage', whereby traders select the exchange to which they report their trades on the basis of which exchange rulebook best accommodates the transaction they wish to execute. As we discuss in section 3.2.1, for example, block traders in French equities will often report trades to London rather than Paris to avoid the latter's price restrictions and/or publication requirements. Likewise, in the case where a continental bourse forbids automatic order matching outside the central trading system (as in Paris), electronic brokerage systems can simply route internally matched trades in continental equities to London. In the future, this sort of arbitrage may become highly significant in Europe, as it will compel exchanges to adapt their trading systems and trading rules to the demands of the more aggressive and innovative intermediaries.

Appendix 2

Table. Percentage Shares of World Market Capitalization, 1982–94

	1982	1983	1984	1985	1986	1987	1988	1989	1990	1991	1992	1993	1994
USA	53.27	52.85	51.95	47.56	38.23	30.59	27.92	28.83	33.24	37.07	39.84	40.87	42.89
Japan	16.69	17.80	20.29	22.12	30.33	41.09	43.20	39.01	33.15	29.99	25.14	24.89	20.52
UK	7.45	7.00	6.92	8.02	7.61	9.12	8.08	7.88	10.42	9.54	9.96	7.53	7.74
Canada	4.24	4.07	3.89	3.62	2.93	2.75	2.53	2.79	2.58	2.36	2.51	3.77	4.34
Germany	2.83	2.74	2.56	4.40	4.29	2.84	2.72	3.46	4.07	3.74	3.48	3.25	3.20
France	1.83	1.23	1.33	1.96	2.63	2.16	2.53	3.27	3.47	3.44	3.48	2.94	3.06
Switzerland	1.70	1.71	1.88	2.15	2.34	1.86	1.65	1.83	1.89	1.97	2.03	1.75	2.59
Hong Kong	0.00	0.00	0.00	0.88	0.88	0.69	0.88	0.77	0.99	1.18	1.84	1.85	1.82
Taiwan	0.00	0.00	0.00	0.00	0.00	0.00	1.28	2.28	0.84	0.92	0.82	1.60	1.71
South Africa	3.95	3.36	2.25	1.26	1.76	1.86	1.34	1.41	1.17	1.23	1.22	1.31	1.48
Netherlands	2.06	2.42	2.10	1.36	2.04	1.84	1.47	1.36	0.92	1.08	1.10	1.41	1.36
Australia	1.70	2.08	1.71	1.57	1.37	1.18	1.56	1.35	1.29	1.38	1.35	0.91	1.29
Korea	0.22	0.28	0.26	0.17	0.24	0.44	1.01	1.36	0.94	0.72	0.89	1.73	1.28
Malaysia	0.69	0.93	0.81	0.55	0.25	0.24	0.25	0.38	0.41	0.42	0.75	0.63	1.25
Italy	0.85	0.66	0.76	1.57	2.44	1.47	1.56	1.54	1.79	1.57	1.26	1.48	1.23
Brazil	0.51	0.53	1.25	0.97	0.71	0.23	0.33	0.43	0.13	0.33	0.37	1.23	0.98
Sweden	0.85	1.00	1.04	1.27	1.27	0.98	0.97	1.06	1.39	1.28	1.84	0.89	0.91
Singapore	0.98	1.23	0.85	0.49	0.59	0.49	0.49	0.58	0.79	0.79	0.48	0.83	0.85
Mexico	0.19	0.12	0.15	0.09	0.10	0.17	0.26	0.44	0.35	0.77	1.14	0.61	0.77
Thailand	0.00	0.00	0.00	0.00	0.00	0.00	0.00	0.00	0.18	0.21	0.47	0.51	0.75
Total	100.00	100.00	100.00	100.00	100.00	100.00	100.00	100.00	100.00	100.00	100.00	100.00	100.00

Source: Fédération Intérnationale des Bourses de Valeurs.

Figure. Percentage of World Market Capitalization, 1985

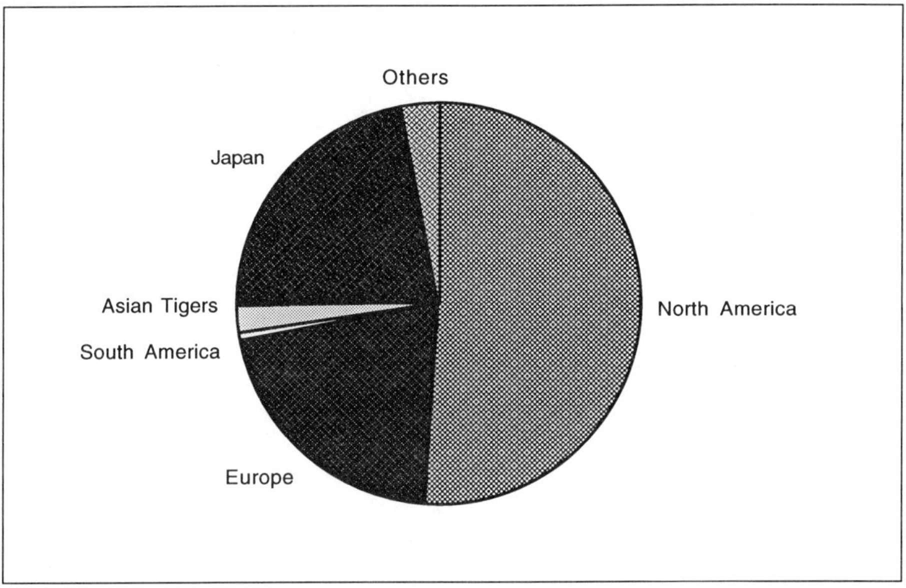

Figure. Percentage of World Market Capitalization, 1994

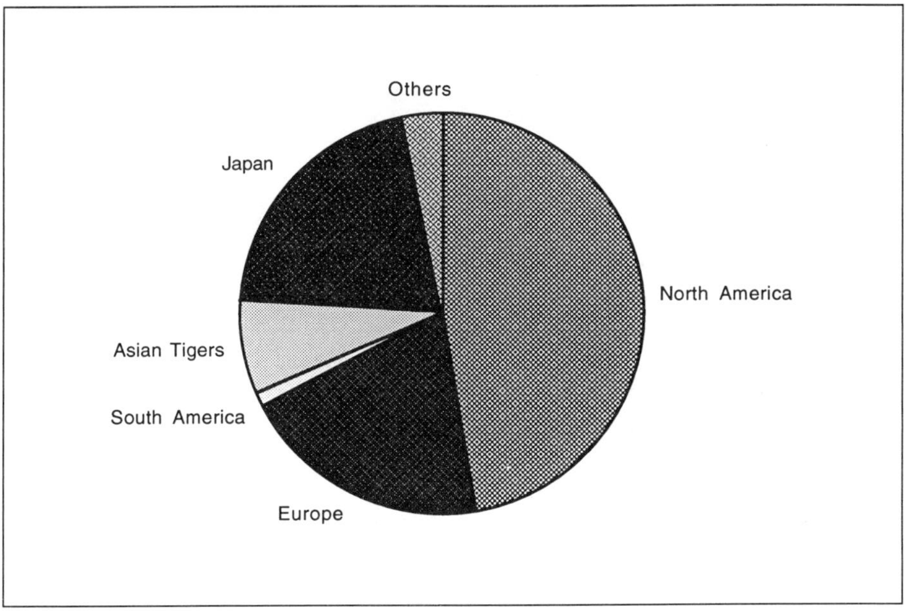

References

Anderson, Ronald W. and Pierre Tychon, 1993. 'Competition among European Financial Markets: The Case of Belgian Cross-listed Stocks', Discussion Paper 9314, Département des Sciences Economiques, Université Catholique de Louvain.

Biais, Bruno, Pierre Hillion and Chester Spatt, 1992. 'An Empirical Analysis of the Limit Order Book and the Order Flow in the Paris Bourse', paper presented at the CEPR workshop on Market Microstructure, 3–4 April, Konstanz.

Booth, G. Geoffrey, Peter Iversen, Salil K. Sarkar, Hartmut Schmidt and Allan Young, 1994. 'Market Structure and Bid-Ask Spread: Nasdaq vs. the German Stock Market', unpublished manuscript.

Breedon, Francis, 1993. 'Intra-day Price Formation on the London Stock Exchange', LSE Financial Markets Group Discussion Paper No. 158, March.

Brown, Nicholas Arthur, 1994. 'Information Links and Liquidity Effects in Parallel German and London Equity Markets', unpublished PhD dissertation, London Business School.

Clemons, E. and B. Weber, 1989. 'International Stock Exchange: Assessment and Recommendations', internal report to the London Stock Exchange.

Cohen, Norma, 1994. 'Paris woos trade with system to speed big share deals', *Financial Times*, 29 July.

Davis, Ruth, 1993. 'London Trading in German Equities', *Stock Exchange Quarterly with Quality of Markets Review*, Winter.

de Jong, Frank, Theo Nijman and Ailsa Röell, 1995. 'A Comparison of the Cost of Trading French Shares on the Paris Bourse and on SEAQ International', European Economic Review, 39:1277–1301.

Financial Times, 1995. 'Amsterdam SE Plans Merger with EOE', 10 October.

Franks, Julian, and Stephen Schaefer, 1991. 'Equity Market Transparency', *Stock Exchange Quarterly with Quality of Markets Review*, Summer.

Franks, Julian, and Stephen Schaefer, 1995. 'Equity Market Transparency on the London Stock Exchange', *Journal of Applied Corporate Finance*, Spring, 8 (1):70–77.

Gemmill, Gordon, 1994. 'Transparency and Liquidity: A Study of Large Trades on the London Stock Exchange under Different Publication Rules', Office of Fair Trading Research Paper No. 7, November.

Global Investment Technology, 1995. 'Chicago Stock Exchange to Shed Ancillary Units', 2 October:12.

Impenna, C., P. Maggio and Fabio Panetta, 1995. 'Innovazioni Strutturali nel Mercato Azionario: gli Effetti della Contrattazione Continua', Banca d'Italia, Temi di

Discussione del Servizio Studi No. 248, January.

Jacquillat, Bertrand, 1995. 'The Diversion of Order Flow on French Shares from the CAC Market to the SEAQ International: An Exercise in Transactions Accounting', Working Paper, Université Paris Dauphine, November.

Kregel, Jan, 1990. 'Changes in Trading Structure and Large Block Trading in Major Stock Markets', English version of Appendix 6 of the Instituto per la Ricerca Sociale's *Terzo Rapporto sul Mercato Azionario*, Il Sole–24 Ore, Milan, March.

Lee, Ruben, 1989. 'Market Making on the UK Stock Exchange', unpublished PhD dissertation, Nuffield College, Oxford University.

McKinsey & Co., 1992. 'Towards a Stronger International Position in Dutch Securities: Summary of Findings, Conclusions, and Recommendations', report submitted to the Board of the Amsterdam Stock Exchange, 6 November.

Madhavan, Ananth, 1995. 'Consolidation, Fragmentation, and the Disclosure of Trading Information', *The Review of Financial Studies*, Fall, 8 (3): 579–603.

Murgia, Maurizio, 1993. 'Il Mercato Telematico Azionario', Istituto per la Ricerca Sociale, Working Paper No. 7, February.

Naik, Narayan, Anthony Neuberger and S. Viswanathan, 1994. 'Disclosure Regulation in Competitive Dealership Markets: Analysis of the London Exchange', London Business School, Institute of Finance and Accounting Working Paper no. 193, July.

Office of Fair Trading, 1994. 'Trade Publication Rules of the London Stock Exchange', Report to the Chancellor of the Exchequer by the Director General of Fair Trading, November.

Pagano, Marco and Ailsa Röell, 1990. 'Trading Systems in European Stock Exchanges: Current Performance and Policy Options', *Economic Policy*, 10, April.

Pagano, Marco and Ailsa Röell, 1991. 'Dually-traded Italian Equities: London vs. Milan,' LSE Financial Markets Group Discussion Paper No. 116, April.

Pagano, Marco and Ailsa Röell, 1992. 'Auction and Dealership Markets: What is the Difference?', *European Economic Review*, 36 (2/3), April.

Pagano, Marco and Ailsa Röell, 1993a. 'Shifting Gears: An Economic Evaluation of the Reform of the Paris Bourse', in V. Conti and R. Hamaui (eds), *Financial Market Liberalization and the Role of Banks*, Cambridge University Press.

Pagano, Marco and Ailsa Röell, 1993b. 'Auction Markets, Dealership Markets and Execution Risk', in V. Conti and R. Hamaui (eds), *Financial Market Liberalization and the Role of Banks*, Cambridge University Press.

Pagano, Marco and Ailsa Röel, 1993c. 'Transparency and Liquidity: A Comparison of Auction and Dealer Markets with Informed Trading', LSE Financial Markets Group Discussion Paper No. 150; Revised version, IGIER Working Paper No. 54, November, forthcoming in the *Journal of Finance*.

Panetta, Fabio, 1991. 'Gli effetti della quotazione internazionale: il caso delle azioni italiane a Londra', Banca d'Italia, Temi di discussione del Servizio Studi no. 156, August.

Reiss, Peter C. and Ingrid Werner, 1994. 'Transactions Costs in Dealer Markets: Evidence from the London Stock Exchange', Stanford University, Graduate School of Business, Research Paper No. 1289.

Röell, Ailsa, 1990a. 'Dual Capacity Trading and the Quality of the Market', *Journal of Financial Intermediation,* 1.

Röell, Ailsa, 1992. 'Comparing the Performance of Stock Exchange Trading Systems', in J. Fingleton and D. Schoenmaker (eds), *The Internationalization of Capital Markets and the Regulatory Response*, Graham and Trotman, London.

Schmidt, Hartmut and Peter Iversen, 1992. 'Automating Germany Equity Trading: Bid-Ask Spreads on Competing Systems', *Journal of Financial Services Research*, 373–97.

Schmidt, Hartmut, Olaf Oesterhelweg and Kai Treske, 1995. 'Deutsche Börsen im Leistungsvergleich – IBIS und BOSS-CUBE', *Kredit und Kapital*, November.

Urrutia, Alfredo, 1990. 'El Paso al Mercado Continuo: Efectos sobre la Volatilidad de los Precios y el Volumen de Contratación', *Moneda y Credito*, 191: 41–71.

Worthington, Peter M., 1991. 'Global Equity Turnover: Market Comparisons', *Bank of England Quarterly Review*, May, 246–9.

Chapter 2

EQUITY TRADING II: INTEGRATION, FRAGMENTATION, AND THE QUALITY OF MARKETS

I. INTEGRATION OF MARKETS

When considering integration and the consolidation of order flow (or its contra-side, fragmentation), it is useful to distinguish between *markets* and *market-places*.[1] Shares may be traded in several different market-places and still be part of a single market. For instance, they may be traded on an exchange floor, in-house at a brokerage firm, or on an exchange in another country. If the *market-places* are sufficiently linked, they effectively comprise one *market*. We consider the European secondary market in the broad sense of 'market', rather than in the more specific sense of 'market-place'. In brief, our position is as follows:

- Integrating separate market-places into a single market is of critical importance to the users of trading systems. Only if markets are integrated will trades be made at low cost and at reasonably accurate prices, and will asset managers achieve appropriate intra- and inter-country portfolio diversification.
- An integrated European market should incorporate a diversity of alternative market-places so as to cater to the varying needs of different investors.
- The most rapidly growing class of participants is the institutional investors. Traditional market-places (the exchanges) may or may not be adaptable enough to service their needs. In any event, proprietary systems should be allowed to offer alternative market-places. Thereafter, it is likely that the competitive pressure the proprietary systems place on the traditional exchanges, along with cross-border trading, will effectively drive the traditional market-places to greater efficiency.
- Cross-border regulatory cooperation is needed between regulatory organizations with regard to manipulation, fraud, money laundering, and other abuses of power and position. But both technology and economic

[1] This distinction is made by Baxter (1996).

considerations are too complicated for any regulatory authority to micro-manage the development of the separate market-places and their integration into a single market. Economic forces should be relied on.

- Impediments to the efficient development of market structure exist. Most importantly, these include the vested interests of sell-side participants, the relative silence of buy-side participants, and regulatory interference. We caution that regulatory attempts to micro-manage market structure may, if unchecked, turn out to be the most serious of the three.

The Natural Tendency of Markets is to Consolidate in a Single Market-place
If allowed to do so, order flow for a specific stock will naturally tend to consolidate in a single market-place. This is because traders comprise a network, and when any transactions network includes a larger number of participants, counterparties can more easily find one another, and transaction prices are in closer alignment with underlying equilibrium values. Because the size of a transactions network contributes positively to the value of the good that is being produced, a securities market may be said to exhibit *positive network externalities*.[2] Positive network externalities in trading explain why order flow tends to attract more order flow, and give a large market-place a strong competitive advantage. Because of network externalities, the natural tendency is for order flow to consolidate, both in space (geographically) and in time.

This does not imply, however, that in a free market environment one securities market will come to dominate trading in Europe, or that a single European stock exchange will evolve. First of all, a home country has an informational advantage in trading shares of its domestic securities. Second, if change is driven by market forces, a menu of trading venues that cater to the varying needs of different investors will be likely to emerge, and both order-driven and quote-driven systems will endure. Third, different issues of securities, depending on their size, average trading volume, and investor base, tend to trade in different types of markets.

However, if one market architecture were to dominate the others, one might expect that system to be emulated in the other national market centres. If so, we expect that the shares of each country will trade predominantly in their home country, but that screens from the home countries will be located throughout Europe, enabling others to access the 'home' country markets. We expect the

[2] Markets with network externalities have received increasing attention in the industrial organization literature in recent years. The approach has yielded new insights in telecommunications, electricity networks, and other high-technology industries.

distribution of screens to proliferate, and trading in shares to become truly pan-European. As this occurs, banks and brokerage houses will likely develop their own cross-border order-routing systems and will increasingly become members, local or remote, of other national exchanges.[3]

Might the national exchanges of some smaller countries and the regional exchanges of other countries weaken and be left with only illiquid, local stocks? It is not possible at this time to state with any certainty which markets will survive and which will perish, but it should be clear that the 'market for markets' may treat some local exchanges harshly: this is a price that must be paid to realize the benefits of competition.

Markets May Also Fragment

Orders can be diverted to a new market-place for two reasons. First, this will occur if the new market-place is more attractive to users as a technologically superior, 'stand alone' system. For instance, the introduction of the IBIS electronic trading system in Germany has resulted in appreciable order flow being taken away from the exchange floors. Second, order flow can fragment spatially if satellite markets offer faster executions for lower commissions while free-riding on the price discovery and other services provided by a major market-place.[4] In the United States, for example, order flow in recent years has increasingly been diverted from the New York Stock Exchange (NYSE) to regional exchanges, to the over-the-counter market, and to proprietary trading and brokerage systems (primarily Instinet, Posit, and the Arizona Stock Exchange). US order flow has also been directed to London, primarily to avoid domestic trading rules.

Fragmentation deriving from competition by market architecture is desirable; fragmentation deriving from free-riding on price discovery is not. Prices can be pirated with relative ease in continuous trading because trading takes place while prices are being set. The trade establishes a price, and the posting of quotes gives the price continuing validity until new quotes and/or a new transaction price are set. Because of its continuing validity, a price established on a major exchange becomes the benchmark against which other orders can be executed in a satellite market. The satellite market trades do not contribute to price discovery, and are of no benefit to those participants who have actively taken part in price discovery by posting quotes on the market.

[3] The operations of a brokerage house could remain centralized in its home country to centralize risk management and to economize on oversight and other management costs.

[4] See Bloch and Schwartz (1978). Note that their analysis of how the order flow can fragment in the absence of an order focusing rule applies to a continuous market, and not to a call market.

The NYSE's response to this threat of losing order flow has been its order focusing rule (Rule 390) which, briefly stated, requires that member firms send their orders for an Exchange-listed stock to the NYSE or to one of the regional exchanges.[5] The Paris Bourse is similarly concerned about orders fragmenting away from its central CAC system. Customers may seek out the other side of a block order, but still have to bring the cross to CAC for execution (as at the NYSE). Additionally, Bourse rules require that orders received by Instinet, a Bourse member, must not be matched automatically through Instinet's electronic system, but rather routed manually to CAC for normal execution. It is clear that the Bourse does not wish Instinet to be considered an alternative market.

Types of Market Integration

Markets may be integrated in different ways and to varying degrees. At one extreme, they can be fragmented, but linked by arbitrageurs. For instance, the *hoekman* (retail market maker) in Amsterdam provides an arbitrage linkage between the exchange floor (which attracts smaller orders) and the upstairs market (which attracts larger orders). At the other extreme, orders can be consolidated in a single *consolidated limit order book* (CLOB). An intermediate solution is to require that the best bids and offers for a stock established in different markets be consolidated, and to disallow trading outside the best consolidated quotes (as with the Intermarket Trading System, ITS, in the United States). Markets may also be integrated by offering a menu of trading venues to participants, with participants being free to choose from the menu as they prefer.

Which form of integration is best? *For a given trading technology*, consolidating orders in a CLOB lowers trading costs and sharpens the accuracy of price discovery. However, as noted above, allowing alternative markets to coexist, side-by-side, encourages intermarket competition, which spurs the development of new trading technologies. A menu of alternatives also gives choices to participants who, because of differences in their sizes and trading styles, require different services from the market.

When not faced with competition, a market-place has little incentive to make innovations that would increase efficiency for its customers. In fact, it has a strong incentive *not* to innovate when a new technology implies lower profits for its members, as is often the case. The evidence is clear in Europe: very little change in market structure occurred in the continental exchanges until they began losing order flow to London's SEAQ-I market. But, since then, change in

[5] Since July 1980, with the institution of SEC Rule 19c.3, Exchange members have been free to trade issues listed after April 1979 away from the Exchange.

most of the European market centres has been dramatic. In addition, competition is just now emerging from proprietary systems, such as those operated by Instinet and Tradepoint. To the extent that competition is sufficient, there is little need to control market design by regulatory intervention.

Barriers to Competition

Although not always conspicuous, serious barriers may exist that keep markets from achieving a desirable degree of integration. The first major impediment to change is the existence of structural arrangements in the securities industry which shield the profitable operations of broker-dealer firms as a group. Sell-side participants, being proficient at finding profits in the inefficiencies of the continuous market, collectively have an incentive to keep markets relatively inefficient.

Exchanges have historically been membership organizations. A membership association's incentive is to maximize the price of membership, not the value of stockholders' equity. The price of membership reflects the value of member access privileges. An innovation that could decrease the cost of trading (for instance, a more efficient order handling procedure) may lower the value of membership (if that system reduced the need to use broker-dealer intermediaries).

Membership dominance in exchange governance is now breaking down in a number of exchanges in Europe (for instance, the Frankfurt Stock Exchange is now an equity-owned, for-profit corporation). Nevertheless, sell-side institutions continue to exert extensive control over market structure (in Frankfurt, only members of the exchange are allowed to own shares and a supervisory board must agree to the sale of shares). In the long run, of course, one would expect that a more efficient way of handling trading would make its way into the marketplace and gain market share. But, in the short run, progress can be blocked. If the regulatory authorities allow competition to be stifled, the long run may indeed be a long time in arriving.

A second significant barrier to technological change has been the relative silence of European buy-side participants. Asset managers, for the most part, have paid insufficient attention to controlling trading costs and to seeking improvements in market structure. This is beginning to change with the growth of unit trusts and pension funds, and the change will accelerate as these funds increasingly invest in equities. Given equity market transaction costs that are significant relative to investment returns, asset managers can be expected to begin demanding more efficient trading venues. As they make their voices heard, they will become a powerful force for change in the European equity markets.

Perhaps the most serious barrier to meaningful change is regulation itself. For instance, in the United States, adherence to the principle that the best quotes on the ITS not be violated has prevented the emergence of any market that would give independent price discovery during the trading day. The 'concentration' provisions (Article 14.3) and limitations on the cross-border expansion of trading systems (Article 15.5) in the Investment Services Directive could potentially have a similar effect in Europe (see Chapter 4).

II. QUALITY OF MARKETS

Can buy-side participants in general, and institutional investors in particular, trade in a liquid, transparent environment with immediacy, without destabilizing the markets, at accurate prices and at low cost? The answer is, unequivocally, 'no' – they cannot. The first step towards developing more efficient trading structures is to recognize this.

Transaction Costs

Assessing transaction costs relative to share *prices* may suggest that transaction costs are of minor importance. Assessing transaction costs relative to the *returns* that can be realized from equity investments shows that these costs are, in fact, substantial.

Consider the following simple example.[6] In a costless trading environment, a stock bought at $30 which is expected to sell at $33 in a year's time has an expected return of 10 percent. Now, assume the following: commissions of 6 cents per share for institutions and 50 cents per share for small investors; a bid-ask spread of 1/8 of a point ($0.125); and a market impact of 1/8 of a point for institutions and zero for retail customers. In total, one-way (either buy or sell) transaction costs are:

	Institutional customer	Retail customer
Commissions	$0.060	$0.500
Bid-ask spread	$0.063	$0.063
Market impact[7]	$0.125	$0.000
Total costs	$0.248	$0.563

With these costs, the prices and returns for a one-year holding period are:

[6] This example is also presented in Schwartz (1994).

[7] One-eighth of a point, the minimum size of a non-zero execution cost, may appreciably understate the magnitude of this cost for a large trader.

	Institutional customer	Retail customer
Purchase price	$30.25	$30.56
Expected selling price	$32.75	$32.44
Expected return	8.28%	6.13%

and the costs in percentage terms are:

	Institutional customer	Retail customer
Costs as a percentage of selling price	0.83%	1.88%
Reduction in expected returns	17.20%	38.70%

As a percentage of share price, the costs represent slightly under 1 percent for institutional traders and slightly under 2 percent for retail traders – seemingly small amounts. However, expected total *returns* are lowered by 17 percent (from 10 percent to 8.28 percent) for the institutional trader, and by 39 percent (from 10 percent to 6.1 percent) for the retail trader. The percentage reduction in the risk premium is even greater. If the risk-free rate is 3 percent, the risk premium without transaction costs is 7 percent (10 percent – 3 percent), and the reduction in the risk premium is 25 percent for an institutional trader and over 55 percent for a retail trader.

Clearly, transaction costs have an appreciable impact on returns. They also affect price discovery and short-period price volatility, as we explain below.

Price Discovery

Transactions would always be made at equilibrium prices in a costless trading environment. Price discovery refers to the dynamic processes by which equilibrium values are found in a non-costless market-place. The process is complex and imperfect.[8] Equilibrium values are not observable; thus, deviations from equilibria are not clearly apparent to participants, and have hardly been acknowledged by academic researchers or regulators. Increasingly, however, the difficulty of achieving accurate price discovery is being recognized by practitioners and by the market centres. The trading systems used by a market-place affect the quality of price discovery. In particular, the opening procedure in any trading session should explicitly be examined in this light.

[8] For further discussions, see Handa and Schwartz (1996a).

Transparency

Transparency has received a great deal of attention in discussions concerning market structure and regulation, and has been considered at length in Chapter 1. Clearly, transparency is of central importance for effective order handling by market participants and for price discovery in the broad market. The UK Securities and Investments Board (SIB) Report, 'Regulation of the United Kingdom Equity Markets' (June 1995), further considers 'transparency to be of fundamental importance to investor protection and market integrity' (p.33). The particular problem faced in the UK market, and addressed in the SIB Report, concerns how relevant information on large trades should be disclosed to market participants.[9]

Transparency is typically understood as meaning that quotes (pre-trade) and last sale (post-trade) information are widely available on a real-time basis. However, this treatment of the issue can be broadened. Transparency also includes buy-side participants disclosing their orders once their trading decisions have been made. The problem is that revealing information before a trade can be detrimental to the participant seeking to trade (a stock's price will rise or fall when it becomes known that a large buy or sell order is in the offing). Thus, participants attempt to hide information about their orders while they feed them to the market in small pieces over extended periods of time.

Transactions can be made only to the extent that a sufficient number of orders are revealed. A market-place should encourage participants, particularly institutional investors, to reveal their orders to the market or, at least, to the trading system. The Paris CAC, for example, allows 'hidden' orders to be entered into the trading system. These orders are not revealed to the market until sufficient trading volume in the stock has occurred, at which point at least part of an order is entered on the open book. The procedure has the advantage of facilitating the careful revelation of an order to the market.

As noted in Chapter 1, dealer reluctance to disclose large proprietary trades is not fundamentally different from buy-side reluctance to disclose full

[9] When a trade is realized, information is produced concerning the particulars of the transaction – the price, the quantity, and the time. A completed trade may be viewed as a joint product: the trade itself and information about the trade. Transparency refers to the publication of this information to the public. In a continuous market, the information component is of no benefit to the transacting parties but, because of the complexity of price discovery, is of considerable value to others who may be transacting in the near future.

However, the consumers of the information – i.e., those who expect to be transacting in the future – are not able to pay its producers – i.e., those who have just transacted. Thus, in the absence of any publication requirements, trade information tends to be undersupplied. For this reason, requirements concerning the timely publication of floor information (quotes, prices, and volume) have economic justification. If faced with meaningful competition, the market centre itself should have sufficient incentive to provide an optimal amount of transparency. If this is the case, no further intervention by a regulatory authority should be needed.

trading intentions, yet the latter is clearly impossible for the exchanges or regulators to compel. Regulation can force dealers to disclose their trades, but it may also result in dealers participating in fewer trades. Unfortunately, the public policy debate over transparency has focused almost exclusively on dealer revelation of transactions, and has largely ignored the evidence on dealer behaviour under different disclosure regimes.

Forcing fast trade publication of dealer trades will not curtail dealer participation in trading to the extent that dealers are currently realizing economic rents from the market. An 'economic rent' is a payment to a factor of production in excess of what is required to keep that factor in its present employment. The 'factor' in question is the dealer capital that provides immediate liquidity. Under delayed publication in London, dealer capital is widely employed in the market. In the United States, on the other hand, where immediate publication is the rule, this factor is used less intensely. Upstairs block facilitators, being more reluctant to provide immediacy because of the publication requirement, commonly offer only to cross trades if and when counterparties are found. And so a factor widely employed in the UK is not as intensively employed in the United States, owing at least in part to the different disclosure rules. Hence, UK dealers cannot be assumed to be extracting economic rents, and strengthening the publication requirement could indeed result in their committing less of their own capital to market making.

Determining the effect of order handling and trade execution rules on investor and intermediary behaviour is a complex matter. Once effective access to alternative trading venues becomes a reality in Europe, regulatory intervention in setting market transparency rules will no longer be either necessary or desirable. In a competitive 'market for markets', we would recommend that the determination be left to the market centres.

Volatility

Transaction costs cause intra-day price movements to be excessively volatile. In the short run, transaction prices bounce between the bid and the ask; they rise and fall with the market impact of large buy and sell orders; and they swing around equilibrium values with the vagaries of the price discovery process. Hasbrouck and Schwartz (1988) have assessed the excess short-period volatility that characterizes a continuous market for three US market centres: the American Stock Exchange, the New York Stock Exchange, and Nasdaq. They found that short-run volatility (measured by the variance of returns over half-hour intervals) was excessive relative to long-run volatility (measured by the variance of returns over two-day intervals) for the large majority of firms in their sample. They observed short-run volatilities that were more than twice what they would have been on expectation in a costless trading environment for 23 percent of Amex firms, 27 percent of NYSE firms, and 60 percent of Nasdaq/NMS[10] firms.

Conclusion

Transaction costs can have a sizeable impact on investment returns, as they do on measures of market quality, such as the accuracy of price discovery and short-term price volatility. This underscores the need for more efficient market structures.

III. LIQUIDITY AND MARKET STRUCTURE[11]

Alternative market structures cater to the different trading characteristics of individual securities (i.e., whether they are large capitalization stocks or small ones). Equally important, alternative market structures are needed to service the different trading needs of investors (whether they are large or small participants, informed or informationless traders, etc.).

Order flow in major market centres around the world is increasingly being dominated by institutional participants. In the United States, an estimated 75 to 80 percent of NYSE trading volume in 1994 was accounted for by institutions.[12] Moreover, institutional orders are large. In the United States, 66 percent of the orders in one database (that of Plexus, a West Coast securities firm) represent more than 50 percent of average daily trading volume, and a remarkable 40 percent represent more than 100 percent of average daily trading volume.[13] These large orders would strain a continuous order-driven system. Because they require considerable liquidity and time to be worked, large orders have typically required the intermediation services of dealers, specialists, and 'upstairs' block facilitators.

Market makers dampen excess volatility caused by temporary buy/sell imbalances by adding liquidity to the market. Do the market makers provide sufficient liquidity at a reasonable price? Can institutions provide liquidity to themselves? Are other innovations in market structure needed?

In this section, we consider three generic market structures: (1) the continuous agency/auction market; (2) the dealer market (which is also a continuous trading environment); and (3) the periodic call market.

The Continuous Agency/Auction Environment

The Paris CAC system is an order-driven agency/auction market. As such, it depends primarily on the limit orders of public participants to 'drive' the market.

[10] NMS = National Market System.
[11] Parts of this section draw on Handa and Schwartz (1996b).
[12] See Becker and Angstadt (1995).
[13] See Wagner and Edwards (1993).

A pure agency/auction environment involves no dealer intervention at all. Agents for buyers and sellers simply meet at a trading post or pit – or through a computer system – where the stocks are traded. With a limit order book in a continuous market, buyers and sellers also meet as the limit orders of some public participants establish the prices at which other public participants can trade by market order. Rules of order execution, such as price and time priorities, encourage limit order traders to compete for incoming market orders by raising their bids or lowering their offers and, in the process, narrowing the inside spread.

Limit order traders must be compensated for providing liquidity to market order traders. They are compensated by transaction prices being relatively volatile (exhibiting mean reversion) in the short run.[14] This is true regardless of the size of customer orders, the sophistication of computer technology, or the speed with which orders can be submitted, withdrawn, or turned into trades.

Evidence on the profitability of limit order trading is presented by Handa and Schwartz (1995). They found, for a sample of US stocks, that returns are significantly higher (*vis-à-vis* market orders) for limit orders that execute. Consequently, limit orders are desirable for patient traders. Handa and Schwartz also observe that returns tend to be lower when an execution is forced at the end of a trading period if a limit order does not execute. Consequently, market orders are preferable for impatient traders. Handa and Schwartz further demonstrate that a pure limit order trading strategy (maintaining a network of buy and sell limit orders on both sides of the market) yields positive returns. These findings suggest that an order-driven market is viable for retail orders, but that it does require accentuated short-period volatility to be so.

Does a continuous agency/auction market provide sufficient liquidity for institutional customers? Very often it does not. Institutional order flow, being lumpy (the orders are large) and at times one-sided (buyers only or sellers only), is more difficult to handle, especially when a market is under stress. Institutional investors generally are not willing to place their large orders on a limit order book because of the adverse effect on market prices the exposure would have. These traders commonly require extra liquidity and time to work their large orders. At a minimum, the agency/auction market must enable them to feed in their orders piecemeal.

Thus, by itself, the pure agency/auction market may not be capable of fully satisfying the needs of the institutional investors. The large investors require a special mechanism that enables them to find one another when they seek to trade. Is dealer intermediation the appropriate mechanism?

[14] For further discussion, see Handa and Schwartz (1995).

The Dealer Market

London's SEAQ system is a quote-driven dealer market. As such, public participants do not trade directly with one another, but through the dealer (market maker) as an intermediary.

Of course, the ultimate source of liquidity for public sellers is public buyers, and vice versa. But public participants do not generally arrive at the market at the same moments in time, which complicates their provision of liquidity directly to themselves. The classic function of a dealer is to accommodate the non-synchronous arrival of public participants by standing ready, continuously, to sell shares to buyers and to buy shares from sellers. In this regard, the market makers supply immediacy – i.e., *immediate private liquidity.*[15] A public participant's decision to demand immediacy, or alternatively to trade patiently, depends on the price of immediate liquidity. The price of immediate liquidity, and the very ability of a public participant to choose to obtain it or not, depend on the architecture of a trading system. The price of immediate liquidity has traditionally been taken to be the bid-ask spread, which is the source of a dealer's compensation.[16] Market makers are thought to compete for order flow by tightening the spread. But two dealer market practices diminish the incentive for market makers to improve their quotes in order to gain order flow. These practices are *preferencing* and *quote matching.*

The financial houses in Britain and the United States may make markets in certain issues for the tactical purpose of being able to provide a broader array of services to their corporate clients: for instance, to gain access to the firm in order to provide consulting and advisory services in corporate finance matters. Reciprocally, providing a broader array of services enriches the market maker's general knowledge of a company, which facilitates his or her market making operations.

Additionally, in the intermediated markets in Britain and the United States, dealers must know their trading customers. In the process of getting to know their clients, dealers commonly develop close relationships with them that result in the customers *preferencing* orders to particular dealers. 'Preferencing' refers to the practice of a customer directing an order to a dealer even if that dealer is not posting the most aggressive quote on the market. When this occurs, the mar-

[15] Intermediaries (but not dealers *per se*) also serve the economic function of eliminating counterparty risk entirely for public buyers and sellers.

[16] UK market makers, however, enjoy a wider range of "privileges" while fulfilling their obligation to provide liquidity on a continuous basis. As enumerated in the SIB Report (1995), the privileges include exemption from stamp duty, exclusive access to stock borrowing and to inter-dealer brokers, delayed publication of large trades, the right to participate in agency crosses outside the best bid and offer, and exemption from having to notify companies of holdings of 3 percent or more.

ket maker will typically accept the preferenced order and *quote match* (i.e., give a transaction at the best quote on the market). A failure to accept the order and/or to quote match could result in that dealer not getting the telephone call the next time the customer wants to trade.

With preferencing and quote matching, market makers need not compete for order flow by tightening their quotes.[17] Alternatively, they may solidify relationships with their customers by other means so as to get preferenced orders. A consequence is that strict price and time priorities are not maintained across the dealer firms – they would disrupt the preferencing behaviour that is inherent in the SEAQ dealer market.[18] The economic result is that posted spreads are widened.

Regardless of how it is provided – by agent, auctioneer, or dealer – immediate liquidity is costly, particularly for large orders. The cost is incurred in the form of bid-ask spreads, market impact, and the inherent tendency of prices to exhibit accentuated volatility in short trading intervals. Recent applications of computer technology in securities trading and the emergence of electronic proprietary trading systems (PTSs) – such as Instinet, Posit, and the Arizona Stock Exchange (AZX) in the United States – have shown that liquidity can be obtained without dealer intermediation. Instinet and Tradepoint are now looking to demonstrate the same thing in London. The emergence of these electronic systems gives rise to the following questions: Do institutional investors really require dealer intermediation? Is *immediate liquidity* demanded by all institutional investors? Would an alternative to the continuous market be desirable?

The Call Market

It has been widely assumed that traders want to be able to transact immediately, and major securities trading systems in Europe (and throughout most of the world) are based on the principle of continuous trading. We suggest that the costs to participants of transacting whenever they choose during a trading session have not been properly understood, and that far too much importance has been attached to providing immediacy. Some investors choose – where a choice is available – not to pay the price for immediacy. The list includes passive investors, limit order traders, and other informationless traders for whom lower transaction costs are more important than immediacy. For instance, mutual funds may trade certain amounts each day, not because of the receipt of news, but for redemptions

[17] London market makers find that actually quoting the best bid or offer (i.e., being on the yellow strip) only weakly increases the probability of receiving the next public order to sell or to buy.

[18] By price priority being violated, we mean that the dealer who is quoting most aggressively does not necessarily receive the next counterpart order, because that order may be preferenced to a dealer whose quote is not at the best bid or offer. With quote matching, the counterpart orders do, however, execute at the best price being bid or offered in the market.

and other cash-flow needs. Large orders brought to CAC's order-driven market are typically fed into the system in small pieces over the course of a trading session (sometimes in an attempt to obtain the volume-weighted-average price for the session). These participants do not need to trade at a particular moment during the day, and they do not need to pay the price of immediacy. For them, a periodic market would offer an attractive alternative. A description of this type of market is provided in the chapter appendix.

The availability of call market trading is desirable, both from the perspective of direct cost and from the wider perspective of market quality, and the call market is particularly suitable for handling institutional order flow. But, for it to operate effectively, a sufficient number of participants must be willing to postpone their orders until the next market call. Will they do this, or is the cost of waiting too consequential? If a trader expects that the price will soon move because of fundamental information, the opportunity cost of waiting may indeed induce that participant to pay for a speedy execution. How often does this happen, and how important is the consideration? The extent to which institutional participants actually do or do not require immediate execution of their large orders has rarely been questioned. Because of this lack of information, a survey of institutional trading practices was conducted for this report (see Chapter 3).

In brief, we found that a substantial proportion of buy-side traders are willing to delay executions if this can reduce their costs of trading. As electronic call markets eliminate bid-ask spreads and generally reduce commissions and market impact, this finding would suggest that call market trading would offer investors an attractive supplement to continuous markets, whether order- or quote-driven.

Many electronic order-driven markets, such as CAC, do open trading with a call. However, little attention has been given to the call market as a desirable facility in its own right, and its broader use in Paris as well as in Switzerland's new electronic system has been resisted.[19] Nonetheless, our interviews in Paris revealed pockets of vocal support even on the sell-side,[20] and plans have been made to include two daily calls in the operation of a new small cap market (Nouveau Marché) to begin operation in February 1996. In Frankfurt, current plans are to incorporate three daily calls with a new electronic trading system.

[19] Orders submitted to CAC's call market opening pay a higher commission than orders submitted to the continuous market. A peak load problem is perceived to exist at the opening because of heavy volume at the call, and the intent is to control it by the commission structure. This may be reasonable if the opening volume is heavy for reasons other than the desirability of the call market procedure. However, if it is attributable to the call being an efficient trading environment, the peak load problem could be dealt with better simply by running the call at least one more time during the trading day (perhaps an hour or two after the opening).

[20] An official with whom we spoke at Cholet Dupont advocated a contraction of the continuous trading period to three hours in the afternoon, supplemented by two daily calls.

IV. PUTTING THE PIECES TOGETHER: IS ONE MARKET-PLACE POSSIBLE?

A diversity of trading systems currently exists in Europe. To highlight the three most prominent markets: London features a dealer system; Paris features a continuous electronic auction system (CAC); and Germany is a hybrid, comprising three main segments of comparable size – intermediated floor trading, 'off-exchange' telephone dealing, and a continuous electronic auction system.

This diversity is highly desirable. The systems should not be forced to conform with one another, nor should they be melded into a single European stock exchange. Diversity offers a menu of alternatives, and it injects much needed competition among viable alternatives.

To achieve the requisite diversity in one market-place, the three generic structures discussed above would have to be integrated under a single roof. Technically, one part of the task is relatively simple: a call market could easily be interfaced with either an order-driven or a quote-driven continuous market. For instance, the continuous market (either agency/auction or dealer) could open with a call, and then offer one or more additional calls during the trading session and/or at the close.

Integrating quote- and order-driven continuous markets, on the other hand, is not as easily accomplished, although it has been done. In Switzerland's SOFFEX, limit orders are integrated into a screen-based dealer market that enforces strict time and price priorities. The system appears to work quite well for options and futures trading (roughly 70 percent of the quotes in SOFFEX are from dealers, and 30 percent are from public customers). Public and dealer quotes also coexist successfully in Instinet's continuous market.

In Paris, dealers appear to be integrated into the CAC system handling the retail order flow, although this integration may be somewhat illusory. For the most part, retail orders are brought directly to the CAC market, while large institutional orders may be handled upstairs with the use of a dealer, before they are brought to the CAC.[21] Further, new rules instituted in the French market in September 1994 allow large proprietary trades to be made outside the best bid and offer on the CAC (although within a 'weighted-average' spread), and the publication of large proprietary transactions can be delayed. While these rule changes facilitate the 'dealerization' of the French market, they do not in any meaningful sense produce a new concentrated 'hybrid' market. French equity dealing goes on in much the same way as it did before, when large trades were only reported to

[21] The same applies at the NYSE, where there is some integration between the trading floor and the upstairs dealer-driven block market.

London to avoid the Paris price limit and transparency rules. Now, those deals which can be accommodated within the liberalized rules are reported to Paris (and often to London as well), while those which are too large to trade within the price limits set by the Bourse are still reported only to London (see Chapter 1, section 3.2.1). Thus, there has been no material change in the way in which French equity dealers *trade* – only in where they *report*.

The classic dealer markets – SEAQ in London and Nasdaq in the United States – have historically resisted introducing a formal, centralized system for handling public limit orders. The dealers, understandably, resist competition from limit order traders.[22] But the roots of the problem go deeper. A limit order facility requires strict price priority along with time priority or some other secondary priority rule to establish the sequence in which limit orders at the same price execute. Unfortunately, these strict rules of order execution conflict with the preferencing and quote matching behaviour that characterizes the SEAQ and Nasdaq markets, as discussed above.

A regulatory authority could, of course, require that a limit order facility be included in a quote-driven market. However, this would undermine the distinctive characteristics of the market, without, in all likelihood, bringing net benefits to investors. Buy-side traders in Nasdaq stocks already have separate (but well integrated) order-driven trading platforms such as Instinet and AZX, and in SEAQ stocks have Instinet and Tradepoint.[23] It is clearly best for each market-place to determine its own structure as it responds to the competitive pressure brought by others, and for a network of separate market-places that comprise one market, as discussed above, to be thereby attained.

V. CONCLUSIONS

Barriers to an integrated European market exist, as they do in many markets around the world. We have highlighted three: the relative silence of buy-side participants, the vested interests of sell-side participants, and the intervention of regulatory authorities in market structure issues.

Regarding the buy-side participants, their emerging recognition of the serious impact of trading costs on portfolio performance is leading them to take a more active role *vis-à-vis* market structure in the United States, and the same development is just starting to happen in Europe. Regarding the sell-side partici-

[22] However, the dealer markets have in the past allowed customer limit orders to be handled by the dealers. Nasdaq now has plans in process to introduce a formal, centralized system, which it calls "Naqcess".

[23] To date, however, the volume received by Tradepoint has been low.

pants, we believe that their control over market structure will weaken appreciably as inter-market competition intensifies, and as market-places increasingly become business enterprises rather than membership organizations.

In the long run, the most formidable barrier to competition may prove to be regulatory intervention itself. Given the complexities of today's technologically sophisticated environment, it is simply not possible to state categorically – on the basis of observation, theoretical analysis, or empirical investigation – which form of market structure is best. The menu of trading venues should not be designed by a regulator, a committee of regulators, or any other interested party. No one knows all the answers to all the questions concerning consolidation, transparency, price discovery, price stability, and liquidity. As one prominent financial economist recently pointed out, 'We are just beginning to understand the enormous complexities of the secondary asset markets. It is not what we do not know about the markets that hurts us the most, but what we think we know but don't.'[24]

The posture of relying on 'market-based solutions' has been underscored in some of our meetings in London, and is emphasized in the SIB Report (1995): 'We have no view on what specific changes in market processes should happen or what mechanisms for equity trading are best. That is for market participants to decide' (p.5). The Report goes on, however, to set forth 'three key aspects of market integrity' that are of regulatory concern: 'fairness, a "clean" market, and efficient price formation' (p.11). Further, it 'stresses the fundamental importance (particularly in today's diverse marketplace) of transparency in promoting efficient price formation and in helping to ensure that investors are treated as fairly and equitably as possible' (p.12). Yet the Report later acknowledges that transparency is a function of (and in turn has a major effect on) market structure. The debate over the proper level of transparency on the LSE derives 'in large part because of the quote-driven nature of the market and the difficulty inherent in reconciling immediacy of post-trade publication with risk-taking by market participants (which helps to provide liquidity to market users)' (p.34). And so the concatenation of thoughts – from fairness to transparency to market structure – illustrates how difficult it is for a regulatory authority to steer clear of market structure issues even when it states, as a matter of principle, that it is the markets which should decide.

In a competitive, diversified environment, the risk of fragmentation will always exist as satellite markets free-ride on price discovery and other services provided by a major market centre. Markets will never be totally transparent. For these and other reasons, certain constituents will not be pleased. Cries for regula-

[24] Allan Kleidon, meeting of the Association of Financial Economists, Washington DC, January 1995.

tory intervention will be heard, largely from the challenged sell-side participants. Seemingly valid points will be made. After all, integration, fairness, liquidity, price stability, and transparency are all desirable, and each, individually, may be improved through regulatory intervention. However, these market attributes cannot *all* be improved by regulation – very significant trade-offs are involved. When the market attributes are viewed as interrelated components of the whole, the best the regulators can do to enhance the long-run prospects of the markets is to resist the temptation to intervene.

Appendix

ORDER HANDLING AND PRICE DETERMINATION IN A CALL MARKET[25]

Order handling and price determination is different in a periodic call market than in continuous trading. The distinction, however, is commonly not understood.

A call market is a point in time meeting place that enables participants to find one another more readily. In call market trading, orders are batched for simultaneous, multilateral executions at predetermined points in time. At a call, a clearing price is determined that maximizes the number of shares traded. All participants trade at this single price, with buy orders at the clearing price and higher, and sell orders at the clearing price and lower, executing. The process can be simply illustrated using integer pricing and round lot (100 share) orders.

Assume that over a relatively brief interval of time, exactly 1 round lot to buy and 1 round lot to sell is conveyed to the market at each price in the interval from $51 to $55. Rather than executing against the limit order book as they arrive, or being placed on the book, the orders are held until the call, at which time they are sorted and cumulated from the highest price to the lowest price for buy orders, and from the lowest price to the highest price for sell orders. The orders and cumulative sums are shown in the following table.

Table. Buy/Sell Orders and Cumulative Orders at a Market Call

Price	Buy orders	Cum. buy	Cum. sell	Sell orders
55	100	100	500	100
54	100	200	400	100
53*	**100**	**300**	**300**	**100**
52	100	400	200	100
51	100	500	100	100

The clearing price is that value which maximizes the number of shares that will transact. In the example, 53 is the clearing price – 300 shares are bought at 53 and 300 shares are sold at 53 (at 54, only 200 shares would be bought, and at 52 only 200 would be sold).[26]

[25] For further discussion about call market trading, see Cohen and Schwartz (1989), Economides and Schwartz (1995), and Schwartz (1996).

[26] In the example presented here, an exact clearing price exists (the number of shares sought for purchase at 53 exactly equals the number offered for sale). A more complex algorithm is needed for determining the clearing price when, owing to price discreteness and quantity discontinuities, an exact cross does not exist. However, the principle can be retained that the price selected is that which maximizes the number of shares that transact.

Market orders in the continuous environment generally execute immediately at the best counterpart quotes. Limit orders in the continuous market generally receive delayed execution, or they may receive no execution at all. If they do execute, limit orders in the continuous market generally execute at the prices at which they are written. In contrast, all orders that execute in the call market do so at a common clearing price, which means that there is no clear distinction between limit orders and market orders. Putting a price on an order simply specifies the conditions under which that order will or will not execute at the call. The more eager a participant is to trade, the more aggressively he or she will price an order to reduce the probability of non-execution. A market order in the call environment is a limit buy with an arbitrarily high price, or a limit sell with an arbitrarily low price.

In a continuous market, limit orders are liquidity supplying and market orders are liquidity demanding. In a call, limit order traders do not, *per se*, provide liquidity to market order traders. Rather, investors who place orders early (both limit and market) provide liquidity to those who place orders after them.

In the aggregation process at a market call, the orders of informed participants are pooled with the orders of liquidity-motivated participants on both sides of the market. Pooling the order flow reduces the cost that limit order traders may incur at the hands of informed traders. This is because in the pooling environment, an order that executes does so at the common clearing price – not at the price of the order, as is the case in the continuous market.[27] Thus, short-run price volatility need not be accentuated to compensate liquidity-providing traders. Moreover, pooling the orders of traders on both sides of the market directly reduces the short-run volatility attributable to temporary liquidity imbalances.

[27] Liquidity traders on the same side of the market as the informed traders clearly do not get 'bagged', but may incur a non-execution cost if their orders are not priced aggressively enough.

References

Baxter, Frank, 1996. 'An Analogue Trader Views the Digital Market and Beyond', in Robert A. Schwartz (ed.), *How Stocks Trade: New Competition in the Market for Markets*, Irwin Professional, Homewood, ILO.

Becker, Brandon and Janet Angstadt, 1995. 'Market 2000: A Work in Progress', in Robert A. Schwartz (ed.), *Global Equity Markets: Technological, Competitive, and Regulatory Challenges*, Irwin Professional, Homewood, ILO.

Bloch, Ernest and Robert A. Schwartz, 1978. 'The Great Debate over NYSE Rule 390', *Journal of Portfolio Management*, Fall.

Cohen, Kalman J. and Robert A. Schwartz, 1989. 'An Electronic Call Market: Its Design and Desirability', in Henry C. Lucas, Jr and Robert A. Schwartz (eds), *The Challenge of Information Technology for the Securities Markets: Liquidity, Volatility, and Global Trading*, Dow Jones Irwin, Homewood, ILO.

Economides, Nicholas and Robert A. Schwartz, 1995. 'Electronic Call Market Trading', *Journal of Portfolio Management*, Winter.

Handa, Puneet and Robert A. Schwartz, 1995. 'Limit Order Trading', New York University Working Paper.

Handa, Puneet and Robert A. Schwartz, 1996a. 'Dynamic Price Discovery', *Review of Quantitative Finance and Accounting*, forthcoming.

Handa, Puneet and Robert A. Schwartz, 1996b. 'How Best to Supply Liquidity in an Electronic Environment: Is Disintermediation a Desirable Route?', *Journal of Portfolio Management*, Winter.

Hasbrouck, Joel and Robert A. Schwartz, 1988. 'Liquidity and Execution Costs in Equity Markets', *Journal of Portfolio Management*, Spring.

Schwartz, Robert A., 1994. 'US Securities Markets Regulation: Market Structure', in Benn Steil (ed.), *International Financial Market Regulation*, John Wiley, Chichester.

Schwartz, Robert A. (ed.), 1996. *How Stocks Trade: New Competition in the Market for Markets*, Irwin Professional, Homewood, ILO.

Securities and Investments Board, 1995. 'Regulation of the United Kingdom Equity Markets', June.

Wagner, Wayne and Mark Edwards, 1993. 'Best Execution', *Financial Analysts Journal*, January/February.

Chapter 3

EQUITY TRADING III: INSTITUTIONAL INVESTOR TRADING PRACTICES AND PREFERENCES

1. INTRODUCTION

A good deal is known about how broker-dealers, the so-called 'sell-side' of the market, execute trades through stock exchange trading systems. However, very little is known about how institutional investors, the 'buy-side' of the market, manage the orders they submit to broker-dealers, or how they might manage them differently if they could bypass traditional sell-side trading systems and intermediaries.

Funds under institutional management in Europe have grown dramatically in recent years. Data compiled by the European Federation of Investment Funds and Companies reveal that the net assets of EU collective investment schemes have grown from ECU 516 billion in 1989 to ECU 1.095 trillion in 1994. Of this 1994 total, ECU 233 billion was invested in equity funds. Given that funds under institutional management are expected to continue expanding at a robust rate, systematic information on the development of buy-side trading practices and preferences should be considered essential for proper sell-side business planning and public policy formulation.

1.1. Background to the Questionnaire

The analysis in this chapter is based on a detailed questionnaire mailed to 400 large European institutional fund managers.[1] This questionnaire was adapted from a previous survey of US institutional equity traders, the results of which are summarized in Economides and Schwartz (1995).[2] We make reference to the US study throughout this chapter, in order to compare responses with the present survey.

Our European questionnaire, reproduced in the chapter Appendix, comprises a preliminary section to be completed by the chief financial officer and a

[1] The authors are grateful to *Institutional Investor* magazine for sponsoring the study analysed in this chapter. The 400 firms selected for the present study were culled from a variety of databases and other sources.

[2] The US questionnaire was mailed to 825 US institutions, producing 150 responses (an 18 percent response rate).

main section to be completed by the head equity trader. We received a total of 59 completed questionnaires in time for inclusion in the analysis; a response rate of 15 percent.[3] Given the disproportionate number of large institutional fund managers based in the UK, and the possible unfamiliarity of certain English-language market terminology on the European continent, it is perhaps not surprising that 32 (54 percent) of the respondents were UK-based.[4] This compares with a UK share of 43 percent of EU equity funds under institutional management. We therefore acknowledge a mild UK bias in our sample.

Unless otherwise indicated in the chapter, those responding 'don't know' (DK) or not answering (NA) were excluded from the sample when calculating the percentage of respondents selecting a given choice for a given question. The percentage of DKs and NAs for each question is provided in footnotes. The 'average responses' cited are figures between 1.0 and 5.0, corresponding to the number value assigned to each possible response. Thus an average response of '3.0' would mean that respondents on average chose the midpoint response for a given question.

The reader will note that a number of questions refer specifically to the London Stock Exchange SEAQ trading system. The reason why some questions focus specifically on SEAQ is that we wanted to ensure that responses were directly comparable across market participants, and this sometimes required focusing their attention on the same trading system. SEAQ was the system we expected the largest number of respondents to be familiar with. Nonetheless, we acknowledge that the lack of familiarity with this system among some continental respondents resulted in a relatively higher number of DKs and NAs for these questions, and may also have reduced the continental response rate on the mailing.

1.2. Purpose of the Study

A number of key areas were investigated in this survey.

First, we examined fund managers' demand for 'immediacy' in trading services, and their willingness to pay for this service. While a demand for immediate trading obviously underlies the operation of continuous trading systems, it is likewise the case that the short-term volatility associated with continuous trading environments encourages a demand to 'nail down' a price by trading immediately. Yet the advent of electronic call market trading (see Chapter 2) – provided by companies such as Instinet, Posit, and AZX, as well as some stock ex-

[3] This understates somewhat the actual response, since some of the 400 firms sampled did not actually manage equity funds.

[4] Of the 27 continental European responses, 8 were from France, 4 from Denmark, 4 from Germany, 3 from Spain, 2 from the Netherlands, 2 from Switzerland, and one each from Austria, Belgium, Ireland, and Sweden.

changes – means that trading can be delayed to pre-determined points in time *if* traders find it desirable to do so. They may find it desirable because trading in a continuous environment generally entails higher explicit costs than call market trading.[5] While the few European call market systems in existence currently attract very low trading volumes, the use of such systems may grow as competition in the asset management industry forces buy-side traders to focus on the costs of trading under different market architectures.

The second major area we examined was investor views of trading through new proprietary electronic trading systems (PTSs). In particular, we sought to gain some insights into how institutions saw the market prospects for such systems, what barriers to PTS growth they foresaw, and how they felt these systems would perform relative to a major existing stock exchange system (SEAQ).

Finally, we looked to assess how buy-side traders view the development of market structure rules at the European level. Specifically, we asked their views on the overall cross-border trading benefits they would secure from implementation of the Investment Services Directive (ISD), as well as their views on the need for specific ISD provisions relating to trading 'concentration' and post-trade transparency.

2. THE DEMAND FOR IMMEDIACY

2.1. Why Do Fund Managers Trade?

In order to assess what fund managers require in trading systems, it is important to know what motivates their trading decisions. For example, some factors, such as the fund manager having knowledge of another order in the market, will almost certainly induce a demand for immediacy, while others, such as a reassessment of portfolio structure, will almost certainly not require this service.

As we see from the results in Table 1, stock-specific information is the factor most often motivating trading decisions, with an average response of 4.19. Clearly, such information can motivate a demand for immediate execution. However, it is significant that the next three most common factors – internal research (3.79), reassessment of portfolio structure (3.47), and external research (3.24) – should not generally require immediacy. The factor most likely to induce a demand for immediacy, knowledge of another order in the market (1.82), was the second-least important factor motivating trading itself: 44 percent said it *never*

[5] A major French broker-dealer with whom we spoke went so far as to describe continuous trading in French equities as 'robbery'. He recommended a return to traditional Paris call market trading (two 'fixings' per day), perhaps supplemented by a three-hour continuous market, operating from 14:00 to 17:00 when US institutions are active in the European markets.

motivated their trades. In fact, many of the factors most likely to require immediacy – such as chartist signals (1.98) and derivatives signals (1.79) – rarely motivated actual trading decisions.

Table 1
Listed below are a number of factors that might motivate investment decisions for individual stocks. Please indicate how frequently your investment decisions are motivated by each of these factors. (For each row, tick a box from 1 to 5, where 5 = 'very frequently' and 1 = 'never'.)[6] (Q11)

	Very frequently (5) %	(4) %	(3) %	(2) %	Never (1) %	Average response
Stock-specific information	50.85	32.20	6.78	5.08	5.08	4.19
Market-wide news	5.45	20.00	34.55	27.27	12.73	2.78
Reassessment of portfolio	12.07	34.48	43.10	8.62	1.72	3.47
Fund redemptions or other cash-flow reasons	3.45	8.62	34.48	44.83	8.62	2.53
Index-tracking	10.17	5.08	18.64	37.29	28.81	2.31
Profit-taking	12.07	25.86	36.21	18.97	6.90	3.17
Bargain-hunting	6.90	20.69	25.86	29.31	17.24	2.71
Cut losses	1.75	12.28	26.32	42.11	17.54	2.39
Chartist signals	0.00	10.34	15.52	36.21	37.93	1.98
Internal research	31.03	34.48	20.69	10.34	3.45	3.79
External research	6.90	37.93	36.21	10.34	8.62	3.24
Trading information (knowledge of another order)	1.82	1.82	16.36	36.36	43.64	1.82
Derivatives motivated	1.72	1.72	15.52	36.21	44.83	1.79

2.2. *Why Do Fund Managers Want to Trade Stocks Quickly?*

Stock-specific information is not only the primary reason why traders wish to trade, but also the primary reason why they wish to trade *quickly* (3.74 is the average response for this factor). The second most common reason is volatile prices (3.45), which means that the market price could move against the trader before his or her order is executed. Interestingly, this factor is a pure function of a continuous trading environment. That is, while the demand for continuous trading derives partly from the demand to trade immediately, the reverse is also true: because of the short-term volatility inherent to the continuous market, many will wish to trade immediately.

[6] Percentage of respondents excluding DK (Don't Know) and NA (No Answer): DK was 5.1% for trading information; NA was 6.8% for market-wide news; all other values for DK and NA were under 2%.

Table 2
Listed below are some possible reasons for wanting to trade a SEAQ stock quickly. How important is each of these factors?[7] (Q20)

	Very important (5) %	(4) %	Somewhat important (3) %	(2) %	Not at all important (1) %	Average response
(1) Stock-specific information	39.62	22.64	16.98	13.21	7.55	3.74
(2) Changing market exposure	7.41	18.52	40.74	24.07	9.26	2.91
(3) Prices are volatile	25.00	23.21	30.36	14.29	7.14	3.45
(4) Raise cash	3.70	18.52	33.33	31.48	12.96	2.69
(5) SEAQ immediate trading is easy	7.55	18.87	22.64	18.87	32.08	2.51
(6) Portfolio manager instructions	14.82	22.22	29.63	18.52	14.82	3.04

2.3. How Immediate is an 'Immediate' Trade?

This question is designed to elicit from buy-side traders an idea of how quickly a trade should be done to be considered 'immediate'. Forty-two percent indicated that such a trade should be within 1 minute, and a further 40 percent indicated that it should at least be within 10 minutes. Only 7 percent said that an 'immediate' trade need only take place within 1 day. These results are very similar to those found in the US study: 72 percent said that 'immediacy' meant less than 10 minutes,[8] and less than 5 percent considered one day sufficiently 'immediate'.

What can we draw from this? Primarily, it illustrates the fact that the typical buy-side trader's sense of an 'immediate' trade is well within the time-frame associated only with a continuous trading environment. That is, call market trading will not generally satisfy those wishing to trade 'immediately': such systems will, by and large, only be used by those making a conscious decision to trade 'patiently'.

[7] Percentage of respondents excluding DK and NA. Out of all respondents: DK was 5.1% for (5) and 1.7% for the other statements; NA was 8.5% for (1), 6.8% for (2), 5.1% for (3), 6.8% for (4), 5.1% for (5), and 6.8% for (6).

[8] The US study did not ask for responses on 'under 1 minute'.

Table 3
What do you consider an 'immediate' trade on a FTSE 100 stock? A trade executed within: (Q18)

	Percentage of respondents[9]
1 minute	42.11
10 minutes	40.35
1 hour	10.52
2 hours	0.00
1 day	7.02

2.4. How Often Do Buy-Side Traders Use Limit Orders?

Placing limit orders indicates a willingness to trade patiently in a continuous market. Limit order traders are making a conscious decision not to demand or pay for immediacy.

Since the London Stock Exchange is a dealer market, limit orders do not feature prominently. We asked the question regarding the frequency with which different types of orders were placed in terms of *total* trading (not just London trading), however, which allows us to include trading practices in the continental auction markets.

'Protected trades' are a London concept, involving the dealer 'guaranteeing' a minimum price, but pledging to work the order over time and possibly achieve a better average price.

Since the question mixes London and continental trading practices, the results are obviously somewhat rough and ready. Given that the majority of respondents were UK institutions, we were nonetheless surprised to find that a substantial 46 percent said that they used limit orders for at least half their trading. The comparable figure from the US study is 53 percent.

These findings have two important implications. The first is that the dynamics of price behaviour in the market must be compensating traders sufficiently for placing limit orders: that is, there must be sufficient short-run mean reversion, or 'bounce' in transaction prices, to ensure that limit order traders do not, on average, lose money in providing 'free options' to market order traders.[10] The second implication is that traders are often willing to trade patiently, indicating that they are (at least implicitly) recognizing the cost of demanding immediacy.

[9] Excluding DK and NA. Out of all respondents: DK was 0%; NA was 3.4%.
[10] See Handa and Schwartz (1995).

Table 4
Relative to your total trading, how often do you use the following?[11] (Q25)

	Never	1-24% of trades	25-49% of trades	50-74% of trades	75-100% of trades
Limit orders	0.00	21.05	33.33	33.33	12.28
Market orders	3.64	16.36	27.27	40.00	12.73
Protected trades	13.73	35.29	39.22	7.84	3.92

How would buy-side traders react if a central limit order facility were brought into the London dealer market? The results are mixed, but certainly do not indicate strong enthusiasm for the idea. Only just over 25 percent said that they would use such a facility for over half their trades, while 30 percent indicated that they would use it for under a quarter of their trades. It is exceptionally difficult to graft major elements of an order-driven market onto a quote-driven market, such as limit order trading; this means that the two systems will, and almost certainly should, continue to operate in parallel rather than in some hybrid merged form.

Table 5
If SEAQ had a central limit order facility, how often would you use it? (Q27)

	Percentage of respondents[12]
Never	6.98
Rarely (1-24% of trades)	23.26
Sometimes (25-49% of trades)	44.19
Regularly (50-74% of trades)	23.26
Frequently (75-100% of trades)	2.33

3. CONCERN FOR TRADING COSTS

3.1. How are Trading Costs Perceived to Affect Portfolio Performance?

The average respondent (2.62) did not believe that trading costs significantly lowered equity portfolio performance. Fifty-four percent seemed to consider the

[11] Percentage of respondents excluding DK and NA. Out of all respondents: DK was 0% for limit orders, 1.7% for market orders, and 3.4% for protected orders; NA was 3.4% for limit orders, 5.1% for market orders, and 10.2% for protected orders.

[12] Excluding DK and NA. Out of all respondents: DK was 20.3%; NA was 6.8%.

effect to be low, while 28 percent indicated some concern. Furthermore, there was no significant difference between UK (2.59) and continental (2.73) responses. Table 6 summarizes the results. Unfortunately, we do not have comparative data from the US survey, although we suspect that US fund managers would express considerably more concern with trading costs.

In any event, we were able to gain further insight into the impact of trading costs by inquiring into the importance of individual components of trading costs. These results are summarized in Table 7.

Table 6
To what extent do trading costs lower the performance of your equity portfolio? (Q13)

		Percentage of respondents[13]
(5)	Very much	5.45
(4)		21.82
(3)		20.00
(2)		34.55
(1)	Insignificantly	18.18
Average response		*2.62*

3.2. How Important are Different Costs of Trading?

There are a number of different components of the cost of trading, broadly conceived: commissions, bid-ask spread, market impact, and the opportunity cost of missing a price through execution delay. The bid-ask spread (3.62) and market impact (3.55) were considered the most significant on average, with commissions (3.34) and opportunity costs (3.30) somewhat less important. This stands in contrast to the US study, where 55 percent of respondents ranked opportunity costs the 'most important', followed by market impact (41 percent), and commissions (only 3.3 percent).

The relevant US question was structured differently, and spread costs were not included, making it difficult to draw direct comparisons. Nonetheless, the different perspective on the significance of opportunity costs is rather striking, and we are unable to offer any simple explanation for the disparity.

[13] Excluding DK and NA. Out of all respondents: DK was 3.4%; NA was 3.4%.

Table 7
How important is each of the following costs of trading to your trading decisions?[14] (Q12)

	Very important (5) %	(4) %	(3) %	(2) %	Not at all important (1) %	Average response
Commission	18.97	27.59	25.86	24.14	3.45	3.34
Bid-ask spread	25.86	25.86	34.48	12.07	1.72	3.62
Market impact	23.21	32.14	23.21	19.64	1.79	3.55
Opportunity cost	20.37	29.63	22.22	14.81	12.96	3.30

3.3. How Willing are Fund Managers to Trade Patiently?

As we indicated above, European fund managers generally do not believe that trading costs significantly lower the performance of their portfolios. However, implicit in the question was the assumption that trading costs were not immutable: that is, that they could be reduced by traders trading *differently* from the way they currently do. For many European fund managers, however, the choice of execution routes is very limited in comparison with their American counterparts. Therefore, we need to enquire whether European fund managers would be *willing* to trade differently *if* this could actually serve to reduce their trading costs.

We asked fund managers how willing they are to trade patiently in order to *try* to reduce trading costs. The findings paint a more subtle picture. The average respondent (3.42) indicated that he or she was moderately willing to trade patiently. Fifty-one percent indicated that they were clearly willing or very willing (i.e., responses 4 or 5) to trade patiently, and only 5 percent said that they were not at all willing. By way of comparison, 69 percent of US fund managers expressed a willingness to trade patiently, while only 4 percent said that they were not at all willing. This accords with what we have heard from European dealers: i.e., that US institutions were considerably less likely than European (particularly UK and Dutch) institutions to demand immediate execution.

[14] Percentage of respondents excluding DK and NA. Out of all respondents: DK was 3.4% for market impact and 5.1% for opportunity cost; NA was 3.4% for opportunity cost, and 1.7% for all the other costs.

Table 8
How willing are you to trade patiently in order to try to reduce trading costs? (Q14)

		Percentage of respondents[15]
5	(very willing)	19.30
4		31.58
3		26.32
2		17.54
1	(not at all willing)	5.26
Average response		*3.42*

The picture becomes even more interesting when we attach monetary figures to the cost of immediacy. Respondents for whom the previous questions were perhaps too abstract now have the opportunity to consider the problem in a more concrete scenario. What if respondents could save 2.5 pence per share in commissions, spread costs, and market impact on a £5 stock by delaying a trade for one hour, three hours, or one day?

Forty-nine percent of respondents indicated that they would regularly or frequently (i.e., on over 50 percent of trades) delay trades *if* they could save 1/2 percent of the cost of shares. This is actually higher than the figure from the US survey, which was 43 percent.[16] When the delay was increased to three hours, a still substantial 43 percent of European respondents indicated that they would wait, compared with 30 percent of US respondents. For a full one-day delay, 24 percent of European respondents were still willing to wait, compared with 15 percent of US respondents. Table 9 provides a summary of the responses.

What these responses would appear to indicate is that European fund managers *would* be willing to trade patiently – at least as much so as American fund managers – *if* they had access to trading vehicles which could save them a fraction of a percent off the cost of shares. US proprietary call market trading systems (Instinet, Posit, and AZX) have, in aggregate, grown substantially in recent years precisely because of their ability to cut buy-side trading costs (despite a loss of immediacy), and the survey responses of European buy-side traders would certainly suggest a latent demand for such systems in Europe.

[15] Excluding DK and NA. Out of all respondents: DK was 1.7%; NA was 1.7%.

[16] The question on the US survey featured a \$0.25 savings on a \$50 stock. As with the European survey, 'Don't Knows' and 'No Answers' have been eliminated from the sample size in presenting the responses.

Table 9

Once you have decided to trade, how often would you accept an execution delay for a SEAQ stock trading at £5.00 if you could save the 2.5 pence *per share* in commissions, bid-ask spread, and market impact? (Q22-24)

	Length of execution delay % of respondents[17]		
	1 hour	3 hours	1 day
Never	12.20	25.00	39.02
Rarely (1–24% of trades)	12.20	10.00	19.51
Sometimes (25–49% of trades)	26.83	22.50	17.07
Regularly (50–74% of trades)	14.63	12.50	0.00
Frequently (75–100% of trades)	34.15	30.00	24.39

4. TRADING LARGE ORDERS

4.1. How Large are UK Share Trades?

Table 10 indicates that average UK trade size is relatively large, particularly in comparison with trades executed through continental auction markets. Fifty-two percent of our respondents' UK share trades exceeded 3 x Normal Market Size (NMS),[18] 33 percent exceeded 5 x NMS, and 14 percent exceeded 10 x NMS. These findings are consistent with data produced by the London Stock Exchange. Clearly, trades of this size can only be handled cost-effectively, on a consistent basis, in a dealer market. If the London Stock Exchange ran an auction market, average trade size would be considerably smaller.

As we discussed in Chapter 1, installation of modern electronic continuous auction markets in continental Europe has led institutional investors to execute a larger percentage of their orders as a series of smaller trades rather than *en bloc* through London dealers. Nonetheless, normal institutional orders can often swamp the public liquidity available in a continuous auction market at any point in time, which leads fund managers to seek out a range of alternative execution vehicles – including 'upstairs' dealer trading and call market trading. The US survey found that 36 percent of respondents indicated that one in every five of their *orders* (not *trades*) exceeds the stock's average daily trading volume (ADTV). Furthermore, data from the US Plexus Group indicate that 40 percent of institutional orders exceed ADTV, and two-thirds exceed 50 percent of ADTV.[19]

[17] Excluding DK and NA. Out of all respondents: DK was 8.5%; NA was 22%.
[18] NMS = approximately 2.5% of average daily trading volume.
[19] Wagner and Edwards (1993).

Table 10
Please indicate, roughly, the breakdown of your UK stock trading by NMS (normal market size) (Q31)

Size of trade	Mean response[20]
Less than 3 x NMS	47.67
3-5 x NMS	19.43
5-10 x NMS	18.55
> 10 NMS	14.36

4.2. How Do Portfolio Managers Expect Large Orders to be Handled?

Do portfolio managers expect rapid executions from their trading desks, or are they willing to be patient? Only 11 percent expected a large FTSE 100 share order – 10 x NMS or more[21] – to be fully executed within one hour, and only 3 percent expected such speed on a small cap stock. Thirty-six percent allowed more than one day for execution of a large cap order, and 73 percent allowed more than one day for a small cap order.

US portfolio managers appeared considerably more patient: 6 percent expected their large orders for large cap stocks to be executed within one hour, and less than 1 percent expected such speed for small cap stocks. Seventy-five percent allowed over one day for a large cap stock, and 95 percent for a small cap stock.

Table 11
How much time does your portfolio manager typically give you to trade a large order – 10 times NMS (normal market size) or more?[22] (Q32)

	Small cap stock	Large cap (FTSE 100) stock
1 hour or less	3.03	11.11
1 hour–1 day	24.24	52.78
1–2 days	18.18	16.67
2–3 days	12.12	5.56
More than 3 days	42.42	13.89

[20] Percentage of respondents excluding NA. Out of all respondents: NA was 28.8% for all the categories.

[21] 10 x NMS = 25% of ADTV, which was the standard used for the question in the US study.

[22] Percentage of respondents excluding NA and Other. Out of all respondents: NA was 37.3% for small cap and 32.2% for large cap, and Other was 6.8% for both.

4.3. How are Large Orders Traded?

Larger orders do not have to be traded immediately, as a block. They can be broken into smaller lots for separate executions over an extended period of time.

For large orders in FTSE 100 shares, 52 percent of respondents break up less than 1 in 5 of their large orders, and nearly 13 percent never break up such orders. In the US survey, for roughly the equivalent size US order,[23] only 34 percent indicated that they would break up fewer than 1 in 5 orders, and less than 6 percent never break up such orders.

It would certainly appear that US institutions in the US markets were demanding immediacy less often than European institutions in the UK market. As we have heard from European dealers, US institutions are also less apt to demand immediacy in European share trading. Nonetheless, we must take proper account of the different regulatory environments in the United States and the UK, and not judge this result as an indication of fundamentally different buy-side trading preferences in US and European institutions. Immediate post-trade publication is required of all dealers in the United States, while delayed publication is permitted for large trades in the UK. As the UK rules present less risk to dealers committing capital, immediacy in size is likely to be *relatively* less costly in the UK, leading to relatively higher demand for the service.

Table 12

How frequently do you break a large FTSE 100 stock order (500,000 shares or more) into smaller lots for separate executions over an extended period of time? (Q34)

	Percentage of respondents[24]
Never	12.50
1–9% of orders	27.08
10–19% of orders	12.50
20% or more of orders	47.92

4.4. How Long Does it Take to Execute a Broken-Up Large Order?

The length of time typically taken to implement an investment decision in the market-place is a direct indication of willingness to trade patiently. For large FTSE 100 share orders (500,000+), 43 percent of respondents indicated that they regularly or frequently (50 percent of the time) take over a full day to execute the

[23] 100,000 average US shares will have very roughly the same monetary value as 500,000 FTSE 100 shares.

[24] Excluding DK and NA. Out of all respondents: DK was 6.8%; NA was 11.9%.

order completely. Again, US investors appear somewhat more patient: 56 percent regularly or frequently took over a full day. As we discussed above, however, we cannot say whether US investors are in some sense 'obliged' to be patient by less US dealer willingness to provide cost-effective trade immediacy under an immediate publication regime.

Table 13
When you break a large FTSE 100 stock order (500,000 shares or more) into smaller lots, how long does it take for the order to be executed completely?[25] (Q35)

	Between 3 hours and 1 day	More than 1 day
Never	3.57	23.33
Rarely (1–24% of instances)	17.86	10.00
Sometimes (25–49% of instances)	32.14	23.33
Regularly (50–74% of instances)	35.71	13.33
Frequently (75–100% of instances)	10.71	30.00

4.5. Is Market Illiquidity a Problem for Portfolio Adjustment?

For a large cap (FTSE 100) stock, buy-side traders very rarely find it necessary to abandon a desired portfolio adjustment because of insufficient market liquidity. Sixty-six percent of respondents indicated that they never abandon portfolio adjustments because a FTSE 100 stock is too illiquid, and 91 percent indicated that this happens less than 10 percent of the time. However, illiquidity can be a problem for smaller (non-FTSE 100) stocks. Forty-two percent of respondents indicated that they abandon desired portfolio adjustments over 10 percent of the time, and 15 percent do so over 20 percent of the time.

For thinly traded stocks, a continuous trading environment is particularly inappropriate, as it allows the limited liquidity which does exist to dissipate through time. Call auctions are therefore a valuable means of ensuring that sufficient liquidity can be maintained by focusing order flow at a specific point in time. This is at the root of Tradepoint's strategy to run a continuous auction market for the largest 400 UK stocks, and a call auction for smaller stocks. Our analysis in this chapter would suggest that call auction trading could be usefully extended to larger stocks.

[25] Percentage of respondents excluding DK and NA. Out of all respondents: DK was 11.9% for between 3 hours and 1 day, and 9.5% for more than a day; NA was 21.4% for between 3 hours and 1 day, and 19% for more than a day.

Table 14
When you wish to adjust your portfolio, how frequently do you decide not to do so because the London market is too illiquid?[26] (Q36)

	Never	1–9% of trades	10–19% of trades	20% or more of trades
FTSE 100 stock	66.04	24.53	7.55	1.89
Non-FTSE 100 stock	31.25	27.08	27.08	14.58

5. PROTECTING INFORMATION AND ANONYMITY

5.1. How Concerned are Buy-Side Traders about Information Leakage?

Maintaining anonymity is often important for a buy-side trading desk, since revelation of their identity can provide others in the market with valuable information, such as the likely size of the full order. Thus, revealing one's identity can produce an immediate adverse price impact. This explains the growing popularity of anonymous proprietary trading platforms, such as that provided by Instinet (particularly in Nasdaq stocks, which are generally dealer-intermediated). Sixty-two percent of respondents indicated that anonymity was either valuable or very valuable, and a mere 5 percent felt that it was not valuable.

Table 15
When you want to trade, how valuable is keeping your identity anonymous? (Q15)

		Percentage of respondents[27]
(5)	Very valuable	28.57
(4)		33.93
(3)		10.71
(2)		21.43
(1)	Not at all valuable	5.36
Average response		*3.59*

[26] Percentage of respondents excluding DK and NA. Out of all respondents: DK was 6.8%; NA was 3.4%.

[27] Excluding DK and NA. Out of all respondents: DK was 3.4%; NA was 1.7%.

Forty-eight percent said that they were either concerned or very concerned about information leakage when they called a broker or market maker, and less than 6 percent were unconcerned. The results were very similar in the United States: 46 percent were concerned or very concerned, although somewhat more (12 percent) were unconcerned.

Table 16
When you call a broker or market maker, how concerned are you about information leakage? (Q33)

		Percentage of respondents[28]
(5)	Very concerned	25.00
(4)		23.08
(3)	Somewhat concerned	30.77
(2)		15.38
(1)	Not concerned	5.77
Average response		*3.46*

6. ALTERNATIVE TRADING SYSTEMS

6.1. Will Trading Migrate to New Proprietary Systems?

To date, virtually all European equity trading has been concentrated on official stock exchange systems, or handled 'off-exchange', through exchange members, over the telephone. Could this change over the next few years? The recent arrival in Europe of proprietary electronic trading and brokerage systems, such as those operated by Tradepoint and Instinet, indicates that new private trading service providers believe that buy-side traders can be tempted away from traditional exchange intermediaries and execution systems.

We asked respondents what percentage of European share trading they expect will be done outside the traditional exchange systems by the year 2000. The results were striking, given the very low base from which we are starting. Sixty-nine percent of respondents expected that over 10 percent of total trading would be done through alternative systems, 35 percent expected this volume to be over 25 percent of trading, and just under 13 percent thought the volume would actually surpass 50 percent. Given that institutional funds under management are expected to grow dramatically in the coming years, stock exchanges and their members should certainly take note of these findings.

[28] Excluding DK and NA. Out of all respondents: DK was 3.4%; NA was 8.5%.

Table 17

In the United States in recent years, there has been significant growth in share trading through alternative electronic trading/brokerage systems – or '*proprietary trading/brokerage systems*' – such as Instinet's electronic broking (continuous auction) system and crossing network, POSIT's crossing network, and the Arizona Stock Exchange's (AZX) call auction. We would like to know your views on the prospects for proprietary systems, such as Instinet and Tradepoint, in Europe.

By the year 2000, what percentage of European share trading do you believe will be transacted outside the traditional trading mechanisms of the national stock exchanges (i.e. through proprietary trading/brokerage systems)? (Q37)

	Percentage of respondents[29]
None	2.08
1–4% of trades	2.08
5–9% of trades	27.08
10–24% of trades	33.33
25–49% of trades	22.92
50% or more of trades	12.50

6.2. What are the Constraints on PTS Growth in Europe?

We identified a number of factors which we felt were *potential* constraints on the growth of PTSs in Europe, and asked respondents how significant they felt these were. Not surprisingly, the existing concentration of liquidity on the national exchanges was considered the most significant: 51 percent considered this a serious or very serious constraint. Worryingly, 40 percent identified the concentration provisions of the Investment Services Directive (see Chapter 4) as a serious or very serious constraint. This is a clear indication that the Directive is not seen as wholly liberalizing. Interestingly, only 12 percent considered existing arrangements with broker-dealers, such as soft commissions, to be a serious constraint. This contrasts with the US study, which found 35 percent indicating that they would use alternative trading systems more if they did not have soft dollar arrangements with their brokers.

[29] Excluding DK and NA. Out of all respondents: DK was 13.2%; NA was 5.1%.

Table 18

Below are some possible external constraints on the growth of proprietary trading/brokerage systems in Europe. How significant do you believe each of these to be?[30] (Q38)

	Very serious constraint (5) %	(4) %	Moderate constraint (3) %	(2) %	No constraint (1) %	Average response
High level of liquidity presently on the national exchanges	27.45	23.52	29.41	13.73	5.88	3.53
Concentration provisions of the Investment Services Directive (Art. 14)	10.00	30.00	36.67	16.67	6.67	3.20
Member-firm trading restrictions imposed by national stock exchanges	15.22	17.39	39.13	21.74	6.52	3.13
Other national regulatory restrictions	10.00	15.00	32.50	35.00	7.50	2.85
Existing investor arrangements with broker-dealers (e.g. soft commissions)	2.04	10.20	42.86	26.53	18.37	2.51

6.3. Will PTSs Provide Improved Trading Services?

We identified 11 trading features which we believed buy-side traders would be concerned with, and asked respondents how they felt PTSs will perform on each of these features relative to SEAQ. The results were again striking. In terms of the average response (below 3.0 favours SEAQ), SEAQ came out better on only two of the 11 trading features: liquidity (2.64) and immediacy (2.78). While these are extremely important features of any trading environment – liquidity undoubtedly being the most important – it is clear that institutions believe that at least some of their trading needs will be better met outside the present SEAQ structure. This is particularly the case for transaction costs (3.93), anonymity (3.83), and spread costs (3.62), where respondents expressed a clear preference for alternative trading mechanisms. With regard to transaction costs, a remarkable 74 percent felt that PTSs would perform better.

[30] Excluding DK and NA. Out of all respondents: DK was 6.8% for existing liquidity on exchanges, 39% for concentration, 11.9% for member-firm restrictions, 20.3% for other national restrictions, and 10.2% for soft commissions etc; NA was 6.8% for existing liquidity on exchanges, 10.2% for concentration and member-firm restrictions, 11.9% for other national restrictions, and 6.8% for soft commissions etc.

We should stress that we do not feel that these findings in any way undermine the case for maintaining and supporting the operation of a London dealer market. The findings do, however, undermine claims, frequently heard from the London Stock Exchange and certain of its members, that the needs of investors cannot be better served outside the present trading structure. No trading system can be all things to all traders, and investors seem to be indicating that they would welcome more choice.

Table 19

Compared with SEAQ, indicate whether you think that proprietary trading/brokerage systems (PTS/B) as a group are, or will be, better, comparable, or worse with respect to the following trading features.[31] (Q39)

	PTS/B much better (5) %	PTS/B better (4) %	PTS/B comparable (3) %	PTS/B worse (2) %	PTS/B much worse (1) %	Average response
Transaction costs	21.43	52.38	23.81	2.38	0.00	3.93
Liquidity	0.00	21.43	33.33	33.33	11.90	2.64
Spread costs	7.69	56.41	25.64	10.26	0.00	3.62
Execution rates	5.26	39.47	26.32	26.32	2.63	3.18
Immediacy of execution	2.44	21.95	34.15	34.15	7.32	2.78
Minimal market impact	7.32	26.83	53.66	12.20	0.00	3.29
Anonymity	25.00	32.50	42.50	0.00	0.00	3.83
Control over negotiation process	9.76	24.39	39.02	19.51	7.32	3.10
Pre-trade transparency (i.e. publicly visible best bid-ask)	4.88	24.39	48.78	14.63	7.32	3.05
Post-trade transparency (i.e. publicly visible last-trade data)	2.44	21.95	56.10	14.63	4.88	3.02
Investor protection	5.13	12.82	66.67	15.38	0.00	3.08

7. EUROPE AND THE INVESTMENT SERVICES DIRECTIVE

7.1. Will the ISD Promote Cross-Border Buy-Side Trading?

The Investment Services Directive (ISD) is the legislative centrepiece of the single market programme for the securities sector. We asked institutional investors

[31] Excluding DK and NA. Out of all respondents: DK was 13.6% for transaction costs, 13.6% for liquidity, 16.9% for spread costs, 18.6% for execution rates, 13.6% for immediacy, 13.6% for market impact, 15.3% for anonymity, 13.6% for control over negotiation, 13.6% for pre-trade transparency, 13.6% for post-trade transparency, and 16.9% for investor protection; NA was 15.3% for transaction costs, 15.3% for liquidity, 16.9% for spread costs, 16.9% for execution rates, 16.9% for immediacy, 16.9% for market impact, 16.9% for anonymity, 16.9% for control over negotiation, 16.9% for pre-trade transparency, 16.9% for post-trade transparency, and 16.9% for investor protection.

how they felt it would affect their ability to trade cross-border cheaply and efficiently.

The results reveal no more than a lukewarm endorsement. Sixty-one percent of total respondents expressed no opinion (in the form of answering 'don't know', or not answering). Of those expressing a view, only 35 percent expected any net improvement as a result of ISD implementation.

Table 20
How will the Investment Services Directive affect your ability to execute cross-border equity trades cheaply and efficiently?[32] (Q40)

Improve it very much (5) %	Improve it somewhat (4) %	No effect (3) %	Harm it somewhat (2) %	Harm it very much (1) %	Average response
4.35	30.43	60.87	4.34	0.00	3.35

7.2. Is Inter-Trading System Competition Good for Investors?

Many continental exchange officials and national treasuries have maintained that parallel trading of their domestic equities in the London dealer market is damaging to the global liquidity of their shares, and is therefore contrary to the interests of investors. This argument was at the root of the debate over the inclusion of 'concentration provisions' in the ISD (see Chapter 4). We have therefore taken the question directly to the investors: is parallel trading of French equities in Paris and London good or bad *for your business*? The question was not abstract, as it asked respondents to comment on the impact of parallel trading on their own firms.

The response indicated a strong endorsement of parallel trading: 57 percent said the effect was positive, while only 4 percent said that it was negative. Only the French response was mixed, with 2 indicating 'fairly good', 2 'irrelevant', and 2 'fairly bad' (accounting for all the negative responses). The results must therefore be seen as a further endorsement of investor choice in trading systems, and a strong statement from the primary customers of trading services against national regulators applying 'concentration' rules against new competition.

[32] Excluding DK and NA. Out of all respondents: DK was 40.7%, and NA was 20.3%.

Table 21
French equities are traded over several European trading systems, such as the Paris Bourse (CAC) and the London Stock Exchange (SEAQ-I). For your business, is this competition:[33] (Q41)

A very good thing (5) %	A fairly good thing (4) %	Irrelevant (3) %	A fairly bad thing (2) %	A very bad thing (1) %	Average response
21.28	36.17	38.30	4.26	0.00	3.74

7.3. Who Should Set Minimum Transparency Rules?

Market transparency, in the form of post-trade publication, also featured prominently in the debates over market structure regulation in the ISD. Again, we put the question to the primary customers of trading services: who should determine the minimum transparency rules for stock exchanges in Europe?

The results may come as a surprise to regulators throughout Europe. Only 23 percent endorsed making such rules at the European level. Just slightly more, 25 percent, wanted the decision left to the home-state regulator. But a majority – 52 percent – wanted the decision left to the individual stock exchanges themselves.

Breaking down the results by nationality provides a somewhat more subtle picture. UK respondents overwhelmingly supported leaving transparency rules to the individual exchanges: 63 percent, as compared with 23 percent for the home-state regulator and 13 percent for pan-European rules. This result would indicate that UK institutions, which operate domestically in a dealer market, endorse the view that there is a real economic trade-off between post-trade transparency and market liquidity. Continental respondents split almost evenly across the three choices: 33 percent for the stock exchanges, 28 percent for the home state regulator, and 39 percent for European rules.[34]

[33] Excluding DK and NA. Out of all respondents: DK and NA were 10.17% each.

[34] 33% of continental respondents did not answer this question, as opposed to only 6.3% of UK respondents.

Table 22
Who should determine the minimum post-trade transparency rules (i.e. trade publication rules) for stock exchanges in Europe?[35] (Q42)

	%
The individual stock exchanges themselves	52.08
The individual home state national regulators	25.00
The European Commission and/or Council of Ministers (i.e. through EC directives)	22.92
Other (please specify):	0.00

8. SUMMARY AND CONCLUSIONS

Given the rapid growth of equity funds under institutional management, it is clear that the trading practices and preferences of professional asset managers are going to become increasingly important in shaping the development of equity market structure. Yet surprisingly little systematic information on buy-side trading exists, and the public policy debate in Europe has therefore been largely uninformed by the views and practices of institutional investors. The study discussed in this chapter goes some way towards rectifying this problem. Our important findings fall into three broad categories.

8.1. Patience and Market Structure

We investigated how well institutional investor trading practices and preferences actually correspond to the menu of trading services currently available in Europe. This menu is, at present, dominated by trading systems and broker-dealer practices designed to facilitate rapid execution of customer orders. In volatile markets, immediate trading offers the advantage of minimizing execution risk, or the risk that prices will move disadvantageously before a buy or sell order can be filled. Yet immediate executions incur direct costs (in the form of bid-ask spreads, market impact, and relatively high commissions) which might be avoided if executions could be delayed and traditional market intermediaries bypassed. Thus it is important to know how European institutional investors currently trade, and how they would trade if alternative services were available, in order to assess whether and how equity market structure could be made more conducive to investor interests.

We discovered the following:

[35] Excluding NA. Out of all respondents: NA was 18.6%.

- Many of the factors which most commonly motivated our respondents' trading – such as internal and external research, and reassessment of portfolio structure – rarely require immediate trading. The reverse holds as well: factors often requiring immediate execution – such as chartist signals or knowledge of other orders in the market – rarely motivate our respondents' trading.
- Forty-six percent of respondents use limit orders for over half their trading – limit orders manifesting patient trading in a continuous market. This figure is particularly impressive as over half our respondents were UK-based institutions, trading primarily in a dealer market where limit orders are less favourably accommodated than in an auction market.
- Fifty-one percent of respondents indicated a clear willingness to trade patiently as a means of keeping down execution costs. Only 5 percent said that they were unwilling to do so.
- Forty-nine percent of respondents indicated that they would regularly or frequently accept a trading delay of *one hour* in order to save 1/2 percent off the cost of shares. Forty-three percent would accept a *three-hour* delay to obtain such a savings, and 24 percent would accept a *full day* delay.
- Thirty-six percent of respondents are given more than one full day by their portfolio manager to trade a large order (25 percent x ADTV) on a FTSE 100 stock, and 73 percent are given more than a day to trade a large order on a small cap stock. Only 11 percent are instructed to trade a large FTSE 100 order within an hour, and only 3 percent are instructed to trade a large order on a small cap stock within an hour.
- Forty-eight percent said that they were concerned or very concerned about information leakage when calling a broker or dealer, and 62 percent said that maintaining their anonymity was valuable or very valuable.

These findings indicate that respondents are aware of and concerned about the costs of immediacy and trade intermediation, and that they would be willing to make considerable use of alternative trading vehicles which provided less immediacy but lower execution costs. Such vehicles do already exist, in the form of non-intermediated electronic call markets, which are handling significant and growing volumes of trading in the US markets. This may be partially a reflection and partially a cause of US respondents to the earlier Economides and Schwartz (1995) study appearing, on balance, more patient than their European counterparts.

A summary of the responses from the European and US surveys is provided in Table 23 below.

Table 23. Summary of European and US Survey Responses

Response	Europe (%)	US (%)
1. Willing to trade patiently (T8)	51	70
2. Willing to accept a 1-hour trading delay to save 1/2% on shares (T9)	49	43
3. Willing to accept a 3-hour trading delay to save 1/2% on shares (T9)	43	31
4. Willing to accept a 1-day trading delay to save 1/2% on shares (T9)	24	15
5. Are given 1 day or more to trade a large order for a small cap stock (T11)	73	95
6. Are given 3 days or more to trade a large order for a small cap stock (T11)	42	45
7. Are given 1 day or more to trade a large order for a large cap stock (T11)	36	75
8. Are given 3 days or more to trade a large order for a large cap stock (T11)	14	14
9. Break up more than 20% of large orders into smaller lots (T12)	48	66
10. Regularly take 3 hours to 1 day to execute a large order completely (T13)	46	76
11. Regularly take more than 1 day to execute a large order completely (T13)	43	56
12. Concerned about information leakage when calling broker or dealer (T16)	48	48
13. Value keeping identity anonymous when wanting to trade (T15)	62	N/A
14. Anonymity is an important motive for trading on an electronic system	N/A	74

T = table number in the text of this chapter.
N/A = question not asked.

8.2. Alternative Trading Systems

Our respondents are extremely sanguine about the prospects for new proprietary trading systems in Europe. Sixty-nine percent expected such systems to handle over 1 in 10 European equity trades by the year 2000, and 13 percent expected such systems to handle over half of all European trades. Respondents also believe that such systems will offer better performance than existing exchange systems along a range of measures: for example, PTSs are expected to outperform SEAQ on 9 of 11 major trading system features. Despite being optimistic about PTS prospects and capabilities, many respondents did see significant external constraints on their growth: in particular, 40 percent considered the concentration provisions of the Investment Services Directive to be a serious or very serious constraint, and 33 percent considered member-firm trading restrictions imposed by stock exchanges to be a serious or very serious constraint.

8.3. European Rules

As we discuss in Chapter 4, the EU Council of Ministers' redrafting of the Commission's original ISD text meant a dilution of the Directive's liberalizing force, as certain Member State governments emerged as partisans for the interests of their respective national stock exchanges. Not surprisingly, the interests of European investors fell by the wayside. Only 39 percent of our respondents expressed any opinion regarding whether the ISD might facilitate their cross-border trading, and of those only 35 percent expected any improvement owing to the Directive. Respondents overwhelmingly rejected the underlying premise of the ISD concentration provisions: that parallel dealer trading of stocks listed on national auction markets was detrimental to market liquidity and investor interests. Fifty-seven percent of respondents said that London trading of French equities was good or very good for their business, while only 4 percent said it was bad. The rest found it irrelevant. Finally, a large majority of respondents (77 percent) rejected the need for minimum market transparency rules to be written into EU directives, while 52 percent did not even want such rules decreed by national regulators – they wished to leave the determination to the individual stock exchanges themselves. On the basis of our study's findings, we believe that there is a clear need for EU national governments to take much more explicit account of the needs of investors when formulating market structure regulations.

References

Economides, Nicholas and Robert A. Schwartz, 1995. 'Equity Trading Practice and Market Structure: Assessing Asset Managers' Demand for Immediacy', *Financial Markets, Institutions, and Instruments*, 4 (4).

Handa, Puneet and Robert A. Schwartz, 1995. 'Limit Order Trading', Working Paper, Leonard N. Stern School of Business, New York University.

Wagner, Wayne H. and Mark Edwards, 1993. 'Best Execution', *Financial Analysts Journal*, January/February.

APPENDIX

EUROPEAN CAPITAL MARKETS INSTITUTE

THE EUROPEAN INSTITUTIONAL INVESTOR SURVEY

PART I: QUESTIONS FOR THE CHIEF INVESTMENT OFFICER

A. CLASSIFICATION DATA (to be used for analysis, not for identification)

1. In what country is your organization based (*ie*, your specific office)?

________________ 05-09

2. What type of organization do you work for?

• Independent investment management firm	❑ 10-1	
• Subsidiary of a commercial bank, investment bank, insurance company, or brokerage firm	❑ -2	
• Department of a commercial bank, investment bank, insurance company, or brokerage firm	❑ -3	
• Corporate pension fund	❑ (see -4 or -5 below)	
If so, are more than 50% of your assets managed internally?	yes ❑ -4	no ❑ -5
• Public pension fund	❑ (see -6 or -7 below)	
If so, are more than 50% of your assets managed internally?	yes ❑ -6	no ❑ -7
• Unit trust (*ie*, SICAV or mutual fund)	❑ -8	
• Other (please specify):		

________________ 11-12

3. With regards to UK share <u>dealing</u> in your organization, who carries out this function?

centralized dealing desk ❑ 13-1 portfolio manager ❑ -2 other (please specify): ________ 14

4. Is your style of asset management primarily:

Active ❑ 15-1 Passive ❑ -2

5. Which of the following best describes your organization's general investment approach? Please indicate your primary investment approach, and - if appropriate - your secondary approach.

(Tick no more than **one box for each column**)

	Primary investment approach	Secondary investment approach
Value-orientated	❑ 16-1	❑ 18-1
Growth-orientated	❑ -2	❑ -2
Quant-driven active	❑ -3	❑ -3
Asset allocation (*eg*, country fund)	❑ -4	❑ -4
Indexation	❑ -5	❑ -5
Other (please specify):		
________	❑ 17	❑ 19

6. What is the total value of your organization's equity assets under management (including own-funds)?

currency (*eg*, £): _____ value: ________________ 20-24

7. Please indicate, roughly, the percentage of your funds invested in the following assets:

Equities	____%	25-30
Fixed income	____%	31-35
Property	____%	36-40
Cash	____%	41-45
Other (please specify):		
________	____%	46-50
________	____%	51-55
	100%	(Categories should total 100%)

8 Please indicate, roughly, the percentage of your <u>equity</u> assets invested in the following areas:

UK	____%	56-57
Continental Europe	____%	58-59
North America	____%	60-61
Far East	____%	62-63
"Emerging Markets"	____%	64-65
	100%	(Categories should total 100%)

66-79=z
80-1

9. Please indicate, roughly, the breakdown of your equity assets by index classification:

<u>UK</u>			**<u>FRANCE</u>**			**<u>GERMANY</u>**		
FTSE 100	____%	05-06	CAC	____%	13-14	DAX	____%	17-18
FTSE Mid 250	____%	07-08	non-CAC	____%	15-16	non-DAX	____%	19-20
FTSE Small Cap	____%	09-10						
non-All-Share	____%	11-12						
	100%			**100%**			**100%**	

(All countries' allocations should total 100%)

10. What is your annual trading volume?

Value of equities traded:

currency (*eg*, £): _____ value: ________________ 21-25

Value of total equity commissions paid:

currency (*eg*, £): _____ value: ________________ 26-30

B. WHY YOU TRADE

11. Listed below are a number of factors that might motivate investment decisions for individual stocks. Please indicate how frequently your investment decisions are motivated by each of these factors. (For each row, tick a box from 1 to 5, where 5 = "very frequently" and 1 = "never".)

		Very frequently				Never	Don't know
a.	Stock-specific fundamental issues	5 ☐ 31-1	4 ☐ -2	3 ☐ -3	2 ☐ -4	1 ☐ -5	☐ -6
b.	Market-wide news	5 ☐ 32-1	4 ☐ -2	3 ☐ -3	2 ☐ -4	1 ☐ -5	☐ -6
c.	Re-assessment of portfolio structure	5 ☐ 33-1	4 ☐ -2	3 ☐ -3	2 ☐ -4	1 ☐ -5	☐ -6
d.	Fund redemptions or other cash flow reasons	5 ☐ 34-1	4 ☐ -2	3 ☐ -3	2 ☐ -4	1 ☐ -5	☐ -6
e.	Need to track a market index	5 ☐ 35-1	4 ☐ -2	3 ☐ -3	2 ☐ -4	1 ☐ -5	☐ -6
f.	Profit taking	5 ☐ 36-1	4 ☐ -2	3 ☐ -3	2 ☐ -4	1 ☐ -5	☐ -6
g.	Bargain-hunting	5 ☐ 37-1	4 ☐ -2	3 ☐ -3	2 ☐ -4	1 ☐ -5	☐ -6
h.	Desire to cut losses	5 ☐ 38-1	4 ☐ -2	3 ☐ -3	2 ☐ -4	1 ☐ -5	☐ -6
i.	Chartist signals	5 ☐ 39-1	4 ☐ -2	3 ☐ -3	2 ☐ -4	1 ☐ -5	☐ -6
j.	Internal research (from portfolio manager)	5 ☐ 40-1	4 ☐ -2	3 ☐ -3	2 ☐ -4	1 ☐ -5	☐ -6
k.	External research (from broker, etc.)	5 ☐ 41-1	4 ☐ -2	3 ☐ -3	2 ☐ -4	1 ☐ -5	☐ -6
l.	Trading information (knowledge of another order)	5 ☐ 42-1	4 ☐ -2	3 ☐ -3	2 ☐ -4	1 ☐ -5	☐ -6
m.	Derivatives-motivated trading	5 ☐ 43-1	4 ☐ -2	3 ☐ -3	2 ☐ -4	1 ☐ -5	☐ -6
n.	Other (please specify): ______ 50-1	5 ☐ 44-	4 ☐ -2	3 ☐ -3	2 ☐ -4	1 ☐ -5	☐ -6

PART II: QUESTIONS FOR THE DEALER

NOTE: "SEAQ" QUESTIONS REFER TO UK STOCKS ONLY (NOT "SEAQI" STOCKS)

A. YOUR VIEWS ON EQUITY TRADING

12. How important is each of the following costs of trading to your trading decisions? (Tick **one box for each row**)

	Very important				Not at all important	Don't know
Broker commissions	5 ☐ 51-1	4 ☐ -2	3 ☐ -3	2 ☐ -4	1 ☐ -5	☐ -6
Bid-ask spread	5 ☐ 52-1	4 ☐ -2	3 ☐ -3	2 ☐ -4	1 ☐ -5	☐ -6
Market impact of trade	5 ☐ 53-1	4 ☐ -2	3 ☐ -3	2 ☐ -4	1 ☐ -5	☐ -6
Opportunity costs of missing a price through trade delay	5 ☐ 54-1	4 ☐ -2	3 ☐ -3	2 ☐ -4	1 ☐ -5	☐ -6

13. To what extent do trading costs lower the performance of your equity portfolio?

Very much				Insignificantly	Don't know
5 ☐ 55-1	4 ☐ -2	3 ☐ -3	2 ☐ -4	1 ☐ -5	☐ -6

14. How willing are you to trade patiently in order to try to reduce trading costs?

Very willing				Not at all willing	Don't know
5 ☐ 56-1	4 ☐ -2	3 ☐ -3	2 ☐ -4	1 ☐ -5	☐ -6

15. When you want to trade, how valuable is keeping your identity anonymous?

Very valuable				Not at all valuable	Don't know
5 ☐ 57-1	4 ☐ -2	3 ☐ -3	2 ☐ -4	1 ☐ -5	☐ -6

16. Which of the following trade execution routes do you use?

	Never	Rarely (1-24% of trades)	Sometimes (25-49% of trades)	Regularly (50-74% of trades)	Frequently (75-100% of trades)	Don't know
Principal (no broker)	☐ 58-1	☐ -2	☐ -3	☐ -4	☐ -5	☐ -6
Agency (broker)	☐ 59-1	☐ -2	☐ -3	☐ -4	☐ -5	☐ -6
Crossing network (*eg*, Instinet or Posit)	☐ 60-1	☐ -2	☐ -3	☐ -4	☐ -5	☐ -6
Other (please specify:) ______	☐ 61-1	☐ -2	☐ -3	☐ -4	☐ -5	☐ -6

17. Listed below are some criteria that might be important in selecting which broker or market maker to deal through. How important is each of these criteria? (Tick **one box for each row**)

	Very important		Somewhat important		Not at all important	Don't know
Execution capability	5☐ 62-1	4☐ -2	3☐ -3	2☐ -4	1☐ -5	☐ -6
Anonymity	5☐ 63-1	4☐ -2	3☐ -3	2☐ -4	1☐ -5	☐ -6
Good research	5☐ 64-1	4☐ -2	3☐ -3	2☐ -4	1☐ -5	☐ -6
Efficient settlement	5☐ 65-1	4☐ -2	3☐ -3	2☐ -4	1☐ -5	☐ -6
Soft commissions	5☐ 66-1	4☐ -2	3☐ -3	2☐ -4	1☐ -5	☐ -6
Directed	5☐ 67-1	4☐ -2	3☐ -3	2☐ -4	1☐ -5	☐ -6
Other (please specify): ______	5☐ 68- 72-1	4☐ -2	3☐ -3	2☐ -4	1☐ -5	☐ -6

73-79=z

80-2

18. What do you consider an "immediate" trade on a FTSE 100 stock? A trade executed within:

1 minute	10 minutes	1 hour	2 hours	1 day	Other (please specify):
❑ 05-1	❑ -2	❑ -3	❑ -4	❑ -5	❑ __________ 06-07

19. Based on your definition of an "immediate" trade in the last question, are your immediate FTSE 100 stock trades mostly buy trades, sell trades, or evenly split between the two?

Much more often buy trades	Mostly buy trades	Evenly Split	Mostly sell trades	Much more often sell trades	Don't know
5 ❑ 08-1	4 ❑ -2	3 ❑ -3	2 ❑ -4	1 ❑ -5	❑ -6

20. Listed below are some possible reasons for wanting to trade a SEAQ stock quickly. How important is each of these factors? (Tick **one box for each row.**)

Factors for trading quickly	Very important		Somewhat important		Not at all important	Don't know
Stock-specific information	5❑ 09-1	4❑ -2	3❑ -3	2❑ -4	1❑ -5	❑ -6
Changing your market exposure on "macro" news (*ie*, non-stock-specific)	5❑ 10-1	4❑ -2	3❑ -3	2❑ -4	1❑ -5	❑ -6
Prices are very volatile, and the market could move against you	5❑ 11-1	4❑ -2	3❑ -3	2❑ -4	1❑ -5	❑ -6
To raise cash	5❑ 12-1	4❑ -2	3❑ -3	2❑ -4	1❑ -5	❑ -6
Simply because SEAQ makes immediate trading easy	5❑ 13-1	4❑ -2	3❑ -3	2❑ -4	1❑ -5	❑ -6
Simply because your portfolio manager wants his/her trade done quickly	5❑ 14-1	4❑ -2	3❑ -3	2❑ -4	1❑ -5	❑ -6
Other (please specify): ____________	5❑ 15-16-1	4❑ -2	3❑ -3	2❑ -4	1❑ -5	❑ -6

21. Please indicate on a scale of 1 to 5 (where 5 = "most preferred" and 1 = "least preferred") how you feel about trading SEAQ stocks at each of the times listed below. (Tick **one box for each row**)

	Most preferred		Neutral		Least preferred	Don't know
Before the market opening	5 ❑ 17-1	4 ❑ -2	3 ❑ -3	2 ❑ -4	1 ❑ -5	❑ -6
Half-hour after opening	5 ❑ 18-1	4 ❑ -2	3 ❑ -3	2 ❑ -4	1 ❑ -5	❑ -6
Remainder of morning	5 ❑ 19-1	4 ❑ -2	3 ❑ -3	2 ❑ -4	1 ❑ -5	❑ -6
Noon until half-hour to close	5 ❑ 20-1	4 ❑ -2	3 ❑ -3	2 ❑ -4	1 ❑ -5	❑ -6
Last half-hour to close	5 ❑ 21-1	4 ❑ -2	3 ❑ -3	2 ❑ -4	1 ❑ -5	❑ -6
After the market close	5 ❑ 22-1	4 ❑ -2	3 ❑ -3	2 ❑ -4	1 ❑ -5	❑ -6

Questions 22-24 are intended to assess how important it is for you to trade stocks quickly: within **one hour**, within **three hours**, and within **one day**.

22. Once you have decided to trade, how often would you accept an execution delay of **one hour** for a SEAQ stock trading at **£5.00** if you could save the following amount *per share* in commissions, bid-ask spread, and market impact?:

(Tick **one box for each row**)

	Never	Rarely (1-24% of trades)	Sometimes (25-49% of trades)	Regularly (50-74% of trades)	Frequently (75-100% of trades)	Don't know
0.5 pence per share	❑ 23-1	❑ -2	❑ -3	❑ -4	❑ -5	❑ -6
1.0 pence per share	❑ 24-1	❑ -2	❑ -3	❑ -4	❑ -5	❑ -6
2.5 pence per share	❑ 25-1	❑ -2	❑ -3	❑ -4	❑ -5	❑ -6
5.0 pence per share	❑ 26-1	❑ -2	❑ -3	❑ -4	❑ -5	❑ -6
7.5 pence per share	❑ 27-1	❑ -2	❑ -3	❑ -4	❑ -5	❑ -6
10 pence per share	❑ 28-1	❑ -2	❑ -3	❑ -4	❑ -5	❑ -6

23. Once you have decided to trade, how often would you accept an execution delay of **three hours** for a SEAQ stock trading at **£5.00** if you could save the following amount *per share* in commissions, bid-ask spread, and market impact?:

(Tick **one box for each row**)

	Never	Rarely (1-24% of trades)	Sometimes (25-49% of trades)	Regularly (50-74% of trades)	Frequently (75-100% of trades)	Don't know
0.5 pence per share	❑ 29-1	❑ -2	❑ -3	❑ -4	❑ -5	❑ -6
1.0 pence per share	❑ 30-1	❑ -2	❑ -3	❑ -4	❑ -5	❑ -6
2.5 pence per share	❑ 31-1	❑ -2	❑ -3	❑ -4	❑ -5	❑ -6
5.0 pence per share	❑ 32-2	❑ -2	❑ -3	❑ -4	❑ -5	❑ -6
7.5 pence per share	❑ 33-1	❑ -2	❑ -3	❑ -4	❑ -5	❑ -6
10 pence per share	❑ 34-1	❑ -2	❑ -3	❑ -4	❑ -5	❑ -6

24. Once you have decided to trade, how often would you accept an execution delay of **one day** for a SEAQ stock trading at **£5.00** if you could save the following amount *per share* in commissions, bid-ask spread, and market impact?:

(Tick **one box for each row**)

	Never	Rarely (1-24% of trades)	Sometimes (25-49% of trades)	Regularly (50-74% of trades)	Frequently (75-100% of trades)	Don't know
0.5 pence per share	❑ 35-1	❑ -2	❑ -3	❑ -4	❑ -5	❑ -6
1.0 pence per share	❑ 36-1	❑ -2	❑ -3	❑ -4	❑ -5	❑ -6
2.5 pence per share	❑ 37-1	❑ -2	❑ -3	❑ -4	❑ -5	❑ -6
5.0 pence per share	❑ 38-1	❑ -2	❑ -3	❑ -4	❑ -5	❑ -6
7.5 pence per share	❑ 39-1	❑ -2	❑ -3	❑ -4	❑ -5	❑ -6
10 pence per share	❑ 40-1	❑ -2	❑ -3	❑ -4	❑ -5	❑ -6

25. Relative to your total trading, how often do you use the following?: (tick **one box for each row**)

	Never	Rarely (1-24% of trades)	Sometimes (25-49% of trades)	Regularly (50-74% of trades)	Frequently (75-100% of trades)	Don't know
limit orders	☐ 41-1	☐ -2	☐ -3	☐ -4	☐ -5	☐ -6
market orders	☐ 42-1	☐ -2	☐ -3	☐ -4	☐ -5	☐ -6
protected trades	☐ 43-1	☐ -2	☐ -3	☐ -4	☐ -5	☐ -6

26. Relative to your total trading, how often do you trade the following?: (tick **one box for each row**)

	Never	Rarely (1-24% of trades)	Sometimes (25-49% of trades)	Regularly (50-74% of trades)	Frequently (75-100% of trades)	Don't know
individual stocks	☐ 44-1	☐ -2	☐ -3	☐ -4	☐ -5	☐ -6
baskets/program trades	☐ 45-1	☐ -2	☐ -3	☐ -4	☐ -5	☐ -6
index futures/options	☐ 46-1	☐ -2	☐ -3	☐ -4	☐ -5	☐ -6

27. If SEAQ had a central limit order facility, how often would you use it?

Never	Rarely (1-24% of trades)	Sometimes (25-49% of trades)	Regularly (50-74% of trades)	Frequently (75-100% of trades)	Don't know
☐ 47-1	☐ -2	☐ -3	☐ -4	☐ -5	☐ -6

28. How often does your portfolio manager give you an order with a price limit?

Never	Rarely (1-24% of trades)	Sometimes (25-49% of trades)	Regularly (50-74% of trades)	Frequently (75-100% of trades)	Don't know
☐ 48-1	☐ -2	☐ -3	☐ -4	☐ -5	☐ -6

29. Do you use index options or futures specifically to reduce your need to trade SEAQ stocks quickly?

yes ☐ 49-1 no ☐ -2 don't know ☐ -3

If you answered "no" or "don't know" on question 29, please skip question 30.

30. When you use index options or futures to reduce your need to trade SEAQ stocks quickly, approximately how long do you wait before buying or selling the shares? (tick **one box for each row**)

	Never	Rarely (1-24% of trades)	Sometimes (25-49% of trades)	Regularly (50-74% of trades)	Frequently (75-100% of trades)	Don't know
1 hour or less	☐ 50-1	☐ -2	☐ -3	☐ -4	☐ -5	☐ -6
1-3 hours	☐ 51-1	☐ -2	☐ -3	☐ -4	☐ -5	☐ -6
3 hours - 1 day	☐ 52-1	☐ -2	☐ -3	☐ -4	☐ -5	☐ -6
more than one day	☐ 53-1	☐ -2	☐ -3	☐ -4	☐ -5	☐ -6

31. Please indicate, roughly, the breakdown of your UK stock trading by NMS (normal market size):

	% of trades	
Less than 3 x NMS	____ %	54-55
3-5 x NMS	____ %	56-57
5-10 x NMS	____ %	58-59
More than 10 x NMS	____ %	60-61
	100%	(Categories should total 100%)

32. How much time does your portfolio manager typically give you to trade a **large order** - 10 times NMS (normal market size) or more - for

A: a large cap stock (FTSE 100 stock) and B: a small cap stock (non-FTSE 100)?

(Tick **one box for each column**)

Typical allowed execution time	Large Cap (FTSE 100) Order	Small Cap (non-FTSE 100) Order
1 hour or less	☐ 62-1	☐ 64-1
1 hour - 1 day	☐ -2	☐ -2
1 - 2 days	☐ -3	☐ -3
2 - 3 days	☐ -4	☐ -4
More than 3 days	☐ -5	☐ -5
Other (please specify): ________________	☐ 63	☐ 65

33. When you call a broker or market maker, how concerned are you about information leakage?

Very concerned		Somewhat concerned		Not concerned	Don't know
5 ☐ 66-1	4 ☐ -2	3 ☐ -3	2 ☐ -4	1 ☐ -5	☐ -6

34. How frequently do you break a large FTSE 100 stock order (500,000 shares or more) into smaller lots for separate executions over an extended period of time?

Never	1-9% of trades	10-19% of trades	20% or more of trades	Don't know
☐ 67-1	☐ -2	☐ -3	☐ -4	☐ -5

35. When you break a large FTSE 100 stock order (500,000 shares or more) into smaller lots, how long does it take for the order to be executed completely? (Tick **one box for each row**)

	Never	Rarely (1-24% of instances)	Sometimes (25-49% of instances)	Regularly (50-74% of instances)	Frequently (75-100% of instances)	Don't know
up to 1 hour	☐ 68-1	☐ -2	☐ -3	☐ -4	☐ -5	☐ -6
1-3 hours	☐ 69-1	☐ -2	☐ -3	☐ -4	☐ -5	☐ -6
3 hours - 1 day	☐ 70-1	☐ -2	☐ -3	☐ -4	☐ -5	☐ -6
over 1 day	☐ 71-1	☐ -2	☐ -3	☐ -4	☐ -5	☐ -6

36. When you wish to adjust your portfolio, how frequently do you decide **not** to do so because the London market is too illiquid? (Tick **one box for each row**)

	Never	1-9% of trades	10-19% of trades	20% or more of trades	Don't know
For a FTSE 100 stock	☐ 72-1	☐ -2	☐ -3	☐ -4	☐ -5
For a small cap stock (*ie*, non-FTSE 100)	☐ 73-1	☐ -2	☐ -3	☐ -4	☐ -5

74-79=z
80=3

B. ALTERNATIVE TRADING SYSTEMS

37. In the United States in recent years, there has been significant growth in share trading through alternative electronic trading/brokerage systems - or "**proprietary trading/brokerage systems**" - such as Instinet's electronic broking (continuous auction) system and crossing network, POSIT's crossing network, and the Arizona Stock Exchange's (AZX) call auction. We would like to know your views on the prospects for proprietary systems, such as Instinet and Tradepoint, in Europe.

By the year 2000, what percentage of European share trading do you believe will be transacted outside the traditional trading mechanisms of the national stock exchanges (*ie*, through proprietary trading/brokerage systems)?

None	0.1-0.9% of trades	1-4% of trades	5-9% of trades	10-24% of trades	25-49% of trades	50%+ of trades	Don't know
❑ 05-1	❑ -2	❑ -3	❑ -4	❑ -5	❑ -6	❑ -7	❑ -8

38. Below are some possible external constraints on the growth of proprietary trading/brokerage systems in Europe. How significant do you believe each of these to be? (Tick **one box for each row**).

	Very serious constraint		moderate constraint		no constraint	Don't know
High level of liquidity presently on the national stock exchanges	5 ❑ 06-1	4 ❑ -2	3 ❑ -3	2 ❑ -4	1 ❑ -5	❑ -6
Member-firm trading restrictions imposed by national stock exchanges	5 ❑ 07-1	4 ❑ -2	3 ❑ -3	2 ❑ -4	1 ❑ -5	❑ -6
Existing investor arrangements with broker-dealers (*eg*, soft commissions)	5 ❑ 08-1	4 ❑ -2	3 ❑ -3	2 ❑ -4	1 ❑ -5	❑ -6
Concentration provisions of the Investment Services Directive (Article 14)	5 ❑ 09-1	4 ❑ -2	3 ❑ -3	2 ❑ -4	1 ❑ -5	❑ -6
Other national regulatory restrictions	5 ❑ 10-1	4 ❑ -2	3 ❑ -3	2 ❑ -4	1 ❑ -5	❑ -6
Other (please specify): ____________	5 ❑ 11-12-1	4 ❑ -2	3 ❑ -3	2 ❑ -4	1 ❑ -5	❑ -6

39. Compared with SEAQ, indicate whether you think that proprietary trading/brokerage systems (**PTS/B**) **as a group** are, or will be, **better**, **comparable**, or **worse** with respect to the following trading features:
(Tick **one box for each row**)

	PTS/B much better	PTS/B better	PTS/B comparable	PTS/B worse	PTS/B much worse	Don't know
Transaction costs	5 ❑ 13-1	4 ❑ -2	3 ❑ -3	2 ❑ -4	1 ❑ -5	❑ -6
Liquidity	5 ❑ 14-1	4 ❑ -2	3 ❑ -3	2 ❑ -4	1 ❑ -5	❑ -6
Spread costs	5 ❑ 15-1	4 ❑ -2	3 ❑ -3	2 ❑ -4	1 ❑ -5	❑ -6
Execution rates	5 ❑ 16-1	4 ❑ -2	3 ❑ -3	2 ❑ -4	1 ❑ -5	❑ -6
Immediacy of execution	5 ❑ 17-1	4 ❑ -2	3 ❑ -3	2 ❑ -4	1 ❑ -5	❑ -6
Minimal market impact	5 ❑ 18-1	4 ❑ -2	3 ❑ -3	2 ❑ -4	1 ❑ -5	❑ -6
Anonymity	5 ❑ 19-1	4 ❑ -2	3 ❑ -3	2 ❑ -4	1 ❑ -5	❑ -6
Control over negotiation process	5 ❑ 20-1	4 ❑ -2	3 ❑ -3	2 ❑ -4	1 ❑ -5	❑ -6
Pre-trade transparency (*ie*, publicly visible best bid-ask)	5 ❑ 21-1	4 ❑ -2	3 ❑ -3	2 ❑ -4	1 ❑ -5	❑ -6
Post-trade transparency (*ie*, publicly visible last-trade data)	5 ❑ 22-1	4 ❑ -2	3 ❑ -3	2 ❑ -4	1 ❑ -5	❑ -6
Investor protection	5 ❑ 23-1	4 ❑ -2	3 ❑ -3	2 ❑ -4	1 ❑ -5	❑ -6
Other (please specify): ____________	5 ❑ 24-26-1	4 ❑ -2	3 ❑ -3	2 ❑ -4	1 ❑ -5	❑ -6

C. EUROPEAN ISSUES

40. How will the Investment Services Directive affect your ability to execute cross-border equity trades cheaply and efficiently?

Improve it very much	Improve it somewhat	No effect	Harm it somewhat	Harm it very much	Don't know
5 ❑ 27-1	4 ❑ -2	3 ❑ -3	2 ❑ -4	1 ❑ -5	❑ -6

41. French equities are traded over several European trading systems, such as the Paris Bourse (CAC) and the London Stock Exchange (SEAQI). For your business, is this competition:

A very good thing	A fairly good thing	Irrelevant	A fairly bad thing	A very bad thing	Don't know
5 ❑ 28-1	4 ❑ -2	3 ❑ -3	2 ❑ -4	1 ❑ -5	❑ -6

42. Who should determine the **minimum post-trade transparency rules** (*ie*, trade publication rules) for stock exchanges in Europe? (Tick **only one box**)

The individual stock exchanges themselves	❑ 29-1
The individual home state national regulators	❑ -2
The European Commission and/or Council of Ministers (*ie*, through EC directives)	❑ -3
Other (please specify):	❑ -4

____________ 30-32

33-79=z
80=4

RETURN TO: DR. BENN STEIL RIIA 10 ST JAMES'S SQUARE LONDON SW1Y 4LE UK
QUERIES? TEL: +44 171 957 5746 FAX: +44 171 957 5710

Chapter 4

EQUITY TRADING IV: THE ISD AND THE REGULATION OF EUROPEAN MARKET STRUCTURE

1. INTRODUCTION

This chapter examines the development and significance of the Investment Services Directive (ISD) in the area of equity *market structure*; or the institutions, rules, and processes through which stocks are traded in Europe. The central tenet underlying the analysis is that the implications of the Directive cannot be accurately gauged by simple reference to its text; rather, it is national competitive interests, as perceived by the Member State negotiators, which will determine how the compromise terms of the Directive are actually applied by the authorities in each national market. Thus, we devote considerable space to a discussion of the arguments made in the Council of Ministers in support of introducing market stucture regulation into the Directive.

2. PRINCIPLES OF EU FINANCIAL REGULATION

The EU legislative framework for financial markets is grounded in a concept known as 'competition among rules', which takes the continuing reality of separate and distinct national legal and regulatory systems as given. The principle outlined in the European Commission's 1985 White Paper supporting competition among rules is that of *mutual recognition*, according to which all Member States agree to recognize the validity of one another's laws, regulations, and standards, and thereby facilitate free trade in goods and services without the need for prior harmonization. Directly derived from this principle is the Second Banking Coordination Directive (2BCD) provision for a *single passport*, under which credit institutions incorporated in any EU Member State are permitted to carry out a full range of 'passported services', detailed in the Directive's annex, throughout the EU.[1] Similar guidelines are laid down for the provision of cross-border in-

[1] The institution must be authorized to carry out an activity in its home state before it can invoke its passport rights to do so in other Member States.

vestment services in the ISD. Reinforcing the market-opening effect of mutual recognition is the assignment of *home country control*, which attributes the primary task of supervising a given financial institution to its home country authorities. Home country control should, in theory, provide some assurance that foreign EU firms will not be put at a competitive disadvantage by host country authorities seeking to protect domestic firms. However, a major exception to the home country control provision exists for 'rules of conduct', which remain the province of the host country.

A second major principle enshrined in the White Paper is *harmonization of minimum standards*, which acts to limit the scope for competition among rules by mandating Member State conformity with some base-level EU-wide requirements. The principle is intended to ensure that 'basic public interests' are safeguarded in a 'single market' with different national rules and standards. Whether this principle facilitates or inhibits the free movement of goods, capital, and labour depends wholly upon the manner in which it is applied. It can, on the one hand, facilitate free competition by stopping Member States from erecting 'standards barriers' against one another's products and services, while on the other it can inhibit free competition by barring certain products or practices from the market altogether.

The minimum harmonization principle represents a major question mark in the drafting of EU legislation. 'I have to confess', wrote a former director-general of DGXV,[2] 'that I find myself cheerfully unrepentant in face of the criticism that the Commission has not made any serious attempt to develop a theory of harmonization.'[3] Yet reading the Commission's version of history in the White Paper, it is at least clear that the minimum harmonization principle is not seen simply as a necessary response to negative externalities deriving from free competition among rules. Rather, competition among rules is itself seen as a necessary but regrettable consequence of the Commission's inability to legislate full harmonization.[4]

[2] Directorate-General XV covers financial institutions and company law.

[3] Fitchew (1991:1).

[4] 'The harmonisation approach has been the cornerstone of Community action in the first 25 years and has produced unprecedented progress in the creation of common rules on a Community-wide basis. However, over the years, a number of shortcomings have been identified and it is clear that a genuine common market cannot be realised by 1992 if the Community relies exclusively on Article 100 of the EEC Treaty. There will certainly be a continuing need for action under Article 100; but its role will be reduced as new approaches, resulting in quicker and less troublesome progress, are agreed. . . . Clearly, action under this Article would be quicker and more effective if the Council were to agree not to allow the unanimity requirement to obstruct progress where it could otherwise be made. . . . In principle, . . . mutual recognition could be an effective strategy for bringing about a common market in a trading sense.' (Commission of the European Communities, 1985:18)

That said, it is readily apparent in the case of the ISD that the Commission attempted to rely far more on mutual recognition than on harmonization. It was only when the draft Directive passed into the control of the Council of Ministers that harmonization took on a significant dimension.

3. THE COMMISSION'S 1988 DRAFT DIRECTIVE

The European Commission presented its proposal for an Investment Services Directive to the European Council of Ministers in December 1988.[5] The primary aim of the draft Directive was to liberalize the cross-border provision of investment advice, broking, dealing, and portfolio management. To accomplish this, the draft Directive sought to define a simple and transparent EU-wide authorization procedure, which would rely primarily on *mutual recognition* in facilitating cross-border access for investment firms. With regard to stock exchanges, the draft Directive aimed merely to liberalize access to membership for all European investment firms, regardless of the Member State in which they were officially authorized.

What the draft Directive did not aim to do was to regulate European *market structure*. There is no definition of a 'stock exchange', no rules regarding on- and off-exchange trading, and no transparency requirements. In this regard, the draft Directive was highly liberal. Home authorities would remain free to set their own national market structure regulations, provided that these did not interfere with the legitimate rights of access of foreign EU investment firms. However, this meant implicitly that different national market structures would operate freely in parallel, and that investors would have the ability to bypass their home state exchanges and execute their transactions according to the rules applying on another Member State exchange. Any attempts by Member States to impose trading 'concentration' rules, restricting transactions to domestic exchanges, would almost certainly have been held by the Commission to violate the 1988 Capital Movements Directive (33/361/EEC).

4. THE 'REGULATED MARKET' CONCEPT

Market structure regulation was introduced into the ISD negotiations following a formal intervention by the French government delegation to the Council of Ministers in December 1989. The French introduced a critical distinction between *des marchés reconnus* (recognized markets) and *des opérations de gré à gré* (OTC

[5] The draft text was amended in January 1990, adding further liberalization measures relating to the cross-border expansion of trading systems via remote membership.

operations). Only the former were said to respect the 'principles' of transparency, fairness, and security, while the latter were held to reduce the 'global liquidity' of the European markets.

Thereafter, the concept of the 'recognized market' (subsequently relabelled 'regulated market') became critical in the development of the Directive. The French delegation insisted that Member States must have the right to require that transactions in domestic securities take place only on a 'regulated market' (so-called 'concentration'), which meant that any market which was not so designated could find cross-border participation in its operations severely restricted. The Capital Movements Directive would no longer offer any protection against such Member State restrictions. The definition of a 'regulated market' thus became critical.

Two essential components of the definition emerged in the Council debates: *transparency*, defined in terms of post-trade publication of transactions details, and formal *listing* of securities. Supporters of the regulated market concept, in particular the French and Italian delegations, held that both a high level of transparency and strict prudential requirements for the listing of securities were central criteria, particularly with regard to investor protection. These two criteria, not incidentally, happened to be ones which the rapidly growing London SEAQ International (SEAQ-I) market did not meet. Individual SEAQ-I transactions were not published, and this segment of the London market did not formally 'list' stocks – it simply traded them.

While the commitment of the negotiating parties to market integrity and investor protection is not in question, it is important to recognize that the motivation behind the introduction of market structure regulation into the Directive lay elsewhere. Specifically, the establishment of 'regulated market' criteria which SEAQ-I could not meet was seen as an effective mechanism to force the repatriation of French share trading back from London to Paris.

5. SHOULD THERE BE CONCENTRATION RULES?

It is, of course, quite often the case that the logic of an argument is correct even when the motivations for raising it are purely self-interested. Since the final text of the ISD gives Member States the *choice* whether or not to require trading in a given security to be concentrated on a 'regulated market', it is important to examine the arguments which the French delegation presented in favour of concentration in order to illuminate the decision which Member States will have to take after 1996.

5.1. Fragmentation

The French delegation expressed enormous concern about the 'fragmentation' of the European stock exchanges, which it claimed was contrary to the interests of issuers, investors, and intermediaries, and 'handicapped' Europe in competing with the great world financial centres. There are several strands to the argument about the costs of fragmentation, and these need to be examined individually.

5.1.1. Intermediary Interests

First, it is certainly reasonable to argue that trading 'fragmentation' *arising from legal or cartel barriers* is detrimental to the interest of issuers and investors. Such fragmentation tends to inflate the cost of access to the equity markets, and consequently raises the cost of equity capital for issuers and reduces net expected returns for investors.

However, fragmentation often *serves* the interests of many local intermediaries. As we pointed out in Chapters 1 and 2, the primary interest of exchange members is to maximize the benefits of exchange membership. This is often best promoted by barring direct access privileges to non-members, thereby obliging investors to bear excessive intermediation costs, and lobbying for protection against alternative trading service providers which seek to expand and integrate different pools of liquidity.

Fortunately, any cartel-like behaviour on the part of local intermediaries can be eliminated simply by dismantling legislation protecting the monopoly status of national stock exchanges. Once this is accomplished, new intermediaries – brokers, dealers, and trading systems – will be able to offer improved services to investors and issuers, thus obliging existing intermediaries to follow suit. However, concentration rules would act to *reinforce*, rather than dismantle, the monopoly status of stock exchanges. In this regard, such rules favour local 'producers' of financial services at the expense of 'consumers' – i.e. the issuers and investors – throughout the EU.

5.1.2. Multiple Exchanges and Market Architectures

Secondly, we would agree with an argument that the existence of three dozen European stock exchanges – almost all of which are operating with the same basic trading mechanism (the continuous electronic auction) – is, at the very least, duplicative and wasteful of resources. The expansion of remote membership access after 1996 will undoubtedly go a considerable way towards facilitating cost-effective cross-border trading, and thereby eliminate significant barriers to creating a common and expanded pool of equity market liquidity. A single European currency would serve to integrate the market even further (see Chapter 10). However, it is important to recognize that the French delegation was not actually expressing concern over excessive *duplication*, but rather over excessive *differences* in modes of trading. This is brought out in frequent and disparaging references to the expansion of 'off-market', or OTC, trading, which clearly points to the London dealer market.

This stands in contrast to our position, developed in Chapters 1-3, that 'fragmentation' brought about by *competition in market architecture* is highly desirable. The London dealer market injected vital 'private liquidity' into continental markets dominated by illiquid public auction markets. Trading in continental equities may not have been *concentrated* on continental market places, but the London and continental markets were well *integrated* – which is the central economic matter. Furthermore, while trade diversion to London was driven by legitimate liquidity concerns, one must not ignore the trade *creation* generated by the new London liquidity pool, part of which had to flow back to the continental market-places as dealers rebalanced their portfolios.

In the survey discussed in Chapter 3, we asked European institutional investors whether competition in French equity trading between the Paris Bourse and the London Stock Exchange was good or bad for their business. Fifty-seven percent said it was a 'fairly good' or 'very good' thing, 38 percent said it was 'irrelevant', and only 4 percent said it was a 'fairly bad' thing.[6] Thus we have virtually no support whatsoever from the consumers of trading services for the elimination of parallel 'OTC' (i.e. dealer) trading of exchange-listed European stocks.

5.1.2.1. A Euro-ITS

In order to produce the 'true unification' of the European capital market, the French delegation called for the creation of an automatic European order-routing and execution system. The parallel operation of an 'OTC' (i.e., dealer) market, they rightly claimed, was incompatible with such a system.

To accomplish this unification, the French delegation recommended following the model of the United States in the 1970s, when Congress mandated the creation of a 'National Market System' (NMS).[7] The centrepiece of the NMS became the Consolidated Tape Association (CTA), the Consolidated Quotation System (CQS), and the Intermarket Trading System (ITS). The CQS and ITS are the electronic price display and order-routing systems linking the primary and regional exchanges.

The CQS and ITS, however, have not actually served to integrate the US markets.[8] This is because the displayed quotes do not, and in fact could not, reveal all of the trading interest on the exchange floors. On the New York Stock Exchange (NYSE) in particular, trades frequently take place within the CQS spread. The only way in which the CQS and ITS could themselves 'integrate' the US markets would be to force the exchanges to adapt to the limitations of these systems. In effect, the US markets would have to permit only two types of orders,

[6] Excluding those indicating 'don't know' and those not answering the question.
[7] See Bronfman, Lehn, and Schwartz (1994) on the development of US securities regulation.
[8] See Blume and Goldstein (1995).

limit and market orders, and all other modes of trading would have to be banned. This would, for example, require the elimination of such common practices as the submission of 'not held' orders, where the investor instructs the floor trader to use his or her discretion in executing them. It would also require the elimination of electronic call auctions and crossing networks, which are rapidly becoming standard trading vehicles for institutions, merely because such systems cannot accommodate the submission of 'firm quotes' to the CQS. The strictures of the CQS have, in fact, been invoked by the NYSE in its legal argument against the launch of a crossing system by a competitor exchange (see section 9).

In order to 'integrate' the US markets according to the rigid CQS/ITS blueprint, the trading floors would have to be shut down and many of the new proprietary systems banned. In effect, the US markets would have to be transformed into a networked version of the Paris CAC system.

The creation of a true Euro-ITS would have the same effect in the EU. Systems incompatible with CAC – e.g., the London SEAQ-I dealer market, the German trading floors and telephone market, and the Amsterdam *hoekman* system – would have to be eliminated. This would remove competition among alternative market architectures. The official 'regulated markets' that would be linked to the Euro-ITS would all be (fundamentally identical) continuous electronic auctions, each of which would trade, almost exclusively, domestic stocks. But under this model, with no inter-market competition, a Euro-ITS serves no purpose. Without direct remote access to national exchanges for new foreign intermediaries, the critical cost barriers to cross-border trading will remain. Yet *with* direct remote access, a Euro-ITS becomes unnecessary. The proposal is, therefore, a non-starter: it would not add anything to the liquidity of the European equity markets.

Far more importantly, if competing trading venues were to emerge, the imposition of a Euro-ITS could actually be expected to *damage* the markets: as Amihud and Mendelson (1991) concluded, 'ITS-like order-routing linkage systems are actually worse than no system at all due to their negative effects on the incentives to provide immediacy and liquidity'(p.90). A Euro-ITS would preclude the possibility of the investor choosing an immediate execution over waiting for the order to be routed, and possibly re-routed, to the market posting the best price (and thereby risking the possibility of the order being returned partially or fully unexecuted). Moreover, an ITS violates *all* secondary priority rules currently existing in the markets, such as time and size priority, in order to maintain strict price priority (which does not always serve investors' interests). As an ITS *by design* encourages quote-matching, a classic form of free-riding on posted limit orders, it may actually serve to *reduce* liquidity provision in the markets.

In short, concentration rules which act to restrict investor access to alternative modes of transacting do not represent a sound basis for integrating the

European equity markets. Provided that it is market-driven, rather than created and sustained by legal or cartel barriers, trading fragmentation across multiple market architectures should not be restricted.

5.1.3. Competition with Other World Financial Centres

Finally, we take up the issue of 'fragmentation' and regional competition. There exists in Europe a widespread notion that the European economy suffers 'in competition' with the United States and Japan because its constituent national economies are smaller. This equation of size with economic effectiveness is a common fallacy in the wider European debate. This is true particularly in the area of monetary policy, where it is often claimed that only a pan-European monetary policy (in the form of a single currency) can be effective.[9] If an effective monetary policy is defined in terms of stable prices and maintaining the external value of the currency, then the Swiss case should be sufficient to establish the contrary.

In the wholesale financial services sector, there are strong economic forces at work promoting the concentration of services provision, in Europe as elsewhere. For a number of reasons which are unrelated to the size of the UK economy, London has been the primary European beneficiary of the operation of such forces – in equity trading as in other areas of wholesale banking. London is, for example, the leading world centre for currency trading, despite the relative insignificance of the pound sterling. To the extent that economies of scale and 'positive network externalities' are operative in trading services, they will emit the same basic centripetal force in Europe as elsewhere (although the results will not necessarily be to every government's liking).

In what sense, then, can Europe meaningfully be said to be 'handicapped' in the 'competition' with other major financial centres, such as New York and Tokyo?

Grand visions of geopolitical monoliths competing for economic supremacy are obscurantist, and certainly unhelpful in establishing a sound economic basis for regulating European market structure. The primary economic role of the equity markets is to facilitate the cost-effective channelling of passive savings to productive investments. Provided that European governments are willing to dismantle regulations protecting local producer interests, competition can be relied on to produce an efficient balance of concentration and fragmentation. Europe will not be 'handicapped' by intra-European trading competition.

[9] See Wolf's (1995) deconstruction of this position.

5.2. Transparency

Transparency is, in the view of the French delegation, the touchstone of a 'regulated market'. More specifically, it is *post-trade* transparency about which they expressed concern. Again, the US markets were used as a model to illustrate their vision.

In the United States, all transactions in major stocks must be published within 90 seconds, regardless of trade size. However, the effects of this requirement are not uniformly positive in terms of the liquidity, efficiency, or volatility of the US markets.

An increasingly popular pastime in the US markets is 'tape shooting'.[10] This involves short-term 'momentum' traders monitoring the electronic transaction tape – which reveals stock, price, volume, and broker – and 'shooting' at trades which indicate the presence of a large investor: i.e., buying or selling in quantity in advance of a large order being fully executed, or worked off by the dealer. This has led to increased short-term volatility, which is then further exacerbated by broker-dealers withdrawing capital and making the market less liquid for large transactions. This makes it more difficult and costly to execute an immediate block trade in New York than in London (as well as increasing volatility risks for small investors). Not surprisingly, therefore, US block transactions are increasingly being executed in London. Firm data are hard to come by, but one major investor – Arco, the investment arm of Atlantic Richfield Company – reports that its brokers now defend against tape shooting by executing 5 percent of its trades overseas (presumably the highest-volume trades). Since US investors do not see these trades at all, this practice makes the US markets *less* transparent than if the US authorities allowed delayed publication of proprietary block transactions.

As we discussed in some detail in Chapter 1, imposing immediate publication rules on an order-driven market is unnecessary (since transparency is integral to the functioning of an auction system), while imposing them on a quote-driven market will reduce the commitment of private dealer capital to accommodating block transactions. As we emphasized in section 4.3.3 of that chapter, requiring dealers to publish large proprietary trades immediately will also generally fail to make the markets more transparent, owing to the avoidance actions it encourages.

Finally, it is frequently argued that delaying publication is unfair in that it privileges market-makers and disadvantages investors. Regarding market-makers – i.e., dealers *required* to post firm two-way quotes in size – it is not possible to create an intermediary role with affirmative *obligations* to the market, which are not borne by others, without providing compensatory *privileges*. One such

[10] See *Wall Street Journal* (1992).

privilege is delayed publication of large proprietary trades; trades to which dealers are generally committing capital in their role as liquidity providers, rather than as investors. If dealers are required to publish such trades immediately, they are in effect being required to publish their immediate trading intentions, and hence will not commit capital to the dealer function in the first place. Thus the role will largely disappear.

If this argument is incorrect, and dealers are generating economic rents from delayed publication, then the European institutional investors who trade in size and require dealer services should certainly endorse the imposition of EU-wide minimum transparency requirements. Yet our survey of buy-side traders, discussed in Chapter 3, found that only 23 percent wanted such requirements set at the EU level, while 52 percent wanted the decision to be left to the *individual stock exchanges themselves*. This is hardly a ringing mandate for EU action from the primary consumers. A very real trade-off between transparency and liquidity-in-size should therefore be acknowledged.

As for the retail investors, they will not be made better off by denying dealer services to the wholesale sector. The buy-side institutions, like the dealers, will not reveal their trading inventory or intentions when they go to the market if it is not advantageous for them to do so. An institution working off a large order piece-by-piece in the market is no different from a dealer doing so. Unless 'thought police' can be installed in the markets, investors will always bear the risk that a large unrevealed order is overhanging the markets – whether that order is being worked by a dealer, having been bought from an institution, or by the institution itself.

In the absence of viable competition to a dealer market from alternative market architectures, we would agree that there is a role for the statutory regulator in vetting transparency provisions, as there may be insufficient competitive pressure on the sell-side to tailor its rules to the requirements of the captive investor clientele. However, an ISD which eliminates barriers to competition among alternative market structures *mitigates* the need for regulatory intervention (as competition does in *any* sector of the economy). Thus, rather than seeing transparency regulation transferred up from the national to the EU level, we would prefer to see an orderly transfer of control *down* to the exchanges themselves. The timing of this transition in each national market should be determined by the level of contestability in each market.

In short, we do not believe that the ISD should seek to define a European 'regulated market' in terms of transparency rules which are only appropriate to an auction market. We would hold that the example of the US markets serves to illustrate the *drawbacks*, rather than the *benefits*, of government-mandated immediate trade publication requirements.

5.3. Equal Treatment of Orders

The French delegation argued that in many countries the diffusion of stock ownership among the general populace is an essential objective of 'financial policy', and that the organization of the markets should be made to serve this aim by providing equal access for large and small orders, without discrimination by price. So-called 'OTC' operations were said to be prejudicial to the public interest, in that they did not guarantee equality of treatment to different bearers of the same securities.

This position is very similar to that taken by the French Treasury with regard to the pricing of retail banking services. The Treasury had long upheld a cartel arrangement operated by the Association of French Banks, wherein all members agreed not to introduce charges for basic services (such as cheque processing) in return for an industry-wide ban on remunerated current accounts. The Treasury supported this arrangement in order to facilitate the cross-subsidization of banking services to the benefit of small account holders. In 1992, UK-based Barclays Bank attempted to invoke 2BCD 'single passport' rights by paying interest on French current accounts, provoking the intervention of the then finance minister Michel Sapin, who argued that such accounts 'would have the biggest impact on the poorest clients, who wouldn't earn anything on the remuneration but would have to pay for services that are free today'.[11] Essentially, the French government took the view that the activities of the financial sector must be circumscribed by the income redistribution goals of the state.

The view that the freedom of private parties to transact must be subordinate to the requirements of the welfare state is not universally shared, either as a principle or in the same form, throughout the EU. Therefore, the primary tools which have been used to construct the single market – mutual recognition, home country control, and minimal harmonization – will be rendered ineffective if each Member State insists on injecting its own political objectives into single market directives, or on imposing them unilaterally to 'trump' directives after they have already been agreed.

With regard to the specific question of 'equal treatment' of orders, there is no economic justification for the requirement that orders of different sizes be transacted at the same price. Wholesale and retail transactions for most commodities take place at different prices, and the size of the price gap will be determined by such factors as the size of the fixed cost component of transacting.

In the case of equity trading, larger transactions will generally receive a better price in the dealer market than in the auction market, because the public

[11] From an interview with *La Tribune*. Sapin is on weak grounds empirically. Neither Barclays nor its major competitors imposes cheque charges in the UK, although they all pay interest on current accounts. See Steil (1995) for details on the Barclays case.

liquidity in the latter is often insufficiently deep to accommodate immediate trading in size. However, even in the dealer market exceptionally large transactions will generally receive the *worst* prices because of the anticipated market impact. Presumably, this would not be widely interpreted as unfair discrimination against large institutional trades. Furthermore, small retail investors are increasingly investing through large institutional fund managers, rather than directly through brokers, and will therefore find themselves disadvantaged by any market structure regulations which act to increase the cost of institutional transactions.

In short, we see no merit in European market structure regulation which seeks to impose artificial incentives for small transactions or penalties for large ones. The goal of diffusing share ownership among the general population would be better served by removing barriers elsewhere – in particular, those which constrain the growth of private pension schemes, including restrictions on domestic and foreign equity investments (see Chapter 6).

We conclude this section on trading concentration by emphasizing that we can find no compelling economic grounds for sanctioning it in the ISD. On the contrary, we believe that the effect of endorsing concentration rules in the Directive is fundamentally anti-competitive, and damaging to the single market effort. It is furthermore wholly unnecessary, as the true goal of the concentration provisions – halting and reversing the European expansion of the London Stock Exchange – has already been achieved by the unilateral competitive reforms on the major continental exchanges. To declare the European segment of the LSE 'unregulated' is simply to render the term 'regulated' meaningless. Protecting the investor requires that the competent authorities regulate the relationship between the broker and the client, such that the former has a fiduciary obligation to act in the best interests of the latter. It certainly does not require that the authorities effectively grant monopoly status to the national stock exchange, as this is apt to *impair* the ability of the broker to secure best execution for the client. We would therefore urge Member States not to apply the concentration provisions.

6. THE 'REGULATED MARKET' IN THE ISD

The Council of Ministers split six to six over the introduction of the 'regulated market' concept, and particularly the restrictions which governments would be allowed to apply to off-'regulated market' transactions. The southern Member States (the so-called 'Club Med Group') – particularly France and Italy – were adamant that the Directive must incorporate the right of Member States to require the concentration of trading on a regulated market, and that such a market should feature near-immediate post-trade transparency. The northern Member States – particularly the UK, Germany, and the Netherlands – were equally adamant that the Directive must allow investors the free choice of how and where to execute their trades. Concern was expressed that a concentration principle would allow Member States to erect protectionist barriers against foreign trading of domestic securities (a particular concern of the UK, which suspected that the sole purpose of incorporating such a principle was to eliminate SEAQ-I), and possibly to curtail the development of OTC derivative products based on exchange-traded securities. The UK delegation also emphasized that the proposed transparency provisions, in focusing wholly on post-trade publication, ignored the fundamental importance of pre-trade transparency (in the form of firm, visible, two-way quotes in size). To the end, the UK expressed severe reservations about the ability of the Directive to safeguard the liquidity of the markets and to maintain their capacity for handling large transactions.

In effect, Member State delegations were locked in a proxy war on behalf of domestic producer interests: each delegation took the negotiating position perceived to be most favourable to its own exchange and intermediaries. France and Italy, the two largest national auction markets in the EU, backed concentration against dealerization, while the UK, Germany, and the Netherlands, the most dealerized markets in the EU, defended the liberty of investors to choose their own trading platform.

The major issues of contention – transparency, concentration, and bank access to regulated markets[12] – kept the parties locked in difficult negotiations until June 1992, when qualified majority approval was finally achieved (Italy and Spain voted against). The delay in reaching agreement led to the Directive's implementation deadline being put back by three years, resulting in an anomalous situation wherein EU credit institutions were granted a single passport from 1 January 1993 (under the 2BCD), while non-bank securities houses were obliged to wait until 1 January 1996. The difficulty in achieving compromise is reflected in the considerable ambiguity of the final text in many areas, and the complicated cross-referencing required to define the critical concept of a 'regulated market'. To assist the reader in following the discussion below, we have reproduced the

[12] Whether the significant restrictions on banks' securities business imposed by the US Glass-Steagall Act are warranted on prudential grounds is a question which has been scrupulously avoided by the EU because of the political need to accommodate universal banking in the single market. Given the importance of securities market activities for major German banks, Germany in particular was adamant that banks be accorded direct access to all EU regulated markets. France, Spain, Italy, and Portugal all resisted this provision, which led to a compromise allowing a lengthy transition period at the end of which such access must be accorded. France, Italy, and Belgium have until the end of 1996 to allow host-country banks to trade directly on their exchanges, while Portugal, Spain, and Greece were given until the end of the century. Article 15 stipulates that such restrictions may be extended by a qualified majority vote in the Council of Ministers. Until the restrictions are lifted, banks wishing to trade directly on these exchanges will only be able to do so through a separately capitalized securities subsidiary (Steil 1993).

relevant sections of the Directive in the Chapter Appendix: i.e., Articles 1.1, 1.2, 1.13, 14, 15.4, 15.5, 16, 20, 21, and the Directive Annex.

6.1. Article 1.13: the 'Regulated Market' Introduced

Article 1.13 purports to define a 'regulated market', but leaves considerable scope for strategic interpretation. Part of the definition is circular, and may lead to conflicts between Member States in the future. Article 1.13 says that a regulated market is, *inter alia*, one which appears on a list to be drawn up by each home Member State in accordance with Article 16, yet Article 16 refers to regulated markets without providing further qualifications for defining them. Therefore Article 16 implicitly refers back to Article 1.13 for the definition, thus creating an endless loop between the two articles. To draw sense from this construction, it should logically (if not necessarily *legally*) be presumed that a regulated market is one which meets the requirements laid out in Article 1.13, or in other parts of the Directive referred to in this Article, while also meeting regulatory requirements as set out by the home Member State (referred to in Article 16).

The main component of the definition which is actually laid out within Article 1.13 is the listing requirement. According to the Article, a regulated market must meet the requirements of the Listing Particulars Directive (79/279/EEC) *where the Directive is applicable.* As we pointed out earlier, the London SEAQ-I dealer market does not formally 'list' equities. Thus, in order for SEAQ-I to be a regulated market, the UK Treasury must hold, at least implicitly, that the Listing Particulars Directive is not applicable. This view is not universally shared. A leading official of the Italian securities regulator, the *Commissione Nazionale per le Società e la Borsa* (Consob), has stated on a number of occasions that he believes that the Directive *is* applicable to SEAQ-I. Tradepoint, which does not 'list' equities either, will almost certainly also find its status subject to different interpretations. Paris Bourse Chairman and Chief Executive Jean-François Théodore (1995) has emphasized publicly his belief in the importance of 'listing procedures' to the determination of a regulated market.

The 'where applicable' clause was clearly necessary to secure UK approval of the ISD, but it does – no doubt deliberately – leave scope for challenges from Member States wishing to invoke the concentration provisions (Article 14, see below) against foreign trading systems. This legal ambiguity may be sufficient to deter market participants from transacting through such systems. One managing director of a major French *société de bourse* with whom we spoke said he believed market participants would be wary of using new trading systems until they had seen that the systems were widely accepted.

6.2. Article 21: Transparency

Article 1.13 requires regulated markets to comply with the transparency provisions elaborated in Article 21. The transparency provisions were the subject of intense controversy in the Council redrafting of the ISD, and in fact still elicit a wide range of interpretations. Article 21 requires all regulated markets to publish 'at least' weighted average prices, high and low prices, and aggregate trading volumes at the start of trading and on a rolling basis throughout the trading session. We are not aware of any European market which publishes weighted average prices *in place of* individual transaction prices (or one which would want to), so this particular provision appears to have been a compromise between those who wanted a requirement for rapid publication of individual transactions and those who wanted no publication requirement at all. We do not, in fact, expect any exchange to start publishing weighted average prices in place of individual transaction prices as a result of ISD implementation.

After consultation with the European Commission, the Federation of European Stock Exchanges (FESE) claims to have arrived at a common policy to require publication of the identity of the security, time of transaction, transaction volume, and transaction price, and has expressed the view that this exceeds the standards laid down by Article 21, thereby obviating the need for any publication of weighted average prices. Furthermore, it is a widely held view within the Federation that publication should be immediate for trades of up to 'normal market size' (NMS), interpreted to mean 'median transaction size' (or, in London and Paris, 2.5 percent of average daily trading volume). Larger trades (6-75 x NMS in London) may be subject to a maximum publication delay of one hour. However, Article 21 does allow for an unspecified additional publication delay or suspension in the case of

- 'exceptional market conditions';
- 'small markets, to preserve the anonymity of firms and investors';
- 'exceptional transactions that are very large in scale compared with average transactions';
- 'highly illiquid securities defined by objective criteria and made public'.

None of these criteria are defined in the Directive.

The Article 21 transparency requirements are, in sum, so vague as to be virtually meaningless, and it is important to recognize that the FESE does not have any formal regulatory enforcement role. In the case of London, 'exceptional transactions' are being defined as those in excess of 75 x NMS, which will be allowed a maximum five-day publication delay. While this is a reasonable interpretation of 'exceptional transactions', one European exchange is reported to hold the view that some component stocks of its own principal market index are 'highly illiquid' – an interpretation which would appear to be rather less reasonable. It is also possible for an exchange to define certain types of trading in its market to be 'off-exchange' (e.g., Frankfurt telephone trading, and floor trading without *Kursmakler* intermediation), and therefore only to impose sufficient publication rules on those parts of its market that it wishes to bear the 'regulated market' imprimatur (which brings certain privileges, as we describe below).

Perhaps reflecting the UK's proclivity for 'over-implementing' directives, London may actually have the most transparent dealer market in Europe come 1996 (see Chapter 1, section 4.3.4). This would represent a rather stunning paradox, given that the UK had fought the most fiercely against including *any* post-trade transparency requirements in the ISD.

6.3. ISD Restrictions on Non-'Regulated Markets'

Article 14.3 explicitly authorizes (but does not *require*) Member States to mandate that transactions in domestically traded securities be carried out only on 'a regulated market'. This is the so-called 'concentration principle'.

The word 'a' before 'regulated market' is critical, because it means that Member States may *not* require that transactions only be carried out on *the domestic* 'regulated market'. Thus, as long as a market qualifies as 'regulated', its freedom to provide services across borders cannot, in theory, be interfered with by a foreign Member State. In practice, a determined domestic market protector, or protectionist, can still unilaterally circumscribe the rights of a foreign 'regulated market' by

- invoking the 'general good' exception;[13]
- invoking Article 15.5 against the creation of a 'new market' within its territory;[14]
- provoking a protracted European Court of Justice challenge.[15]

However, those markets not officially stamped as 'regulated' still have certain rights against foreign interference in their freedom to provide services. A Member State invoking concentration may only do so to restrict transactions

[13] 'Rules of conduct', for example, are considered to be in the interest of the 'general good', and fall under the responsibility of the *host* Member State. See Ferrarini (1994: sections 3.4.2 and 4.3-4.3.2).

[14] See section 6.4.

[15] This appears to have been the Italian strategy with regard to the SIMs law (see section 7).

- by investors 'habitually resident or established in that Member State';
- by investment firms carrying out such transactions within the territory of that Member State;
- in securities 'dealt in on a regulated market in that Member State'.

Furthermore, a Member State invoking concentration must give domestic investors the right to authorize transactions on their behalf being carried out off a regulated market (Article 14.4). The exact form of this 'opt out' may be made subject to the Member State's view of the degree to which the investor is believed to require 'protection': essentially, a distinction may be drawn between individual 'retail' investors and professional (or institutional) investors. Reflecting the suspicions of Member States opposing Article 14.3 that supporters would make the opt out too cumbersome to be effective, there is a further clause specifying that it must not be subject to conditions which 'jeopardize the prompt execution of investors' orders'. Reflecting the determination of supporters of Article 14.3 to make concentration effective, Jean-François Théodore called publicly in July 1995 for an assurance 'that legislation adopted in France to implement the Directive includes provisions for equity transactions to take place on a regulated market' (1995:4). 'Assuming that being a regulated market represents a competitive advantage,' he continued, 'great care must be taken in awarding such status' (p.5).

6.4. ISD Privileges for 'Regulated Markets'

Being a 'regulated market' does indeed represent a competitive advantage if that market wishes to provide for remote access in other Member States. Under Article 15.4, regulated markets are entitled to provide trading screens to 'investment firms'[16] based in other Member States without having to seek approval from the relevant foreign authority. Thus, for example, the Paris Bourse would have the right to provide CAC screens for remote members in the Netherlands without prior approval from Dutch regulators. This provision of the Directive is popularly viewed as the European 'single passport' for screen-based trading systems.

The rights associated with this passport are strictly limited, however, by the following paragraph, Article 15.5, which was inserted at the insistence of the French Treasury. 'This Article', it states, 'shall not affect the Member States' right to authorize or prohibit the creation of new markets within their territories.' This naturally begs the critical question as to what precisely constitutes a 'new' market, as the establishment of such a market may still be prohibited.

As recently as January 1995, the Dutch Ministry of Finance had expressed the view that a foreign screen-based trading system wishing to provide for re-

[16] See Article 1.2 in the Appendix to this chapter.

mote access in the Netherlands was seeking to create what was, from the perspective of the Netherlands, a 'new' market. Thus, such systems would have to continue to apply for a licence as a recognized foreign investment exchange from the Ministry. This interpretation elicited considerable criticism from market participants and regulators in France and Germany, as it effectively negated the automatic cross-border access for CAC and IBIS screens which they believed had been provided for under Article 15.4. The Dutch Ministry of Finance formally abandoned its interpretation after discussions in Brussels, but the ambiguity of Article 15.5 may generate further disputes in the future.

Consider the case of a regulated market based in Member State X which decides to provide for remote access in Member State Y. Assuming that the regulated market does not begin trading the domestic securities of Member State Y, this market should (notwithstanding the abandoned Dutch interpretation) face no substantial difficulties in invoking 'single passport' rights under Article 15.4. However, should this regulated market then decide to begin trading securities already listed on a market based in Member State Y, there exists the serious possibility that Member State Y would invoke Article 15.5 to stop this, using the argument that a 'new' market was being established within its territories. We suspect that Tradepoint would face such difficulties if it tried to trade non-UK equities outside the UK, in direct competition with existing continental exchanges. We base this judgment partly on the responses of institutional investors to the question (no. 38) we posed in the survey discussed in Chapter 3, regarding possible constraints to the growth of proprietary trading systems in Europe: 77 percent of those responding[17] said that the concentration provisions represented a 'moderate' to 'very serious' constraint.

7. IS EUROPEAN MARKET STRUCTURE REGULATION LESS OR MORE LIBERAL POST-ISD?

This may be a surprising question to many readers, who understandably believed that the purpose of the ISD was to eliminate barriers to competition in the investment services sector. However, the answer is far from clear. The Article 15.4 single passport is potentially a significant weapon against the maintenance of regulatory barriers to the cross-border operation of trading systems. Yet this weapon is significantly dulled by the Article 15.5 new market provisions, the Article 14.3 concentration provisions, and indeed the very concept of a 'regulated market' as enshrined in the Directive, which poses a serious potential bar-

[17] Excluding those indicating 'don't know' and those not answering the question.

rier to the expansion of dealer markets and proprietary trading systems. It can be argued that European market structure regulation would be more liberal *without* the ISD, since trading systems would be able to invoke existing European law to challenge barriers to cross-border access. The Capital Movements Directive could have been invoked to challenge Member State concentration provisions. Furthermore, Articles 52 (freedom of establishment) and 59 (freedom to provide services) of the 1957 Treaty of Rome could have been invoked to challenge Member State restrictions against foreign trading systems seeking to facilitate remote cross-border access. In fact, it was precisely on this basis that the European Commission launched a European Court action in 1994 against the Italian 'SIMs' law, which requires foreign securities houses to establish a separately capitalized Italian subsidiary (at a cost of approximately $3-4 million)[18] in order to carry out securities market activities in Italy.[19] In the Commission's judgment, then, the ISD was not necessary to compel Italy to allow cross-border access for foreign intermediaries.

8. DIRECTIVES AS A TOOL OF LIBERALIZATION

It is important to recognize the practical reality that directives – even the most liberal ones – do not a single market make.

First of all, national market structure regulations will remain which apply restrictions on activities beyond those authorized in the ISD, but which are not *necessarily* in strict violation of the ISD. For example, the Italian SIMs law contains its own 'concentration' provisions (Article 11) which allow little scope for an investor opt-out. An Italian investor may opt out of the requirement that his or her trade be executed on a 'regulated market' through a prior written authorization. '. . . but in addition to that,' according to a leading Consob official,

> it is necessary to comply with an *objective* parameter (which may *easily be verified*): whether it would be possible for the client to have access to a *better price* compared with that which could be obtained if the transaction were to be performed on the regulated market (Biancheri 1994:13, my italics).

In fact, this parameter cannot 'easily be verified', and is certainly not 'objective'. Different types of orders and trades are characteristic of different types of markets and trading strategies: e.g., market orders, limit orders, program

[18] *The Economist* (1994).
[19] See Steil (1995).

trades, protected trades (UK), stopped trades (US), and not-held orders (US). It is simply not meaningful to compare prices across markets unless the investor is demanding the same service. For example, if the investor demands an immediate execution, the price may be less favourable than if he or she were willing to bear the execution risk associated with a delay. Yet since the SIMs law requires that an 'off-market' trade be done at a demonstrably *better* price than an 'on-market' trade, any broker believing that his or her client is better served by the former would probably still be unwilling to bear the associated legal risk. The SIMs law concentration rules furthermore make no allowance for the ability of institutional investors to look after their own trading interests.[20] Yet while the SIMs rules would appear to go beyond what is permissible under the Directive, the aforementioned Consob official opined that it will be for 'the Italian lawmaker . . . to determine the extent to which the national law and the contents of art.14 paragraphs 3 and 4 of the directive actually match'.[21]

Secondly, 'escape clauses' are routinely inserted into directives to allow Member States to maintain strict control over the parameters and pace of reform. In the case referred to earlier in which the French Treasury attempted to stop Barclays from paying interest on current accounts,[22] the Treasury defended its position with the Commission by invoking Article 14.2 of the 2BCD, otherwise known as the 'monetary policy escape clause':

> Without prejudice to the measures necessary for the reinforcement of the European Monetary System, host Member States shall retain complete responsibility for the measures resulting from the implementation of their monetary policies. Such measures may not provide for discriminatory or restrictive treatment based on the fact that a credit institution is authorized in another Member State.

The second sentence is clearly intended to stop Member States from using monetary policy considerations as a disguise for protectionism. It does not work. The French Treasury maintained that remunerated current accounts involve disturbance in the flows of liquidity within the banking system, and therefore interfered with the conduct of monetary policy. This logic could, in fact, be used to ban virtually *any* financial product. Article 15.5 of the ISD, the 'new

[20] 'It should also be added that, unlike the [Investment Services] Directive, the law in abstract terms does not envisage the possibility of a different approach for institutional investors' (Biancheri 1994:13).

[21] Biancheri (1994:13).

[22] Ultimately the Treasury did not succeed, but this was due to a loophole in French domestic banking regulations successfully exploited by Barclays, rather than Barclays' successful invocation of 2BCD single passport rights. See Steil (1995).

market' exception to the single passport for trading systems, is perhaps the most obvious and significant escape clause in that Directive.

Finally, the transformation of directives into national law is a very uneven process. The Commission's last annual assessment of the single market, made public in June 1995, detailed 'serious problems' stemming from Member States' failure to implement directives, to apply them correctly, or to sanction offenders. In the words of one official, 'There is often a clear distinction between an agreement within the council of ministers and implementation on the ground.'[23] Effective implementation was often severely hindered by wide differences in national interpretation.

Chapter 7 illustrates by reference to the Capital Adequacy Directive how critical national interpretation is to the manner in which a directive is transposed into national law. There is also a marked variation in the timeliness of implementation across Member States. As of the end of 1994, over 60 percent of Member States had yet to implement '1992' single market provisions relating to public procurement and intellectual property. Less than one-third of Member States will have fully implemented the ISD by the deadline of 1 January 1996, and a number are significantly behind schedule. This combination of differential interpretation and dilatory implementation gives rise to strategic defensive action by Member States, who are understandably anxious to see that domestic businesses are not put at a competitive disadvantage by the action or inaction of other Member States.

The enforcement powers of the Commission and the Court are largely ineffective. In 1994, the Commission issued 546 'reasoned opinions' (which have no force) against Member States failing to implement EU law, and formally filed 89 Court actions against them. Court judgments can take several years (as with the Italian SIMs law case), after which they are often simply ignored. The Commission has never pursued a recalcitrant Member State after a second condemnation by the Court, partly for fear of publicly undermining the authority of a primary institutional pillar of the European Union.[24]

The European Commission has traditionally placed considerable emphasis on the need for harmonization of (at least minimum) rules and standards in constructing a 'single market'. Yet international agreements, such as directives, necessarily emerge from a *political* process in which national actors are seeking to protect perceived national competitive interests, regardless of whether these may be reconciled with publicly stated goals, such as increasing the efficiency and

[23] *Financial Times* (1995). The Commission's report showed France to be the country most likely to erect barriers to trade. In 1994, the Commission received 53 complaints from companies and individuals whose products were rejected in France.

[24] See Hunter (1995).

stability of the larger market. Thus international rules and standards will not necessarily enshrine 'best practice', and are considerably more likely merely to entrench existing practice.

No amount of institutional or legislative process reform will ensure that directives serve to open markets if this is not what Member State governments wish to happen. It is simply endemic to multinational institutions that sovereign members will seek to have their perceived interests reflected in policy, and to allow themselves scope for opting out where this is not possible. To a large degree, then, the effective liberalization of the European equity markets rests with the enlightened self-interest of Member State governments, and the pressure generated by market participants aggressively pursuing cross-border commercial opportunities.

9. A EUROPEAN SEC?

> It seems to me that there is a very sound element in the widespread disinclination to confer sovereign powers, or at least powers to command, on any international authority. What we need are not international authorities possessing powers of direction, but merely international bodies (or, rather, international treaties which are effectively enforced) which can prohibit certain actions of governments that harm other people (Hayek 1978:229).

Friedrich Hayek's statement on international bodies well encapsulates our view on the possible creation of a European Securities and Exchange Commission (SEC). We do not see benefits flowing from the construction of a new central regulatory body with 'powers of direction'.

As the European markets become increasingly integrated, there will undoubtedly be greater need for cross-border cooperation, coordination, and information-sharing among national regulators in order to combat instances of fraud and market manipulation. Money laundering is already a large and rapidly expanding cross-border business. Yet it is difficult to see how deterring criminal practice will be abetted by the establishment of a remote, centralized European SEC.

As for market structure regulation, the creation of a European SEC is apt to do more harm than good. As the 'market for markets' in European equity trading becomes more competitive, there will be correspondingly less need for *any* market structure regulation. The fact that governments are still so intimately involved in the setting and vetting of trading rules is an unfortunate relic of an era when exchanges were natural monopolies. Tremendous advances in computerization over the past twenty years, however, have made possible many new modes of transacting – in particular, electronic continuous auctions, call auctions, and crossing networks. As competition increasingly moves into the trading services sector, basic principles of industrial economics would suggest that government controls over modes of transaction and information dissemination should be dismantled, rather than passed upwards to a new supranational body.

The absurdities of involving a central regulator in the micro-details of trading structure in a competitive market are well illustrated by the case of 'Chicago Match', an electronic midday order match system established by the Chicago Stock Exchange (CHX).[25] The US SEC is required to pass judgment on any and all proposals for new public trading systems. In deciding whether to approve Chicago Match, the SEC was forced to address numerous legal objections from a major competitor, the New York Stock Exchange, which were based not on whether the system was good for investors, but rather on whether it was consistent with anachronistic legal definitions and intermarket quote dissemination systems. Among the critical but senseless questions on which the SEC was forced to adjudicate were:

- whether Chicago Match would legally be a 'facility' *of* a registered 'Exchange' (which is OK), or an 'exempt exchange' (i.e., PTS) operated *by* a registered 'Exchange' (which is not OK);[26]
- whether the proposal should be rejected on the grounds that Chicago Match orders, which are necessarily submitted unpriced, will not be reported to the CQS – notwithstanding the fact that CQS facilities were designed by the NYSE, and are *incapable* of handling indications without prices.

In the end, the SEC gave its blessing to Chicago Match, but appeared often at pains to rebut the legal objections posed by the NYSE. 'In analyzing the CHX proposal,' the SEC explains, 'the Commission recognizes that the Chicago Match is a mixture that brings together features of a call market with the market making capabilities of the CHX floor. Obviously, such systems represent certain challenges in fitting into the traditional regulatory mold envisioned for an exchange system under the [1934 Securities Exchange] Act.'[27] This is certainly an understatement. The combination of the 1934 Act, the 1975 National Market System (NMS) amendments, and the post-1975 creation of the ITS, CQS, and CTA has locked the SEC into the job of regulating an equity market structure

[25] See Steil (1996).

[26] To date, the SEC has not allowed national securities exchanges to operate so-called proprietary trading systems (PTSs).

[27] See SEC Release No. 34-35030 (30 November 1994).

which no longer requires or benefits from such regulation. We see no reason to extend such regulation to the EU.

10. SUMMARY AND CONCLUSIONS

This chapter has examined the development of the Investment Services Directive, the arguments used in the Council of Ministers to support the introduction of market structure regulation into the Directive, the implications of the Directive for the further development of European market structure, and wider issues related to the effectiveness of European single market directives in the financial services area.

On the basis of the discussion in this chapter, as well as in Chapters 1-3, we wish to highlight the following conclusions:

- With regard to issues of market structure, the final ISD text which emerged from the Council in 1992 is considerably less liberalizing than the original draft text presented to the Council by the Commission in 1988 (and amended in 1990). The Article 15.4 'single passport' provisions for screen-based trading systems represent a potentially significant weapon against the maintenance of regulatory barriers to the cross-border expansion of national markets. However, the Article 15.5 'new' market provisions, the Article 14.3 'concentration' provisions, and indeed the very concept of a 'regulated market' as enshrined in the Directive pose serious potential barriers to the expansion of dealer markets and proprietary trading systems in Europe. If Member States choose to exploit the protectionist potential of these provisions, European market structure may be *less* liberal than it would have been without an ISD.
- Rules which act to restrict access to alternative modes of transacting do not represent a sound basis for integrating the European equity markets. Provided that it is market-driven, rather than created and sustained by legal or cartel barriers, trading 'fragmentation' across multiple market architectures should not be restricted.
- EU-wide minimum post-trade transparency rules are neither necessary nor desirable, and have very little support among institutional investors (see Chapter 3). An ISD which serves to eliminate barriers to competition among alternative market structures should *mitigate* the need for regulatory intervention (as competition does in *any* sector of the economy). Rather than seeing transparency regulation transferred up from the national to the EU level, we would prefer to see an orderly transfer of control *down* to the exchanges themselves.

- Securities 'listing' should not be made a touchstone of an EU 'regulated market' – the imprimatur from which single passport privileges flow. While stock exchanges have traditionally performed the listing role, listing is *not* an essential function of a well-regulated *trading system*: such quality control measures can be equally well performed by separate institutions, such as ratings agencies. Any legal challenges to the status of SEAQ-I, Tradepoint, or other trading systems which are based wholly on the listing criterion in Article 1.13 should be dismissed as anti-competitive in intent.
- European single market directives reflect political compromises which invariably allow a considerable degree of protectionism to persist. This is then aided and abetted by uneven implementation, lax enforcement, and strategic circumvention. Ultimately, we believe that the effective liberalization of the European equity markets lies not with directives themselves, but rather with the enlightened self-interest of the Member State governments, and particularly with the pressure generated by market participants aggressively pursuing cross-border commercial opportunities.

References

Amihud, Yakov and Haim Mendelson, 1991. 'How (Not) to Integrate the European Capital Markets', in A. Giovannini and C. Mayer (eds), *European Financial Integration*, Cambridge University Press.

Biancheri, Carlo, 1994. 'The Implementation of European Union Regulations on the Provision of Investment Services in Italy', paper presented at a conference entitled *The Investment Services and Capital Adequacy Directives: Practical and Strategic Implications for Securities Firms*, City & Financial Conferences, 8 December.

Blume, Marshall and Michael A. Goldstein, 1995. 'On the Integration of the US Equity Markets', Working Paper, The Wharton School, University of Pennsylvania, January.

Bronfman, Corinne, Kenneth Lehn and Robert Schwartz, 1994. 'US Securities Markets Regulation: Regulatory Structure', in Benn Steil (ed.), *International Financial Market Regulation*, John Wiley, Chichester.

Commission of the European Communities, 1985. 'Completing the Internal Market: White Paper from the Commission to the European Council', June.

The Economist, 1994. 'A New Broom for Europe's Capital Markets', 5 November.

Financial Times, 1995. '"Serious Problems" Hinder the EU's Single Market', 16 June.

Fitchew, Geoffrey, 1991. 'Political Choices', in R. Buxbaum *et al.* (eds), *European Business Law: Legal and Economic Analysis on Integration and Harmonization*, Walter de Gruyter, Berlin.

Hayek, Friedrich, 1978. 'The Campaign against Keynesian Inflation', *New Studies in Political Economy and the History of Ideas*, Routledge, London.

Hunter, Rod, 1995. 'The EU's Great and Radical Vice', *The Wall Street Journal Europe*, 18 August.

Steil, Benn, 1993. *Competition, Integration and Regulation in EC Capital Markets*, Royal Institute of International Affairs, London.

Steil, Benn, 1995. *Illusions of Liberalization: Securities Regulation in Japan and the EC*, Royal Institute of International Affairs, London.

Steil, Benn, 1996. 'Call Market Trading: History, Economics, and Regulation', in Robert A. Schwartz (ed.), *How Stocks Trade: New Competition in the Market for Markets*, Irwin Professional, Homewood, ILO.

Théodore, Jean-François, 1995. 'The Establishment of Regional Financial Areas and Perspectives on Regulatory Harmonization', speech presented at the 20th annual conference of the International Organization of Securities Commissions, Paris, 13 July.

Wall Street Journal, 1992. 'Heard on the Street: Investors Irked by "Tape-Shooting"', 11 September.

Wolf, Martin, 1995. 'On Monetary Sovereignty', *Financial Times*, 12 June.

Appendix

EXCERPTS FROM COUNCIL DIRECTIVE 93/22/EEC ON INVESTMENT SERVICES IN THE SECURITIES FIELD

TITLE I
Definitions and scope

Article 1
For the purposes of this Directive: ... ...

1. *investment service* shall mean any of the services listed in Section A of the Annex relating to any of the instruments listed in Section B of the Annex that are provided for a third party;

2. *investment firm* shall mean any legal person the regular occupation or business of which is the provision of investment services for third parties on a professional basis.

For the purposes of this Directive, Member States may include as investment firms undertakings which are not legal persons if:

– their legal status ensures a level of protection for third parties' interests equivalent to that afforded by legal persons, and
– they are subject to equivalent prudential supervision appropriate to their legal form.

However, where such natural persons provide services involving the holding of third parties' funds or transferable securities, they may be considered as investment firms for the purposes of this Directive only if, without prejudice to the other requirements imposed in this Directive and in Directive 93/6/EEC, they comply with the following conditions:

– the ownership rights of third parties in instruments and funds belonging to them must be safeguarded, especially in the event of the insolvency of a firm or if its proprietors, seizure, set-off or any other action by creditors of the firm or of its proprietors,
– an investment firm must be subject to rules designed to monitor the firm's solvency and that of its proprietors,
– an investment firm's annual accounts must be audited by one or more persons empowered, under national law, to audit accounts,
– where a firm has only one proprietor, he must make provision for the protection of

investors in the event of the firm's cessation of business following his death, his incapacity or any other such event.

No later than 31 December 1997 the Commission shall report on the application of the second and third subparagraphs of this point and, if appropriate, propose their amendment or deletion.

Where a person provides one of the services referred to in Section A (1) (a) of the Annex and where that activity is carried on solely for the account of and under the full and unconditional responsibility of an investment firm, that activity shall be regarded as the activity not of that person but of the investment firm itself;

13. *regulated market* shall mean a market for the instruments listed in Section B of the Annex which:

- appears on the list provided for in Article 16 drawn up by the Member State which is the home Member State as defined in Article 1 (6) (c),
- functions regularly,
- is characterized by the fact that regulations issued or approved by the competent authorities define the conditions for the operation of the market, the conditions for access to the market and, where Directive 79/279/EEC is applicable, the conditions governing admission to listing imposed in that Directive and, where that Directive is not applicable, the conditions that must be satisfied by a financial instrument before it can effectively be dealt in on the market,
- requires compliance with all the reporting and transparency requirements laid down pursuant to Articles 20 and 21;

TITLE V

The right of establishment and the freedom to provide services

Article 14

1. Member States shall ensure that investment services and the other services listed in Section C of the Annex may be provided within their territories in accordance with Articles 17, 18 and 19 either by the establishment of a branch or under the freedom to provide services by any investment firm authorized and supervised by the competent authorities of another Member State in accordance with this Directive, provided that such services are covered by the authorization.

   This Directive shall not affect the powers of host Member States in respect of the units of collective investment undertakings to which Directive 85/611/EEC[28] does not apply.

[28] OJ No L 375, 31. 12. 1985, p. 3. Directive last-amended by Directive 88/220/EEC (OJ No L 100, 19. 4. 1988, p. 31).

2. Member States may not make the establishment of a branch or the provision of services referred to in paragraph 1 subject to any authorization requirement, to any requirement to provide endowment capital or to any other measure having equivalent effect.

3. A Member State may require that transactions relating to the services referred to in paragraph 1 must, where they satisfy all the following criteria, be carried out on a regulated market:

- the investor must be habitually resident or established in that Member State,
- the investment firm must carry out such transactions through a main establishment, through a branch situated in that Member State or under the freedom to provide services in that Member State,
- the transaction must involve a instrument dealt in on a regulated market in that Member State.

4. Where a Member State applies paragraph 3 it shall give investors habitually resident or established in that Member State the right not to comply with the obligation imposed in paragraph 3 and have the transactions referred to in paragraph 3 carried out away from a regulated market. Member States may make the exercise of this right subject to express authorization, taking into account investors' differing needs for protection and in particular the ability of professional and institutional investors to act in their own best interests. It must in any case be possible for such authorization to be given in conditions that do not jeopardize the prompt execution of investors' orders.

5. The Commission shall report on the operation of paragraphs 3 and 4 not later than 31 December 1998 and shall, if appropriate, propose amendments thereto.

Article 15

4. Subject to paragraphs 1, 2 and 3, where the regulated market of the host Member State operates without any requirement for a physical presence the investment firms referred to in paragraph 1 may become members of or have access to it on the same basis without having to be established in the host Member State. In order to enable their investment firms to become members of or have access to host Member States' regulated markets in accordance with this paragraph home Member States shall allow those host Member States' regulated markets to provide appropriate facilities within the home Member States' territories.

5. This Article shall not affect the Member States' right to authorize or prohibit the creation of new markets within their territories.

Article 16

For the purposes of mutual recognition and the application of this Directive, it shall be for each Member State to draw up a list of the regulated markets for which it is the home Member State and which comply with its regulations, and to forward that list for information, together with the relevant rules of procedures and operation of those regulated markets, to the other Member States and the Commission. A similar communications shall be effected in respect of each change to the aforementioned list or rules. The Commission shall publish the lists of regulated markets and updates thereto in the *Official Journal of the European Communities* at least once a year.

No later than 31 December 1996 the Commission shall report on the information thus received and, where appropriate, propose amendments to the definition of regulated market for the purposes of this Directive.

Article 20

1. In order to ensure that the authorities responsible for the markets and for supervision have access to the information necessary for the performance of their duties, home Member States shall at least require:

(a) without prejudice to steps taken in implementation of Article 10, that investment firms keep at the disposal of the authorities for at least five years the relevant data on transactions relating to the services referred to in Article 14 (1) which they have carried out in instruments dealt in on a regulated market, whether such transactions were carried out on a regulated market or not;

(b) that investment firms report to competent authorities in their home Member States all the transactions referred to in (a) where those transactions cover:

- shares or other instruments giving access to capital,
- bonds and other forms of securitized debt,
- standardized forward contracts relating to shares or
- standardized options on shares.

Such reports must be made available to the relevant authority at the earliest opportunity. The time limit shall be fixed by that authority. It may be extended to the end of the following working day where operational or practical reasons so dictate but in no circumstances may it exceed that limit.

Such reports must, in particular, include details of the names and numbers of the instruments bought or sold, the dates and times of the transactions, the transaction prices and means of identifying the investment firms concerned.

Home Member States may provide that the obligation imposed in (b) shall, in the case of bonds and other forms of securitized debt, apply only to aggregated transactions in the same instrument.

2. Where an investment firm carries out a transaction on a regulated market in its host Member State, the home Member State may waive its own requirements as regards reporting if the investment firm is subject to equivalent requirements to report the transaction in question to the authorities in charge of that market.

3. Member States shall provide that the report referred to in paragraph 1 (b) shall be made either by the investment firm itself or by a trade-matching system, or through stock-exchange authorities or those of another regulated market.

4. Member States shall ensure that the information available in accordance with this Article is also available for the proper application of Article 23.

5. Each Member State may, in an non-discriminatory manner, adopt or maintain provisions more stringent in the field governed by this Article with regard to substance and form in respect of the conservation and reporting of data relating to transactions:

- carried out on a regulated market of which it is the home Member State or
- carried out by investment firms of which it is the home Member State.

Article 21

1. In order to enable investors to assess at any time the terms of a transaction they are considering and to verify afterwards the conditions in which it has been carried out, each competent authority shall, for each of the regulated markets which it has entered on the list provided for in Article 16, take measures to provide investors with the information referred to in paragraph 2. In accordance with the requirements imposed in paragraph 2, the competent authorities shall determine the form in which and the precise time within which the information is to be provided, as well as the means by which it is to be made available, having regard to the nature, size and needs of the market concerned and of the investors operating on that market.

2. The competent authorities shall require for each instrument at least:

(a) publication at the start of each day's trading on the market of the weighted average price, the highest and the lowest prices and the volume dealt in on the regulated market in question for the whole of the preceding day's trading;
(b) in addition, for continuous order-driven and quote-driven markets, publication:

- at the end of each hour's trading on the market, of the weighted average price and the volume dealt in on the regulated market in question for a six-hour trading period ending so as to leave two hours' trading on the market before publication, and
- every 20 minutes, of the weighted average price and the highest and lowest prices

on the regulated market in question for a two-hour trading period ending so as to leave one hour's trading on the market before publication.

Where investors have prior access to information on the prices and quantities for which transactions may be undertaken:

(i) such information shall be available at all times during market trading hours;
(ii) the terms announced for a given price and quantity shall be terms on which it is possible for an investor to carry out such a transaction.

The competent authorities may delay or suspend publication where that proves to be justified by exceptional market conditions or, in the case of small markets, to preserve the anonymity of firms and investors. The competent authorities may apply special provisions in the case of exceptional transactions that are very large in scale compared with average transactions in the security in question on that market and in the case of highly illiquid securities defined by means of objective criteria and made public. The competent authorities may also apply more flexible provisions, particularly as regards publication deadlines, for transactions concerning bonds and other forms of securitized debt.

3. In the field governed by this Article each Member State may adopt or maintain more stringent provisions or additional provisions with regard to the substance and form in which information must be made available to investors concerning transactions carried out on regulated markets of which it is the home Member State, provided that those provisions apply regardless of the Member State in which the issuer of the financial instrument is located or of the Member State on the regulated market of which the instrument was listed for the first time.

4. The Commission shall report on the application of this Article no later than 31 December 1997; the Council may, on a proposal from the Commission, decide by a qualified majority to amend this Article.

ANNEX

Section A

Services

1. (a) Reception and transmission, on behalf of investors, of orders in relation to one or more of the instruments listed in Section B.
   (b) Execution of such orders other than for own account.
2. Dealing in any of the instruments listed in Section B for own account.

3. Managing portfolios of investments in accordance with mandates given by investors on a discriminatory, client-by-client basis where such portfolios include one or more of the instruments listed in Section B.
4. Underwriting in respect of issues of any of the instruments listed in Section B and/or the placing of such issues.

Section B

Instruments

1. (a) Transferable securities.
   (b) Units in collective investment undertakings.
2. Money-market instruments.
3. Financial-futures contracts, including equivalent cash-settled instruments.
4. Forward interest-rate agreements (FRAs).
5. Interest-rate, currency and equity swaps.
6. Options to acquire or dispose of any instruments falling within this section of the Annex, including equivalent cast-settled instruments. This category includes in particular options on currency and on interest rates.

Section C

Non-core services

1. Safekeeping and administration in relation to one or more of the instruments listed in Section B.
2. Safe custody services.
3. Granting credits or loans to an investor to allow him to carry out a transaction in one or more of the instruments listed in Section B, where the firm granting the credit or loan is involved in the transaction.
4. Advice to undertakings on capital structure, industrial strategy and related matters and advice and service relating to mergers and the purchase of undertakings.
5. Services related to underwriting.
6. Investment advice concerning one or more of the instruments listed in Section B.
7. Foreign-exchange service where these are connected with the provision of investment services.

Chapter 5

CORPORATE GOVERNANCE

1. INTRODUCTION

Within a matter of two weeks during the summer of 1995, 'shareholder activism' – a phenomenon previously almost unheard of in France – had brought down the board of the large French conglomerate Navigation Mixte and imposed severe limits on the chief executive officer of the even larger conglomerate Suez. These reactions followed a period of intense debate in the French establishment over issues of corporate governance. The recently published Viénot Report severely criticizes a number of features of French corporate governance, in particular the widespread crossholdings of shares, and recommends limiting the number of boards a director can sit on. Similar calls for reforms, largely directed towards the large banks, have been heard in Germany, following such governance failures as Metallgesellschaft and the Schneider empire. In Belgium, the holding companies are coming under increasing scrutiny, and control arrangements are being challenged in the Netherlands. The United Kingdom has already seen a follow-up to the path-breaking Cadbury Code of Best Practice which criticized institutional investors for not making use of their votes. Corporate governance is back on the agenda in many European countries.[1]

At the level of the European Union, another debate is gathering momentum. This debate concerns the relatively poor liquidity – and ultimately the sustainability – of many of Europe's three dozen stock exchanges. While most observers argue that greater integration of secondary equity markets would promote liquidity by bringing in more traders to each exchange, previous attempts to bring about such integration have not been very successful. An early ambitious effort to link exchanges, the IDIS (Interbourse Data Information System), with moral and some financial support from the European Commission, failed due to lack of resources. Private initiatives, such as Euroquote, have been abandoned

[1] The different national debates, as seen from the perspective of lawyers and accountants, are nicely summarized in *International Corporate Governance: Who Holds the Reins?*, a recent report from the International Capital Markets Group (1995).

because of disagreements among exchanges. In fact, liquidity-enhancing reforms on the Continental exchanges have come about largely through competitive pressure, rather than through collaboration.[2] This book, and this chapter, are about the impediments to such integration.

We argue that while the two issues – corporate governance and liquidity of markets – are often treated as independent of each other, they are in fact closely related. Corporate governance is commonly believed to benefit from the concentration of holdings of debt and equity in individual firms. Of course, concentrated ownership is hardly a guarantee of good corporate governance: there are many examples on the European continent of inactive and entrenched controlling investors. However, ownership concentration can serve to mitigate free-rider problems, better align incentives of owners with those of the firm, and make intervention more effective. Liquidity, on the other hand, may benefit from dispersion of ownership: the more traders in the market for a given instrument, the argument goes, the more liquid the instrument. The fact that corporate governance is linked to the liquidity of markets, and ultimately to the integration of these markets, makes it an issue of not only national but also Community-wide concern.

Casual observation also suggests a link between the liquidity of stock markets and corporate governance. The markets in western Europe differ dramatically in terms of number of companies listed, total market value, liquidity, and price volatility: the United Kingdom is at one extreme with a relatively large, liquid market, and Germany is at the other with a much smaller share of large corporations listed and less liquid exchanges. The United Kingdom and Germany also occupy opposite ends of the spectrum in terms of corporate governance arrangements. The German system relies heavily on concentrated shareholdings and active involvement by investors in corporate strategic decisions. In the United Kingdom, ownership is more dispersed, and issuers and investors typically prefer to maintain arm's-length relationships.

In addition, there is a widespread perception that, as activity levels and liquidity have increased on most stock exchanges in western Europe over the past decade, weaknesses in existing corporate governance systems have become more pronounced, or at least more apparent. This chapter examines the liquidity/control tradeoff and its implications for the integration of secondary equity markets in Europe. Two crucial questions are addressed. Are existing corporate governance patterns constraining the development of more uniform, and thus supposedly more liquid, markets for equity? If so, what are the prospects for change in these patterns, either through evolution or through institutional reform? In

[2] See Chapter 1.

particular, what effects, if any, would improved liquidity on European exchanges have on corporate governance patterns?

The observation of a link between corporate governance and liquidity of stock markets is not new in the economics literature. Almost thirty years ago Harold Demsetz (1968) pointed out that concentration of ownership, often believed to be a precondition for effective corporate governance, reduces the number of traders – and thus liquidity – in secondary markets. Amir Bhide (1993) posits that when ownership of a firm is fragmented, liquidity of its stock is better, and vice versa: when liquidity of a stock is high, ownership tends towards fragmentation. In an examination of a broad range of regulations in the United States affecting ownership concentration and liquidity, Bhide finds a strong bias in favour of liquidity, and against concentrated ownership. In his view, restrictions on the exercise of control by financial institutions and the strong enforcement of liquidity improving measures by the Securities and Exchange Commission have severely impeded corporate governance.

Recent theoretical work suggests that while corporate governance and liquidity are related, the link may be more complicated and less direct than suggested by Bhide. First, issuers have found ways of increasing capital and maintaining liquidity without dispersing control, although these mechanisms may have reduced the incentives of investors to maximize profits and exercise control. Secondly, improvements in liquidity do not necessarily reduce the effectiveness of corporate control; indeed, enhanced liquidity of a firm's stock may in fact improve governance by facilitating the concentration of control in the market. Finally, Bhide's argument is closely tied to the regulatory experience of the United States; ownership and control patterns, the organization and operation of markets, and regulatory frameworks have evolved quite differently on the European continent.

This chapter revisits the liquidity/control tradeoff in light of the new theoretical contributions and the empirical evidence from Europe. The basic argument is that prevailing corporate governance structures have constrained the liquidity of stock markets, and that variations in these structures across Europe impose costs on companies and investors wishing to transcend national boundaries. Furthermore, this chapter argues that the evidence on convergence of existing corporate governance arrangements is mixed, and the direction of change is not obvious. The scope for corporate governance reform at the level of the European Union is also limited, at least in the short and medium terms. Ownership and control patterns are therefore likely to remain an important constraint on the liquidity of secondary markets for equity in Europe, and an obstacle to the integration of these markets. However, this does not imply, as suggested by Bhide, that improvements in the liquidity of secondary equity markets necessarily come at the expense of corporate governance. On the contrary, increases in the number of traders – for example, through integration of national equity markets or improved incentives to hold equity relative to other assets – are likely to improve corporate governance by facilitating the accumulation of control blocks.

The chapter starts by providing some stylized facts on variations in ownership and control patterns, and the liquidity of stock exchanges in Europe (Section 2). Section 3 develops a framework for interpreting the observed differences, in particular the link between the concentration of ownership and liquidity of stock markets, based on some recent contributions in corporate finance. In section 4, existing corporate laws are related to the basic financing patterns in some European countries. In most west European countries, with the exception of the United Kingdom, existing regulation and practices appear biased towards ownership concentration, rather than liquidity. The differences in governance patterns *per se* also reduce the liquidity of secondary equity markets. In section 5, we examine the prospects for increased liquidity through convergence in, or deliberate reform of, governance patterns. Section 6 summarizes the main points, and section 7 draws some policy implications.

2. INTERNATIONAL VARIATIONS IN FINANCIAL SYSTEMS

Most of the comparative finance literature has focused on international variations in the relative importance of different sources of finance, i.e. on the role of the financial system in supplying capital. Even though the initial reactions to these studies emphasized the differences across systems, the similarities are at least as striking. Using aggregate flow-of-funds statistics, Mayer (1990) finds a strong universal dominance for internally generated funds, and finds bank loans to be the most important external source of finance in all the countries studied. Intermediated finance strongly dominates direct finance with the possible exception of United States – the only country where corporate bonds play an important role in financing the corporate sector.[3]

It is tempting to conclude that the observed similarities imply that there are no economically significant differences between financial systems, but this would be a mistake. Instead, we argue that it is the relative importance of markets and institutions in monitoring the use of funds, rather than their roles in the supply of funds, that distinguishes financial systems. These differences are not cap-

[3] Mayer's study suggests that the United Kingdom and the United States rely more heavily on internal funds than France, Germany, and Japan. However, Corbett and Jenkinson (1994), using the same methodology but more recent data, do not observe these differences for France and Germany – Japan stands out as the exception with a much higher share of external finance. Rajan and Zingales (1994), on the basis of firm-level data for large corporations in the G7 countries, find little difference in the relative importance of debt and equity finance.

Table 1. Ownership Concentration in Listed Firms (the Largest Owner's Share)

<table>
<tr><th></th><th>(1)</th><th>(2)</th><th>(3)</th><th>(4)</th><th>(5)</th><th>(6)</th><th>(7)</th><th>(8)</th></tr>
<tr><th>Largest owner's share</th><th>France (1982)</th><th>Germany (1985)</th><th>Italy (1993)</th><th>Spain (1990)</th><th>Sweden (1987)</th><th>UK (1990)</th><th>Japan (1983)</th><th>US (1981)</th></tr>
<tr><td>> 50</td><td>55</td><td>66</td><td>89</td><td>49</td><td>42</td><td>5</td><td>5</td><td>9</td></tr>
<tr><td>30-50</td><td rowspan="6">42</td><td rowspan="4">23</td><td rowspan="3">9</td><td rowspan="6">49</td><td>31</td><td rowspan="3">29</td><td rowspan="6">70</td><td rowspan="4">29</td></tr>
<tr><td>25-30</td><td rowspan="2">12</td></tr>
<tr><td>20-25</td></tr>
<tr><td>15-20</td><td rowspan="3">2</td><td rowspan="2">11</td><td rowspan="2">27</td></tr>
<tr><td>10-15</td><td rowspan="3">12</td><td>10</td></tr>
<tr><td>5-10</td><td rowspan="2">4</td><td>30</td><td>29</td></tr>
<tr><td><5</td><td>2</td><td>2</td><td>9</td><td>25</td><td>23</td></tr>
</table>

Sources : (1)-(2), (5)-(8) from Berglöf (1988); (3) from Barca (1995); (4) from Galve Gorriz and Salas Fumas (1993).

tured by traditional financial statistics and therefore require other data. Here we focus on two aspects: the concentration of equity ownership and the liquidity of markets for these instruments.

Unfortunately, the data on ownership in European firms are still rather poor, and comparability is limited. Table 1 summarizes some studies of ownership of equity in non-financial corporations in eight OECD countries. The samples and methodology differ across studies, but one feature stands out – the high concentration of ownership in Continental European and Scandinavian countries, as compared with the United Kingdom and the United States. If only quoted companies are considered, 79 and 85 percent of the companies in France and Germany, respectively, had one owner with stakes larger than 25 percent.[4] The corresponding figure for the United Kingdom was 16 percent. In effect, the overwhelming majority of listed companies on the European continent are closely held. Comparisons over time are not always available, but evidence from France, Germany, and Sweden shows an increase in ownership concentration over the 1970s and 1980s.[5]

Establishing the identity of controlling holders is even more difficult. Only a few studies have been undertaken, and what constitutes a controlling shareholder varies across countries and should ultimately depend on the dispersion of shares in the individual firm. Pyramiding[6] and other arrangements separating

[4] Franks, Mayer, and Rennebog (1995).

[5] Berglöf (1988).

[6] Chains of firms (sometimes as many as 10 or 15) owning one another, allowing the ultimate controlling owner to minimize its capital stake without affecting the concentration of control.

Table 2. The Identity of Controlling Owners (%)

	France[a] 1982	Germany[b] 1980	Sweden[c] 1985
Individuals	42.3	34.5	36.0
Non-financial enterprises		17.3	25.0
Investment companies			26.0
Banks		12.2	
Insurance companies		2.5	6.0
Government	18.0	14.2	
Foreign owners	39.6	17.3	
Others		2.0	7.0
Total	100.0	100.0	100.0

Notes:
a. Data refer to 249 firms with a majority shareholder (out of 500 largest firms).
b. Majority shareholder in listed firms.
c. Largest shareholder in 107 largest privately-owned firms.
Source: Berglöf (1988).

capital contribution and control further complicate the interpretation of data. Nevertheless, these studies reveal the strong influence of family and entrepreneurial ownership on the European continent, here represented by France and Germany[7] (see Table 2). The continuing importance of families in the control of corporations is one of the central features distinguishing continental European systems from those of the United Kingdom, and the United States for that matter. Institutional shareholders, in particular non-financial corporations and banks, also play an important monitoring role in continental Europe. The significance of family control does not seem to have markedly decreased over the past two decades, whereas non-financial corporations in many countries have become more important as large blockholders.[8]

In practically all European countries, institutional shareholders have become more important at the expense of private individuals (Table 3). However, the types of institutions holding shares, and possibly exercising control, are quite different. In the United Kingdom, the growth of pension funds over the past two decades has been spectacular, whereas increases in institutional shareholdings in Germany have come primarily from non-financial enterprises and foreign investors. The strong portfolio-orientation of institutional investors in the United Kingdom

[7] Barca (1995) shows a similar picture for Italy.

[8] With the exception of France, where tax subsidies have provided households with strong incentives to own equity, share ownership has become increasingly institutionalized in Europe. However, on most of the European continent the accumulation of institutional shareholdings has taken place either in the banks themselves or in institutions controlled by the banks (here the Netherlands is an exception).

Table 3. Ownership of Listed Stocks By Sector (as of 31 December)

		Households	Non-financial corporations	Government institutions	Financial institutions	Foreign owners
France	1977	41	20	3	24	12
	1992	34	21	2	23	20
Germany	1970	28	41	11	11	8
	1993	17	39	3	29	12
Italy	1993	32	22	28	14	4
United Kingdom	1969	50	5	3	36	7
	1993	19	2	1	62	16
Japan	1970	40	23	0	35	3
	1993	20	28	1	42	8
United States	1981	51	15	0	28	6
	1993	48	9	0	37	6

Sources: Barca (1995); Berglöf (1988); Lannoo (1994); International Capital Markets Group (1995).

contrasts sharply with the control-orientation of this investor category in, for example, Germany. This difference in the orientation of institutional investors is closely linked to the observed variations in the functioning of financial markets.

The concentration of ownership seems to be related to the liquidity of equity markets, and to the willingness to list firms on public exchanges. Table 1 in Chapter 1 shows the differences in the number of listed firms, the total market value, and the turnover of major stock exchanges in relation to GDP in EU countries. Unfortunately, owing to differences in reporting, these figures are often hard to interpret, and sometimes directly misleading.[9] However, the United Kingdom clearly stands out in a European comparison, with a large number of firms listed and a high market value relative to GDP. In general, the markets of continental Europe seem to play a more limited role, with the Netherlands and Switzerland as important exceptions.[10] Sweden is characterized by a relatively large and active stock market despite heavily concentrated ownership.

There are also differences in the nature of the market for corporate control. In the United Kingdom, hostile takeovers mounted through purchases in the

[9] For example, the high velocity in Germany and Switzerland primarily seems to be a reflection of the narrowness, rather than liquidity, of the markets. The way in which trades are reported in Germany also severely overstates market liquidity (see Chapter 1).

[10] The high market capitalization and relatively high liquidity of the Dutch market can be attributed primarily to a small number of very large multinational firms. Royal Dutch Shell alone accounted for 34 percent of capitalization in 1991. Together with four other large international Dutch companies Shell had 33 percent of the turnover. In Switzerland the high capitalization and turnover are primarily reflections of the country's well-developed financial sector. In Germany, the top five companies accounted for 47 percent, and the 10 largest companies for 63 percent, of total turnover (Wymeersch 1994).

official market play an important role. On the European continent, such transactions are rare. In Germany, as in the Netherlands, no truly hostile takeover attempt has succeeded. Since the regulatory changes in the wake of the failed takeover attempt of Société Générale, hostile takeovers of larger firms in Belgium have basically come to a halt. Sweden had only four successful hostile offers during the 1980s, a period characterized by substantial corporate restructuring.[11] However, French authorities have made a point of activating the market for corporate control, and a considerable number of takeovers have taken place against the will of incumbent management. In general, takeovers in continental Europe are used as a mechanism to withdraw firms from the stock exchange rather than as a device to change control. Most control-related trading in Europe occurs in large blocks outside official markets.

3. CORPORATE FINANCE AND GOVERNANCE

Corporate governance and market liquidity have both been important topics in the finance literature over the past decade. They have typically been addressed independently of each other. However, attempts have been made recently to link the two. This section discusses some of these contributions and develops a simple conceptual framework for classifying financing patterns and financial systems.

The starting point of the corporate governance literature is the basic agency problem of capitalism: the credibility problem facing entrepreneurs or firms when they seek to convince outside investors to contribute funds. In its most extreme form, the agency problem is about how to ensure that investors, once they have contributed their money, receive anything at all in return. Management could steal resources outright or pay themselves handsome salaries and decorate lavish offices. Competition in factor and output markets may mitigate this agency problem, but in itself competition is insufficient: market signals are generated after funds have been committed, and have little impact on the *ex post* bargaining problem between the firm and its investors. The role of corporate governance is to ensure that these signals and other relevant information are actually translated into investment decisions – for instance, by replacing management following poor performance, or closing down unprofitable units.

There are two generic approaches to the classic agency problem: either one or more investors are given influence over strategic decisions in the firm (control-oriented finance), or management finds ways of committing to efficient actions and to share in the proceeds from these actions (arm's-length finance).[12]

[11] Isaksson and Skog (1994).

[12] For example, Aghion and Bolton (1992) and Hart and Moore (1994), respectively.

Control has a value because not all future actions and contingencies are written into contracts enforceable in court, or anticipated in some external legal framework: control is the right to make decisions when contracts are incomplete.[13] Under control-oriented finance, investor intervention typically is based on a control block of equity or a position as exclusive or dominant creditor. Intervention can take many forms: for example, vetoing or blocking particularly inefficient investment decisions, or using voting majority to oust incumbent management. Under arm's-length finance, investors do not intervene in the company, at least not as long as payment obligations are met: intervention, if it comes, typically involves some external mechanism such as the market for corporate control, or a court in the case of bankruptcy. The firm attempts to commit to behave efficiently and repay investors; for example, by providing collateral in the form of contingent property rights to individual well-specified, and verifiable, assets or cash flows.

Control-oriented and arm's-length finance are often combined in the individual firm.[14] The combination of the two forms of finance may give rise to additional agency problems – in particular between controlling shareholders and minority shareholders. The basic issue of the two agency problems is the same: how to convince investors that they will be repaid in the future. However, the concrete manifestations of agency problems in a widely held firm often differ substantially from those in a closely held firm with a controlling shareholder, and conflicts in owner-managed firms are different from those in firms with professional management without substantial ownership stakes: the choice of ownership structure thus has important implications for the nature of conflict in a firm.

Both forms of finance rely on concentration of ownership for effective corporate governance: when holdings are widely and evenly dispersed, no single investor has incentives, or the capability, to exercise control. In the case of control-oriented finance, control is concentrated from the outset, but arm's-length finance relies on the accumulation of controlling stakes in the market. Holding large blocks not only requires wealth but also implies abstaining from diversification opportunities: controlling owners in large corporations are seldom well-diversified, not even in the United States.[15] If the possibilities to diversify portfolios, and the distribution of wealth, differ across financial systems, so do the opportunity costs of holding control. To induce investors to give up diversification opportunities and hold, or assemble, control blocks to exercise corporate governance, other investors

[13] Grossman and Hart (1986).

[14] There are by now several contributions to the literature attempting to model the combination of different forms of finance (see, e.g. Holmström and Tirole, 1994).

[15] Demsetz and Lehn (1985).

may have to allow large stakeholders to extract private benefits from the firm. Such rent extraction is also a cost of concentrating ownership.

Here the focus is on yet another cost of control-oriented finance. When financial instruments are concentrated in a few hands, they are often viewed as more difficult to trade: stocks of closely held companies are less liquid than those of widely held corporations, and stocks that form part of control blocks are less liquid than those that do not.[16] But some observers, as Bhide (1993), go even further: not only does fragmented ownership lead to greater liquidity, but greater liquidity also leads to ownership fragmentation. If this claim is correct, it would have far-reaching implications for public policy. Not only should we worry about measures directly constraining the concentration of ownership, but *all* improvements in liquidity come at the expense of concentration, and thus by implication effective corporate governance.

A recent article by Patrick Bolton and Ernst-Ludwig von Thadden (1995) provides one of the first steps towards a formal analysis of the tradeoff between concentration of ownership and liquidity. The authors address two crucial choices facing a firm: whether to concentrate shareholdings, and whether to list its stock on a public exchange.[17] By concentrating holdings the firm can ensure that (presumably) value-increasing monitoring will take place. Dispersion of shareholdings, or arm's-length financing, does not preclude effective monitoring – a control block can still be formed in the secondary market – but the likelihood is lower.

The decision to go public affects the tradeoff between control and liquidity in at least two ways. The greater anonymity of transactions in a public market makes it easier for controlling investors to unwind their positions. As a result, their ability credibly to commit *ex ante* to monitoring is reduced; this makes concentration of ownership less attractive. A public listing is also likely to affect the degree of informational asymmetry between large blockholders and minority shareholders. If information becomes more asymmetric, as the authors find most likely, this has a negative impact on liquidity in a firm with a controlling block. On the other hand, if the small investors in the public firm know more about the controlling

[16] The most conspicuous evidence is perhaps the difference between different classes of the same stock: high-voting shares are normally much less liquid than low-voting shares.

[17] Pagano and Röell (1995) address a similar problem in a firm where control remains in firm hands, but where the controlling owner has to decide whether to sell the rest of the shares to a single monitoring investor or disperse the shares through a public offering. In order to avoid excessive monitoring by a large investor, and a corresponding reduction in his private consumption out of the firm, the owner may decide to incur the costs of going public. An interesting implication of the Pagano-Röell analysis is that improved monitoring by stock markets – e.g. stricter securities regulation – increases the likelihood that a firm will go public. Restrictions on the consumption of private benefits improve the ability of controlling owners to commit when going public. This finding goes against the common argument that firms avoid going public because of all the restrictions imposed by exchanges.

owners and their intentions than they would in the private firm, going public with a controlling block is always better than doing so with dispersed shareholdings.

In Bhide's view, going public with a concentrated block is always optimal. Bolton and von Thadden suggest that the situation is more complicated. They find that, when listing costs are not prohibitively high, a publicly listed firm always dominates a private firm with dispersed ownership: accumulating large blocks is more costly when the firm is not listed, and this leads to a loss of effective control. However, in a closely held private firm, the decision to go public involves a tradeoff between control and liquidity. The public exchange, with greater anonymity and, by assumption, greater asymmetries of information, offers higher liquidity but also greater possibilities for the controlling owner to sell off his control block secretly. If the informational asymmetry is more pronounced in private firms, the public company with concentrated ownership always dominates (as in Bhide).

However, the link between liquidity and control is less direct than suggested by this discussion. Investors and issuers have found a number of ways of keeping control concentrated while increasing liquidity and limiting the capital committed. In most countries, at least some firms issue shares with differentiated voting power. Holding companies and pyramidal ownership structures are other ways of maintaining control while expanding the capital base. Crossholdings of shares, and proxy votes on behalf of small shareholders, serve a similar purpose. These mechanisms allow firms to escape, to some extent, the liquidity/control tradeoff, but at the cost of incentives. Controlling owners now hold a smaller share of the firm's cash flows, and should thus be more inclined to consume private benefits at the expense of profit-maximization.

In addition, the liquidity of one firm's financial instruments may be related to the liquidity of those of other firms traded on the same exchange. Public markets with more stocks allow better diversification of portfolios and thus attract more traders, and more traders bring down volatility and increase liquidity.[18] Such contagion effects, or 'thick market' externalities, may be quite important in explaining the observed, and persistent, differences across countries in the degree of liquidity of markets. The existence of such externalities also suggests that analysing the liquidity/control tradeoff of a single firm in isolation could be misleading. Furthermore, exogenous changes in liquidity – e.g. through an increase in the number of traders – do not necessarily lead to a control loss.

The liquidity of financial markets may also be linked to the liquidity of markets for real assets. For example, the scope for arm's-length finance depends on the availability of collateral, which in turn is a function of how easily real assets can

[18] Pagano (1993).

be sold. The liquidity of real assets, in turn, is affected by firm organization – for instance, the ease with which individual units can be sold off without damaging the rest of the firm, and the strength of the association between physical and human assets. When employees develop skills specific to a particular machine or workplace, separating these physical assets and transferring them to a new owner is more difficult. In other words, the organization of production and skill acquisition of workers, but also the connection between labour law and company law, may affect the finance decision and ultimately the nature of the financial system. The close association of workers and physical assets forces investors to exercise control. When worker skills are highly specific to a firm, or mobility for other reasons is low, shareholders and creditors are also – by the need to raise outside finance beyond the collateral base – transformed from outsiders into insiders.

The tradeoff between corporate governance and liquidity has implications at the level of the financial system. When many firms have chosen arm's-length finance – for example, because legal rules discourage concentration of ownership – financial markets are likely to be more liquid. If there are liquidity externalities across firms, such differences should be reinforced. On the other hand, the use of mechanisms allowing the capital base to expand without the loss of control should weaken, but does not eliminate, the link between corporate governance and liquidity. The analysis thus suggests a strong interconnectedness between different aspects of the financial systems, with one type of system predominantly based on arm's-length finance and another with a more important role for control-oriented finance (see Table 4). Arm's-length systems have dispersed ownership of both debt and equity, and more liquid markets for these instruments. Investors are prone to portfolio-orientation, and the market for corporate control operating over the public exchanges is an important mechanism for the correction of managerial failure. Systems where control-oriented finance dominates have more concentrated ownership structures in individual firms and less liquid markets. Control-oriented financial systems also breed control-oriented investors; opportunities for diversification are less and the costs of trading tend to be high. The market for corporate control operates outside the public exchanges in the form of occasional trades in large blocks.

4. CORPORATE FINANCE AND CORPORATE LAW

The observed variation in corporate governance structures in Europe reflects, at least to some extent, the different choices made by issuers, investors, and intermediaries in the tradeoff between the liquidity of financial instruments and concentration of ownership. These choices influence – and are influenced by – company law and related regulation, self-enforced rules, and social norms in such

Table 4. Financial Systems and Capital Structure

	Type of financial system	
	Control-oriented	Arm's-length
Share of control-oriented finance	High	Low
Financial markets	Small, less liquid	Large, highly liquid
Share of all firms listed on exchanges	Small	Large
Ownership of debt and equity	Concentrated	Dispersed
Investor orientation	Control-oriented	Portfolio-oriented
Turnover of control blocks	Low	High
Use of mechanisms for separating control and capital base	Frequent	Limited, often by regulation
Dominant agency conflict	Controlling vs. minority shareholders	Shareholders vs. management
Role of external board of directors	Limited	Important
Role of hostile takeovers	Very limited	Potentially important

areas as disclosure requirements, insider trading, and procedures for mergers and acquisitions. This section briefly characterizes two types of legal systems in Europe and relates them to existing corporate finance patterns.

4.1. A Two-Way Relationship

The relationship between corporate finance and governance, on the one hand, and corporate law and securities regulation on the other, is still poorly understood. Both control-oriented finance and arm's-length finance rely on a legal system enforcing property rights, but the role of courts differs with regard to the two forms of finance. Also, understanding the rules themselves is not sufficient to determine their effect on the control/liquidity tradeoff; it is also important to see to what extent existing regulation is actually enforced or agents have managed to circumvent rules. There is, however, a general perception that arm's-length finance places greater demands on courts, in that it requires detailed enforcement of specific rights to assets and cash flows, whereas control-oriented finance merely requires the protection of voting rights. However, the viability of control-oriented finance is also related to the protection of arm's-length investors: when ownership is concentrated, controlling owners rely on the legal protection of minority shareholders in order to commit *ex ante* not to exploit them.

A recent survey of the corporate governance literature by Andrei Shleifer and Robert Vishny (1995) argues that concentration of ownership is an unavoidable outcome of shortcomings in the legal system: in the absence of well-functioning securities regulation, concentration of ownership is the only way to commit not to steal from the company. Companies in countries with poor protection of minority shareholders should therefore have more concentrated ownership structures than countries with more protective, and better enforced, rules. While this idea seems to capture the observed correlation between the degree of elaboration of securities regulation and the concentration of ownership, it does not explain the widespread use of various mechanisms for increasing control beyond the level of capital contributed – for instance, through pyramiding or dual-class shares. If anything, the share of capital, relative to the amount of control exercised, seems to be lower in countries with concentrated ownership.

More importantly, implicit in the Shleifer-Vishny article is the view that ownership and control patterns are ultimately determined by existing laws. The legal framework does influence the viability of different financial arrangements and the tradeoff between corporate governance and liquidity: either *directly*, for example through restrictions on the size of stakes or type of control mechanisms allowed; or *indirectly*, by affecting investors' incentives to take on controlling blocks. However, financing patterns also influence the evolution of the legal system. They determine the nature of conflicts between the firm and its investors, and between investors, which, in turn, has implications for the structure and function of the board of directors and general shareholders' meeting. In a similar vein, the importance attached to fiduciary duties and rules for minority protection reflects the capital structure of firms and the liquidity of markets for the instruments issued.

Equally important, when there are clearly identifiable owners with controlling stakes, lawmakers may choose to abstain from regulation and court involvement. By definition, control is the right to decide in situations not contracted upon, or constrained by regulation. For example, instead of providing detailed rules for how many members there should be on the board, how they should be elected, and when they should be fired, lawmakers may choose to delegate these decisions to controlling owners, when there are such owners. Furthermore, in contrast to the claims in Shleifer and Vishny, legal frameworks on the European continent are in many respects at least as complete or detailed as those of the United States: the important difference is often the extent of involvement of the courts in conflict resolution.

4.2. Corporate Law Traditions in Europe

At first glance it may appear that EU countries have similar legal structures for limited liability companies. While there is some variation, most corporate laws or self-enforced codes regulate minimum capital requirements, the structure and composition of boards, and responsibilities of the general shareholders' meeting.

However, the relative importance of private and public limited liability companies differs substantially, and underlying the superficial similarities of existing legal structures are deep-rooted differences. Wymeersch (1994) identifies two broad traditions in Europe – a company-based and an enterprise-based legal system. This classification may exaggerate differences between systems and obscure important variations within each category, but it seems to capture significant elements of existing regulation, self-enforced rules, and social norms. In the company-based system, the firm is viewed as a nexus of legal contracts among investors, while in the enterprise-based tradition the focus is on the firm as a physical entity. The company-based system is primarily associated with the United Kingdom, while the enterprise-based system is best represented by Germany and the Netherlands, but can also be found in Switzerland and Austria.[19] Wymeersch argues that some legal systems on the European continent – primarily France and Belgium – find themselves in transition, largely in response to government intervention. We will return to these transitional systems, but for now we will focus on the two systems corresponding most closely to the two types – the United Kingdom and Germany, respectively.

4.2.1. The United Kingdom: A Company-Based System

Regulation in the United Kingdom – whether statutory or self-enforced codes of conduct – views securities markets as playing an important role in monitoring and disciplining firms. The market provides an objective valuation of the firm and protects shareholders against the abuses of management, primarily through the takeover mechanism. An active, liquid market is a prerequisite for efficient monitoring, and market manipulation and insider dealings are severely punished. Securities regulation in areas such as disclosure requirements, accounting standards, and auditing procedures is ambitious. The City Takeover Code, with its strong protection of minority shareholders, is one of the most elaborate pieces of regulation of its type. Furthermore, legislation discourages holdings of large stakes by institutional investors, while such investors also generally respect self-imposed limits on the concentration of ownership.

In such a system, the structure and functioning of the board of directors is viewed as crucial to corporate governance, as reflected in a vast literature on the optimal size and composition of boards. In the absence of a controlling shareholder, boards of directors are essentially self-appointed. The increasing equity

[19] In an interesting passage, Baums (1994) describes how during the nineteenth century and early twentieth century there was also a 'nexus of contracts' view in German law, at least in legal theory, but after the Second World War this view was abandoned. Under the current doctrine other stakeholders, in particular employees, are members of the firm (*Unternehmen*).

ownership by institutional investors with a tradition of portfolio-orientation has further intensified the discussion, and led to the establishment of audit committees and special committees reviewing corporate policies in such areas as remuneration and business ethics.[20] Boards in UK companies have also become more non-executive, with technical expertise and general industry knowledge, rather than financial stake, being viewed as important criteria in the selection of directors. The positions of chairman of the board and chief executive officer are becoming separated in an increasing number of firms.

Conflicts of interest in corporate governance are viewed as serious and highly undesirable. For example, while equity holdings by banks are allowed, the Bank of England strongly discourages controlling stakes in manufacturing companies. Stakeholders other than shareholders, such as creditors or employees, are seldom represented on the board. Such board representation is perceived as driving the firm away from maximization of shareholder value. In particular, takeovers are typically initiated and negotiated by management without involving other stakeholders, not even major shareholders. As compared with German law, English corporate law is characterized by few explicit provisions for the protection of minority interests: group law – the legal rules applying when one firm is controlled by another – is merely viewed as a special case of company law.[21]

4.2.2. Germany: An Enterprise-Based System

The German-style enterprise-based legal system places less emphasis on the role of the market. This is a reflection of the relatively small number of firms listed, and the even smaller share of listed firms with a majority of shares actively traded.[22] Securities market regulation has, in Wymeersch's words, been the subject of 'benign neglect'. Supervision is weak and enforcement rare. For example, German authorities have been reluctant to require officially organized supervision of public issues, other than initial public offerings, semi-annual disclosure of information, and regulation of insider dealings.[23] There is no explicit takeover regulation, and no strong need for such regulation seems to be perceived (no hostile takeover in the traditional sense has succeeded; and given the concentrated ownership structure of German firms and the extensive use of proxy shares, no dramatic increase in such takeover activity should be expected).

[20] International Capital Markets Group (1995).

[21] Prentice (1993).

[22] Baums (1994) estimates that only 38 German firms are actively traded, in the sense that more than 75 percent of the shares are not in close hands.

[23] Germany has now accepted disclosure of large transactions and large block holdings in line with the EC directive (Wymeersch, 1994).

The well-known two-tier board structure in Germany, with a supervisory board (*Aufsichtsrat*) and a management board (*Vorstand*), has been extensively described and analysed in the legal literature. Company law assigns a key strategic role to the *Aufsichtsrat*, which appoints the *Vorstand*. However, even though the supervisory board can play an important role in some critical situations, and has done so historically, the current consensus seems to be that its role in monitoring management is limited. The management board is not bound to accept instructions from the *Aufsichtsrat*, and some companies have removed from their by-laws rules requiring supervisory board approval of certain material transactions.[24] Some recent corporate governance failures have led to calls for reform and activation of the *Aufsichtsrat*. However, this institution cannot be expected to function as an independent board of directors in the Anglo-American sense. In large companies, half of the members are representatives of the employees, and the rest of the board is, *de facto*, appointed by the controlling owner, if there is such an owner.

A comparatively large share of equity holders is legally represented at general shareholders' meetings; this is largely a function of the system of proxy votes, whereby holders of bearer shares delegate voting to the banks through which they do their brokerage business.[25] In the relatively small number of firms where ownership is widely dispersed, these proxy votes give the three large commercial banks – Deutsche Bank, Commerzbank, and Dresdner Bank – potential control over voting at these meetings. Legislation allows banks to combine debt and equity holdings within certain broad limits.[26] The large banks also organize the most important markets for securities trading. Whether or not banks have used their positions to exercise corporate governance, and the possible effects of such bank intervention, are currently subjects of intense debate in Germany, but few observers question the banks' potential influence.[27]

There is a stark discrepancy between the rudimentary securities markets regulation and the elaborate laws affecting the structure of enterprises and groups

[24] ICMG (1995).

[25] Gottschalk (1988) adds up the shares held by the banks on their own account, their proxy holdings, and the shares held by the banks' investment companies. He finds that banks represented more than four-fifths of all votes in shareholder meetings. In the case of Siemens, a widely held firm by German standards, 60 percent of all shares were represented at the general shareholders' meeting in 1987. Deutsche Bank voted 17.8 percent, Dresdner Bank 10.7 percent, Commerzbank 4.1 percent, and all other banks 32.5 percent. Foreign owners are less likely to be less represented at the general shareholders' meeting. As in many other large German firms, foreign ownership increased substantially in Siemens over the 1980s, and in 1990 it accounted for 43 percent of total equity (Baums 1994).

[26] In 1990, combined bank exposures in individual firms were not allowed to exceed 50 percent of the bank's capital base (Borio 1990). This limit has since been lowered to 25 percent.

[27] For example, Edwards and Fischer (1994) ascribe a limited role to banks in corporate governance, while Gorton and Schmid (1995) find empirical support for positive bank influence.

of companies.[28] Wymeersch suggests that the well-developed group law should be viewed as an attempt to compensate for the lack of protection of minority shareholders. The legislation on co-determination is another example of the emphasis placed in German law on the enterprise itself and its stakeholders, rather than on the nexus of contracts between investors.[29]

4.2.3. Systems in Transition

The legal system of the Netherlands has some of the features of a company-oriented system; for example, securities regulation is close to UK practice. This is largely due to the presence on the Dutch stock market of the large binational companies listed on international exchanges. However, in most other respects the system is enterprise-based, but in a rather different way from Germany. Control over most companies remains in firm, mostly Dutch, hands, but banks play a less pronounced role in corporate governance. A number of specific control instruments, such as voting trusts and golden shares, have been developed to preserve this pattern: a large number of hostile takeovers have been attempted, but have all failed. The legislation on insider trading is of recent date, and its enforcement has been weak.[30] At least until recently, the large institutional investors have not pushed for reform to the same extent as their British counterparts. Dutch law requires a two-tier board structure where the supervisory board elects itself. The Netherlands also has elaborate co-determination laws, but they work through a separate co-determination committee rather than through the supervisory board.

Sweden, like the other Scandinavian countries, has had a control-oriented financial system strongly influenced by German corporate law. During the 1980s the Swedish financial system underwent considerable deregulation, and financial markets expanded rapidly. Securities regulation has developed in the direction of the United Kingdom. However, ownership patterns remain concentrated, and the dominant position of the two largest banks – SE Banken and Handelsbanken – has been reinforced by the recent financial crisis. Corporations only have one tier of boards, and employee representation is required in large and medium-sized firms.

[28] The significance of the law on groups of companies, *Konzernrecht*, reflects the ownership structure of German firms. According to a study referred to in Baums (1994), as much as 90 percent of all domestic stock corporations and more than 50 percent of all German partnerships are members of groups of two or more firms.

[29] The Co-determination Acts (*Mitbestimmungsgesetze*) apply to firms with more than 500 employees. In companies with more than 2000 employees, one half of members are elected by the employees. In groups of firms, the employees of dependent firms are allowed to co-elect the employee board members of the top (governing) company (Baums 1994).

[30] Wymeersch (1994).

Some countries on the European continent, primarily Belgium and France, find themselves in transition, with features of their legal systems being altered. Belgium has become increasingly enterprise-oriented, in particular after the takeover legislation in the wake of the failed attempt on Société Générale de Belgique. This legislation largely emulates the UK City Takeover Code; but rather than fostering takeover activity, it has led controlling shareholders to reinforce their positions, essentially ruling out hostile takeovers on the bulk of Belgian enterprises. The increasing foreign influence – mostly Dutch, German, and French – has further reinforced the enterprise-based nature of the system. This orientation is reflected in the operation of the market for corporate control, with most transactions taking place outside the largely dormant Brussels stock exchange.

The situation in France is rather different. Even though most of the legal thinking is still strongly influenced by an enterprise-based doctrine, regulators have since 1965 systematically attempted to introduce elements of company-based systems.[31] The attempts to open up the market have primarily been motivated by a desire to protect minorities. Disclosure requirements and accounting standards have been comparatively strict, and rules on insiders and takeovers have evolved considerably in response to changes in the operation of markets. State agency supervision is important. Strong tax subsidies have attracted large numbers of small shareholders to the stock exchange, and the large-scale privatizations have been another important instrument in changing ownership and trading patterns.[32] The traditionally strong position of the *président-directeur-général* (PDG) has also increasingly been challenged, and recent shareholder activism has put unprecedented pressure on management in some firms to consider the interests of smaller shareholders.[33]

The recent attempt to separate the positions of chairman of the board and president has not been successful; very few companies have undertaken such a separation.[34] The French government has also outlawed a number of specific control techniques. In particular, autocontrol by parent company through holdings by subsidiary, or crossholdings, has been restricted. Double voting rights and voting caps for loyal investors have been forbidden, and preferential subscription rights can no longer be waived. As a result, the financial system has become more open, but issuers and investors have found ways of circumventing many of the restrictions. There is also strong emphasis on the desirability of a

[31] Wymeersch (1994).

[32] However, the initial dispersion of shares has been reduced considerably by subsequent trading.

[33] As witnessed, for example, in the Viénot Report on corporate governance in France.

[34] French company law allows both two-tier and single-tier boards, but the chief executive officer is considered the dominant authority.

controlling core group of shareholders (*noyeau dur*) with privileged information rights. The restrictions on the concentration of credits are limited, and combinations of debt and equity holdings are allowed and common among larger banks.

4.3. Reform at the EU level

Attempts at harmonizing corporate governance legislation within the European Union have generally been unsuccessful.[35] The ambition has also been lowered from the total harmonization of the 1970s to minimal harmonization and mutual recognition of additional requirements through the Single Market programme. Corporate governance is one of the areas targeted for the application of the subsidiarity principle, i.e. regulation is left to Member States. A major initiative from the Commission seems even less likely after the recent enlargement.

Previous initiatives to unify the structure and control of public listed companies, takeover bid procedures, and employee rights have effectively been stopped. A number of proposals are still on the table such as the draft fifth, tenth, and thirteenth company law directives. The draft fifth directive requires harmonization of the structure of public companies. Among other things, this draft provides two forms of board structure and requires employee representation and control of the board. Amendments in 1990 introduced several measures concerning control, such as the 'one-share-one-vote' principle and majority voting in the general assembly. The draft tenth and thirteenth directives aim at facilitating cross-border mergers and harmonizing takeover procedures, respectively.

The most ambitious harmonization project at the EU level is the European company statute – *Société Européenne*. This statute would provide an optional structure for companies recognized in all Member States, but subject to the law of its home state. The regulation specifies terms of incorporation, minimum capital requirements, two options for board structure, allowable restrictions on voting rights, and reporting requirements. A related draft directive defines the rights of the employees in a company which chooses this form of incorporation.

The overall prospects for these and other attempts at the European level to reform corporate governance are generally perceived to be poor. Recently, some large corporations operating at the European level have attempted to reactivate the European company statute, but the project is stalled, in particular over the issue of employee rights. On this issue, as on many other matters relating to corporate governance, the disagreements primarily between Germany and the United Kingdom are effectively blocking progress. There is an increasing realization that the lack of progress stems from deep-rooted institutional differences.

[35] Lannoo (1994).

If, as is argued here, corporate governance arrangements are linked to firm organization and the operation of markets for real assets, the scope for reform may be quite limited. This realization has led some lobbying organizations to call for Europe-wide codes of conduct which could be adopted by large firms on a voluntary basis. There is some question as to the demand for, and exact content of, such a voluntary code, but more importantly the Commission is unlikely to abdicate completely its regulatory ambitions in the area of corporate law.

4.4. Some Comparisons

There is a close correspondence between the control/liquidity tradeoff as reflected in the financial system and the nature of the legal system. Control-oriented financial systems for the most part have enterprise-based legal systems, and arm's-length systems have company-based systems. This basic compatibility impedes convergence and institutional reform, in particular at the level of the European Union.

Another observation concerns potential regulatory biases affecting the control/liquidity tradeoff. Bhide (1993) argues that government policy in the United States has acted systematically to constrain concentration of ownership and to promote liquidity directly. The situation in western Europe is less clear. Though different from its US counterpart, regulation in the United Kingdom – whether self-enforced or based on government enforcement – also appears to have a liquidity bias. The more lenient disclosure requirements and insider regulation suggest that lawmakers on the European continent have gone, if anything, in the opposite direction. In addition, supervision is less vigorous, and enforcement rare. With some notable exceptions, regulators have also taken a hands-off approach to the various ways in which financial institutions have managed to circumvent existing regulation limiting their role in corporate governance. The liquidity bias has probably been mitigated by the use of control mechanisms, such as dual-class shares, allowing them to raise capital without giving up control.

The control mechanisms in use cover a broad spectrum of arrangements. Holding companies are important ingredients in corporate governance in many countries, particularly in Belgium and Germany.[36] Closed-end mutual funds and dual-class shares have been the prime vehicles of control in Sweden.[37] In Germany and Sweden, and particularly in Italy, pyramiding plays an important role.[38] Proxy votes held by banks on behalf of small investors, and crossholdings of shares, are other ways of concentrating control in Germany.[39] Voting trusts and special golden shares serve the same purpose in Dutch corporate governance.

[36] Wymeersch (1994).

[37] Isaksson and Skog (1993).

[38] See, for Germany, Franks and Mayer (1994); and for Italy, Barca (1995).

[39] Wymeersch (1994).

Despite legal restrictions, corporations in France have complicated crossholding arrangements to ensure concentration of control, and the government has maintained potential influence in large privatized firms through golden shares.

While these arrangements differ substantially, giving each financial system its specific characteristics, their ultimate objective is the same: to allow investors to increase the span of control without a corresponding capital contribution, or to raise additional capital without diluting control. Unfortunately, available theory and data do not yet allow us adequately to measure their relative effectiveness in this respect, or the extent to which they have been fully exploited. Neither do we know the costs of these mechanisms in terms of poorer incentives for controlling owners, but there is some evidence that shares in firms with these types of arrangements trade at considerable discounts.[40]

Most countries in Europe have some restrictions on the ownership of equity by financial institutions, but in many cases these investors have found ways of circumventing the rules. For example, Swedish banks were until recently prevented from holding equity in non-financial corporations, but nevertheless found ways of exercising considerable control through closely related investment companies. While formal restrictions on bank ownership in Germany have been lax, political pressure has been strong on the large commercial banks to limit their holdings of equity in individual companies. Nevertheless, as shown in Table 3, the banks' share of outstanding stock increased during the 1970s and 1980s. More importantly, through the extensive use of proxy votes banks have managed to exercise substantial potential control in large companies. All this suggests strong forces sustaining existing governance arrangements, and a willingness by governments to accommodate them.

5. COMPETITION AND CONVERGENCE OF FINANCE SYSTEMS

The basic tenet of this chapter is that the observed corporate governance patterns and legal systems in Europe impede the liquidity of secondary equity markets. There are two primary reasons why this may be the case. First, many of the existing corporate governance arrangements in Europe are anathema to the development of liquid secondary markets: issuers and investors have deliberately traded off liquidity against control. Second, the differences in corporate governance arrangements *per se* impose costs on issuers and investors wishing to transcend

[40] For example, shares in Belgian holding companies trade at discounts sometimes as high as 50 percent. The price of closed-end mutual funds in Sweden – the control vehicles of the large bank-centred corporate groupings – also reflects substantial discounts. The Amsterdam Stock Exchange claims that Dutch stocks trade at discounts of between 10 and 20 percent owing to the widespread use of mechanisms separating control from capital contribution (Wymeersch 1994).

national boundaries. This section discusses the scope for change in existing governance patterns through either evolution or reform, but first we briefly elaborate why these patterns matter to the creation of more uniform, and more liquid, exchanges in Europe.

The choices made by individual issuers and investors in the liquidity/control tradeoff have implications for the entire national market: when most stocks are illiquid, so is the entire market. This, in turn, affects the gains from further integration: integrating very illiquid exchanges may do little to improve overall liquidity. Differences across national markets in the individual tradeoff decisions are reinforced by liquidity externalities: when one firm's stock becomes more liquid, this improves the liquidity of other stocks listed on the same exchange. While issuers and investors have found mechanisms for improving liquidity without dispersing control, the relative illiquidity on many continental European markets suggests that they have not been entirely successful. There is also an issue as to whether the power of these mechanisms has been exhausted, and future capital increases may have to come at the expense of concentration of ownership.

The existence of differences in corporate governance patterns *per se* does not necessarily prohibit, or even impede, trading on an exchange. Firms with very different ownership and control structures coexist on most exchanges, seemingly without negative consequences for volatility and liquidity. Indeed, such variation is desirable to the extent that it increases the range of options open to investors. Even having firms incorporated under different state company laws does not seem to have a negative effect on trading on the New York Stock Exchange. However, the differences in corporate governance arrangements and supporting legal structures in Europe are much greater and qualitatively different from, for example, those among states in the United States. An admittedly UK-biased study by the UK Department of Trade and Industry identified a number of structural differences impeding cross-border transactions in the EU. The list includes availability of information, the relative influence of different stakeholders, taxation, accounting standards, and supervisory practices. To this one could add variation in listing requirements (and thus in the information conveyed by a listing), takeover regulation, and minority protection. Such differences are likely to be particularly important for small investors. However, there is evidence that large sophisticated investors also suffer from these impediments.[41] Furthermore,

[41] For example, the case of the attempted takeover of the German tyre manufacturer Continental by its Italian competitor Pirelli illustrates that the costs can also be considerable for large investors. As described by Baums (1994), Pirelli committed several severe legal errors in the course of the negotiations, and may well have lost the battle as a result. The company also misjudged the defensive capabilities of Continental and the closeness of its ties to various other stakeholders. The planned merger between Volvo and Renault, and Agnelli's attempt to gain control over Perrier, are other examples where misunderstandings of local corporate governance arrangements played an important role in the outcome.

the cross-country differences are likely to be more severe for control-oriented transactions than for transactions involving arm's-length finance.

5.1. Competition Between Systems

One way of bringing about greater uniformity in corporate governance arrangements would be through competition. Systems can compete in two ways: either by attracting firms or simply by being more efficient. Firms could, for example, be attracted through regulatory competition: issuers would move to the jurisdiction where the rules were most favourable to them. In the United States, 80 percent of changes in the state of incorporation are to Delaware, suggesting that corporate laws play an important role in this decision.[42] Migration of firms from one system to another is much more difficult in Europe, primarily for cultural reasons, but this is also due to the strong interconnectedness between financing arrangements, legal rules, and the rest of the economy. In addition, unlike the United States where statutory domicile is the dominant principle, the European Union follows the physical-presence rule based on location of activities. In the absence of mobility of firms across systems, adjustments would have to come from within.

The lack of migration and the persistence in differences between types of financial systems within the European Union would clearly be less of a concern if one type of system were gradually gaining ground simply as a result of its greater efficiency. If, in addition, the 'winning' system were one where liquid markets played an important role, this would be good news for the liquidity of secondary equity markets in Europe. However, changes in national corporate governance patterns, if they come, are unlikely to be brought about by competition among financial systems. Leaving aside the issue of whether competition among systems makes economic sense – at least the notion of competitiveness at this level is problematic – it is in corporations, not systems, that corporate governance arrangements compete. When corporations are not competitive owing to governance failure, any correction will be brought about by the mechanisms of that particular system. Only if the financial system of a country repeatedly failed to undertake such corrective actions would we see something like one system losing out. But even then it is not clear what forces would bring about change in the inferior system: a system that fails to undertake corrective actions in individual firms may do even worse when attempting to make a radical alteration in its own way of functioning.

There is no evidence of major differences in the effectiveness of corporate governance arrangements of large firms in different countries, at least not between

[42] Romano (1993).

those of the United States, Japan, and Germany.[43] Management is equally likely, or unlikely, to be replaced following poor performance or shortage in cash flows in these three systems. But the processes whereby this discipline operates may be quite different. In Japan, a company's main bank, as the largest lender and a significant shareholder, is instrumental in initiating change by sending out directors and coordinating corporate stakeholders.[44] In the United Kingdom, corrective actions could originate in the board of directors, which may or may not contain representatives of important investors. However, non-financial corporations holding or acquiring large stakes in the company seem to play a role in correcting managerial failure, at least in medium-sized firms: the market for corporate control, in the sense of hostile takeovers, appears to be less important in this respect.[45]

Each system thus has its own specific set of mechanisms for bringing about change. For example, when confronted with increasing international competition, in particular from Japan, during the 1970s and early 1980s, US and German corporate governance arrangements appear to have responded quite differently. In the United States, the number of takeovers, including hostile takeovers, increased dramatically and attempts were subsequently made to activate the board of directors. In Germany, on the other hand, substantial restructuring was associated with increased concentration in shareholdings and less influence from supervisory boards.

Yet another problem with the view that competition will bring about convergence is that efficiency as such seems to have played a limited role in determining the evolution of financial systems. The institutional arrangements appear to be as much an outcome of political processes. Mark Roe's work provides ample illustration of the importance of populist pressures in the United States in bringing about the regulatory framework which has been so important in shaping corporate governance patterns in that country.[46] The German system of co-determination is largely a product of the political climate after the Second World War. A discussion of the politics of financial system evolution is beyond the scope of this chapter, but it is probably a good guess that the constituencies in favour of protecting the status quo are at least as strong as those pushing towards convergence.

5.2. The Forces of Convergence

If one system is not going to overtake the other, perhaps the different systems will converge under the pressure from outside forces. Claims of convergence are often heard but seldom substantiated. Financial systems have many dimensions,

[43] Kaplan (1994).
[44] Kaplan and Minton (1994).
[45] Franks, Mayer, and Rennebog (1995).
[46] For elaboration of this argument, see Coffee (1991) and Roe (1994).

and convergence in one dimension does not imply convergence in another. There are nevertheless some common external factors affecting the evolution of financial systems.

Internationalization. The most frequently mentioned, and possibly most important, force towards convergence is internationalization. Obviously, large corporations are becoming increasingly international, and flows of real and financial capital across borders have reached previously unimaginable proportions. Corporate financing patterns have followed suit, with large firms seeking to raise ever greater shares of their finance in international markets, and investors becoming more global in their investment behaviour. These developments have left imprints in the ownership structure of individual corporations. The share of the capital stock owned by foreign investors, mostly institutions, has increased in most countries in the European Union (see Table 3). The fact that the same investors are active in many different financial systems should foster convergence of governance patterns.

Competition in many product markets is also becoming increasingly international, and strategic behaviour more global, with stronger interdependence across national markets. The effects on corporate governance are difficult to foresee. On the one hand, the increasing size and complexity of these corporations make control-oriented finance more costly. On the other hand, the more intense strategic interaction and speed in competitive responses are likely to increase the need for investor intervention. Globalization notwithstanding, most multinational corporations have clearly identifiable home countries, and the conditions in the home country have often been an important explanatory factor in their success.[47] One of the roles of a home country may be to provide effective corporate governance.

Despite the internationalization of corporate finance, corporate governance remains remarkably national. For example, in Sweden, with one of the most internationalized industries, the national financial system still plays an important role in monitoring the large multinational firms. Corporations like SKF, Electrolux, and Sandvik, heavily reliant on exports and with most of their employees outside Sweden, are controlled by Swedish investors. Even ABB – often claimed to be the archetype of the global corporation, with its headquarters in Switzerland and a complex international organization – remains firmly in the hands of the Swedish Wallenberg group. The multinational corporations originating in countries with arm's-length financial systems also seem to retain the corporate governance patterns of their home countries.

[47] Porter (1990).

Institutionalization. Over the past two decades direct household share ownership has decreased in importance in most European countries: in several national markets their share of total stocks outstanding is now below 20 percent (see Table 3). Institutionalization typically reflects both an increase in the share of total wealth managed by institutions, and a shift in the portfolio of households away from direct holdings of equity.[48] The effect of increasing institutional ownership on corporate governance is less clear. The orientation of institutions often reflects the general nature of the financial system in which they operate. In control-oriented financial systems, institutional investors tend to be control-oriented. Large banks and insurance companies, but also pension funds to the extent that they exist, often get actively involved in governance. In arm's-length financial systems, institutions typically stay on the side-line. During the 1980s the increase in institutional ownership in countries with control-oriented systems came largely in control-oriented institutions; and in arm's-length systems portfolio-oriented institutions became more important.[49] In other words, institutionalization has until now, if anything, reinforced existing differences between financial systems.

There are, however, also important signs of convergence. In many countries institutional investors have come under severe criticism. The national debates largely reflect the differences in financial systems. In the United States and the United Kingdom, the primary concern has been with the lack of monitoring by institutions with large holdings in individual firms. The German discussion, on the other hand, has focused on the *excessive* influence exercised by large institutions, in particular the main commercial banks. To some extent the corporate governance approaches of institutional investors have responded to these pressures.

Institutional shareholder intervention has often been triggered by shareholder activism, as in the cases of, for example, General Motors and American Express in the United States, and Navigation Mixte and Suez in France. However, whereas shareholder activism in arm's-length systems has involved investors more in corporate governance, the same phenomenon in control-oriented systems may come to undermine existing governance arrangements. One price paid for greater and more effective investor involvement in monitoring has in many cases been less minority protection. With more powerful non-controlling shareholders, possibly reinforced by improved legal minority protection, controlling owners in closely held listed firms may face a choice between selling off their blocks and taking the firms private. This may be a contributing factor to the many withdrawals from European exchanges in recent years, with some exchanges experiencing a net reduction in the number of listed firms.

[48] Berglöf (1988).
[49] Ibid.

Reactions by institutional investors have also come by default. Institutions in the United States and the United Kingdom have increasingly found themselves so large that they can no longer trade without affecting the price, and thus, reluctantly, have taken on more long-term positions in individual firms. As a result, incentives to monitor have been strengthened, and in some highly publicized cases institutional investors have played an important role in bringing about change. In Germany, on the other hand, better access of corporations to alternative sources of finance has weakened the ability of the large banks to exert influence.

The net effect of institutionalization on the degree of control-orientation is thus unclear, but the significance of the strategic governance choices of institutional investors will increase dramatically as a result of national pension reforms in Europe. As a result of ageing populations, most countries are moving towards funded schemes, with far-reaching consequences for corporate ownership.[50] These new institutional investors should be expected to account for more than 25 percent of total shareholdings in many European countries within the next decade, although this would still be less than the current share of pension funds in the United Kingdom and the United States. If these institutions become more like other institutional investors operating in the same system, the effects on corporate governance will be small. The Dutch experience with capitalized pension funds and large insurance companies also suggests that their impact may be limited. If, as is more likely, the new pension funds choose to emulate their UK and US counterparts, changes may be substantial, pushing the Continental systems towards a greater arm's-length orientation and more liquid equity markets. This, in turn, would give rise to a whole new agenda of corporate governance reform in these countries.

Financial innovation. The past two decades have seen a rapid development of new financial instruments and new markets for previously existing instruments. Derivatives are steadily gaining in importance, in particular in international finance. Securitization has dramatically changed credit markets and the nature of banking. These developments have been more pronounced in countries with arm's-length financial systems, but they have also increased the role of arm's-length finance in traditionally control-oriented systems. However, despite deeper and more liquid financial markets, ownership of corporations has become more concentrated in many control-oriented countries; one interpretation being that controlling investors have reacted by fortifying their positions to ward off potential takeover threats.

[50] Davis (1993).

Financial innovation can also support control-oriented arrangements. The mechanisms designed to raise capital without diluting control can be viewed in this light. A recent example may indicate where the process is going. To circumvent restrictions on shareholdings by foreign investors in Qantas Airlines, New Zealand banks have created synthetic shares which replicate dividend characteristics and price movements of underlying shares without conferring voting rights. These synthetic instruments are then sold to foreign investors. While still resisted by issuers, the creation of such instruments may become an important tool for them to increase liquidity without changing control structures. Some investment banks have also developed products which allow investors to unwind, and create, large controlling blocks at low cost. It is in the nature of financial innovation that the future is hard to foresee, but the process is, at least in part, driven by demand within a given financial system. These demands are likely to reflect existing institutional arrangements.

Technological and regulatory developments may also affect the role of banks in corporate governance. In countries with arm's-length financial systems, in particular in the United States, banks have been severely restricted in the exercise of corporate governance: commercial and investment banking have been separated and banks have been curtailed in their growth by various regulations. In the United Kingdom, universal banking is allowed, but banks have been discouraged from holding large equity holdings in individual firms. The internationalization and rapidly changing technologies of banking have undermined much of this regulation. Regulatory competition has led to the spread of universal banking. Many of the emerging economies in Eastern and Central Europe have also adopted such legislation, largely modelled on the German system. Again, the net effect on corporate governance is uncertain – it depends on the strategic choices of these universal banks. However, more sophisticated corporate customers and an eroding informational advantage of banks over markets may trigger a change in the role of banks, from monitoring to providing *ex post* flexibility in cash-flow fluctuations: bank finance is easier to renegotiate than bond finance.

Thus while there are important forces pulling, or pushing, financial systems in the same direction, we conjecture that they will take time to work their way through, and change may not always go in the direction of convergence of systems. Moreover, these forces will have to be channelled through the internal mechanisms in each system. New practices will have to spread, and ownership and control structures change. Existing financial systems have, by definition, demonstrated some survival properties, and the strong interconnectedness between the different dimensions of a financial system suggests significant inertia.

5.3. Convergence or Not, and to What?

We cannot, therefore, rely on competition among systems to bring about the institutional changes necessary to increase the liquidity of secondary equity markets and reduce the differences among financial systems in Europe; the forces towards convergence are also, at least to some extent, offset by countervailing influences reinforcing traits of existing systems. Moreover, even where there is pressure towards convergence it may not always go in the direction of less control-orientation and more arm's-length features. Indeed, along some important dimensions the opposite appears to be true. There is some undisputed convergence in governance practices: the use of specialized committees has spread from the United States and Canada to the United Kingdom and is now being considered in, for example, Germany; the German-style separation of the positions of chairman and chief executive officer is becoming increasingly common in Anglo-Saxon countries; and the accountability of directors is being strengthened in many countries.[51]

However, the widely held view that corporate governance arrangements are slowly converging towards some Anglo-American-style system is a rather empty, or even misleading, one. First of all, there are important differences between the United States and the United Kingdom: for instance, US banks still face considerably more legal restrictions on the activities in which they can engage. Second, both these systems, and that of the United States in particular,[52] are undergoing considerable change, with fundamental restructuring and reorientation of the banking sector accompanied by adjustments in the regulatory framework. It is very hard at this point to picture the new institutional arrangements emerging out of this process.

Despite the tradeoff between ownership concentration and the liquidity of markets there are signs that new hybrid systems are emerging, with strong control-orientation but liquid markets for financial instruments. Such hybrid systems may be able to combine some of the benefits of arm's-length and control-oriented finance: exogenous increases in liquidity bring down the costs of concentrating control. However, the long-term survival properties of these systems are still unknown. A corporate governance vacuum could develop, leaving management more scope to build empires and enjoy the fruits of power. Hybrid systems may also get 'stuck in the middle' for lack of mechanisms to achieve institutional change.

[51] International Capital Markets Group (1995).

[52] In the United States, lawmakers are currently debating draft bills to liberalize restrictions in the Glass-Steagall Act.

6. CONCLUSIONS

The basic issue addressed in this chapter is whether existing corporate governance arrangements impede the liquidity of secondary equity markets in Europe and, if so, what the implications are for policy-makers. This section summarizes the main conclusions.

- **There is a strong correlation between corporate financing patterns and the liquidity of equity markets in Europe.** In control-oriented financial systems, such as the German one, ownership is concentrated and markets relatively illiquid. Arm's-length financial systems of the type found in the United Kingdom are characterized by dispersed shareholdings and high market liquidity.
- **Existing corporate governance arrangements in Europe severely impede the development of more uniform, and more liquid, secondary equity markets.** Not only are certain corporate governance arrangements anathema to the development of active markets, but the large differences *per se* impose substantial costs on investors.
- **There is a fundamental tradeoff between concentration of ownership and liquidity of shares.** Concentration reduces liquidity by limiting the number of traders in the market. If ownership concentration is a necessary (but of course not sufficient) condition for effective corporate governance, improvements in liquidity may involve costs in terms of less effective monitoring of corporations.
- **Issuers can escape the liquidity/control tradeoff through various mechanisms, but only at the cost of worsening incentives for controlling owners.** These mechanisms – e.g. dual-class shares, pyramiding, and proxy votes – reduce controlling owners' share of cash flows, and thus may make them less likely to take value-maximizing decisions, and more prone to exploit other stakeholders. This can explain the frequent claims of inactivity and misguided governance among controlling investors on the European continent.
- **The reverse is also true: i.e. attempts to strengthen incentives of controlling owners have costs in terms of liquidity.** For example, eliminating dual-class shares in order to better motivate investors will most likely make the stock less liquid.
- **But, despite frequent claims to the contrary, improvements in liquidity do not necessarily come at the expense of corporate governance.** In fact, improved liquidity achieved, for example, through the elimination of barriers to cross-border trading should facilitate the accumulation of controlling blocks in secondary markets.

- **The nature of conflicts between stakeholders of the firm, and thus the legal framework required, depend on ownership patterns.** In closely held firms, most conflicts will be between controlling owners and other suppliers of capital: i.e. among investors. When firms are widely held, the overriding conflict is between management and investors.
- **The roles of different corporate institutions are also radically different when ownership is concentrated than when it is widely dispersed.** For example, voting procedures in the general assembly and the composition of the board of directors are of limited importance when one owner, or group of owners, controls the majority of votes. Outside directors should not be expected to take independent stands when the controlling owner can hire and fire them at will.
- **Financing arrangements and legal systems also appear to be closely interrelated in practice.** Systems dominated by control-oriented finance tend to have enterprise-based legal systems. However, there are some countries, such as Belgium and France, where legal systems are in transition, and others, such as Sweden and the Netherlands, that combine elements of different financial systems. It is too early to evaluate the long-term sustainability of these systems.
- **Concentration of ownership may both substitute for and complement the legal framework.** In the absence of a well-functioning legal framework, a large personal stake may be the only way for an entrepreneur to commit not to steal from the company. On the other hand, and possibly more importantly, lawmakers may not need to regulate and involve courts when decisions can be delegated to clearly identifiable investors with large controlling stakes.
- **The market for corporate control is important in most countries, but its functioning differs across countries.** The United Kingdom is the only country where hostile takeovers play a significant role, and where most control transactions take place on an official exchange. In many countries on the European continent, takeovers are primarily an instrument for withdrawing companies from the stock exchange. Trade in controlling blocks is nevertheless important and typically takes place outside exchanges.
- **Institutional ownership has become increasingly important in virtually all countries in western Europe, but it has taken different forms of expression.** In the United Kingdom, portfolio-oriented pension funds dominate, but on the European continent commercial banks and non-financial corporations are still the most important institutional owners.
- **Common shocks may lead to very different responses in different**

financial systems. In an arm's-length system, an outside shock may give rise to increased takeover activity and activation of outside directors, while in a control-oriented system ownership is likely to become more concentrated and boards, if anything, may lose in importance.

- **Competitive pressure may reinforce rather than alter basic features of systems.** Change, if it comes, is likely to be driven largely by other forces. For example, the ongoing and planned reforms of pension systems on the European continent are likely to alter dramatically the structure of ownership in firms and, as a result, corporate governance patterns.
- **Recent research suggests, however, that the evolution of financial systems is as much a political process as it is an economic one.** Even if fundamental reform of financial systems were economically feasible, and desirable, it is not clear that the necessary constituencies for change could be formed. Indeed, the various stakeholders may have an interest in the preservation of the status quo.
- **There are strong forces for persistence in corporate governance systems.** The bias towards the political status quo, the interrelatedness of different aspects of the financial system, and the system-specific ways of dealing with external shocks suggest that changes in fundamental features will be slow.

7. POLICY IMPLICATIONS

If existing corporate governance patterns constrain the liquidity of European equity markets, there may be a role for public policy-makers. This section draws some policy implications:

- **Restrictions on ownership concentration or the exercise of control are likely to be costly ways of improving liquidity.** Voting caps and limits on the share of equity in individual firms of certain investors, such as insurance companies and pension funds, may be justified for other reasons, but possible gains in liquidity will be achieved at the expense of corporate governance.
- **Prohibitions on the use of mechanisms for separating control from capital contribution will, if anything, reduce liquidity.** Forbidding deviations from 'one-share-one-vote' will force controlling owners to hold larger stakes and thus reduce the number of traders in secondary markets.
- **In general, corporate governance reform is a risky way of improving liquidity.** For such reform to have a positive impact on liquidity it would have to go in the direction of arm's-length financial systems and company-

based legal systems. The evidence on the relative advantages of different systems is still inconclusive, and we do not know much about the interdependence between financing patterns and other socio-economic variables.

- **Liquidity should be addressed directly, rather than through restrictions on concentration of ownership.** Further integration of equity markets, achieved despite the impediments arising from existing ownership and control patterns, will improve liquidity by bringing in more traders. This, in turn, is likely to have a beneficial impact on corporate governance by facilitating the accumulation of controlling blocks.
- **Regulators cannot rely on competition between regulatory systems to harmonize corporate governance patterns.** The apparent interconnectedness between legal systems and financing arrangements, and between these arrangements and other aspects of the economy, impedes such competition. The physical presence rule for determining the legal domicile further limits the mobility of companies.
- **Efforts to harmonize the structure and control of corporations at the level of the European Union are unlikely to succeed.** Corporate governance reform, if undertaken, would most probably extend beyond issues of finance to the functioning of labour markets and firm organization. Finding the necessary political support for such changes is difficult.
- **Even if adopted against all odds, the 'European Company' (*Société Européenne*) is unlikely to have a positive impact on liquidity.** While some firms may opt out of other forms of incorporation – for example, to avoid co-determination requirements – ownership structures are unlikely to change. Indeed, new untested corporate forms could conceivably reduce liquidity, at least temporarily.
- **The subsidiarity principle should generally apply with regard to corporate governance regulation.** Most of the issues involved are best settled at the level of the individual Member States.
- **But the European Union should not, and is unlikely to, completely abdicate its regulatory role in the general area of corporate governance.** There may still be scope for further Community-wide regulation in areas such as disclosure requirements and insider trading.
- **A voluntary 'code of conduct' for firms, suggested by some lobbying groups, is most probably a non-starter.** Such a proposal fails to address the fundamental differences in corporate governance arrangements. Moreover, a voluntary code would affect only a small number of large companies, most of which already span borders, and therefore would be of little consequence for liquidity. In any case, the Commission is unlikely to endorse this initiative.

- **The market might benefit considerably, however, if firms were merely obliged to disclose their governance practices.** Annual reports should contain information on such things as the composition of the board (executive versus non-executive directors, relationship to major shareholders etc.), existence and role of additional committees, procedures for appointment of directors, managerial compensation schemes, and internal and external control practices. Increased corporate transparency brings down barriers to integration, and thus improves liquidity.
- **If the Commission is to play a role in corporate governance reform, the present deadlock over legal harmonization must be broken.** One way of achieving this objective would be to involve not only Directorate General XV (internal market and financial services), but also Directorate General III (industry) and possibly Directorate General II (economic and financial affairs). Corporate governance is about decisions directly affecting the management and organization of companies. Approaching the issue as one of horizontal industrial policy, as many Member States and parts of the OECD already do, could pave the way for a new and more constructive debate where governance arrangements are viewed in their proper context. Improving the effectiveness of such arrangements is a task of utmost importance to the long-term efficiency and growth of European industry.

References

Aghion, Philippe and Patrick Bolton, 1992. 'An "Incomplete Contract" Approach to Bankruptcy and the Financial Structure of the Firm', *Review of Economic Studies*, 59: 473–94.

Barca, Fabrizio, 1995. 'On Corporate Governance in Italy: Issues, Facts and Agenda', paper presented at OECD Conference 'The Influence of Corporate Governance and Financing Structures on Economic Performance'.

Baums, Theodor, 1994. 'Corporate Governance in Germany – System and Recent Developments', in Isaksson and Skog (eds), *Aspects of Corporate Governance*, Juristforlaget, Stockholm.

Berglöf, Erik, 1988. *Owners and Their Control over Corporations – A Comparison of Six Financial Systems*, Ministry of Industry, Stockholm.

Bhide, Amir, 1993. 'The Hidden Costs of Stock Market Liquidity', *Journal of Financial Economics* 334: 31–51.

Bolton, Patrick and Ernst-Ludwig von Thadden, 1995. 'The Ownership Structure of Firms: the Liquidity/Control Trade-Off', paper presented at the Nobel Symposium on 'Law and Finance' in Stockholm.

Borio, Claudio, 1990. 'Leverage and Financing of Non-financial Companies: An International Perspective', Bank for International Settlements Economic Papers.

Cadbury Report, 1992. 'Report of the Committee on the Financial Aspects of Corporate Governance', Gee, London.

Coffee, Jack, 1991. 'Liquidity vs. Control: The Institutional Investor as Corporate Monitor', *Columbia Law Review* 91: 1277–1368.

Corbett, J. and T. Jenkinson, 1994. 'The Financing of Industry, 1970-89: An International Comparison', Working Paper 948, Centre for Economic Policy Research, London.

Davis, E. P., 1993. 'The Development of Pension Funds: An Approaching Revolution for Continental Europe', American Express Awards.

Demsetz, Harold, 1968. 'The Cost of Transactions', *Quarterly Journal of Economics* 82: 33–53.

Demsetz, Harold and Kenneth Lehn, 1985. 'The Structure of Corporate Ownership: Causes and Consequences', *Journal of Political Economy* 93: 1155–77.

Edwards, Jeremy and Klaus Fischer, 1994. *Banks, Finance and Investment in Germany*, Cambridge University Press.

Franks, Julian and Colin Mayer, 1994. 'The Ownership and Control of German Corporations', mimeo, London Business School.

Franks, Julian, Colin Mayer and Luc Rennebog, 1995. 'The Role of Takeovers in Corporate Governance', mimeo, London Business School.

Gilson, R., 1992. 'The Political Ecology of Takeovers: Thoughts on Harmonizing the European Corporate Governance Environment', *Fordham Law Review,* 61.

Gorton, Gary and Schmid, 1995. 'Universal Banking and the Performance of German Firms', mimeo, Wharton School.

Galve Gorriz, Carmen and Vicente Salas Fumas, 1993. 'Propriedad y resultados de la gran empresa Española', *Investigaciones Economicas*, 17 (2): 207–38.

Gottschalk, A., 1988. *Der Stimmrechtseinfluss der Banken in den Aktionarsversammlungen von Grossunternehmen*, WSI–Mitteilungen.

Grossman, Sanford and Oliver Hart, 1986. 'The Costs and Benefits of Ownership: A Theory of Vertical and Lateral Integration', *Journal of Political Economy* 94: 691–719.

Hart, Oliver and John Moore, 1994. 'A Theory of Debt Based on the Inalienability of Human Capital', *Quarterly Journal of Economics* 109, 841–79.

Holmström, Bengt and Jean Tirole, 1994. 'Financial Intermediation and the Real Sector', mimeo, Centre for Economic Policy Research, London.

International Capital Markets Group, 1995. *International Corporate Governance. Who holds the Reins?*, ICMG, London.

Isaksson, M. and R. Skog, 1993. 'Corporate Governance in Swedish Listed Companies', in Baums *et al.* (eds), *Institutional Investors*, Walter Greuyt & Co, Berlin.

Kaplan, Steven N., 1994. 'Top Executive Rewards and Firm Performance: A Comparison of Japan and the U.S.', *Journal of Political Economy*, 102 (3): 510–46.

Kaplan, Steven N. and Bernadette A. Minton, 1994. 'Appointments of Outsiders to Japanese Boards: Determinants and Implications for Managers', *Journal of Financial Economics*, 36 (2): 225–58.

Lannoo, Karel, 1994. 'Corporate Governance in Europe', mimeo, Centre for European Policy Studies.

Mayer, Colin, 1990. 'Financial Systems, Corporate Finance, and Economic Development', in Glenn Hubbard (ed.), *Asymmetric Information, Corporate Finance, and Investment*, National Bureau of Economic Research, Chicago, Chicago University Press, 307–332.

Morin, Franççois, 1994. 'Liaisons financières et cooperation des acteurs-systèmes', *Revue Economique,* 45 (6): 1459–70.

Pagano, Marco, 1993. 'The Flotation of Companies on the Stock Market: a Coordination Failure Model', *European Economic Review* (Special Issue on Finance), 37(5), 1101–25.

Pagano, Marco and Ailsa Röell, 1995. 'The Choice of Stock Ownership Structure: Agency Costs, Monitoring and Liquidity', mimeo, Université Libre de Bruxelles.

Porter, M., 1990. *The Competitive Advantage of Nations,* Macmillan, London and Basingstoke.

Prentice, David, 1993. *Groups of Companies in the EC*, De Greuyter, Hamburg.

Rajan, Raghuram and Luigi Zingales, 1994. 'What Do We Know About Capital Structure? Some Evidence from International Data', mimeo, University of Chicago.

Roe, Mark, 1994. *Strong Managers, Weak Owners: The Political Roots of American Corporate Finance*, Princeton University Press, Princeton, NJ.

Romano, Roberta, 1993. *The Genius of American Corporate Law*, American Enterprise Institute Press, Washington, DC.

Shleifer, Andrei and Robert Vishny, 1995. 'A Survey of Corporate Governance', paper presented at the Nobel Symposium on 'Law and Finance' in Stockholm.

Wymeersch, Eddy, 1994. 'Elements of Comparative Corporate Governance in Western Europe', in Isaksson and Skog (eds), *Aspects of Corporate Governance*, Juristforlaget, Stockholm.

Chapter 6

PENSION FUND INVESTMENTS

INTRODUCTION

This chapter analyses the determinants of equity holdings of pension funds in the EU, with particular reference to the influence of regulation on equity investment – both domestic and international. In a nutshell, pension funds could provide a major stimulus to the development of equity markets in the EU, and this would in turn offer benefits such as improved liquidity, a lower cost of capital, provision of risk capital, and finance for privatizations,[1] but this requires a more appropriate regulatory framework to be adopted in a number of countries.

The argument follows several steps. First, we examine the likely role of equities in the portfolio of pension funds, in the absence of restrictive regulation. This gives an indication of the potential for existing pension funds to contribute to the development of equity markets. Second, we outline the degree to which regulations, particularly those relating to portfolio restrictions and funding rules, may limit the degree to which funds may invest in equities. In a third section, we focus on the effects of such regulations on actual portfolios, as well as assessing the degree to which other extraneous factors may influence equity holdings. Estimates of the returns on actual portfolios relative to the portfolios that might be adopted in the absence of regulation are shown in a fourth section; this analysis enables the economic costs of regulatory and other barriers to be identified. Last, we briefly consider the question of the determinants of the development of funds *per se*, as opposed to pay-as-you-go social security. This is justified since the size of funds is itself a major main influence on the growth of equity markets, and is directly amenable to policy action. The concluding section includes a summary and outlines some issues for policy-makers. It considers in particular action at the EU level in the Pension Funds Directive, why it failed, and what the prospects are for further deregulation at a Union level.

We will focus largely on pension funds in the United Kingdom, Germany, the Netherlands, Denmark, Belgium, Ireland, and Sweden – the principal

[1] Davis (1993a) and Davis (1995).

Table 1. Assets of Pension Funds, end-1993 (US$ bn)

	Stock of assets (end-1993) $ bn	% of GDP	% foreign assets	Equity market cap/GDP
United Kingdom	717	82	31	79
Germany	106	6	8	22
Netherlands	261	85	21	42
Sweden (1991)	39	16	1	n/a
Denmark	26	19	4	28
Ireland	18	44	41	28
France	41	3	2	36
Italy	12	1	4	16
Belgium	7	3	37	31
Spain	10	2	10	24
Portugal	5	7	10	14

Source: European Federation for Retirement Provision/EU Committee. Includes only independent (private- and public-sector) funded schemes.

EU countries in which private pension funds are currently established (see Table 1), but information is also provided, where possible, for other countries – notably France and Italy – where funds are likely to develop strongly in the coming years as pay-as-you-go social security or supplementary pension systems are cut back.[2]

Before commencing, we offer four key definitions. In a *funded pension plan*, pension commitments are covered in advance by accumulation of real or financial assets. In *pay-as-you-go plans*, in contrast, contributions of employers and current employees are relied on to pay pensions directly. Social security systems are pay-as-you-go in most countries, while private pension plans tend to be funded. In a *defined-benefit pension plan,* which still predominate in most EU countries other than Denmark, the pension formula is defined in advance by the sponsor, independently of the contributions and asset returns. There is a distinction between the pension *plan*, which sets out rights and obligations, and the pension *fund* which guarantees that finance for such promises is available. In contrast, in *defined-contribution pension plans* only contributions are fixed, and benefits therefore depend solely on the returns on the assets of the fund; the plan and the fund are the same. A key economic difference between defined-benefit and defined-contribution plans is that with the former there can be risk-sharing between worker and company as well as between younger and older members.[3] These risk-sharing features are absent with defined-contribution plans.

[2] See Federal Trust (1995).

[3] In effect, younger members may accept occasional shortfalls in the coverage of their pension rights while the older workers continue to receive their pensions.

1. HOW MIGHT FUNDS BE INVESTED IN THE ABSENCE OF REGULATION?

This section seeks to trace the economic influences on portfolio distributions of pension funds, which would operate freely in the absence of portfolio and funding regulations. In general, equity holdings must be viewed in the context of portfolio optimization on the part of pension funds in the same way as for any other wealth-holder – seeking an optimal trade-off of risk and return – but clearly the nature of liabilities influence the asset holding that is selected.

In the context of such general portfolio considerations, a first point to note is that in most cases pension funds already hold a greater proportion of capital in uncertain and long-term assets than households. For example, equity holdings of pension funds in 1992 varied from 80 percent of the portfolio in the UK to 2 percent in Sweden (Table 2). But in most cases they compared favourably with personal-sector equity holdings. In the EU, foreign assets of pension funds are concentrated in UK, Irish, Belgian, and Dutch funds (such investment is itself limited by regulation for funds in countries such as Germany), but personal-sector foreign-asset holdings are relatively minor. On the other hand, the personal sector tends to hold a much larger proportion of liquid assets than pension funds do.

These differences can be explained partly by *time-horizons*, which for persons are relatively short, whereas given the long-term nature of liabilities, pension funds may concentrate portfolios on long-term assets such as equities and property yielding the highest returns (see section 3). Second, pension funds have a comparative advantage in compensating for the increased risk of holding equities, by pooling across assets whose returns are imperfectly correlated. A third point is that the portfolio distribution and the corresponding return and risk on the assets held, in relation to the growth of earnings, determine the cost to a company of providing a pension in a defined-benefit plan[4] and the replacement ratio[5] obtainable via an occupational or personal defined-contribution fund.[6] Implicitly, liabilities are typically defined in real terms. This link of liabilities to earnings points to a crucial difference between pension funds and insurance companies as well as households, in that the former face the risk of increasing nominal liabilities (for example, owing

[4] Under full funding, the contribution rate to obtain a given 'defined-benefit' replacement rate depends on the difference between the growth rate of wages (which determines the pension needed for a given replacement rate) and the return on assets, as well as the passivity ratio (the number of years of retirement relative to working age).

[5] The replacement ratio is the ratio of pension to earnings at the time of retirement.

[6] The growth of receipts under funding with 'defined contributions' depends on the rate of return on the assets accumulated during the working life. The actual pension received per annum again varies with the 'passivity ratio'.

Table 2. Pension Funds' Portfolio Distributions (percentage allocations), 1992

	Equities	Fixed income	Property	Liquidity and deposits	Of which: foreign assets[a]
UK	80	11	6	3	30
Germany	6	80	13	1	8
Netherlands	24	60	14	2	17
Sweden	2	91	2	6	1
Denmark	19	67	12	2	4
Ireland	66	24	7	3	35
France	20	67	11	2	2
Italy	14	72	10	5	4
Belgium	31	50	8	11	31
Spain	3	94	2	1	1
Portugal	(18)	(57)	5	19	3

[a] Foreign assets are included in the categories to the left.
Data in brackets are estimated.
Source: European Federation for Retirement Provision/EU Committee.

to wage increases), as well as the risk of holding assets, and hence need to trade volatility with return. The importance of pension liabilities as a cost to firms, and hence the benefit from higher asset returns, is underlined by estimates by the European Federation for Retirement Provision that a 1 percent improvement in asset returns, if risk is constant, may reduce companies' labour costs by 2–3 percent, where there is a fully funded, mature, defined-benefit pension plan.

The implication of this discussion is that growth of pension funds, other things being equal, would *increase the supply of long-term funds to capital markets*, and reduce bank deposits, even if saving and wealth do not increase, so long as households do not increase the liquidity of the remainder of their portfolios fully to offset growth of pension funds. And there is a clear correlation in Table 1 between the importance of pension funds and equity market capitalization. They may also have an *effect on saving and wealth per se*, particularly if a funded system replaces one based on pay-as-you-go.[7] Such results justify a particular focus on pension funds in an analysis of the future development of equity markets in the EU.

[7] As noted by James (1994), the conditions under which funding will have a positive effect on saving – namely myopia, limited access to credit, and lack of credibility of the pension scheme – are precisely those whose absence will lead pay-as-you-go to reduce saving. So a switch from pay-as-you-go to funding is *unambiguously* likely to raise saving.

Various factors will influence the attractiveness of equities to pension funds. *Maturity* – the ratio of active to retired members – is a key underlying factor for both defined-benefit and defined-contribution funds. Blake (1994) suggests that, given the varying duration[8] of liabilities, it is rational for immature funds having 'real' liabilities as defined above to invest mainly in equities (long duration), for mature funds to invest in a mix of equities and bonds, and for funds which are winding up to invest mainly in bonds (short duration).

Apart from such shifting to lower-risk assets for older workers as they approach retirement, a *defined-contribution pension plan* would seek to diversify, aiming to maximize return for a given risk, and thus following closely the standard portfolio optimization schema outlined above. Since the objective is typically as high as possible a replacement ratio at retirement – while contributions are usually a fixed proportion of salary – the fund must, as noted, seek, if possible, a return in excess of average earnings growth. The superior returns on equities will probably ensure that they account for a significant share of the portfolio (estimates of risk and return using artificial portfolios in the various national markets are given in Section 4).

More complex considerations arise for *defined-benefit funds*. First, there is an incentive to overfund in order to maximize the tax benefits, as well as to provide a larger contingency fund, which, as noted, is usually counteracted by government-imposed limits on funding. Meanwhile, appropriate investment strategies will also depend on the nature of the obligations incurred, which are themselves strongly influenced by the minimum funding rules imposed by the authorities. Certain definitions are useful as background to a discussion of such funding rules. The 'wind-up' definition of liabilities – the 'solvency' level at which the fund can meet all its current obligations[9] ignoring any projections of salary – is known as the accumulated-benefit obligation (ABO). The assumption that rights will continue to accrue, and to be inflation-indexed up to retirement, as is normal in a final salary plan, gives the projected-benefit obligation (PBO). The indexed-benefit obligation (IBO) assumes indexation after retirement.[10] An important argument in favour of the PBO over the ABO is that it ensures advance provision for the burden of maturity of the plan, when there are many pensioners

[8] Duration is the time to the discounted cash flow on an asset.

[9] Projections of inflation will be needed when benefit indexation is a contractual or legal obligation. Another important factor in determining the ABO is whether early leavers' benefits are guaranteed in real terms, as in the United Kingdom, Ireland, and the Netherlands.

[10] This is a legal obligation in Germany and Sweden and soon will be in the UK up to 5 percent inflation. It is generally provided in the Netherlands.

and fewer workers, by spreading costs over the life of the plan.[11] This may be better for the financial stability of the sponsor.

If a fund seeks to finance the accumulated-benefit obligation, and *the obligation is purely nominal, with penalties for shortfalls* – i.e. with no indexation – it will be appropriate in theory to match (or 'immunize') the liabilities with bonds of the same duration to hedge the interest-rate risk of these liabilities, or at least to hedge using derivatives against the risk of shortfall when holding more volatile securities such as equities. Unhedged equities will merely provide unnecessary risk to the fund.[12]

With a *projected-benefit obligation target*, an investment policy based on diversification may be most appropriate, in the belief that risk reduction depends on a maximum diversification of the pension fund relative to the firm's operating investments.[13] Moreover, if the liability includes an *element of indexation*, then fund managers and actuaries typically assume that it may be appropriate to include a significant proportion of equities and property in the portfolio as well as bonds, to minimize the risk of longer-term shortfall of assets relative to liabilities[14] – implicitly diversifying between investment risk and liability risk (which are largely risks of inflation).[15] An essential counterpart to such an approach is that regulators allow gradual amortization of shortfalls, or even focus in solvency calculations on income from assets rather than on market values. Allowing inflation indexation of pensions to be discretionary is another way to reduce the risk of shortfall: implicitly, it is a form of risk-sharing between firms and workers.

Not that theory suggests that funds should invest solely in equity, even if the above arguments point in that direction. As shown by Black (1980), for both defined-benefit and defined-contribution funds, there is a *fiscal incentive* to maximize the tax advantage of pension funds by investing in assets with the highest possible spread between pre-tax and post-tax returns. In many countries this tax effect gives an incentive to hold bonds. Second, the risk of a portfolio of equities may be reduced sharply, at little cost in terms of return, by holding a proportion of bonds (see Tables 4 and 6).

[11] Frijns and Petersen (1992). The ease with which funds of declining industries in the UK financed on a PBO/IBO basis (such as coal mining and railways) coped with maturity are a case in point.

[12] Bodie (1995).

[13] Ambachtsheer (1988). This approach, while being fully consistent with a 'prudent man' rule (obligation of pension managers to invest as a prudent investor would on his own behalf; in particular, with appropriate diversification), highlights the high-risk nature of book reserve or pay-as-you-go provision for private firms.

[14] See the discussion of equities and inflation later in this section.

[15] Such insights are formalized in so-called asset-liability modelling exercises – an actuarial technique involving comparison of forecasts of liabilities in coming years with asset returns under various scenarios, which shows both risks to the employer and possible changes to portfolio strategy that may be warranted (Blake 1992). See also Daykin (1994).

Third, many financial economists disagree with the implicit assumptions which may underlie a strategy of equity investment; namely that *equity is a hedge against inflation, and that raising the share of equity reduces costs*, as opposed to merely raising expected returns, and offering benefits of diversification.[16] Suffice to note here that Tepper (1992) suggests that the debate may hinge on whether returns on equity are statistically independent from year to year. If they were, it is quite conceivable that a long series of bad returns could lead to significant real losses from equities even over a long time-horizon relevant to pension funds. But proponents of the view that equities outperform bonds over long time-horizons would maintain that there are reversals in trends in returns to ensure owners of capital are compensated over the long term. They suggest that although underperformance of equities is quite common in the short term, long-term underperformance would entail economic collapse, which governments would seek to resist, and/or there may be self-correcting tendencies in economies, both of which lead to forms of 'mean reversion' in equity returns.[17]

Also of interest in this context is the suggestion that the premium in returns of equities over bonds is more than can be explained by relative risk,[18] which if correct implies that risk-neutral investors such as pension funds can gain from holding equities.[19] In addition, there is evidence that purchasing shares at regular intervals, as is typical of a pension plan, may significantly reduce risk by evening out rises and falls in valuation. Nevertheless it is important to note that finance theory shows equities should not be assimilated with real long-term bonds; there is no guarantee of value, whether real or nominal, at any time in the future. At most, the value of equities is uncorrelated with inflation; this implies it does not provide a hedge, which would imply a negative correlation.

International equities are of particular relevance in the context of this general discussion. Modern portfolio theory[20] suggests that holding a diversified portfolio of equities in a domestic market can eliminate unsystematic risk resulting from the different performance of individual firms and industries, but not, in a given domestic equity market, the systematic risk resulting from the performance of the economy as a whole.[21] In an efficient and integrated world capital market, systematic risk would be minimized by holding the global portfolio, wherein assets are held in proportion to their distribution by current value be-

[16] See Bodie (1990, 1995).

[17] Bodie (1995) still notes that the cost of insuring a certain return on equities is independent of time-horizon and mean reversion, indicating that the element of risk is unavoidable.

[18] Mehra and Prescott (1985).

[19] However, Blanchard (1993) notes that the premium is tending to decline.

[20] See Solnik (1991).

[21] See, for example, Frost and Henderson (1983).

tween the national markets. In effect, the improvement in the risk/return position from diversification more than compensates for the additional element of volatility arising from currency movements. Several ways may be envisaged whereby a strategy of international diversification should reduce risk. Crucially, to the extent that national trade cycles are not correlated, and shocks to equity markets tend to be country-specific, the investment of part of the portfolio in other markets can reduce systematic risk for the same return. In the medium term, the profit share in national economies may move differentially, which implies that international investment hedges the risk of a decline in domestic profit share and hence in equity values.[22] And in the very long term, imperfect correlation of demographic shifts should offer protection against the effects on the domestic economy of ageing of the population.[23]

Supporting arguments for international investment may be derived from the special circumstances of individual countries or from inefficiencies in global capital markets. There may be industries offshore (oil, gold mining, etc.) which are not present in the domestic economy, investment in which will reduce unsystematic risk even if trade cycles were correlated. The domestic stock market may itself be poorly diversified, being dominated by a small number of large companies (as in the Netherlands), or unduly exposed to one type of risk (as Finland is with raw materials). If the domestic currency tends to depreciate (as in the UK), real returns on foreign assets will be boosted correspondingly, and vice versa for appreciation (though in the long run, real returns will be equalized if purchasing power parity holds). Other economies (e.g. Japan, and latterly the Pacific Rim and Latin America) may be more successful in terms of growth than the domestic economy – or in this case, the EU as a whole – and hence offer higher total returns, given that stock market returns ultimately depend on dividends, which in turn are a function of profits and GDP growth. Similarly, there may be a higher marginal productivity of capital in lower-wage countries (such as Korea) which may be attractive to investors.[24] For investors in certain markets, international investment may be stimulated by the unavailability of certain

[22] This will be of particular importance to defined-benefit pension funds, where liabilities are tied to wages and hence rise as the profit-share falls. Similarly, at an individual firm level, investment in competitors' shares hedges against a loss of profits due to partial loss of the domestic market.

[23] Note that in a closed economy, if there is no benefit to capital formation from funding, there is an equivalence between funding and pay-as-you-go, since pensions must be paid out of a given national income. It is merely the means (returns on capital or tax on labour) which will differ.

[24] Technically these results imply inefficiency and/or slow adjustment of global capital markets. Feldstein and Horioka (1980) suggested this was certainly the case prior to 1980, though more recent research has shown a weakening of this result.

instruments in the home market, such as, until recently, commercial paper and floating rate notes in Germany.

Section 4 shows estimates of the benefits of diversifying between equities and bonds and into international securities. Actual strategies and techniques of international investment are described in Davis (1995).

2. WHAT ARE THE PRINCIPAL PENSION FUND REGULATIONS AFFECTING FINANCING?

A key factor that may influence the portfolio holding of equities, independent of the fundamental factors outlined above, is regulation. This section assesses the main regulations affecting pension fund financing, namely portfolio regulations and regulation of funding. The following section considers their influence, together with other factors, on the portfolio distribution (which affects returns and hence the cost of providing a given level of benefits). In effect, portfolio regulations seek to influence the nature of the return to funding, while funding rules can be seen as ensuring that assets actually are accumulated to cover benefit promises under funding. The basic regulations for EU countries are summarized in Table 3.

Quantitative regulation of portfolio distributions is imposed in a number of countries, with the ostensible aim of protecting pension fund beneficiaries, although motives such as ensuring a steady demand for government bonds may also play a part. As a side effect, it may also protect government agencies set up to insure the benefit obligations of bankrupt firms, since it reduces the likelihood that assets will fall short of liabilities. Limits are often imposed on holdings of assets with relatively volatile returns, such as equities and property, as well as foreign assets, even if their mean return is relatively high. There are also often limits on self-investment,[25] to protect against the associated concentration of risk in the event of insolvency of the sponsor. Apart from the control of self-investment – which is clearly necessary to ensure that funds are not vulnerable to bankruptcy of the sponsor – the degree to which such regulations actually contribute to benefit security is open to doubt, since pension funds, unlike insurance companies, may face the risk of increasing liabilities as well as the risk of holding assets, and hence need to trade volatility with return.[26] Moreover, appropriate diversification of assets can eliminate any idiosyncratic risk from holding an individual security or type of asset, thus minimizing the increase in risk. Again, if

[25] These limits do not, of course, apply to reserve funding systems such as those common in Germany, Luxembourg, and Sweden, where 100 percent of assets are invested in the sponsor.

[26] Indeed, in several countries, a false parallel seems to be drawn by regulators between life insurers and pension funds.

Table 3. Summary of Pension Asset Regulations[a]

	Portfolio regulations	Regulation of funding[b]
United Kingdom	Prudent man concept; 5% self-investment limit, concentration limit for defined-contribution plans.	Maximum 5% overfund of PBO or IBO. Funding only obligatory for contracted-out part of social security.
Germany	Guidelines: maximum 30% EU equity, 25% EU property, 6% non-EU shares, 6% non-EU bonds, 20% overall foreign assets, 10% self-investment limit.	Funding obligatory up to PBO. Option of book-reserve funding.
Netherlands	Prudent man concept, 5% self-investment limit.	Funds are expected to cover PBO; maximum 15% overfund of ABO, minimum is ABO itself.
Sweden	Majority to be in listed bonds, debentures and retroverse loans to contributors.	For ATP, IBO is funded. Contribution rate adjusted 5-yearly to balance fund.
Denmark	Property loans, shares and investment trust holdings limited to 40%, foreign assets to 20%; 60% to be in domestic debt. No self-investment.	Irrelevant as defined contribution; benefits must be funded externally.
France	Assets of supplementary funds (ARRCO/AGIRC) to be invested 50% in EU government bonds and less than 33% in loans to sponsors. Insured funds maximum 40% property and 15% Treasury deposits.	Funded company schemes forbidden; book-reserve funding subject to tax discrimination.
Italy	No pension law for self-administered schemes. Most schemes are insured, investments may be in state bonds (maximum 90%), bank deposits, property, mortgages, securities, investment funds.	No pension law for self-administered schemes; draft law proposes payments equal to 7% of salary. Insured plans must be fully funded on a 15-year projection.
Ireland	Schemes must diversify prudently, any self-investment to be declared.	Funding of ABO required; deferred rights indexed.
Belgium	15% to be invested in government bonds, no more than 15% in sponsor, 40% limit on real estate, 10% deposits.	Funding obligatory of ABO based on current salary, interest rate 7%.
Spain	90% in stocks, bonds, mortgages, property, deposits.	Funding obligatory of ABO plus 4% margin; maximum interest rate 6%.
Portugal	Maxima of 50% real estate, 15% self-investment, 40% equities and bonds not listed in Portugal, but limited to large markets.	Funding obligatory of ABO.

[a] Note that although the table reflects information available to the author at the time of writing, regulations are not infrequently subject to amendment.
[b] ABO refers to the accumulated-benefit obligation; PBO the projected-benefit obligation.
Source: Davis (1995), EFRP.

national cycles and markets are imperfectly correlated, international investment will reduce otherwise undiversifiable or 'systematic' risk.[27]

Portfolio limits may be particularly inappropriate for defined-benefit pensions, given the additional 'buffer' of the company guarantee and risk-sharing between older and younger workers,[28] and if benefits must be indexed. Clearly, in such cases, portfolio regulations may affect the attractiveness to companies of providing pension funds if it constrains managers in their choice of risk and return, forcing them to hold low-yielding assets and possibly increasing their risks by limiting their possibilities of diversification.[29] It will also restrict the benefits to the capital markets from the development of pension funds. And, in the case of restrictions which explicitly or implicitly[30] oblige pension funds to invest in government bonds, which must themselves be repaid from taxation, there may be no benefit to capital formation, and the 'funded' plans may at a macroeconomic level be virtually equivalent to pay-as-you-go.

German externally financed pension funds (*Pensionskassen*), besides a 10 percent self-investment limit, remain subject to the same regulation as life insurers (20 percent limit on foreign asset holdings, 36 percent limit on equities, 25 percent on property). Although these regulations have been eased in recent years, it is arguable that they remain particularly inappropriate for German pension funds, given that they are obliged to offer a form of inflation indexation.[31]

Scandinavian portfolio restrictions for externally funded schemes are in many ways even tighter than Germany's, in that minima are also specified. The Swedish ATP (funded social security) scheme, as well as externally financed private pension funds, have historically been obliged to hold the majority of their assets in domestic listed bonds, debentures, and retroverse loans to contributors (i.e. loans of pension assets back to the sponsoring companies). However, recent deregulations have permitted limited investment in property, equities, and foreign assets, of which some private plans have reportedly taken advantage. Historically, restrictions on equity investments were justified on the additional ground that for ATP they would involve backdoor nationalization and worker control. Danish funds have to hold 60 percent in domestic debt instruments, although since 1990 they have been allowed to hold 20 percent in foreign assets. Investment in the sponsor is forbidden. Belgian funds must invest at least 15 percent of their assets in govern-

[27] Davis (1995).

[28] See footnote 3.

[29] Technically, portfolio restrictions are likely to prevent managers reaching the *frontier of efficient portfolios*, which indicates where return is maximized for a given risk.

[30] For example, by closing down all alternative investment strategies such as international diversification.

[31] One way to avoid the regulations on equities and foreign investment is reportedly to invest via special security funds, whose investments are not subject to restriction.

ment bonds, although international investment is liberalized, with funds often holding 50 percent of their portfolios in foreign assets.

Restrictions are also severe in a number of countries where pension fund development to date has been relatively minor (Table 1). Mutual societies providing pensions in France (via group-insurance policies) must follow insurance regulations which insist that they invest at least 34 percent in public bonds, and a maximum of 40 percent in property and five percent in shares of foreign insurers. Fifty percent of the assets of the supplementary funds ARRCO and AGIRC must be invested in EU public bonds. Greek compulsory auxiliary pension funds are obliged to invest 80 percent of their assets with the Bank of Greece (or a commercial bank acting as its substitute), which would mean virtually all of the assets are invested in state securities. The remaining 20 percent may be invested in property (up to 40 percent), with the rest being in bonds or shares. Portuguese funds may invest in a variety of domestic assets (although they must reportedly hold 30 percent in government bonds), while foreign investment is restricted to 40 percent. Spanish rules are rather flexible, with investment permitted in bonds, equities, real estate, and bank deposits; other assets may not exceed 10 percent of the portfolio. International investment has reportedly been liberalized since the abolition of exchange controls.

Such quantitative limits are not, however, imposed in all the countries studied. For example, UK pension funds are subject to trust law and implicitly[32] follow the 'prudent man'[33] concept: as long as trust deeds are appropriately structured, they are not constrained by regulation in their portfolio distribution, except for limits on self-investment (five percent) and concentration. Dutch private funds face no legal restrictions, except for a five percent limit on self-investment.[34] In contrast, the Dutch public-service fund (ABP) faces strict limits, being able to invest only 10 percent abroad, and 20 percent in shares or real estate (these are to be liberalized soon). Irish funds are obliged to invest prudently and diversify, and are obliged to announce any investment in excess of 5 percent of the scheme's assets in any firm (including the sponsor).

Regulation of the *funding of benefits* (Table 3) and associated accounting rules[35] is a key aspect of the regulatory framework for defined-benefit pension funds, which as noted in Section 1 may strongly influence the scope for equity

[32] There is no explicit 'prudent man' rule, but the duty of prudence to trustees can be interpreted as requiring diversification.

[33] 'Prudent man' concept: obligation of pension managers to invest as a prudent investor would on his own behalf (in particular, with appropriate diversification).

[34] See Van Loo (1988).

[35] Regulation of funding is typically carried out by periodic submission of accounts and actuarial reports to the authorities.

investment, both by influencing asset holdings and the degree of volatility that can be accepted. Note that, by definition, a defined-contribution plan is always fully funded, as assets equal liabilities, whereas, as noted, with defined-benefit plans there is a distinction between the pension plan (setting out contractual rights to the parties) and the fund (a pool of assets to provide collateral for the promised benefits). When the fund is worth less than the present value of promised benefits there is underfunding; when the opposite is the case, there is overfunding. Calculation of appropriate funding levels requires a number of actuarial assumptions; in particular, the assumed return on assets, projected future wage growth (for final salary plans), and future inflation (if there is indexing of pensions), as well as estimates of death rates and the expected evolution of the relative number of contributors and beneficiaries over time.

Minimum funding limits set by regulation seek to protect the security of benefits against default risk by the company, given that unfunded benefits are liabilities on the books of the firm, and therefore risk is concentrated and pensioners (or pension insurers) may have no better claim in case of bankruptcy than any other creditor.[36] Funding offers a diversified and hence less risky alternative backup for the benefit promise, as well as offering the possibility of unplanned benefit increases if the plan is in surplus. Extra protection against creditors of a bankrupt firm is afforded when the pension fund is independent of the firm and when self-investment is banned or severely restricted. There are usually also upper limits on funding, to prevent abuse of tax privileges (overfunding). Bodie (1990) suggests that the three main reasons why firms fund, besides regulations *per se*, are the tax incentives, provision of financial slack (when there is a surplus) that can be used in case of financial difficulty, and because pension benefit insurance may not cover the highest-paid employees.

In Germany, various laws or court decisions have enforced minimum standards of funding for pension funds and what amounts to inflation indexing of pensions. Tax relief is not provided for assets held to cover inflation risks. These provisions were felt to be particularly burdensome, and have helped blunt the growth rate of externally funded private pension plans as opposed to 'booked' benefits,[37] thus limiting pension funds' potential contribution to secondary equity markets in that country. In Germany, accounting conventions also have an impact on funding decisions, as shortfalls of pension funds' assets relative to liabilities (with asset values defined at the lower of cost and market value) are included in the company accounts.[38] It is suggested that this helps to account for

[36] Adequate provision of unfunded pensions is likely to be particularly difficult for declining industries, as the worker/pensioner ratio falls.

[37] Deutsche Bundesbank (1984), Ahrend (1994).

[38] Hepp (1992).

conservative investment strategies based on bond holdings, independently of portfolio regulations discussed below, despite the fact that funding of projected 'real' obligations should make equities attractive.

A particular feature of German private pensions which should also be highlighted in this context is the large volume of reserve financing, where pension liabilities are held directly on the balance sheet of the sponsoring firm and not externally funded. By offering tax privileges to such 'booking', Germany effectively imposes no limits on self-investment of book reserves (although the Germans do insist on insurance of such reserves). Moreover, it can be argued that such booked benefits are highly inimical to the growth of secondary equity markets, since they provide firms with greater internal cashflow, but do not provide any stimulus to equity markets. Cash flow is retained in the firm and not spread to new firms that could otherwise float on the equity market. Such reserves also are by nature highly undiversified, and hence require a compulsory mutual insurance system to be viable. In effect, encouragement of booked benefits allows firms to avoid any external funding of their pension obligations.

Reserve funding is also common in Luxembourg, Austria, and Sweden. It used to be the rule in Spain and Portugal, until reforms in each country in 1987 led to a switch to funding. In Belgium, reserve funding was forbidden under a reform of 1985, owing to fears for the security of pensions in the case of insolvency.

In the UK, plans which contract out of earnings-related social security have historically been obliged only to fund sufficiently to provide an equivalent 'guaranteed minimum pension' (GMP), but this is far below actual benefit promises. Funding above this level is not legally required – although trustees are bound by their duty of care to ensure funding is in place – nor is there a requirement to include deficits in company balance sheets. In practice, a continuance basis such as the PBO or IBO tends to be used, on which overfunding is limited to five percent. Use of the more 'dynamic' PBO (which allows for future wage growth) instead of the ABO may encourage equity holdings. A crucial difference from other countries is that adequacy of funding is judged by current and projected cash flows from assets and not current market values; this allows volatile assets such as equities to be heavily used. This is reflected in accounting standard SSAP24, which also bases fund valuation on such actuarial valuations and long-run smoothing. Historically, this has not conflicted with the need to cover obligations if the fund were wound up, since the PBO has tended to exceed the ABO. But compulsory indexation of pensions, currently being introduced,[39] will increase the ABO and could put the system under threat.[40] Meanwhile, although

[39] Given the cost of this measure, a decline of the company pension fund sector is predicted, but there is little evidence of this to date.

[40] Riley (1993).

the government guarantees to pay the GMP if a plan fails, there has to date been no system to guarantee non-GMP pension benefits in the UK; partly for this reason regulations have historically been less strict than elsewhere, and managers could adopt a high-return/high-risk portfolio strategy.

However, the Goode Committee on UK pension law – set up to investigate regulatory shortcomings in the wake of the Maxwell scandal, and which reported in 1993 – has recommended a minimum funding rule based on the ABO and market-value-based accounting, with only a three-month grace period to top up the fund (albeit with a 10 percent shortfall being permitted without the immediate need to top up). Insurance against fraud was also recommended, as well as indexation and abolition of the GMP. The government launched a bill in late 1994 seeking to implement these proposals, although funding rules will be less strict for immature funds. This might alter quite significantly the asset mix of UK funds, towards bonds rather than equities.

Funding rules in other countries, such as the Netherlands, usually have the ABO as a floor, but the authorities assume (and tax authorities allow) that the PBO will actually be funded, usually with an allowance for (non-compulsory) indexation. In Spain there is a formal margin of 4 percent over the ABO which is set as a minimum. The Netherlands, Ireland, and the UK oblige funds to index deferred pensions, which thus raises the ABO.

The discount rate set for discounting future liabilities is a key influence on funding. In the Netherlands, the government sets a maximum real interest-rate assumption of four percent, which may encourage funds to hold bonds, since their real returns have typically been in this range, while equities yield more (Table 4). Since in practice Dutch funds have been able to earn over this level – surpluses estimated at 30 percent existed by 1990 – a special tax levy is planned. In Belgium, the discount rate is set at a nominal 7 percent, while in Spain there is a maximum rate of 6 percent (the lower the rate, the more assets are required). In the UK, the government accepts the (varying) judgment of the actuaries as to asset returns and discount rates.

Since Danish funds are generally defined-contribution, the issue of funding does not arise. However, the issue of limiting tax privilege does, and is dealt with via taxation of real returns on bonds.

To conclude, portfolio and funding regulations differ quite significantly. The division for portfolio regulations, between countries with prudent man rules and regulations, is stark. For funding, some countries are using only accumulated-benefit based funding, and others projected benefits, while others again rely partly on booked benefits. In the next sections we probe further the consequences of such rules for portfolios.

Table 4. Returns on Pension Funds' Portfolios 1967-90 (Mean (Standard Deviation) of Annual Real Total Returns in Local Currency)

	United Kingdom		Germany		Netherlands		Sweden		Denmark		Ireland		France		Italy		Belgium	
Estimated portfolio return[a]	5.8	(12.5)	5.1	(4.4)	4.0	(6.0)	0.2	(7.6)	3.6	(12.7)	5.0	(11.9)	n/a	n/a	n/a	n/a	n/a	n/a
Average earnings growth	2.6	(2.5)	4.0	(3.1)	2.4	(3.2)	1.5	(3.5)	2.8	(3.6)	2.0		4.0		3.1	(4.3)	n/a	
Portfolio return less average earnings growth	3.2		1.1		1.6		-1.3		0.8		3.0		n/a		n/a		n/a	
Inflation (CPI)	8.9	(5.3)	3.5	(2.1)	4.9	(3.1)	8.1	(2.7)	7.7	(3.2)	10.0	(6.0)	7.1	(4.1)	11.3	(5.9)	5.5	(3.2)
Returns on:																		
Loans	1.4	(5.0)	5.3	(1.9)	3.8	(3.6)	3.4	(3.1)	6.1	(3.6)	n/a	n/a	2.6	(3.2)	2.7	(3.7)	n/a	n/a
Mortgages	2.0	(5.2)	4.7	(1.4)	4.3	(2.6)	2.6	(3.0)	5.8	(3.7)	n/a	n/a	3.7	(2.6)	n/a	n/a	n/a	n/a
Equities	8.1	(20.3)	9.5	(20.3)	7.9	(28.2)	8.4	(23.3)	7.0	(27.5)	8.5	(25.9)	9.4	(26.9)	4.0	(35.9)	6.3	(16.7)
Bonds	-0.5	(13.0)	2.7	(14.9)	1.0	(13.1)	-0.9	(8.5)	3.4	(16.1)	-0.1	(15.3)	1.0	(13.1)	-0.2	(18.3)	1.3	(11.7)
Short-term assets	1.7	(4.9)	3.1	(2.1)	1.6	(4.0)	1.3	(3.5)	1.6	(1.8)	n/a	n/a	2.4	(3.4)	-2.2	(4.2)	n/a	n/a
Property	6.7	(11.4)	4.5	(2.9)	4.6	(15.0)	n/a	n/a	n/a	n/a	n/a	n/a	n/a	n/a	n/a	n/a	n/a	n/a
Foreign bonds	-0.1	(15.0)	3.0	(11.2)	-0.7	(11.2)	-0.2	(12.6)	-2.0	(11.6)	-1.4	(11.4)	-0.2	(12.8)	-1.5	(10.7)	0.2	(11.1)
Foreign equities	7.0	(16.2)	10.4	(13.5)	6.6	(14.4)	7.1	(14.0)	5.5	(14.3)	5.9	(14.2)	7.0	(13.5)	6.0	(12.5)	7.5	(13.7)
Memo: portfolio return[b]	6.3	(10.7)	5.5	(3.0)	4.3	(5.5)	2.8	(2.9)	5.8	(3.0)	n/a	n/a	n/a	n/a	n/a	n/a	n/a	n/a

[a]Using holding period returns on bonds.
[b]Using redemption yields on fixed-rate instruments.
Source: Davis (1995), using National Flow of Funds Data (for portfolio distributions, see Table 2) and BIS macroeconomic database (for asset returns).

3. PORTFOLIO DISTRIBUTIONS OF PENSION FUNDS

Table 2 shows the patterns of portfolio distributions in 1992 for the UK, Germany, the Netherlands, Sweden, Ireland, Denmark, Spain, Belgium, France, Italy, and Portugal. Swedish data are for the funded social security (ATP) scheme. There are marked differences: for example, in 1992 equity holdings varied from 2 percent in Sweden to 80 percent in the UK, and foreign assets from one percent in Spain to 35 percent in Ireland. As background, estimates of real total returns and their standard deviations for 1967-90 are shown in Table 4. Davis (1995) offers a detailed analysis of these patterns of portfolio distributions and their determinants. Here we offer an overview of certain key determinants, grouping by type of influence, and focusing on those which influence domestic and international equity holdings. A number of factors emerge which are additional both to portfolio optimization and to portfolio and funding regulations.

In line with the discussion in Section 1 above, *liabilities* are a major influence, for example, on the share of bonds. In the UK, where bond-holding is low, a degree of inflation protection both before and after retirement is expected. The same point applies to Dutch, Irish, and Belgian funds, which hold a significant proportion of equities and international assets. It is notable that UK, Irish, and Dutch funds tend to index pensions in practice, but have not historically been obliged to do so. This means that the ABO is typically below the PBO, and volatile assets may be held. In contrast, German funds are obliged to index, implying a high ABO and risk of shortfall if volatile assets are held. This may be partly reflected in a greater share of fixed-interest assets in portfolios in that country, although regulation also plays a role. Again, indexation promises are made by the Swedish supplementary national plan, despite which the bond share is extremely high, suggesting an inefficient portfolio allocation.

Historically, the higher *taxation* on bonds than on equities made the former an attractive investment to tax-exempt investors such as pension funds. But this is not the case in Denmark, where bonds are subject to a tax on real returns, from which equities are exempt. There, portfolio regulations force funds to hold tax-disadvantaged assets, as funds must hold 60 percent fixed-interest assets, despite the tax disadvantage to such assets.

Asset returns, both absolute and relative to other assets, are a key influence on the structure of any portfolio. This is generally confirmed by econometric analyses of the influences of portfolio distributions of pension funds,[41] which shows they are strongly influenced by relative asset returns – particularly where there are few regulations governing portfolio distributions and low transactions

[41] See, for example, Davis (1988).

costs, as in the UK. Econometric analysis shows that adjustment to a change in such returns is generally rapid. Assuming adequate information and appropriate incentives to fund managers, this should imply an efficient allocation of funds and correct valuation of securities. In Davis's research, these results did not all hold where transactions costs are high and regulations are strict, as in Germany. There, adjustment to a change in returns is somewhat slower and allocation of funds consequently less efficient. The results also contrast with those for households and companies,[42] where adjustment to changes in returns tends to be much slower than for pension funds in all countries, owing to higher transactions costs and poorer information. Historical examples of responses to relative returns[43] include the high levels of liquidity held temporarily after stock market collapses, as in the UK in the mid-1970s, and in the longer term due to structural changes in yields arising from deregulation and expansion of short-term markets. Inter-country differences in bond-holding may also relate to asset returns, as opposed to portfolio restrictions: partly owing to low and stable inflation, real returns on bonds and other fixed-interest assets are relatively high in Germany, Denmark, and the Netherlands, thus motivating a high portfolio share. In the UK and Ireland, bond returns have been historically low, and pension funds correspondingly hold few bonds. But in Sweden, portfolio regulations ensure that bonds have a high portfolio share, despite poor returns.

Risk reduction is the main motivation for portfolio diversification, as well as being required by prudent man rules. For example, the fall in the UK bond share which has occurred since 1980 partly reflects alternative means of diversification: after abolition of exchange controls UK funds sold bonds to buy foreign assets (although the contraction in the supply of public debt in the late 1980s also played a role). Portfolio regulations may operate contrary to this: Swedish and Danish funds have considerable exposure to housing markets via mortgage-related bonds and loans to housing credit institutions. Together with mortgages, these amounted to around 55 percent of Swedish funds' assets in 1992, while Danish funds had around 60 percent of assets in mortgages or mortgage association bonds. These imply an enormous exposure to potential effects of recession and falling house prices. Meanwhile, as discussed below, UK funds may have portfolios excessively concentrated on equities.

As discussed in Section 1, *international diversification* can offer a better risk/return trade-off to fund managers, by reducing the systematic risk of investing in domestic markets arising from the economic cycle or from medium-term shifts in the share of profits in GDP. In a longer-term context, international in-

[42] Davis (1986).
[43] Davis (1995).

vestment in countries with a relatively young population may be essential to prevent battles over resources between workers and pensioners in countries with an ageing population.[44] Foreign asset holdings have grown sharply over the 1980s in the UK, and more recently in Ireland. This pattern followed abolition of exchange controls at a time when the economy was generating current account surpluses and overseas investment returns looked attractive. Meanwhile, Dutch and Belgian funds have long held a significant proportion of assets abroad. For funds in Belgium, Ireland, and the Netherlands, international investment is particularly attractive owing to the large volume of pension fund assets compared with domestic security and property markets, and the thinness and lack of diversification of equity markets (compare the standard deviations of equity returns in Table 4). Growth has been much less marked in the other countries: in Germany, Denmark, Spain (until recently), Portugal, and Sweden this is partly due to portfolio restrictions. Note that in most of these cases the argument for diversification noted for Belgium, the Netherlands, and Ireland applies with equal force.

Risk aversion of trustees or managers may limit portfolio distributions, and at times appears directly counter-productive. In the Netherlands equity holding remains low – 24 percent – despite the absence of portfolio restrictions. Van Loo (1988) suggests that this may relate to risk aversion of pension fund trustees. Also, according to Wyatt (1993) there are unofficial tolerance limits for equity exposure of 30 percent imposed by the supervisors. This is, of course, contrary to the spirit of the prudent man rule. Partly reflecting portfolio regulations, although probably also owing to the conservatism of managers (since the limits do not currently bind), the equity share in countries such as Sweden and Denmark is exceptionally low – despite the Danish tax on real returns to debt instruments, which encourages substitution of equities for bonds. Risk aversion may also play a role in many countries in limiting international investment, whereas it actually reduces risk over a time-horizon relevant for pension funds (Table 6). Risk aversion appears particularly marked for defined-contribution funds; this is partly rational, given the lack of risk-sharing, and the fact that workers nearing retirement will be anxious for low-risk assets to be held.[45] But this risk aversion may be excessive. Indeed, evidence from the United States[46] suggests that when employees have control over investment – as is often the case for defined-contribution funds – the vast majority goes into fixed-interest bonds: when equities are held

[44] Davis (1994, 1995).

[45] This point indicates the inflexibility of company-based defined-contribution plans seeking to cater both for risk-seeking young workers and risk-averse older ones. Some funds, such as BT in Australia, overcome this by offering four separate funds at different levels of risk.

[46] Rappaport (1992).

and their value declines, dissatisfaction is often expressed.[47] Even for defined-benefit funds, pressures to hold low-risk assets may be sizeable with an ageing membership and employee trustees. But such pressures also seem to occur when the fund is composed of younger workers.[48] Again, for personal pensions, there is anecdotal evidence in the UK that persons free to choose their asset backing often select highly cautious combinations of assets (though those which are managed on a discretionary basis by insurance companies hold high proportions of equities). These considerations suggest that a shift to defined-contribution and personal pensions in the EU would reduce the benefit to equity markets relative to defined-benefit funds.

Portfolio regulations, as already documented, have a clear and widespread influence on portfolios. Bonds constitute over two-thirds of pension fund assets in Sweden and Denmark: this is largely due to portfolio regulations and the nature of the domestic financial markets, which require 60 percent of Danish assets to be invested in domestic debt instruments, while the majority of Swedish assets are to be in listed bonds, debentures, and retroverse loans. Investment of almost a quarter of the Swedish quasi-public funds' assets in government bonds casts some doubt on their efficacy as a means to protect against future risks to social security; given that the bonds are to be repaid by the taxpayer, they entail similar obligations for taxpayers to those implied in the financing of future social security burdens via pay-as-you-go. Similar comments can be made about the Dutch civil servants' pension fund (ABP), which has until recently been subject to severe portfolio restrictions, such that at end-1991 it held 48 percent of its assets in the form of public-sector bonds and loans. Funds in Belgium, France, and Portugal are forced to hold a certain proportion of government bonds, although their actual holdings tend to exceed these ceilings, suggesting that other influences are at work. As regards equities, it was noted above that German funds are limited to a maximum of 36 percent by regulation – since the portfolio share was only at 6 percent in 1992, the German ceiling was not binding.

Funding rules also have an effect. In the UK, where the rules have been flexible, with a low minimum funding level well below actual liabilities, holdings of equities have ranged up to 80 percent. In countries such as Germany, the

[47] In the United States, only 25 percent of the assets of personal defined-contribution '401(k)' plans, where individuals are free to choose their portfolio allocations, are invested in equity (Frijns and Petersen 1992). Mitchell (1994) expresses concern that as a consequence of conservative approaches to investment, future retirees may find their pensions inadequate.

[48] Research by Mitchell (1994) suggests that inclusion of employee representatives among the board of trustees of a pension fund reduces returns even for defined-benefit funds, although in principle the employer is bearing the risk.

effect of minimum funding rules may be overwhelmed by that of accounting rules and portfolio regulations. But an indicator of their effect is shown in the United States, where minimum funding regulations, based on the ABO, make it optimal to hold a large proportion of bonds to protect against shortfall risk, despite their weakness as an inflation hedge, and there is a prudent man rule for investment. There, bonds form around 40 percent of pension funds' portfolios.

As regards *accounting standards*, as noted in Section 2, Hepp (1990, 1992) suggests that in Germany application of strict accounting principles – which are more appropriate to banks than pension funds – restrains equity holdings by funded plans independently of the portfolio regulations. These conventions, for example, insist on positive net worth of the fund at all times, carry equities on the balance sheet at the lower of book value and market value, and calculate returns net of unrealized capital gains. In contrast, the UK accounting standard permits long-run smoothing and focuses on dividends rather than market values, and hence enables funds to accept the volatility of equity returns. The concern of some commentators in the UK is rather whether equity holdings are too high given the risks: however, note that 22 percent of the 80 percent equity share in 1992 was actually in foreign equities, thus reducing risk somewhat. No other country has anything comparable to this portfolio share of equities. And as noted, new legal proposals may lead funds to reduce their equity shares.

The *structure of fund management* in some countries has had counterproductive effects, according to some commentators. This may be particularly the case in Spain and Portugal, where delegation to foreign fund managers is forbidden, and in Germany, where *Pensionskassen* are obliged to manage their funds internally. Other factors which may discourage pension funds from holding equities are features typical of equity markets in bank-dominated financial systems, such as restrictions on transferability of shares, lack of market transparency, entrenched management, and lack of information on firms' development and prospects. This is because they increase the perceived risks of equity holdings, reduce returns, or reduce liquidity.[49]

4. FUNDS' PERFORMANCE

It is evident from the discussion above that a wide variety of often-extraneous influences impinge on pension funds' portfolios, which may in turn restrict funds from portfolio optimization, reduce return, increase risk relative to feasible alter-

[49] Nevertheless, Davis (1993a) suggests that deregulation and growth of pension funds will tend in themselves to ameliorate these features, creating a virtuous circle in formerly bank-dominated systems for equity-holders such as pension funds.

native investment strategies, and hold back the general development of secondary equity markets. We suggest that a useful means of judging the cost of these regulations and market imperfections – and hence the potential benefit to funds of liberalization – is to assess pension funds' performance both relative to that in other countries and to that of artificial portfolios. The patterns of portfolio distributions (Table 2) and risks and returns on assets can be used to derive estimates of the returns and risks on portfolios (Table 4[50]), and hence the cost to the firm of providing a given level of pension benefits (for a defined-benefit fund), or the return to the member (for a defined-contribution fund).

The estimates suggest that pension funds in the UK obtained the highest real return over the period 1967-90, and those in Sweden the lowest. Irish funds' performance was similar to that in the UK. The result, of course, partly reflects risk and the share of equity and property – the UK having the highest standard deviation of returns (together with Denmark), and by far the highest share of real assets. Meanwhile, Swedish funds held high proportions of bonds, which performed poorly over this period. Interestingly, portfolios in Germany and the Netherlands had a high real return and low volatility, despite their focus on bonds and loans. This relates to relatively high returns on fixed-rate instruments in those countries. However, as discussed below, Table 6 shows that real returns for German and Dutch funds could have been boosted significantly by an increased share of equities. Investment in international equities would have ensured that the associated increase in risk were mitigated.

Several observations can be made regarding these results. The publicly sponsored Swedish fund does poorly. Membership of the low-return Swedish ATP is also compulsory, thus in principle reducing competitive pressures on fund managers. In the case of Denmark, occupational defined-contribution funds imply that those who select the managers – the companies themselves – do not bear the high level of portfolio risk. Germany has generally had little competition in fund management,[51] and suffers from inappropriate accounting standards. But as shown by the results for Germany, good economic performance – or international diversification – can overcome a number of handicaps. Comparison, in Table 4, of the results with (nominally) risk-free yields suggest that the funds generally outperformed government bonds, albeit only narrowly in Denmark. However, in Sweden the portfolio return is below that on short-term money mar-

[50] Annual holding period returns on marketable fixed-rate instruments are used, as in Table 6, instead of redemption yields. In our view, the holding period returns are the more relevant measure for an ongoing portfolio, since they take full account of losses or gains due to interest-rate changes (although other assumptions regarding holding periods could also be made).

[51] Davis (1995).

ket paper (it is, of course, open to doubt whether the markets were deep enough to absorb pension funds' size). Returns are generally below those on equities, but at the benefit of much lower risk.

The most crucial test is the *ability of a fund to outperform real average earnings*, given that liabilities of defined-benefit plans are basically indexed to them. Similarly the replacement ratio a defined-contribution fund can offer will depend on asset returns relative to earnings growth.[52] The margin is sizeable (over three percent per annum) in the UK[53] and Ireland, and between one percent and two percent in Germany and the Netherlands. Except for Germany, these countries have prudent man rules. The margin remains positive in Denmark, albeit only 0.8 percent. But in Sweden it is actually negative, implying that the returns on assets need to be constantly topped up to meet their target. It was noted above that this may relate to inefficient asset allocations, arising from portfolio restrictions. Taking the results at face value, and disregarding demographic issues, pay-as-you-go would have offered a higher rate of return than funding over this time period in that country.

Risk (measured crudely as the standard deviation of the annual real return) should not be disregarded: as noted, it is quite high in a number of countries. But defined-benefit pension funds are well placed to accept a degree of volatility, as there can be risk-sharing between worker and company as well as between younger and older members. Risk is more important for defined-contribution funds, as there is no backup from the sponsor and pensions must typically be taken in a lump sum (to buy an annuity) at the precise point of retirement. In contrast, annuities from defined-benefit funds typically come from the fund itself, or at least the rate is guaranteed. In the light of this, the high levels of risk in Denmark, where funds are mainly defined-contribution, are of potential concern.[54] Note that the risk in this case is not equity-related, since Danish funds have historically held very little equity (Table 2).

[52] It also indicates whether in practice the return to funding (the asset return) exceeds that on pay-as-you-go in a steady state (the growth rate of average earnings).

[53] The data for the United Kingdom allow a further comparison of effects of ownership and management methods to be made, this time in the same markets, in that portfolios of public (local-government) fund data can be identified separately from those of private-sector funds. Local-government funds obtain lower returns than private funds. This can be related to more conservative portfolio distributions and in some cases portfolio regulations. UK local-authority funds held an average of 52 percent equity over the sample, while private funds held 56 percent. Interestingly, the risks in real terms were higher for the local-government funds, partly as a consequence of the volatility of real returns on bonds (see Table 4).

[54] Knox (1993) shows that returns on a fund based on 12 percent contributions with 45 years of payment invested will obtain an average replacement rate of 61 percent, but the range of statistical probability of returns based on asset volatility in the past (in this case for Australia) is between 35 percent and 96 percent.

Table 5. Targeted Replacement Rates with Indexed Pensions (%)

	Replacement ratio assuming indexation of pensions to prices	Percentage contribution rate for 40% replacement rate	Replacement ratio assuming indexation of pensions to wages
United Kingdom	60	6.7	50
Germany	39	10.3	27
Netherlands	44	9.1	37
Sweden	14	28.6	11
Denmark	36	11.1	27
Ireland	60	6.7	50

Source: Vittas (1992) and estimates of average earnings, inflation and real returns on pension funds shown in Table 4. There is assumed to a working life of 40 years followed by 20 years of retirement.

In order to estimate the *benefits/contributions trade-off*, in the context of these portfolio choices, Table 5 shows the results of illustrative calculations on the relationship between costs of providing pensions, average earnings, and real returns.[55] This gives an alternative expression of the cost of equity restrictions. The table shows the replacement rate that would be attainable – given the real returns attained by funds in each country and the corresponding growth rates of wages shown in Table 6 (assuming indexed pensions, a 10 percent 'defined'-contribution rate, 40 years of contributions, and 20 years of retirement). Abstracting from risk, the table illustrates clearly the benefits of a higher return relative to real earnings: assuming pensions are indexed to prices, UK and Irish funds can obtain a replacement ratio of 60 percent, and Swedish funds only 14 percent. Conversely, to obtain a pension equal to 40 percent of average earnings, UK and Irish funds need a contribution rate of 6.7 percent, and Swedish funds 29 percent.

As a further experiment, Table 6 shows the *returns on artificial diversified portfolios* holding 50 percent equity and 50 percent bonds between 1967 and 1990, implicitly assuming quantitative portfolio restrictions are replaced by prudent man rules. As noted, equity holdings for EU pension funds are generally below 50 percent (Table 2); in fact, these portfolios approximate closely those of pension funds in the United States, where a prudent man rule is in operation. Compared with Table 4, the results confirm that returns may be boosted by raising the share of equity, at some cost in terms of risk, although the estimates sug-

[55] As provided in Vittas (1992).

Table 6. Artificial Diversified Portfolios (Mean (Standard Deviation) of Real Total Return in Local Currency), 1967–90

	Domestic[a]		Domestic minus estimated portfolio return (Table 4)	Domestic and international[b]		Domestic and international minus estimated portfolio return (Table 4)	Domestic and international minus average earnings
United Kingdom	3.8	(14.8)	-2.0	3.7	(14.1)	-2.1	+1.1
Germany	6.1	(15.2)	+1.0	6.2	(13.4)	+1.1	+2.2
Netherlands	4.5	(17.0)	+0.5	4.2	(15.2)	+0.2	+1.6
Sweden	3.8	(13.5)	+3.6	3.7	(15.2)	+3.5	+2.2
Denmark	5.3	(18.9)	+1.7	4.6	(13.4)	+1.0	+1.8
France	5.2	(18.0)	-	4.9	(15.9)	-	+0.9
Italy	1.9	(22.1)	-	2.0	(18.7)	-	-1.1
Ireland	3.8	(13.3)	-1.2	3.8	(12.4)	-1.2	+1.8
Belgium	4.2	(18.4)	-	3.8	(16.7)	-	

[a] 50% domestic equity, 50% domestic bonds.
[b] 40% domestic equity, 40% domestic bonds, 10% foreign equity, 10% foreign bonds.
Source: Davis (1995).

gest that risk is mitigated by international diversification.[56] Only for the UK and Ireland are returns consistently below those actually obtained (Table 4). Several of the countries which fell below a satisfactory return on assets relative to average earnings (such as Denmark and Sweden) would have found provision of funded pensions less costly – of itself and relative to pay-as-you-go – if they had followed such a rule. German funds would also have boosted their portfolio returns relative to average earnings considerably.

Summarizing this section, it is suggested that support is given to a prudent man rule, backed by flexible accounting and funding standards (perhaps, as in the UK, focusing on income rather than on market value) to permit holding of a proportion, varying with the maturity of the fund, of high-return but volatile assets. (It is not, of course, implied that a 100 percent equity portfolio would be anything but imprudent.) Since foreign investment is shown invariably to reduce risk, albeit often with a slight reduction in return, limits on such holding appear to be particularly counter-productive. Meanwhile, decentralized fund management may be superior to centralized, if the poor performance of the Swedish ATP fund can be generalized.

5. WHAT DETERMINES THE SCALE OF PRIVATE PENSION FUNDING?

A further issue that must be addressed in considering the contribution of pension funds to EU equity markets is the degree to which the overall structure of retirement income provisions has prevented funds from developing in certain countries. Clearly, if funds remain marginal, the patterns of regulation of funding and portfolios are of secondary importance.

The data in Table 1 showed pension fund assets in the countries studied (excluding funds managed by life insurance companies). For each measure, a contrast is apparent between the role of pension funds in the UK, Sweden, Ireland, the Netherlands, and Denmark – where they account for a sizeable part of personal-sector wealth and GDP – and those in other EU countries such as Germany, Spain, France, and Italy.

[56] The table shows international diversification only up to 20 percent of the portfolio, holding bonds and equities for the 'rest of the world' in proportion to global portfolio weights in the 1980s. A full 'global portfolio', where domestic holdings are reduced to their weight in the global index, would imply 95 percent international investment for the small countries, and over 80 percent even for the UK and Germany. Similar calculations for such a strategy (not shown in detail), again with 50 percent bonds and 50 percent equities, also shows lower risk in domestic currency, although the change in return may be in either direction.

Taking the asset/GDP ratio as an imperfect proxy for the size of the funded sector, *what types of influences could account for the differences in the importance of funded sectors in the provision of pensions?* The most crucial point is that privately funded plans cannot usefully be viewed in isolation: the principal alternative to a private pension fund is the state social security pension system. Not surprisingly, the growth of private plans can be related to the scale of social security pension provision, which imposes limits on private-sector plans, particularly if there is generous provision for individuals at higher income levels. Second, where provision is voluntary, taxation and regulatory provisions make it either more or less attractive for the firm to offer a pension fund. For example, exemption of funds from taxation and, as noted above, prudent man rules for asset management and flexible funding rules, will increase funds' attractiveness. However, in some countries these factors may be overridden by imposition of compulsory pension plans on employers.

Since accrued rights within occupational pension plans comprise assets of the employees, it is natural also to consider their motivations. For example, high marginal tax rates may increase the attraction to employees of tax deferral via pension funds. Employees will also be attracted by the quality of retirement income insurance that is on offer, which differs between defined-benefit and defined-contribution plans, and varies with factors such as indexation of pensions to prices or wages.[57] Note that regulations making funds attractive to employees, such as compulsory indexation and short vesting periods (before rights accrue), may make them less attractive to employers. But not all funds are company-based.

Personal pensions, which are invariably defined-contribution, have grown in importance in a number of countries in recent years, notably the UK and Belgium. These personal plans provide the tax incentives of pension plans to those not in company plans, enable company plans to be supplemented, and/or to offer greater portability than is available from company plans. A further factor influencing the size of pension fund assets at a given point in time is maturity. Relatively new, immature funds, which have many contributing workers and few pensioners, will have less assets but more rapid growth than a mature fund with the same number of members but there is an equilibrium ratio of pensioners to contributing members. Coverage, i.e. the proportion of employees covered by pension plans, is obviously also important. However, this is a consequence of the economic features discussed below, rather than a separate cause of growth in itself.

[57] Bodie (1990).

Accrual of pension rights in a defined-contribution plan is synonymous with accumulation of assets – which will thus be larger the higher the contribution rate, coverage of the workforce, and rates of return. But a defined-benefit plan is not necessarily synonymous with a fund: rather it is a way to collateralize the firm's benefit promise. In order for assets to be built up, it is essential for fiscal or regulatory provisions to encourage funding of defined benefits – otherwise defined-benefit plans may be unfunded. Only if external funding is encouraged, as opposed to 'booking' of pension liabilities on the balance sheet, will funds be available in the form of assets of the capital market intermediated via pension funds. And only then can one also assert for defined-benefit funds that the more generous the benefits offered, and the wider the coverage, the more financial assets funds will require.

Table 7 shows the scale of social security, whether schemes are mandatory, the tax regime, and maturity for each EU country.

As regards social security, replacement ratios for low earners are shown to be broadly comparable in most EU countries. In such cases, the shape of the replacement ratio/final earnings relation is a crucial determinant of the scope of private funds: if social security provides high replacement ratios to high-earners, there will be little incentive to develop private-funded plans at all. In line with this assertion, the replacement ratio declines rapidly with earnings in Denmark, Ireland, the Netherlands, and the UK – all countries with large funded sectors. Italy, Portugal, and Germany, by contrast, are notable for similar social security pension replacement ratios for high and low earners. Their private-funded sectors are consequently much less important.

Turning to taxation, there is a clear correlation between generosity of treatment of private pensions and the size of the private-funded sector. The Netherlands, Ireland, and the UK, where funded sectors are large, offer generous so-called 'expenditure tax' treatment. (An expenditure tax falls only on consumption, which ensures a post-tax rate of return equal to the pre-tax rate and hence does not distort choice between consumption now and in the future.) Contributions and asset returns are tax-exempt and only pensions are taxed. Such a regime is denoted EET ('Exempt–Exempt–Taxed') in the table. 'Booking' is discouraged in these countries by the withholding of tax privileges from reserve-funded plans. High general tax rates of up to 68 percent, as in Denmark, can encourage private funding even if their fiscal treatment is less generous (a tax is imposed on real asset returns to pension funds above a certain level). In Germany, tax incentives to 'booking' of corporate pension liabilities and some tax disadvantages to pension funds have, at least until recently, accompanied smaller funded plans. Recent imposition of taxes on contributions in Belgium may stunt growth, according to some commentators.

Table 7. Determinants of the Size of Funded Sectors

	Social security replacement rate (1992), based on final gross salary of $20,000 and $50,000[a] (%)	Form of taxation[b]	Coverage of funded schemes	Maturity of funded schemes
UK	50 - 26[c]	EET – Contributions and asset returns tax-free. Benefits taxed,except for tax-free lump sum.	50% (company) 25% (personal); (voluntary)	Mature
Germany	70-59	TET – Employers' contributions taxed as wages; employees' contributions and asset returns tax-free. Benefits taxed at low rate. (For booked benefits, employers' contributions tax-free, benefits taxed at normal rate.)	42% (voluntary)	Immature
Netherlands	66 - 26	EET – Contributions and asset returns tax-free. Benefits taxed.	83% (voluntary)	Mature
Sweden	69 - 49	ETT – Contributions to ATP tax-free; contributions to ITP/STP subject to social security tax. Tax on asset returns of ITP/STP. Benefits taxed at low rate.	90% (ATP compulsory; ITP/STP voluntary)	Mature
Denmark	83 - 33	ETT – Contributions tax-free. Tax on real asset returns. Benefits taxed, including 40% of lump sum payments.	Over 50% (voluntary)	Mature
Ireland	47 - 19	EET – Contributions and asset returns tax-free, benefits taxed.	46% (voluntary)	Mature
France	67 - 45[d]	E(E)T – Contributions to unfunded ARRCO/AGIRC tax-free; separate funded schemes discouraged; insured pension contributions tax-free.	Under 10% (voluntary)	Immature
Italy	77 - 73	EET – Contributions and asset returns tax-free, benefits taxed.	5% (voluntary)	Immature
Spain	90 - 60	EET – Contributions and asset returns tax-free, benefits taxed.	8% (225,000 pension funds, 875,000 personal pensions)	Immature
Belgium	63 - 40	TTT – Asset returns taxed, benefits taxed, employee contributions partly tax deductible.	37% (voluntary)	Mature
Portugal	69 - 68	EET – Contributions and asset returns tax-free, benefits taxed.	5% (voluntary)	Immature

[a] For married man; source Wyatt (1993). [b] The abbreviations refer to taxation of contributions, returns and benefits, hence EET means contributions and returns are exempt and benefits are taxed. [c] Includes state earnings related pension scheme (SERPS). For those contracted out, the ratios are 35% and 14%. [d] Includes ARRCO.
Source: Davis (1995)

Mandatory membership of private-funded schemes is a feature of the Swedish public system, which is designed in the light of demographic concerns to provide a sizeable proportion of retirement benefits. Coverage is hence extremely high: only in the Netherlands do voluntary plans reach similar levels of coverage. Because the plans are compulsory, the tax regime is less important. The French supplementary plans are also compulsory, but pay-as-you-go financing is enforced.

Funded sectors differ in terms of maturity, which also influences the current and prospective asset/GDP ratio. In the UK, Sweden, and the Netherlands, defined-benefit plans are largely mature and hence the asset/GDP ratio is near a peak, although personal and defined-contribution funds could spur further growth in the UK. In Denmark and Germany, immaturity of company plans indicates that further growth is likely.

A simple regression analysis (using the broader group of OECD countries covered in Davis (1995)) was carried out to test the main influences on the size of the pension asset/GDP ratio (see Table 1), using as independent variables the key factors identified above: namely the scope of social security, the tax regime, whether the scheme is mandatory, and maturity of the scheme. Of course, such a regression cannot prove causality. Subject to this caveat, the equation does indicate the importance of these factors in discriminating between countries with small and large private-funded sectors. It suggests that (1) the generosity of social security has a negative effect on the size of pension funds; (2) reducing the favourability of tax treatment on pensions reduces the size of funds; (3) mandatory provision increases the size of funds; and (4) system maturity is associated with a larger size of funds.[58]

Detailed study of national funded sectors[59] suggests that other important factors in the development of occupational pension funds are the ability of employees to opt out of earnings-related social security for an equivalent private pension (as in the UK), funding of civil service pensions (Netherlands), and widening of coverage via encouragement of personal pensions (UK) – as well as encouragement of supplementary defined-contribution plans, as in the United States. On the other hand, development can be stopped by simply banning com-

[58] More specifically, (1) an increase of one percent in the difference between social security replacement ratios at $20,000 and $50,000 (i.e. increasing generosity to higher earners) is associated with a 1.2 percent higher pension asset/GDP ratio, (2) a deviation from favourable 'expenditure tax' treatment of pensions is related to 21 percent lower funding, (3) countries with compulsory membership have a 23 percent higher pension asset/GDP ratio, and (4) those with 'mature' systems have a 27 percent higher ratio. All variables were significant at the 95 percent level.

[59] Davis (1995).

Table 8. Old Age Pensions and Dependency Ratios for the EU-12

	Social security pension benefits as percent of GDP	Old age dependency 1990[a]	Old age dependency 2040
Belgium	8.2	21.9	41.9
Denmark	10.4	22.2	43.4
Germany	8.3	23.7	47.1
Greece	10.4	20.5	41.7
Spain	5.9	17.0	41.7
France	9.9	21.9	39.2
Ireland	6.1	18.4	27.2
Italy	10.7	20.4	48.4
Luxembourg	8.3	20.4	41.2
Netherlands	9.2	17.4	48.5
Portugal	5.4	16.4	38.9
UK	8.9	23.5	39.1
EU-12	9.0	21.4	42.8

[a] Persons of 65+ as a percentage of those in the age group 15-64.
Sources: OECD, Eurostat.

pany-based externally funded plans, as in France.[60] And funding of.social security in Sweden limits the growth of private funds.

A striking feature of this analysis of the determinants of private funding is that development of funding (Table 1) appears to be tenuously related to the underlying fundamentals. There is little correlation to the future ageing of the population in the different countries (Table 8). These should predispose countries such as France, Italy, and Germany to extend the scope of funding. Taxation costs and transition problems, as well as preference for the 'social solidarity' of comprehensive pay-as-you-go, are among the reasons.

But it is widely suggested that, owing to future demographic difficulties, there is likely to be a major shift to funded schemes in these countries. For example, the OECD estimates that if social security systems are unchanged, expenditure on social security pensions will rise over the next 40 years by 30 percent in Belgium and the UK, 40 percent in Germany and Italy, and 70 percent in France. Implicit debts of governments arising from social security liabilities would amount to several times GDP.[61] Davis (1995) offers some illustrative calculations of the potential size of pension funds in these countries. He shows that, for example, if French pension funds were to reach the size of their UK counterparts in terms of

[60] Wyatt (1993).
[61] OECD (1993).

shares of personal-sector assets, they would total \$528bn.[62] Similar calculations for Germany give \$570bn in assets, which compares with the \$703bn market capitalization of the German stock market. In practice, personal-sector financial wealth would probably be boosted by a switch from pay-as-you-go to funding, so the increase in value of funds – and consequent stimulus to capital markets – would probably be significantly greater. It is notable that in the UK, where social security is less comprehensive, the ratio of personal financial wealth to GDP is more than 2, whereas in France and Germany it is below 1.5. If French financial wealth reached the same level as the UK in relation to GDP, not only would pension funds attain the same share of personal wealth, but the stock of pension assets would be over \$750bn. To a degree depending on portfolio regulations and the investment climate, this should in turn boost demand for equities (as discussed above). If funded sectors developed in France and Germany on a par with those in the UK, and equity proportions were similar to US funds, the increase in demand for equities would be \$243bn and \$262bn, respectively.

6. CONCLUSION AND POLICY ISSUES

The *main conclusions* are simply stated. Besides the nature of liabilities and portfolio optimization *per se*, equity holdings of EU pension funds are shown to be influenced by regulations such as those of minimum funding and portfolio composition, as well as features such as taxation, accounting standards, and the competitiveness of fund management.

In effect, these prevent funds from reaching an optimal trade-off between risk and return. It is suggested that streamlining of such regulations so as to allow prudent man rules and flexible funding limits may increase coverage of private pensions by increasing their attractiveness to the sponsor or member, or, in the case of compulsory provision, reduce the unavoidable cost to companies of providing a given level of private pensions.

Meanwhile, development of externally invested, privately funded pension schemes is held back in a number of countries by factors such as the generosity of social security, taxation provisions, incentives to reserve-funding, or even outright banning of company-based schemes. There is an urgent need for reform of these regulations to resolve the future demographic difficulties likely to face EU countries; their resolution would clearly, as a side-effect, help to boost demand for equities as long as regulations are set appropriately.

[62] Calculations are based on 1991 data.

These benefits would spread to the equity market more generally. *Issuers* would benefit from the resultant increased demand for equity capital. This should reduce the cost of equity finance for established issuers, and enable a wider range of issuers to access the markets – issuers that are at present effectively rationed out of the market. Privatizations would also be facilitated. Besides benefits in terms of overall cost and availability of capital for investment, the potential for an increase in equity relative to debt should make the corporate sector, and hence the economy as a whole, less vulnerable to recession. This is because dividends may be passed in adverse financial conditions in a way that is not possible with interest.

The active approach to investment by pension funds should ensure an efficient allocation of funds, with equity prices sensitively reflecting the prospects of firms. Moreover, a related point is that increased financing activity by pension funds may make for better corporate governance, as the funds obtain extra leverage to put pressure on underperforming managers and firms. This might occur either directly, via funds' influence in company boards, or indirectly, via encouragement of takeovers of badly performing firms.[63]

Intermediaries such as broker-dealers will benefit from pension-fund liberalization in terms of both increased turnover and increased market capitalization (as more equity is issued). This should increase their profitability, entail better terms for retail investors, and further benefit the corporate sector via lower liquidity premia on equity. For fund managers, there will be a greater volume of business available on competitive terms, particularly cross-border. There is likely to be a particular premium placed on skills in equity and international investment. Meanwhile, those who are used to protected situations will have to develop their technical abilities rapidly or go out of business.

As regards policy issues, one possible resolution of the difficulties for equity markets set out in this chapter is *action at a European Union level*. Under the Treaties of Rome and Maastricht, the EU has the objectives, *inter alia*, of ensuring free competition, free movement of capital, and mobility of labour. This has led to an increasing interest by the Commission in retirement income provision. Improvements will be hindered where free competition among fund managers is limited by requirements to employ local managers, where free movement of capital is limited by investment restrictions such as those set out in Section 2, and where mobility of labour is limited by restrictions on cross-border membership of pension funds. The progress of proposals for EU reform is of key relevance to the equity and international investment of existing pension funds.[64]

[63] See Davis (1995: Chapter 8).

[64] See Commission of the European Communities (1991), Kollias (1992), European Commission (1994), and Goldby (1995).

However, appropriate regulation at a Union level could clearly also facilitate development of pension funds in continental European countries currently dependent on pay-as-you-go schemes.

Until mid-1994, the European Commission attempted to liberalize funded retirement provision through the vehicle of a Pension Funds Directive. A draft Directive was drawn up on funded pension schemes which addressed, first, the freedom to offer services across borders (in other words, conduct of administration and fund management in another member state); and, second, the liberalization of investment throughout the Community (although some commentators noted that this freedom should already exist, especially for personal retirement provisions, under the Capital Movements Directive). Freedom to offer services cross-border is of course an integral part of the EU Single Market; it has already been introduced for banking[65] and insurance, and agreed for investment services. Proposed liberalization of investment restrictions in the Directive aimed to eliminate unwarranted limits on certain investments: there was to be no privileged access of governments to finance by pension funds, no requirements to localize assets in individual Member States, and no currency-matching requirements that could not be justified on prudential grounds. The Directive also established principles of investment which would set the context for these rules. These broad guidelines stressed security (necessitating consistent asset/liability matching, diversification, and limited self-investment), liquidity, and profitability. These are clearly in line with the concept of a prudent man rule (Section 2), although they were deliberately not set out in detail. They could nonetheless provide a basis for challenging the limits to domestic equity investment.

Under the draft Directive, countries were to be permitted to require matching of domestic liabilities with domestic assets of up to a certain percentage. This was the point on which the Directive foundered (although there were also concerns about the ability to freeze assets managed by a foreign fund manager). The UK, Ireland, and the Netherlands considered 60 percent (i.e. a 40 percent limit on foreign investment) to be a maximum acceptable degree of matching and preferred no limits at all, while other countries wanted 80 percent, which is the same as in the insurance directives. A proposal by the Commission for a compromise on 70 percent was not acceptable.

It is notable that the countries seeking the more liberal approach were those with the larger established funded sectors (accounting for 82 percent of pension fund assets in the EU, and 93 percent of international investment). In contrast, countries which are heavily dependent on pay-as-you-go sought to

[65] See Davis (1993b).

establish a restrictive approach from the start. Denmark was the exception, taking the illiberal approach despite sizeable pension funds. The motivations of the liberal countries were clear; namely that their funds were already often investing over 20 percent of their assets internationally, and hence any reduction would be unacceptable. As regards the more restrictive countries, some were keen to ensure that when pension funds were established, they would help to finance government deficits and expand the domestic securities markets more generally, while the Germans were reportedly concerned that more liberal investment regulations for pension funds, by increasing risk, would lead to pressure for extension of insolvency insurance that currently applies only to reserve-funded schemes. It was often considered that tax privileges gave grounds for treating pension funds differently from other types of financial institution. A false parallel also seems to have been drawn between pension business (where the liabilities are long-term and usually defined in real – inflation adjusted – terms) and insurance (where liabilities are shorter-term, and typically nominal).

The current approach of the Commission seems to be one of applying the existing Capital Movements Directive to the problem of international investment, and attacking the current regimes in the more restrictive member states as not constituting 'reasonable prudential restrictions' as defined in the Directive. To this end, the Commission issued a communication in which it sought to clarify the Rome Treaty rules on the free movement of capital, which Member States were asked to obey,[66] with a threat of action in the European Court. These guidelines suggest that imposition of both minima and maxima for asset classes, as well as more than 60 percent currency matching, is contrary to the Treaty. But at the time of writing France has challenged this communication as going beyond the rights of the Commission. One major reason for French concern with the Commission's position would appear to be fear of competition on the part of domestic insurance companies, who are tied to 80 percent matching. Additionally, proponents of liberalization have suggested that requirements to invest in government bonds are not consistent with the provisions of the Maastricht Treaty against privileged access of governments to finance.

Meanwhile, discussions continue on a third proposal contained in a recent consultative paper; namely the freedom for pension schemes to operate across national boundaries on the basis of home-state authorization, and for individuals to join schemes in other member states. This is seen as a very difficult issue, particularly because of the need for countries to agree on funding standards, which, as noted in Section 2, differ sharply due to differences in the tax treatment of

[66] Cohen and Tucker (1995).

pension funds. Progress on these issues is essential for the completion of the single market; particularly for increasing labour mobility, which is exceptionally low in Europe in comparison with the United States. A first step may be to cover only migrant and 'frontier' workers – i.e. those living in one state and working in another – and to provide for mutual recognition of pension funds based in other member states. It is hoped that existing provision for cross-border membership of social security schemes for a limited period will provide the basis for such an agreement.

The EU may not, however, be the only international forum where restrictions on equity investments may be challenged. The OECD has a Code on the Liberalization of International Capital Movements, to which all members are obliged to subscribe. Deviations from the principle of free movement of capital are required to be justified ('give reservations' in legal jargon). This requires them to submit to forms of 'peer group pressure' to liberalize. In recent years there have been moves to tighten the requirements of the Code in relation to institutional investors,[67] but the initiative has yet to bear fruit.

Autonomous pressure on governments is also likely, on the one hand from the demographic pressures on their pay-as-you-go pension systems, which will lead them increasingly to adopt initiatives to expand funding, and on the other from their own companies, which will seek minimum cost means of providing such privately funded pensions. Abolition of limits on equity and international investment has been shown in this chapter to be an efficient means for companies to reduce the costs of provision.

[67] See, for example, Gusen (1993).

References

Ahrend, Peter, 1994. 'Pension Financial Security in Germany', Working Paper 94–2, Pension Research Council, University of Pennsylvania.

Ambachtsheer, Keith, 1988. 'Integrating Business Planning With Pension Fund Planning', in R. Arnott and F. Fabozzi (eds), *Asset Allocation: A Handbook*, Probus, Chicago.

Black, Fischer, 1980. 'The Tax Consequences Of Long-Run Pension Policy', *Financial Analysts Journal*, September-October, 17–23.

Blake, David, 1992. *Issues In Pension Funding*, Routledge, London.

Blake, David, 1994. 'Pension Schemes as Options on Pension Fund Assets: Implications for Pension Fund Asset Management', mimeo, Birkbeck College, London.

Blanchard, Olivier J., 1993. 'The Vanishing Equity Premium', in R. O'Brien (ed.), *Finance and the International Economy*, 7 (winners of the 1993 Amex bank essay competition), Oxford University Press.

Bodie, Zvi, 1990. 'Pensions as Retirement Income Insurance', *Journal of Economic Literature*, 28: 28–49.

Bodie, Zvi, 1995. 'On the Risk of Stocks in the Long Run', mimeo, Harvard University.

Cohen, Norma and Emma Tucker, 1995. 'Fund investment rules "a matter of sovereignty"', *Financial Times*, 10 May.

Commission of the European Communities, 1991. 'Proposal for a council directive relating to the freedom of management and investment of funds held by institutions for retirement provision', Brussels, 12 November.

Davis, E. Philip, 1986. 'Portfolio Behaviour of the Non-Financial Private Sectors in the Major Economies', Economic Paper No. 17, Bank for International Settlements, Basle.

Davis, E. Philip, 1988. 'Financial Market Activity of Life Insurance Companies and Pension Funds', Economic Paper No. 21, Bank for International Settlements, Basle.

Davis, E. Philip, 1993a. 'The Development of Pension Funds, an Approaching Financial Revolution for Continental Europe', in R. O'Brien (ed.), *Finance and the International Economy*, 7, Oxford University Press.

Davis, E. Philip, 1993b. 'Problems of banking regulation, an EC perspective', Special Paper No. 59, Financial Markets Group, LSE.

Davis, E. Philip, 1994. 'International Investment of Pension Funds in Europe: Scope and Implications for International Financial Stability', *Finanzmarkt und Portfolio Management*, forthcoming.

Davis, E. Philip, 1995. *Pension Funds, Retirement-Income Insurance and Capital Markets: An International Perspective*, Oxford University Press.

Daykin, Christopher, 1994. 'Occupational Pension Provision in the UK', Working Paper 94–1, Pension Research Council, University of Pennsylvania.

Deutsche Bundesbank, 1984, 'Company Pension Schemes in the Federal Republic of Germany', *Deutsche Bundesbank Monthly Report*, August, 30–37.

European Commission, 1994. 'Supplementary Pensions in the European Union: Developments, Trends and Outstanding Issues', Report by the EC's Network of Experts on Supplementary Pensions.

Federal Trust, 1995, Dick Taverne (ed.). 'The Pension Time Bomb in Europe', The Federal Trust, London.

Feldstein, Martin and Charles Horioka, 1980. 'Domestic Saving and International Capital Flows', *Economic Journal*, 90: 314–29.

Frijns, Jan and Carel Petersen, 1992. 'Financing, Administration and Portfolio Management: How Secure is the Pension Promise?', in *Private Pensions and Public Policy*, OECD, Paris.

Frost, A.J. and I.J.S. Henderson, 1983. 'Implications of Modern Portfolio Theory for Life Insurance Companies' in D. Corner and D.G. Mayes (eds), *Modern Portfolio Theory and Financial Institutions*, Macmillan, London.

Goldby, Ron, 1995. 'Clarifying the Latest Developments in the EU Pension Fund Regulations', mimeo, DGXV, European Commission, Brussels.

Gusen, Peter, 1993. 'Foreign Investment by Institutions and the OECD Code of Liberalisation of Capital Movements', paper DAFFE/INV(93)14, OECD, Paris.

Hepp, Stefan, 1990. *The Swiss Pension Funds*, Paul-Haupt, Berne.

Hepp, Stefan, 1992. 'Comparison of Investment Behaviour of Pension Plans in Europe – Implications for Europe's Capital Markets' in Jurgen Mortensen (ed.), *The Future of Pensions in The European Community*, Brassey's, London, for the Centre for European Policy Studies, Brussels.

James, Estelle, 1994. *Income Security in Old Age*, The World Bank, Washington, DC.

Knox, David M., 1993. 'An Analysis of the Equity Investments of Australian Superannuation Funds', Research Paper No. 6, Centre for Actuarial Studies, University of Melbourne.

Kollias S., 1992. 'The Liberalization of Capital Movements and Financial Services in the Internal Market: implications and challenges for pension funds', in Jurgen Mortensen (ed.), *The Future of Pensions in the European Community*, Brassey's, London, for the Centre for European Policy Studies, Brussels.

Mehra, R. and Ed. C. Prescott, 1985. 'The Equity Premium: a Puzzle', *Journal of Monetary Economics*, 15: 145–61.

Mitchell, Olivia S., 1994. 'Public Pension Governance And Performance', paper presented at a conference on 'Pensions Privatization', Santiago, Chile, 26–27 January 1994.

OECD, 1993. 'Pension Liabilities in the Seven Major Industrial Countries', mimeo for

Working Party 1, Organization for Economic Cooperation and Development, Paris.

Rappaport, Anna M., 1992. 'Comment on Pensions and Labor Market Activity', in Zvi Bodie and Alicia Munnell (eds), *Pensions and the US Economy*, Pension Research Council, University of Pennsylvania Press, Philadelphia.

Riley, Barry, 1993. 'Why Pension Funds Are Glum At The Bull Market', *The Financial Times*, 6 December 1993.

Solnik, B.H., 1991. *International Investments*, Addison Wesley, Reading, MA.

Tepper, I., 1992. 'Comments on Bodie and Papke', in Zvi Bodie and Alicia Munnell, (eds), *Pensions and the US Economy*, Pension Research Council, University of Pennsylvania Press, Philadelphia.

Van Loo, Peter D., 1988. 'Portfolio Management of Dutch Pension Funds', De Nederlandsche Bank, Reprint 197.

Vittas, Dimitri, 1992. 'The Simple(r) Algebra Of Pension Plans', mimeo, The World Bank, Washington DC.

Wyatt Data Services, 1993. '1993 Benefits Report Europe USA', The Wyatt Company, Brussels.

Chapter 7

CAPITAL STANDARDS

The EU Capital Adequacy Directive (CAD),[1] which officially came into effect on 1 January 1996, establishes common minimum capital requirements for securities business carried out by banks and investment firms. The underlying purpose of the Directive is twofold: to ensure that securities business is conducted prudently in the interests of both financial stability and investor protection; and, secondly, to secure competitive equality between EU financial institutions that undertake securities activities. In addition, European policy-makers are concerned to achieve these aims in a manner that safeguards the competitiveness of EU securities markets *vis-à-vis* third countries.

It is important to stress, however, that the CAD does not impose a uniform regulatory regime on securities business conducted within the EU. On some regulatory matters the CAD is silent; in other instances the text is open to interpretation; and, above all, the CAD sets out only minimum requirements which national regulatory authorities may wish to exceed. The manner in which the CAD requirements are implemented at the national level therefore has a crucial bearing on the issue of competitive equality within the single European market.

This chapter examines the likely impact of the CAD on European securities markets, focusing in particular on the competitive consequences for institutions engaged in the trading of equity securities. Section 1 identifies differences in the *cost* of capital facing financial institutions, underlining the point that such differences (which may themselves be driven by regulatory factors) can have competitive implications just as important as those arising from differences in minimum capital requirements. Section 2 considers the various ways in which differential regulatory arrangements may lead to competitive distortions in securities markets. Section 3 offers a critical assessment of the detailed CAD rules relating to the equity business of banks and investment firms. Section 4 explores the issues raised by national implementation of the CAD, drawing on the imple-

[1] Council Directive (93/6/EEC)

mentation rules adopted in the UK by the Bank of England (BoE) and the Securities and Futures Authority (SFA). Section 5 highlights differences between the CAD regime and the regulatory approach adopted by the Basle Committee on Banking Supervision, and the US Securities and Exchange Commission (SEC). Section 6 provides a summary and conclusion.

1. THE COST OF CAPITAL

The main focus of this chapter is the competitive implications for securities markets of capital adequacy requirements. However, it should be recognized at the outset that competitive conditions in financial markets may be influenced not only by capital requirements but also by differences in the cost of capital, which are not related to capital requirements. Furthermore, the cost of capital may be determined in part by regulatory and institutional factors that constitute potential sources of competitive distortion. This point is borne out by two recent analyses of the cost of capital for banks and securities firms undertaken by the Federal Reserve Bank of New York.[2]

As far as banks are concerned, empirical evidence suggests that the average pre-tax cost of equity capital (after adjusting for inflation) for banks from different countries over a sample period 1984-90 was as follows:[3]

Country	%
US	11.9
Japan	3.1
Germany	6.9
UK	9.8
Canada	10.3
Switzerland	5.3

Source: Zimmer and McCauley (1991).

In order to convert these cost of capital estimates into a required spread over the cost of funds for a corporate loan, it is necessary to take account of taxes in home and host countries, the structure of tax treaties, and the corporate form of banking organization (branch or subsidiary). Figure 1 incorporates these adjustments in estimating the required spread on a standardized loan to a US

[2] McCauley and Zimmer (1991); and Zimmer and McCauley (1991).

[3] The figures provided are for illustrative purposes only. Since 1990 the cost of equity capital for Japanese banks has risen, as reflected in the collapse of share prices, but the disparity between these countries remains even if the magnitude has altered. See Steil (1995: 11).

Figure 1. Spread Required to Cover the Cost of Equity on a Loan to a US Company

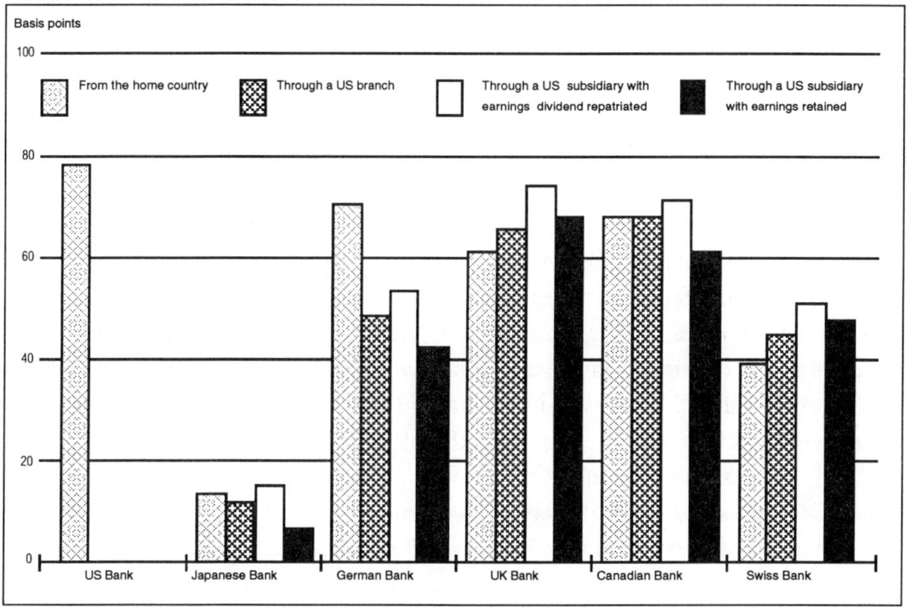

Source: Federal Reserve Bank of New York, *Quarterly Review*, Winter 1991.

company, on the assumption that non-capital funding costs do not vary significantly across banks.

The spread requirements shown in Figure 1 are expressed in terms of bank loan pricing, but the underlying cost of capital differentials could equally well be expressed in terms of required returns on securities activities. The essential point is that banks' post-tax cost of capital appears to vary considerably, depending on country of origin and organizational form. These important differences are largely independent of the capital adequacy requirements of the countries concerned.

The same study also examines the cost of subordinated debt across banks from different countries. The conclusion is that for US banks the cost of such debt rises more quickly in response to lower credit ratings than is the case for foreign banks. The main explanation for this difference appears to be that, since the failure of Continental Illinois in 1984, it has been the stated policy and practice of the US regulatory authorities *not* to extend the official safety net to holders of bank subordinated debt – whereas in Europe and Japan official safety net arrangements have tended to protect all bank creditors. In addition, it is suggested that 'banks with strong links to their industrial customers, including shareholdings, may enjoy a built-in market for subordinated debt that holds down debt costs at higher risk'.[4] Furthermore, the lower sensitivity of subordinated debt costs to bad news itself limits earnings volatility and thereby lowers risk to equity holders. This in turn lowers the cost of equity capital.

These conclusions are important because they show how the lender of last resort function can influence the competitive position of financial institutions – even (or perhaps especially) when prudential regulations have been harmonized.

The same point emerges from a parallel study by the Federal Reserve Bank of New York of the cost of capital for securities firms in the United States and Japan.[5] The authors note that securities firms' non-capital funding costs may be very similar in countries where there is an active 'repo' market because 'the secured nature of this financing technique lessens creditor demands for substantial differences in interest rates based on the creditworthiness of the borrower'.[6] On the other hand, the authors found that the cost of equity capital for Japanese securities firms was significantly less than that for US firms during the period 1982-91. One explanation offered for this competitive disparity is that '... a comparison of the experience of troubled securities firms in the United States and Japan suggests a wider safety net in Japan that may lower equity costs'.[7] Again, the lender of last resort function is seen as a possibly crucial determinant of rival firms' competitive status.

In summary, these empirical studies of the cost of capital suggest that a common capital adequacy framework will not in itself be sufficient to establish a 'level playing field' within the single European financial market. Institutional factors, tax disparities, and the scope of the official safety net will have a crucial bearing on the cost of capital for institutions from different countries, and therefore on the competitive balance within European banking and securities markets. In this context, recent initiatives to harmonize deposit insurance and investor compensation within the EU are of only marginal relevance: Member States are free to provide protection to bank depositors and investors in excess of the EU minimum standards, or may prefer to bail out troubled financial institutions rather than rely on depositor/investor protection schemes.

2. CAPITAL ADEQUACY AND THE LEVEL PLAYING FIELD

The capital adequacy requirements laid down in the CAD are intended to establish minimum prudential standards for investment firms and the securities opera-

[4] McCauley and Zimmer (1991: 45).
[5] McCauley and Zimmer (1991: 14-27).
[6] McCauley and Zimmer (1991: 15).
[7] McCauley and Zimmer (1991: 19).

tions of banks. However, the CAD is also intended to provide conditions of competitive equality for financial market participants throughout the European Union. In view of this second objective it is appropriate to identify the various ways in which uneven capital requirements may distort the competitive balance in financial markets.

The most obvious potential distortion arises from the possibility that financial institutions that are subject to uneven capital requirements may face different overall funding costs. Two qualifications are, however, necessary. In the first place, finance theory suggests that – under conditions of perfectly competitive capital markets, no asymmetries of information between different agents, and no variations in the tax treatment of different forms of finance – a firm's financing is a matter of indifference. In other words, given these assumptions, a firm's weighted average cost of capital should be independent of its capital structure or leverage. In practice, of course, differential tax treatment of interest and dividends, as well as agency costs, mean that firms are not indifferent to their level of gearing.

In this context, banks are special because bank deposits are protected. Deposit interest rates do not therefore reflect the risk characteristics of the deposit-taking bank. This means that banks have a natural bias in favour of low-priced deposit funding, the cost of which is largely independent of the degree of leverage.

Non-bank investment firms, on the other hand, do not enjoy the preferential credit status accorded to banks and are therefore subject to normal market constraints on leverage. However, investment firms are characterized by large fluctuations in their balance sheets and funding needs. For investment firms, therefore, permanent capital in the form of equity may be especially costly because it lacks the elasticity of short-term debt finance. Investment firms will also be concerned to ensure that the capital requirements to which they are subject are no more restrictive than those applied to bank competitors. Therefore, both banks and investment firms have special reason to be concerned about capital structure and regulatory limits on leverage.

A second qualification is that minimum capital standards may be set lower than management's own preferred level of capital: i.e. capital ratios set by regulators may not be binding. In other words, financial markets may reward banks for achieving capital ratios in excess of the regulatory minimum and thereby encourage banks to target those higher ratios. For instance, it appears that US banks' capital raising after 1990 – which took the industry well beyond the Basle requirements – was partly motivated by business rather than regulatory considerations. This strategy was duly rewarded by the stock market.[8] Evidence from

[8] See Cantor and Johnson (1992).

the United States also suggests that securities firms typically maintain levels of capital far above the regulatory minimum.[9] To the extent that it is the markets rather than the regulators' perception of capital adequacy that determines capital targets, regulatory requirements may be of less consequence for the competitiveness of financial institutions.

Notwithstanding the above qualifications, there is a widespread view among regulators and practitioners that capital adequacy requirements impose real costs on financial institutions and that differential capital rules may seriously distort competition. In order to examine the potential for such distortions, and to assess the impact of the CAD, it is necessary to consider the various ways in which capital rules may upset the competitive balance in financial markets.

Most obviously, uneven capital requirements may affect the competitive position of financial institutions from different countries. Such concerns lay behind the 1988 Basle Accord on capital adequacy – the main target of this initiative being Japan, which allegedly allowed its banks to operate on advantageously low capital ratios. Parallel concerns about competitive distortions in securities markets have shaped the capital adequacy provisions of the CAD.

The direction of such competitive distortions will, however, depend on the way in which financial groups are supervised. If foreign subsidiaries (as well as branches) are subject to full consolidated supervision by the home country for capital adequacy purposes, any competitive effects will be felt at the parent company level. However, where, in addition, the foreign subsidiary is subject to solo supervision by the host country in accordance with host country capital rules, a subsidiary (unlike a branch) cannot benefit directly from lower capital requirements in its parent company's country of origin.

On the other hand, if a foreign subsidiary is in effect subject *only* to the capital requirements of the host country it can take advantage of a situation in which capital requirements are lower in the host country than in the home country. Under this regime, the competitive effects associated with uneven capital rules will be reflected *not* in the market share of institutions of differing nationality, but rather in the volume of business attracted by rival financial centres. This is because financial institutions will route their international operations through subsidiaries located in the most accommodating jurisdictions – as, indeed, German banks did in the 1970s when taking advantage of the lower capital requirements imposed by Luxembourg prior to the introduction of consolidated supervision in Germany.

These questions about the direction that competitive distortions might take are important in the European context because, as indicated below, the consolidation rules of the CAD leave considerable discretion to national authorities.

[9] See Haberman (1987).

Capital requirements may also affect the competitive relationship between banks and non-bank investment firms. There appears to be a general consensus among regulators that the securities activities of both types of institution should be treated alike for capital adequacy purposes. This is so despite the fact that bank failures are likely to have more serious systemic consequences than the failure of investment firms. Furthermore, as pointed out below, since banks have access to the lender of last resort, they enjoy a non-capital funding advantage compared with non-bank investment firms. Therefore, equal treatment for capital adequacy purposes does not amount to regulatory parity.

Yet another way in which capital requirements may distort competition is through their impact on securities issuers or borrowers from different countries. Where differential capital requirements are applied to financial institutions' securities positions, and these requirements vary according to the national market on which the securities are listed or traded, the effect may be to increase costs for some issuers relative to others. Alternatively, where the riskiness (price volatility) of securities quoted on national markets differs significantly, and these differences are *not* reflected in capital charges, securities issuers in the riskiest markets may enjoy an unwarranted competitive benefit.

Finally, capital adequacy rules may cause market distortions by discriminating between different types of financing. Differential capital charges may affect the incentives for financial institutions to take positions in equities or debt securities, and may also influence banks' preferences as between debt securities and conventional bank loans. Correspondingly, the cost of raising funds in these alternative forms may be distorted.

Differential capital adequacy requirements may cause competitive distortions in any or all of the ways described above. The types of capital rules that can give rise to such distortions need also to be considered briefly.

Capital requirements are generally expressed as a minimum ratio of capital to risk-weighted assets. If different jurisdictions apply different minimum ratios, financial institutions from some countries could be disadvantaged. Of course, it may be argued that those institutions subject to more stringent capital requirements will be perceived to be less risky and will therefore enjoy lower funding costs that offset the higher capital requirement. For non-bank investment firms there may be some force in this argument, but for banks and bank-related investment firms, which have the implicit support of the official safety net, markets are less likely to differentiate risks in this way.

The risk weights used to calculate the capital ratios may also be a cause of competitive distortion – affecting both financial intermediaries and the issuers of securities subject to variable capital charges. Differential risk weights accorded to bank credits on the one hand, and securities issues by the same category of borrower on the other, may also tilt the playing field in favour of either direct financing (through the securities markets) or indirect financing (through the banking system).

The extent and nature of consolidated supervision practised by different countries may be a further cause of competitive distortion. This is most obviously the case where particular entities within a financial group fall outside the regulatory net altogether. But, as explained above, consolidation procedures will also determine whether competitive distortions primarily affect the relationship between financial institutions from different countries or the relationship between competing financial centres.

Finally, the precise definition of regulatory capital has a direct bearing on the competitiveness of financial firms. The most important distinction here is between equity and near-equity capital on the one hand and subordinated debt on the other. In this context it is interesting to note that for a financial institution the cost of equity-type capital may be two percentage points or more above the cost of subordinated debt.[10] It appears that the composition of regulatory capital can therefore have a major impact on an institution's overall cost of funding.

3. THE CAPITAL ADEQUACY DIRECTIVE[11]

Background Negotiations and the 'Trading Book' Concept

The fundamental conflict in negotiating the CAD was between those countries, notably Germany, with a universal banking tradition and others, in particular the UK, that were concerned to protect the competitive position of investment firms. The underlying difficulty here was that Germany's regulatory arrangements had been designed conservatively to safeguard the solvency of banks, so that subordinated debt, for instance, was excluded altogether from the definition of regulatory capital. In the UK, on the other hand, the regulatory authorities recognized for investment firms (but not for banks) the legitimacy of sophisticated risk management techniques that minimized capital requirements, and the active use of short-term subordinated debt as regulatory capital.

Germany was understandably concerned that if the more finely tuned capital rules appropriate to investment firms were adopted in the CAD, the securities operations of its own universal banks could be placed at a competitive dis-

[10] A recent convertible issue by Barclays Bank was priced on terms that implied a two percentage point difference in financing costs for Tier I (equity-type) capital and Tier II (subordinated debt) capital. See Richard Waters, 'Barclays launches $300m bond in US', *Financial Times*, 17/18 April 1993.

[11] Some of the material in this section is drawn from Dale (1994a), Dale (1994b) and Dale (1994c).

advantage. Equally, the UK was concerned that if the conservative bank-type regulation favoured by Germany were followed in the CAD, then UK-based investment firms would be put at a competitive disadvantage *vis-à-vis* their non-European rivals (in effect encouraging a migration of foreign investment firms from London). Nor was Germany predisposed to abandon its approach to regulation in the interests of uniformity, because that could threaten the stability of its universal banking regime.[12]

The negotiators eventually found a way out of this deadlock, by enlarging the scope of the CAD. Originally it was intended that the Directive would apply to a particular class of financial *institutions* – namely, non-bank investment firms. But in order to meet the conflicting concerns of negotiating parties, it was agreed that the capital adequacy rules should be applied on a *functional* basis to cover certain types of risk taken on by both banks *and* investment firms.[13] For this purpose each type of institution would need to segregate its securities 'trading book' from the rest of its business, and the trading book alone would then be subject to the more permissive capital adequacy rules appropriate to securities trading. In this way a level playing field would be established between universal banks and non-bank investment firms.

Article 2.6 defines the trading book to include the following positions, which must be marked to market daily: (a) proprietary positions in financial instruments held for the short-term or for resale, whether this be for trading, arbitrage, market-making, or hedging purposes; (b) exposures due to unsettled transactions, free deliveries, and over-the-counter derivatives; and (c) exposures due to repurchase agreements and securities borrowing, subject to a number of conditions designed to draw a clear distinction between these trading activities and conventional secured lending by banks – which does not fall within the trading book.

Annex V of the CAD states that the capital of both banks and investment firms shall be defined in accordance with the Own Funds Directive (OFD)[14] – that is, the banking definition of capital. However, national authorities are given the option of permitting banks and investment firms to use an alternative definition of capital in respect of their trading book (only). The alternative definition of capital differs from the banking definition in the following key respects:

[12] A Bundesbank director has stated that, in the context of Germany's restrictive definition of capital, 'we were ... very unhappy to see that the relevant EC Standard is based on a much more diluted concept of capital'. Gaddum (1992: 152).

[13] See Scott-Quinn (1994), Chapter 6, 121-65.

[14] Own Funds Directive (OFD), 1989, 89/299/EEC.

(1) A new class of short-term subordinated debt is eligible for inclusion in regulatory capital. This must have an initial maturity of at least two years (compared with a minimum of five years under the OFD). As an additional safeguard, such debt must incorporate a 'lock-in' clause under which neither principal nor interest can be repaid if this would result in the institution's regulatory capital falling below the required minimum.

(2) The ceiling on the amount of subordinated debt that can be included in regulatory capital is more generous under the trading book option than under the banking rules of the OFD. Whereas the OFD sets this ceiling at 50 percent of 'Tier I' (essentially equity) capital and 25 percent of total regulatory capital, the CAD establishes a ceiling of 60 percent of total regulatory capital backing the trading book. However, for both banks and investment firms the CAD ceiling on subordinated debt may be raised to over 70 percent (250 percent of Tier I capital) if the authorities judge this to be prudentially adequate and, in the case of investment firms, specified 'illiquid assets' are deducted from capital.[15]

Apart from allowing a more permissive use of subordinated debt in regulatory capital, the trading book regime is also subject to less stringent capital adequacy requirements than those applicable to banks under the Bank Solvency Ratio Directive (BSRD),[16] as described below.

In terms of securing an agreed capital adequacy framework that meets the demand for a level playing field between banks and investment firms, the trading book concept is ingenious. However, on closer examination this shift towards functional regulation is open to serious objection.

Most fundamentally, the idea of segregating one part of a bank's business – that is, its securities trading operations – and applying separate and distinct definitions of capital and capital adequacy to the different parts appears to make little prudential sense. As explained in section 1 above, the primary objective of bank regulation is to protect a bank's solvency so as to sustain it as a going concern, but the primary purpose of securities regulators is to ensure that an investment firm can wind down its operations in an orderly manner if need be – hence the emphasis on liquid assets. The CAD's alternative definition of capital allows more liberal use of subordinated debt to support a bank's trading book,

[15] Annex V (8) defines 'illiquid assets' to include fixed assets, holdings of other financial institutions' capital instruments (subject to a waiver in cases of rescue operations), 'not readily marketable' investments, deficiencies in subsidiaries, deposits and loans with a maturity of over 90 days, and physical stocks.

[16] Bank Solvency Ratio Directive (BSRD), 1989, 89/647/EEC.

but to this extent the burden of absorbing losses on the trading book may have to be borne by the equity capital that supports the rest of the bank's business.[17]

In this context the mandatory 'lock-in' provision applicable to short-term subordinated debt does not provide the protection that is evidently intended: a bank which is forced to invoke this clause in respect of its trading book (in effect defaulting) would immediately become suspect in the eyes of the marketplace, thereby risking a deposit run. Accordingly a bank would feel compelled to make good any capital shortfall arising on its trading book so as to prevent the triggering of the lock-in. The presence of significant amounts of 'outside' short-term subordinated debt to back the trading book therefore increases solvency risk for the bank. On the other hand, a parent bank that provides 'inside' subordinated debt to its securities subsidiary would have to hold bank capital against this exposure. In short, it makes little sense to segregate a bank's securities assets for capital adequacy purposes if the risks in this part of the business cannot also be segregated from the bank.[18]

A second objection to the CAD's trading book concept is that while it segregates *assets* used for trading purposes, as well as the regulatory capital used to back such assets, it does not segregate non-capital liabilities. This means that a universal bank is free to use its deposit base to fund its securities trading book. The difficulty here is that because bank deposits are generally protected through deposit insurance and/or other official safety net arrangements, deposit rates do not incorporate a risk premium, even when the bank concerned is engaging in high-risk business. In a sense, banks' risky activities are subsidized.[19] This separation of risk-bearing from risk-taking is one reason why banks are subject to such extensive regulation.

If banks are permitted to use protected deposits to fund their trading book, then the trading operations are also being 'subsidized'. That in turn provides incentives for excessive risk-taking within the trading book – risks that will eventually have to be borne, if not by the bank itself, then by the deposit insurance fund or taxpayers. The moral hazard problem and the associated need for com-

[17] See Dale (1990).

[18] However, if a bank's securities subsidiary is not consolidated with the parent bank, and the latter's holding of subordinated debt in the securities subsidiary is instead deducted from bank capital, then the intra-group capital funding has the effect of reducing required regulatory capital for the group as a whole. See IOSCO (1992), Appendix II.

[19] The risk subsidy accorded to bank deposits is reflected in bank credit ratings, which typically incorporate a judgment on the part of the credit rating agency as to whether or not a particular bank is likely to be officially supported if it runs into financial difficulties. Since the cost of debt finance is closely related to the rating of the borrower, the premium rating that is attributable to the prospect of official support can be viewed as a risk subsidy.

prehensive regulation is then extended from the bank to its securities arm. In this context it may be noted that Barings used depositors' funds to finance its Far East derivatives trading activities prior to its collapse in February 1995.

These difficulties could, in principle, be avoided or at least alleviated by funding rules that prevent or limit the use of deposits to support a bank's trading book and require, instead, funding in the form of outside 'risk money', the cost of which would depend on the perceived risk characteristics of the institution concerned. In this way greater market discipline would be imposed on banks' securities operations and the burden on regulators thereby reduced. Current US proposals to repeal the Glass-Steagall Act adopt this approach in (a) requiring that securities activities be undertaken by a separately incorporated affiliate of the bank; and (b) imposing funding firewalls between the bank and its related securities unit.

Finally, the trading book concept can be criticized on the grounds that it is open to regulatory arbitrage in the form of switches between the banking and trading books. The authors of the CAD were clearly alert to this possibility, which is why they have given such careful attention to the definition of trading book assets, particularly reverse repurchase agreements. Nevertheless, given the existence of very large incentives in terms of differential capital rules, banks have a powerful incentive to present their longer-term investments as trading assets. In this context it should be emphasized that any financial instruments (defined in Annex B of the ISD[20] to include all 'transferable securities') which are held with the *intention* of ultimate resale or for short-term gains can be classified as trading book assets. The subjective nature and generality of this definition suggests that policing the boundary between the banking and trading book will be both costly and difficult.

All things considered, therefore, the trading book concept is best viewed as a device designed to meet a single overriding negotiating objective – namely, competitive equality between banks and non-banks. It appears to serve no useful prudential purpose and indeed gives rise to a number of serious problems. Moreover, even in level playing field terms, there are potential competitive distortions arising from the deposit funding of trading activities.

Capital Requirements under the CAD

The minimum capital requirements imposed on investment firms by the CAD can be considered under six headings: initial capital (Article 3), position risk requirements for debt (Annex I), position risk requirements for equities (Annex I), Settlement and Counterparty Risk (Annex II), Foreign Exchange Risk (Annex

[20] Investment Services Directive (93/22/EEC), 10 May 1993.

III), Other Risks (Annex IV) and Large Exposures (Annex VI). Apart from the initial capital and 'other risks', these requirements are additive. However, whereas Annexes I, II, and VI apply to the trading book only, the remaining requirements apply to the firm as a whole (see Figures 2 and 3).

The level of protection aimed for in each of the various market risk categories is based on a 95 percent confidence level, a 10-day holding period, and volatility data covering the last five years.[21] The 95 percent confidence level was selected because it was judged extremely unlikely that an institution would simultaneously face losses in respect of each of the five main categories of market risk: i.e. interest rate, equity market, foreign exchange, settlement, and large exposures risks. The main focus of this section is on the position risk requirements for equities, although other provisions of the CAD that may affect the competitive status of investment businesses are also considered.

Equity Position Risk

The position or market risk on both debt and equity instruments is divided into two components in order to calculate the required capital. The first is *specific* risk, representing the risk of a price change in the instrument owing to factors related to the issuer; and the second is *general* risk, representing the risk of a price change due (in the case of a debt instrument) to a change in the level of interest rates or (in the case of equities) a broad movement in the equity market unrelated to the specific attributes of individual securities. The requirements for specific and general risk are then added – this being the so-called 'building block' approach.

The overall capital requirement for equity positions therefore consists of separately calculated charges for (a) the specific risk of holding a long or short position in an individual equity, and (b) the general market risk of holding a long or short position in the market as a whole. The minimum standard for the trading book can be expressed as a '4 percent plus 8 percent' formula in which the 4 percent, representing specific risk, applies to the gross equity position (i.e. the sum of all long equity positions and of all short equity positions) and the 8 percent, representing general market risk, applies to the difference between the sum of the longs and the sum of the shorts (i.e. the overall net position in a particular equity market).

An important concession is, however, allowed to equity portfolios that meet the following conditions:

(i) the equities shall not be those of issuers which have issued debt securities attracting an 8 percent specific risk requirement;

[21] See Clarotti (1992: 23).

Figure 2. Capital Adequacy Directive

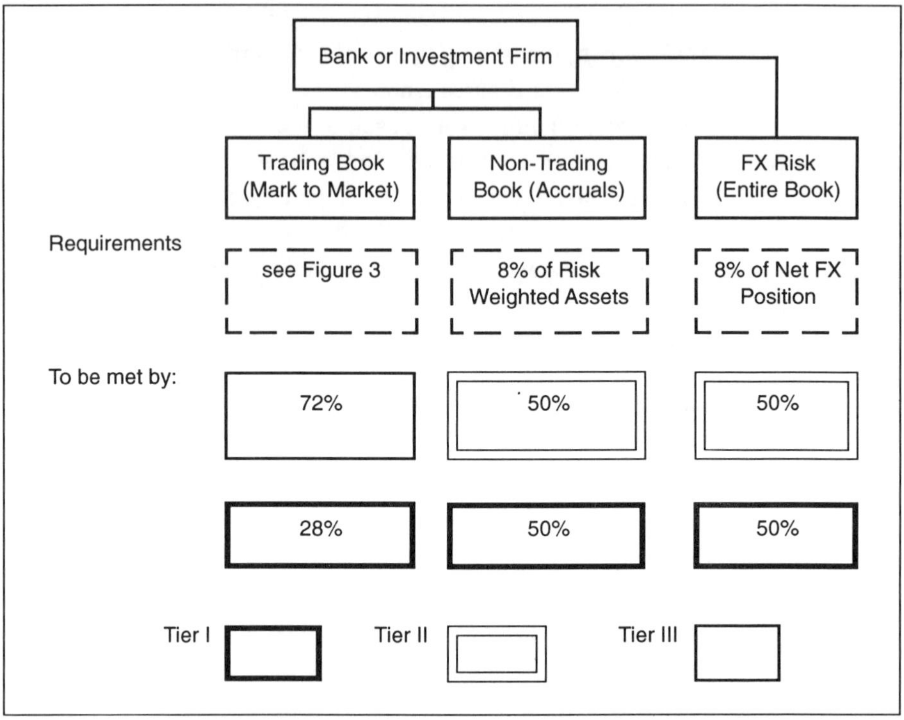

(ii) the equities must be judged 'highly liquid' by national authorities;

(iii) no individual position may exceed 10 percent of the value of the portfolio and the total of such positions must not exceed 50 percent of the value of the portfolio.

If equity portfolios meet these conditions, national authorities may apply a capital requirement against specific risk of 2 percent rather than 4 percent.

Finally, the underwriting of both debt and equity securities is subject to special concessionary arrangements designed to reflect the transient nature of underwriting positions. Under these arrangements a reduction factor may be applied to the net position, ranging from 100 percent on 'working day zero' to 25 percent five days after this date (with no reduction factor thereafter). However, 'working day zero' has been defined as that day 'on which the institution becomes unconditionally committed to accepting a known quantity of the securities at an agreed price'. Therefore, the reference point is not the date on which the underwriting commitment is entered into, but rather the date on which the underwriting firm's actual take-up is known. In other words, the underwriting commit-

Figure 3. Capital Adequacy Directive

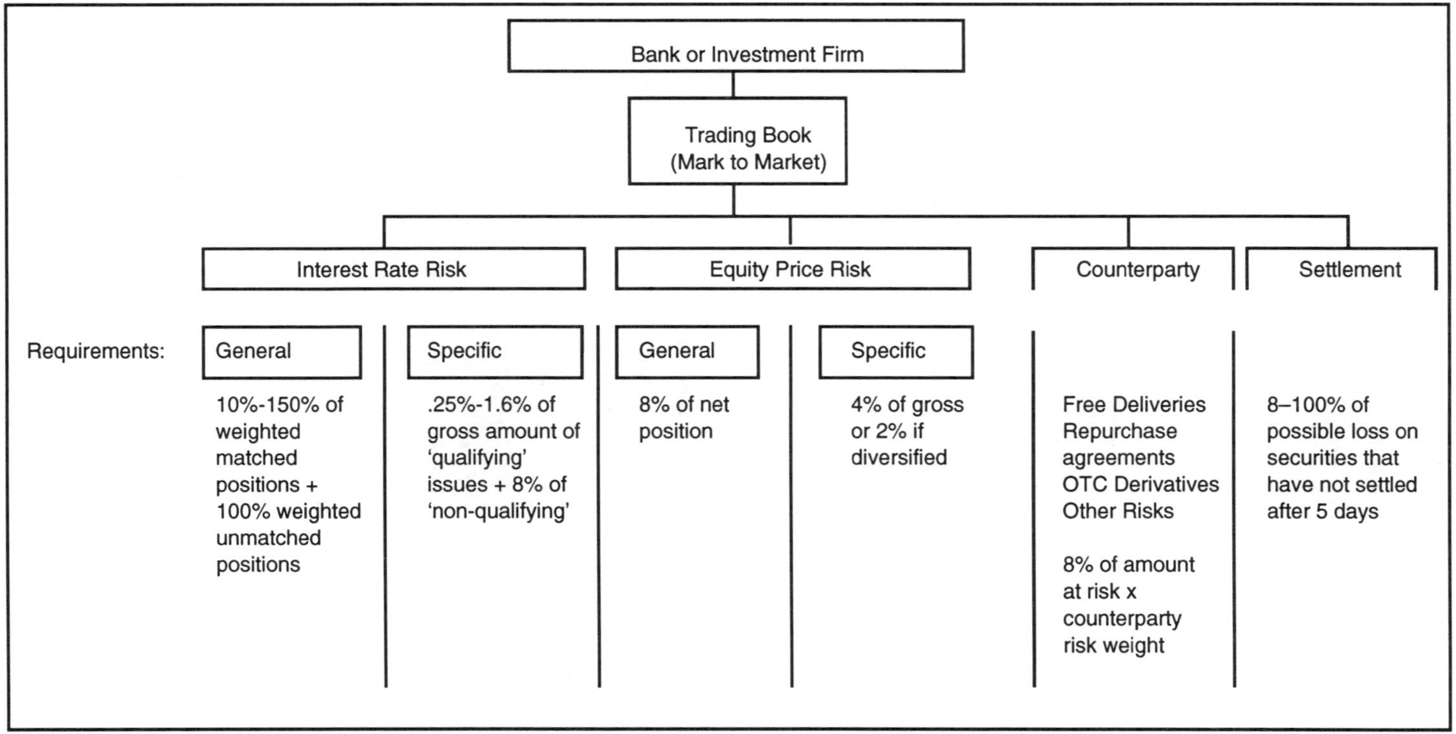

Figure 4. The Equity Position Risk Framework

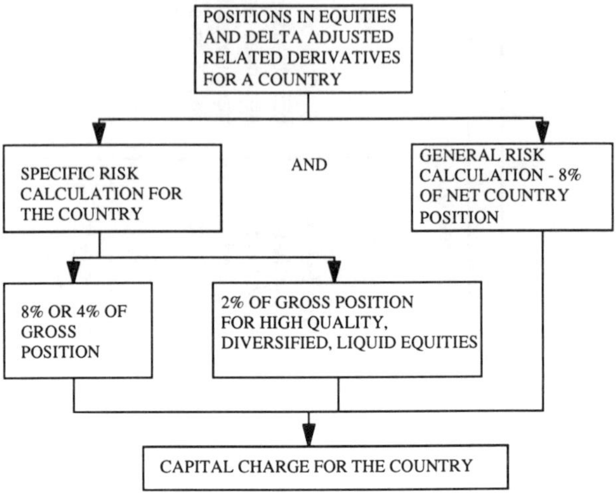

Source: Coopers & Lybrand (1995: 28)

ment period is exempt from any position risk requirements under Annex I[22] – a result that can be attributed to representations on the part of both the securities industry and European banks which had not previously been subject to capital requirements on underwriting commitments.

The CAD's treatment of equity position risk presents several areas of difficulty. In the first place the concessionary 2 percent capital charge against specific risk applicable to liquid and diversified portfolios is loosely formulated. The condition that the equities be judged 'highly liquid' appears to be largely subjective (how, for instance, does this requirement relate to the requirement that qualifying debt securities be 'sufficiently liquid'?), and the condition relating to portfolio concentration appears to be unnecessarily crude (see below).

The second, and much more serious, difficulty in the CAD's approach to equity position risk concerns the building block methodology. The problem here has been identified by Dimson and Marsh, who have investigated the efficiency

[22] This underwriting exposure 'gap' in the CAD also creates a lacuna in the large exposures provisions of Annex VI. Accordingly, Section (ii) of this Annex states that 'pending further co-ordination, the competent authorities shall require institutions to set up systems to monitor and control their underwriting exposures *between the time of the initial commitment and working day one* in the light of the nature of the risk incurred in the markets in question' (italics added).

of three alternative capital adequacy regimes.[23] These are: the *comprehensive* approach, as applied by the US Securities and Exchange Commission (SEC), under which firms are required to have capital equal to a specified proportion of the value of their long positions, plus a proportion of the value of qualifying short positions; the *building block* approach, as adopted by the EU and proposed by the Basle Committee, which bases the capital requirement partly on the net value of the trading book (market risk) and partly on the gross value (specific risk); and the *portfolio* approach, favoured by UK regulatory authorities, which uses the precepts of modern portfolio theory to estimate the volatility of portfolio values.

Dimson and Marsh assess the efficiency of these three alternative regimes by measuring the extent to which each methodology links capital requirements to the risk or volatility of 58 specimen securities portfolios held by UK-based securities firms. The results of this investigation are as follows:

1. The SEC's comprehensive approach performs very poorly because it takes virtually no account of either (a) offsetting long and short positions or (b) the degree of portfolio diversification.
2. The building-block approach performs better because it takes account of offsetting long and short positions. However, the correlation between capital requirements and risk is still low because the risk-reducing benefits of diversification are ignored.
3. In contrast, the UK's portfolio approach, which takes into account both the balance of a portfolio (long versus short positions) and its diversification level, demonstrates a high correlation between capital requirements and portfolio risk.

The overall conclusion is that the SEC is perversely adhering to an inefficient capital adequacy regime; that the Basle Committee and the EU have both opted for an inferior methodology in their attempts to assess market risk; and that elementary principles of modern portfolio theory are being largely ignored by national regulatory authorities. According to Dimson and Marsh, the consequences could be 'the imposition of a worldwide framework which provides perverse incentives for securities businesses, and which would fail to encourage prudence amongst institutions such as market makers, broker-dealers, and banks acting as principals in the securities markets'.[24]

[23] See Dimson and Marsh (1994: 7-14).

[24] Dimson and Marsh (1994: 2).

Consolidated Supervision

Any bank or investment firm which has a bank or investment firm subsidiary – or which holds a 'participation' (equity holding of at least 20 percent) in such a firm – shall be subject to consolidated supervision. Financial holding companies, whose subsidiaries include banks and/or investment firms, must also be supervised on a consolidated basis.

The consolidated supervision requirements are subject to a number of exemptions. Subsidiaries whose operations are *de minimis* may be left out of consideration, as may subsidiaries located in third countries where there are legal impediments to the transfer of the necessary information. Furthermore, a subsidiary/participation may be omitted from consolidation if its inclusion is considered to be 'inappropriate or misleading' from a supervisory standpoint. Finally, in the case of financial groups that do *not* include a bank, consolidated supervision may be waived provided that each investment firm in the group (a) uses a restricted definition of capital (including the deduction of illiquid assets); (b) meets the CAD's capital adequacy requirements and large exposure limits on a solo basis; and (c) sets up systems to monitor and control the sources of capital and funding of all other financial institutions within the group.

The principles of consolidated supervision laid down in the CAD imply that risks within financial groups are interdependent and that losses incurred by one unit are to be made good by other units within the group. This point is underlined by the discretion given to national authorities not to apply the capital adequacy and large exposure rules to a parent bank or to its individual subsidiaries on a solo basis where the parent institution is itself subject to consolidated supervision.

On the other hand, the option to exempt from consolidated supervision financial groups that do not include a bank appears to be based on the view that investment firms, as distinct from banks, can be protected from financial problems arising elsewhere in the group – if necessary through the imposition of 'funding firewalls', in the form of restrictions on intra-group transfers of capital.

The rules on consolidated supervision therefore allow for the coexistence of divergent supervisory regimes. In the general case, where consolidated supervision applies, it is implicitly assumed that the operating units stand or fall together. However, where supervisory authorities exercise the waiver on consolidated supervision, risks within the group are to be segregated and losses incurred by one operating unit should not be allowed to jeopardize the solvency of other units (at least where these are investment firms). The fact that the waiver option is not available to financial groups that include banks is, furthermore, a recognition of the fact that banks are uniquely vulnerable to contagious financial disorders.

Given this implicit acceptance in the consolidation rules of the differing vulnerability of banks and investment firms, it is all the more surprising that the CAD should treat the two businesses equally for all other purposes. Thus, when calculating capital requirements against counterparty risk, investment firms are given the same privileged (20 percent) risk weighting as that accorded to banks. Similarly, when calculating large exposures under the CAD, claims on investment firms may be accorded the same concessionary treatment as inter-bank loans. This parity of treatment is inconsistent with risk weightings incorporated in the Basle Accord on capital adequacy, and is surely anomalous unless it is supposed that investment firms have access to the lender of last resort and the official safety net arrangements that underpin national banking systems. Here is an example of equality of treatment that gives rise to competitive distortion by encouraging financial markets to ignore differences in default risk.

4. IMPLEMENTING THE CAD

Although the CAD is intended to establish a level playing field between institutions undertaking securities business within the EU, implementation of the CAD rules by Member States may nevertheless give rise to competitive distortions. This may occur if there are differing interpretations of the CAD rules, or where the CAD is silent on some regulatory issue. More importantly, since the CAD establishes only minimum regulatory requirements, individual Member States may choose to apply rules more stringent than (or 'superequivalent' to) those laid down by the CAD. In this section we examine implementation of the CAD by the UK in order to identify areas of potential competitive distortion. The UK has been chosen for this purpose because it is one of the first EU Member States to have published implementation rules in final form.

Within the UK there are two key regulatory authorities responsible for implementing the CAD. The Bank of England (BoE) is responsible for regulating banks, including securities business undertaken by bank entities; while the Securities and Futures Authority (SFA) is responsible for regulating securities firms, including the securities subsidiaries of banks. Both the BoE and the SFA published CAD implementation proposals in 1994.[25] These initial consultative documents contained numerous superequivalent items and also diverged from each other in certain important respects. However, in response to industry comments[26] as well

[25] SFA Board Notice 200 (1994); and BoE Consultative Document (1994).

[26] Those industry comments include The British Bankers' Association (BBA) and The London Investment Banking Association (LIBA).

as concerns about regulatory disparities, the final implementation rules issued in the spring of 1995 were significantly modified.[27] In particular the SFA noted industry concerns that 'if other states implement no more than the minimum requirements of the CAD, UK firms could become vulnerable to competitive distortions or the removal of financial services business from the UK'.[28] The SFA also noted that although the approach of other EU Member States to implementation remained uncertain, it would be prepared to examine particular aspects of its own rules 'quickly' if they appeared to be giving rise to serious competitive distortions.

It would seem, therefore, that there are powerful regulatory convergence forces at work, independent of the CAD. That is to say, within the context of the single European financial market, national authorities are becoming increasingly sensitive to the competitive effects of regulatory disparities and are watching one another closely to see whether rival jurisdictions may gain some competitive advantage through the adoption of more permissive regulatory arrangements. At the same time, UK experience with CAD implementation suggests that bank and securities regulators are coming under greater pressure to align the capital adequacy rules of banks to those of securities firms, despite the very different historical traditions of these two businesses and the different theoretical arguments underpinning their respective capital requirements (see section 2). The particular concern in this context is that if the SFA rules are more concessionary than the BoE rules, banks may be induced to subsidiarize their securities activities under the jurisdiction of the SFA.

Notwithstanding the fact that several superequivalent proposals have been removed from the BoE's and the SFA's final CAD implementation rules, there are a number of important respects in which UK implementation is more stringent than the CAD's minimum requirements. Those areas of superequivalence that may cause competitive distortions in equity markets are considered below under five headings: namely, target and trigger capital ratios, the trading book definition, equity position risk, consolidation, and the use of models.

Target and Trigger Capital Ratios

The BoE has consistently followed a superequivalent approach to banks' minimum capital requirements – first under the Basle Accord and now under the CAD – by setting 'target' and 'trigger' ratios for individual banks at or above the 8 percent level. The trigger represents the threshold below which supervisory action is taken, while the (higher) target ratio acts as a regulatory early warning system. Where the target ratio is in the 8-10 percent range, the trigger ratio is set

[27] The final rules implemented are: Bank of England (1995), policy notice S&S/1995/2; and SFA Board Notice 249 (1995).

[28] SFA Board Notice 249 (1995), paragraph 3.

half a percent below the target, but for higher target ratios of, say, 15 percent, the trigger is set as much as 1 percent below the target. Under its CAD implementation rules the BoE is to apply separate trigger ratios to banks' banking and trading books. In the case of the banking book the target/trigger ratios (which may be as high as 20 percent for risky banks) will be applied in the usual way. However, in view of the CAD's comprehensive coverage of trading book risks, banks with diversified trading books and good internal risk management systems are likely to have trading book triggers close to 8 percent, while for other banks trading book triggers will not generally exceed 12 percent.[29]

The SFA's implementation rules also incorporate a secondary capital requirement with a view to capturing (a) liquidity risk arising from high levels of undiversified illiquid assets; (b) unusual operational risks; and (c) other unusual risk profiles – for example, concentration of risks in one business area. This secondary requirement is comparable to the BoE's trigger/target ratio regime; but whereas all banks will be subject to a trigger ratio, the SFA secondary requirement is expected to apply only to a minority of institutions. This is an area, therefore, where banks could be placed at a competitive disadvantage relative to investment firms.

The implicit justification for the UK authorities' trigger/secondary capital requirement regime is that the CAD does not adequately capture the risk characteristics of individual institutions. The UK approach has been criticized by industry representatives on the grounds that it may handicap UK financial firms in a situation where other EU Member States are likely to apply the CAD minimum requirements. At the same time, the discretionary nature of the regime, and the absence of definitive criteria for establishing trigger ratios, is open to the objection of lack of transparency.[30] Nevertheless, it is worth pointing out that the BoE has for some time imposed capital adequacy requirements over and above (and in some cases substantially above) the Basle Accord minimum apparently without prompting an exodus of foreign banks from London.

Definition of Trading Book

The definition of the trading book is important because non-trading book items may attract a higher capital requirement and are also subject to a more restrictive

[29] The capital requirement for supervisory purposes is calculated as follows:
- Multiply banking book risk weighted assets by the banking book trigger ratio.
- Multiply trading book notional risk weighted assets by the trading book trigger ratio.
- Sum the banking book and trading book requirements.
- Determine eligible capital, taking care to respect gearing limits and restrictions on the use of Tier III capital.
- Capital adequacy is then expressed as total eligible capital as a percentage of total capital requirements: where the percentage is greater than 100 percent, the bank is deemed adequately capitalized.

[30] See British Bankers' Association (1995), p.15 Section 4.13.

definition of capital (see section 3 above). Furthermore, some categories of financial instrument are eligible to be included in either the trading or the banking book, depending on the purpose for which the instrument is held. The BoE elaborates on the CAD definition by stating that positions in eligible instruments will be treated as being held with a trading intent if (a) they are marked to market daily; (b) the position-takers have autonomy in entering into transactions within set limits; or (c) they satisfy any other criteria which a bank applies on a consistent basis to the composition of its trading book. In this context each bank must agree a policy statement with its supervisor about which activities are normally considered part of the trading book.

The problem of defining the boundary between the banking and trading book becomes even more troublesome where a trading book exposure is hedged outside the trading book, where a banking book exposure is hedged through the trading book, or where risks are transferred between the banking book and trading book through 'internal' transactions (see Box 1). The treatment of these exposures has proved to be one of the most difficult aspects of the CAD implementation process, although the issues raised primarily affect the trading of debt instruments and control of interest rate risk, rather than position-taking in equities. Furthermore, the precise definition of the trading book is much more important for banks than for investment firms, since the latter typically hold a relatively small volume of non-trading book assets.

Equity Position Risk

The CAD's capital requirements in respect of equity position risk have been described above (see section 3 on 'equity position risk'). Under the BoE and SFA implementation rules the CAD's 8 percent minimum requirement is applied to general market risk. However, the SFA/BoE capital charges for specific risk are more controversial (see Box 2).

The concept of 'non-qualifying' countries, for which the CAD's 4 percent minimum specific risk charge is doubled, is superequivalent and is unlikely to be followed elsewhere in Europe. The UK authorities believe that countries whose equity markets are felt to be either illiquid or particularly volatile should attract a higher specific risk charge in order to satisfy prudential concerns. The real difficulty with the UK approach, however, is that 'qualifying countries' are for this purpose crudely defined as *all* EU and G10 markets plus (in the case of the BoE) Australia.[31] Clearly there are equity markets in the EU where liquidity

[31] Group of Ten industrial countries. The ten members are: Belgium, Canada, France, Germany, Italy, Japan, the Netherlands, Sweden, the United Kingdom and the United States.

Box 1. Bank of England Rules on Hedging and Internal Deals

SITUATION	RULE AND BASIC TREATMENT
Trading book exposure hedged by a non-financial instrument (i.e. bank loan or deposit)	Include non-financial instrument in trading book for general market risk but not specific risk; apply counterparty risk charge
Banking book interest rate risk hedged directly by a financial instrument with an external counterparty	Take financial instrument out of trading book and subject it to banking book rules (i.e. counter-party risk charge)
Banking book interest rate risk transferred to trading book via 'internal deal' (i.e. an FRA or swap)	Include trading book leg of internal deal in trading book for general market risk charge, but not specific risk; no counterparty risk charges on internal deal; banking book charge unchanged

Source: LIBA (1995: 6).

Box 2. Equity Specific Risk Charges

Equities in non-qualifying countries	8 %
Equities in qualifying countries	4 %
'Highly liquid' equities indiversified portfolios	2 %

Source: LIBA (1995: 19).

is lower and volatility higher than in some equity markets outside the EU/G10, but for political reasons it has been felt necessary to group all EU markets together. On the other hand, the BoE and SFA have indicated a willingness to expand (but not contract) the list of qualifying countries based on an empirical assessment of volatility.

The CAD allows a concessionary 2 percent specific risk charge for 'highly liquid' equities held in diversified portfolios, and this is followed in the BoE/SFA requirements. However, whereas the diversification conditions specified by the CAD are adopted by the BoE/SFA, the Directive is silent on the definition of 'highly liquid'. The UK authorities have therefore developed their own criteria for this purpose, their final ruling being that any equities will be considered highly liquid if they are included in either (a) specified major stock market indices or (b) the FT Actuaries World Indices (although in this latter case the equities must be those of qualifying countries). Significantly, it has been stated that the list of eligible indices will be added to as other Member States' definitions of highly liquid equities become available.

The UK approach to implementing the CAD's specific risk requirements for equities has proved highly contentious. The London Investment Banking Association (LIBA) has stated that the doubling of the specific risk charge for equities in non-qualifying countries 'is one of the most serious cases of super-equivalence and is a major source of concern to the investment banking industry'.[32] Similarly the British Bankers' Association (BBA) has expressed 'very considerable concern' over this issue, arguing that if (as it expects) other Member States do not follow the UK approach 'UK banks would face a severe competitive disadvantage in operating in some of the most competitive and dynamic markets in the world'.[33]

It seems highly unlikely that a unilateral UK approach in this area is sustainable, since it could severely affect UK firms' equity trading in Southeast Asia and in emerging markets generally. The lesson is clear: where differential CAD implementation rules threaten major competitive distortions, a second-stage alignment of national regulations seems inevitable. Indeed, in some areas this is openly recognized, as in the UK authorities' stated willingness to reopen their definition of highly liquid equities in response to developments elsewhere in Europe.

Finally, for the purpose of calculating the equity position risk charge it should be noted that both the BoE and the SFA allow a 'hybrid' methodology that combines the CAD and existing SFA rules. Under this alternative method, an institution is required to meet a capital charge equal to the higher of the CAD *minimum* rules and the current SFA ('Sharpe')[34] rules based on modern portfolio theory. This option may confer some advantage in the form of capital savings because the CAD rules do not include the doubled specific risk charge for non-qualifying countries. Furthermore, the retention of the Sharpe approach is viewed as important to some institutions which believe (understandably) that the CAD regime represents a regressive move away from the modern portfolio approach to capital adequacy assessment.[35]

Consolidated Supervision

Banks and investment firms are required to meet the CAD's capital requirements on a consolidated basis. Both the capital requirements and the capital resources

[32] See LIBA (1995: 20).
[33] BBA Document (1995), p. 39, paragraph 10.4.
[34] William Sharpe is one of the architects of modern portfolio theory. See Sharpe (1970).
[35] See LIBA (1995: 22).

Box 3: Scope of Consolidation

	Bank of England	SFA	
	EU and non-EU	EU	Non-EU
Parent			
• Financial Holding Company[1]	Y	Y	D
• Other	D	Y	D
Firm's Subsidiary or Participation			
• Bank	Y	Y	D
• Investment Firm	Y	Y	D
• Financial Institution[2]	Y	Y	D
• Other	D	D	D
Parent's Subsidiary or Participation[3]			
• Bank	Y	Y	D
• Investment Firm	Y	Y	D
• Financial Institution	Y	Y	D
• Other	D	D	D

Y = Yes, always subject to consolidation.
D = Subject to consolidation at discretion of supervisor.

[1]A financial holding company is an entity whose subsidiaries are exclusively or mainly banks, investment firms or financial institutions.
[2]A financial institution is an entity other than a bank which carries out a 'listed activity' as defined in EC law.
[3]A participation means a direct or indirect 20 percent holding.

Source: LIBA (1995: 49).

of the group must be consolidated, although it should be emphasized that on the key issue of techniques of consolidation the CAD is largely silent – except that it explicitly permits the intra-group netting of consolidated position risks, large exposures, and foreign exchange risks.

Under the UK implementation rules, group entities are subject to consolidation depending on their type of business and, in the case of the SFA, their place of incorporation or the location of their head office (see Box 3).

The two alternative consolidation techniques adopted by the UK authorities are 'line-by-line' consolidation and 'aggregation plus'. Under line-by-line or full accounting consolidation, the capital requirement for each individual banking book or trading book exposure is calculated by considering the combined positions of all group entities taken together. This approach offers the fullest potential for offsetting intra-group positions. Under aggregation plus, group capital requirements are calculated as the sum of the individual capital requirements of each group entity – except that under the SFA's rules a parent's investment in a subsidiary is used for aggregation purposes where this exceeds the subsidiary's capital requirement.

Under the BoE rules, banks' banking books are subject to line-by-line consolidation, while their trading books, foreign exchange exposures, and investment firm subsidiaries will usually be consolidated using aggregation plus. The SFA, on the other hand, adopts the aggregation plus approach to consolidation in nearly all cases, reserving the right to require line-by-line consolidation only in limited circumstances.

A key question under the aggregation plus methodology is whose capital requirements are to be applied to each group entity. For UK banks or investment firms the relevant rules are the BoE or SFA CAD implementation requirements. For group entities incorporated in another EU country the relevant rules are those applied by the local regulator. For group entities incorporated in non-EU countries the local rules are again applied so long as these rules are deemed broadly equivalent to the CAD (this is a CAD requirement), while for group entities incorporated in other non-EU countries (i.e. whose local rules are not considered to be broadly equivalent to the CAD) the BoE or SFA implementation rules apply (again a CAD requirement).

The BoE's rules include a list of non-EU countries whose regulations for investment firms are deemed to be broadly equivalent to the CAD.[36] However, the BoE states that for the purpose of consolidating the trading books of third country banking subsidiaries no local bank regulators can be considered to meet the 'broadly equivalent' test until they have implemented the Basle market risk proposals (when finalized).

In an important exception to these consolidation rules, the SFA has determined that in relation to non-EU group companies it 'does not consider that it is bound by the CAD to insist on global consolidation' and that it 'prefers to delay adopting global consolidation until there is international agreement that this should be done'.[37] The SFA will therefore generally limit consolidation to EU entities, while reserving the right to include non-EU subsidiaries when there are compelling prudential reasons for doing so. The SFA cites an offshore booking vehicle for OTC derivatives as one example of an entity which might need to be included in consolidated supervision but which does not fall within the scope of the CAD under the SFA's interpretation of the Directive.

[36] Investment firms from these recognized countries attract a 20 percent counterparty risk weighting, whereas investment firms from non-recognized countries attract a counterparty risk weighting of 100 percent. See BoE policy notice, S&S/1995/2, Chapter 11.

[37] See SFA Board Notice 249 (1995), paragraphs 105-7.

The UK's implementation rules on consolidation have an important bearing on the potential for competitive distortions under the CAD regime. It has been pointed out that aggregation plus creates opportunities for regulatory arbitrage, in that UK firms may avoid superequivalent elements of the BoE or SFA rules by conducting business in those group entities subject to CAD minimum requirements.[38] In particular, the doubled position risk requirement for equities in non-qualifying countries could encourage UK institutions to conduct relevant equity business either in European subsidiaries governed by the CAD minimum requirements or in non-EU subsidiaries. More generally, the SFA's decision not to consolidate non-EU subsidiaries (except in limited circumstances) is surely an open invitation for UK investment firms to escape not merely superequivalent UK requirements, but any or all UK rules that are found to be onerous, simply by routing business offshore.

Models

Models may be used to price transactions prior to applying CAD capital charges, to calculate capital requirements for specific types of instrument, or to calculate overall capital requirements.

The CAD specifically allows for the use of the first two categories of model. In particular, such models may be used (as an alternative to the standard approach) to cover option and interest rate risk in derivatives held on the trading book, and foreign exchange risk in the banking and trading books. Use of models for these purposes will normally result in lower capital requirements for a given level of position or foreign exchange risk.

The real problem in implementing the CAD has arisen in connection with 'value at risk' (VAR) models which apply a portfolio approach to measurement of the overall riskiness of an institution's trading positions. Here, the question is whether such models, which are not specifically provided for in the CAD, can be used to calculate overall capital requirements for the trading book. The Basle market risk proposals do give an important role to such internal risk models and regulators have been under pressure to interpret the CAD in a way that accommodates VAR models – the more so as the CAD will, for practical reasons, probably have to be brought into line with the final Basle capital adequacy regime for market risks. Accordingly regulators within the EU have reached a broad understanding that VAR models may be used to calculate CAD capital requirements.

The BoE, unlike the SFA, has spelt out in some detail the conditions under which it will approve the use of VAR models.[39] The underlying principle

[38] See LIBA (1995: 50).
[39] See the BoE (1995) policy notice, S&S/1995/2, Chapter 11.

is that a bank opting for the VAR approach should calculate its CAD capital requirement on a date randomly chosen by the supervisor, together with the capital requirement specified by its own VAR model. The bank is then required to hold capital based on the higher of two capital requirements: the CAD one resulting from the latest benchmark test (scaled by any increase in the bank's current VAR capital requirement compared with the benchmark date), and the VAR one set out in the Basle consultative proposals on market risk (see Box 4).

The advantage of allowing VAR models to be used in this way is that for many institutions which already have such models in place it will save on systems costs. However, the VAR approach is not designed to bring immediate capital savings, since the CAD benchmark requirements still have to be met. There are therefore no important short-term competitive implications. Nevertheless, if (as seems inevitable) the CAD is in due course amended to conform to Basle, there will be potential for important capital savings through the use of proprietary models – as intended under the Basle approach (see below).

5. THE CAD AND NON-EU REGULATORY REGIMES

The competitive position of European financial institutions is affected not only by EU regulatory arrangements but also by the rules of non-EU supervisory bodies. In particular, the Basle proposal on market risk, when finalized, will have a direct impact on European banks which will be subject to the more stringent of the Basle or CAD rules in any particular area.

The Basle market risk proposals, as presently formulated, are generally more restrictive than the CAD, reflecting the cautious approach favoured by bank regulators. For instance, under Basle the use of Tier III capital can be used only to cover market risks arising in the trading book (not counterparty or settlement risks); Basle imposes a 2 percent specific risk charge on stock market indices, in contrast to the CAD's 0 percent; and, most importantly, Basle's specific risk charge for equity positions risk is 8 percent, reducing to 4 percent for diversified portfolios, whereas the CAD's charge is 4 percent reducing to 2 percent.

However, in one key area Basle is more flexible than Brussels. The proposed Basle rules explicitly recognize the use of internal VAR models for the calculation of overall capital adequacy requirements – subject to the specification of various risk parameters (e.g. 99 percent confidence interval, 10-day holding period, and minimum one-year duration period). In contrast, the CAD requirements have been *interpreted* to allow use of internal VAR models, but subject to CAD benchmarking (see section 4 on 'models' above). The result is that whereas Basle provides a positive incentive for banks to use and develop internal models, since capital savings can be achieved thereby, under the present CAD approach

Box 4. Use of VAR Models Under the CAD

- VAR models can be used to calculate capital requirements on a daily basis.
- Institutions are still required to complete a full CAD capital calculation every six months. The date for this benchmark calculation is to be set by the supervisor. Institutions will have longer than normal to complete this calculation.
- Capital requirements are set as the highest of:
  - the benchmark CAD requirement
  - the benchmark CAD requirements × $\frac{\text{current portfolio VAR}}{\text{benchmark portfolio VAR}}$
  - the VAR number x the scaling factor set by Basle
- The VAR model parameters are those set by Basle

(These are the guidelines set by the BoE. At the time of writing, some of these guidelines were yet to be agreed by the SFA.)

Source: LIBA (1995: 32).

financial institutions which use their own VAR models are subject to the minimum CAD capital requirements in any event.

If the Basle proposals were to be implemented as they stand, and the CAD not amended, the regulatory disparities between the two regimes would create serious competitive distortions. European Union banks and investment firms would be subject to CAD benchmarking, whereas non-EU banks would enjoy greater benefits from the use of internal models. At the same time all banks would be subject to the more restrictive Basle rules in respect of eligible capital and equity position risk requirements. These regulatory asymmetries would have implications for the competitive position both of EU banks versus EU investment firms and of EU banks versus non-EU banks.

It is also interesting to compare the CAD's requirements with those imposed on US securities firms by the SEC under its Net Capital Rule.[40] Such a comparison reveals a number of important differences. First, the SEC definition of regulatory capital is distinctly 'softer' than the CAD definition (in particular, the treatment of subordinated debt is more permissive) – subject, however, to one important qualification, in that the SEC's requirements for the deduction of illiquid assets are more stringent. Second, the response to shortfalls of regulatory capital is

[40] For a more detailed comparison of SEC and CAD regimes see Dale (1995a) and (1995b).

different under the two regimes, with the SEC but not the CAD treating breaches of minimum requirements as a trigger for automatic wind-down of the securities firm. Third, the SEC's minimum capital requirements are generally higher than those imposed by the CAD, particularly in relation to (a) naked positions in equities; and (b) allowances for portfolio diversification and offsetting positions. Finally, the SEC regime, unlike the EU framework, does not incorporate the principle of consolidated supervision, one important consequence being that OTC derivatives business can, in the United States, be conducted through unregulated entities.

Many of these differences can be explained by the SEC's traditional focus on investor protection rather than systemic stability, and the related objective of ensuring that troubled broker-dealers are wound down rapidly. This underlying philosophy is reflected in the SEC's definition of capital (including its strict treatment of illiquid assets), the mandatory wind-down for capital-impaired firms, and the absence of consolidated supervision.

The different regulatory approaches adopted by the CAD and the SEC will have important competitive consequences. In particular, the absence of consolidated supervision under the SEC regime means that US securities firms will be able to conduct derivatives business, in direct competition with their European counterparts, free from the panoply of official controls governing the operations of European derivatives traders. More generally, the extent of SEC/CAD regulatory disparities highlights the futility of trying to establish competitive equality within a limited area such as the EU, given that EU securities activities can migrate to more accommodating regulatory jurisdictions outside the EU. The competitive distortions generated by EU/non-EU regulatory differences will, furthermore, become more acute as international financial markets become increasingly integrated.

6. SUMMARY AND CONCLUSIONS

One of the major purposes of the CAD is to establish conditions of competitive equality within the single European financial market. In this chapter we have shown that the CAD regulatory regime cannot itself be expected to achieve this objective, and is open to a number of serious objections on other grounds.

In the first place, it was shown that common regulatory standards concerning the *quantum* of capital are not sufficient to create a level playing field. This is because financial institutions' *cost* of capital varies considerably due to a variety of institutional factors, including in particular tax arrangements and the extent of the official safety net. These institutional factors will continue to have a crucial bearing on the cost of capital for institutions from different countries and therefore on the competitive balance within European banking and securities markets.

Secondly, in seeking to establish competitive equality between banks and securities firms, the CAD 'trading book' regime is open to several criticisms. The separation of banking and trading books serves no useful prudential purpose because the risks incurred on each book are not segregated. The boundaries between the two books will be virtually impossible to police, with consequential implications for competitive distortions. Furthermore banks are free to fund their securities operations with 'protected' bank deposits – thereby creating intractable moral hazard problems (a point highlighted by the Barings collapse). Finally, it is anomalous that, whereas the special vulnerability of banks to contagious collapse is recognized in the CAD's consolidation requirements, elsewhere the rules apply parity of treatment between the two types of institution.

The methodology adopted by the CAD to calculate capital requirements is also flawed. The building block approach to equity position risk fails to take proper account of portfolio diversification and therefore provides perverse incentives for securities businesses. Recognition of internal VAR models for the purpose of capital adequacy assessment represents a move towards acceptance of more sophisticated risk management techniques but, so long as internal models have to be benchmarked against CAD capital requirements, this concession offers no inducement to sound management of overall risk exposures.

Furthermore, major potential for competitive distortions arises with CAD implementation at the national level. It has been shown that UK authorities' implementation rules are 'superequivalent' in a number of important respects, particularly in the application of target and trigger capital ratios for treatment of equity position risk for non-qualifying countries. Such rules may encourage UK financial institutions to conduct equity business in European subsidiaries governed by the CAD minimum requirements or in non-EU subsidiaries. The UK merely exemplifies the competitive disparities that can arise under a CAD regime that leaves an important residual discretion with national supervisory authorities. Indeed, it seems inevitable that there will be a second-stage realignment of CAD implementation rules as Member States assess the competitive consequences of their own regulatory arrangements in relation to others.

The CAD itself will need to be amended to bring it into line with the Basle rules for regulatory market risks when these have been finalized. Furthermore, some of the more detailed CAD rules relating to risk weights and offsetting may have to be adjusted in the light of experience. This need to adapt regulation to changing circumstances highlights a further weakness of the current Brussels approach: namely, the rigidity of a regulatory regime which requires all rules to be incorporated in Directives which then have to be implemented as legislation at the national level. This contrasts, for instance, with the Basle approach based on internationally agreed guidelines and recommendations which can be amended or supplemented as circumstances require.

Finally, given the international mobility of financial activity, it needs to be emphasized that a single European financial market can be undermined by competitive disparities between the EU and non-EU financial centres as well as between EU Member States. In this context the contrasting EU and SEC approaches to the regulation of securities markets could prove troublesome, especially to the extent that US securities firms are permitted to conduct derivatives business through unregulated derivative product companies. More fundamentally, a regional approach to regulating global markets must inevitably run into difficulties, given the ease with which financial activity may be routed through non-EU financial centres and non-EU institutions.

In the short term there is little that can be done to remedy these deficiencies of the CAD regime. However, in the medium and longer term the following steps should be taken:

1. As a matter of priority the CAD should be amended to incorporate the Basle approach to recognizing internal risk management models, without the need for CAD benchmarking.
2. The European Commission should be more active in examining the competition implications of bank bail-outs. (The Crédit Lyonnais rescue package is the first occasion on which Brussels has ruled on a state aid payment in the banking sector.)
3. The European Commission should look at the possibility of introducing more flexible regulatory arrangements. For instance, under a two-tier regime the general regulatory framework could be incorporated in primary legislation (i.e. Directives) and detailed capital 'rules' left to recommendations which could be readily amended.
4. There needs to be much greater clarity as to what is meant by 'consolidated supervision'. In this context, too, the question of whether and how banks should be consolidated with investment firms should be explicitly addressed, since confusion in this area was a contributory factor in the Barings collapse.
5. Different national approaches to what constitutes illiquid or 'highly liquid' equities may distort cross-border investment decisions and/or favour some EU financial centres at the expense of others. Member States' implementation rules in this area will perhaps converge over time, but it is in the interests of competitive equality that Brussels should develop appropriate criteria for assessing the liquidity of equities.

References

Bank of England (BoE), 1994. 'Implementation of the CAD for UK Incorporated Institutions Authorised under the Banking Act 1987', Consultative Document, December.

BoE, (1995). 'Implementation in the United Kingdom of the Capital Adequacy Directive', Policy Notice: S&S/1995/2, April.

British Bankers' Association (BBA), 1995. 'BoE Consultative Document on the Implementation of the CAD – Comments of the British Bankers' Association', February.

Cantor, R. and Johnson, R., 1992. 'Bank capital ratios, asset growth and the stock market' in Federal Reserve Bank of New York, *Quarterly Review*, 17 (3): 10–24.

Clarotti, Paulo, 1992. *The Completion of the Internal Financial Market: Current Position and Outlook*, Head of Banking and Financial Institutions (Internal Market), DG XV, Brussels.

Coopers and Lybrand, 1995. *The Banking Passport: Implementation of the Capital Adequacy Directive*, Bank of England.

Commission of the European Communities, 1989. 'Council Directive on the own funds of credit institutions' *Official Journal of the European Communities*, No. L 299, 17 April, 16–20.

CEC, 1989.'Council Directive on a solvency ratio for credit institutions', *Official Journal of the European Communities*, No. L 386, 30 December, 14–22.

CEC, 1993. 'Council Directive on the capital adequacy of investment firms and credit institutions' *Official Journal of the European Communities*, No. L 141, 15 March, 1–26.

CEC, 1993. 'Council Directive on investment services in the securities field', *Official Journal of the European Communities*, No. L 141, 10 May, 27–46.

Dale, R., 1990. 'The EEC's Approach to Capital Adequacy for Investment Firms', *Journal of International Securities Markets*, Autumn, 211–18.

Dale, R., 1994a. 'The Regulation of Investment Firms in the European Union' (Part 1), *Journal of International Banking Law*, 9 (10), October, 394–401.

Dale, R., 1994b. 'The Regulation of Investment Firms in the European Union' (Part 2), *Journal of International Banking Law*, 9 (11), November, 464–73.

Dale, R.,1994c. 'Regulating Investment Business in the Single Market', *Bank of England Quarterly Bulletin*, November, 333–40.

Dale, R.,1995a. 'The Capital Adequacy Regulation of US Broker-Dealers: A Comparative Analysis', (Part 1), *Journal of Financial Regulation and Compliance*, 3 (1): 11–27.

Dale, R., 1995b. 'The Capital Adequacy Regulations of US Broker-Dealers: A Comparative Analysis', (Part 2), *Journal of Financial Regulation and Compliance*, 3 (2): 153–75.

Dimson, E. and P. Marsh, 1994. 'City Research Project: The Debate on International Capital Requirements – Evidence on Equity Position Risk for UK Securities Firms', London Business School, Subject report VIII, February.

Gaddum, J., 1992. 'The Regulation of German Financial Markets in an EC Context', *Journal of International Securities Markets*, 6, Summer.

Haberman, G., 1987. 'Capital Requirements of Commercial and Investment Banks: Contrasts in Regulation', *Federal Reserve Bank of New York Quarterly Review*, Autumn, 1–10.

International Organization of Securities Commissions, 1992. *Principles for the Supervision of Financial Conglomerates*, IOSCO, October.

London Investment Banking Association (LIBA), 1995. *LIBA CAD Guide*, June, 1–64.

McCauley, R.N. and S.A. Zimmer, 1991. 'The Cost of Capital for Securities Firms in the United States and Japan', *Federal Reserve Bank of New York Quarterly Review*, Autumn, 14–27.

Scott-Quinn, B., 1994. 'EC Securities Markets Regulation', in Benn Steil (ed.), *International Financial Market Regulation*, John Wiley.

Securities and Futures Authority, 1994. 'Implementation in the UK of the EC Capital Adequacy Directive', Board Notice 200, August.

SFA, 1995. Implementation by SFA of the EC Capital Adequacy Directive', Board Notice 249, May.

Sharpe, William F. (1970) *Portfolio Theory and Capital Markets*, McGraw Hill.

Steil, B., 1995. *Illusions of Liberalization: Securities Regulation in Japan and the EC*, Royal Institute of International Affairs, London.

Zimmer, S.A. and R.N. McCauley, 1991. 'Bank Cost of Capital and International Competition', in *Federal Reserve Bank of New York Quarterly Review*, Winter, 33–59.

Chapter 8

ACCOUNTING DIVERSITY

I. RESEARCH QUESTION

European equity investors are increasingly willing and able to invest across national borders. Enhanced security returns reflecting higher rates of growth abroad, together with improved stock market clearance and settlement systems made possible by advances in computer and information technology, are providing much of the impetus. Paralleling this development, corporate issuers in Europe are becoming more inclined to seek out new investors and market venues as they attempt to expand and diversify their sources of external capital.

While trends towards the globalization of capital markets are clearly evident, this book has shown that significant barriers to European market integration do remain. In this chapter, we examine one particular question with which market participants and policy-makers have shown increasing concern: do differences in European accounting and disclosure standards represent a serious barrier to the integration of Europe's secondary equity markets?

As we will shortly demonstrate, national accounting and disclosure norms vary across Europe. Does this diversity discourage investors or institutional fund managers from investing in particular national markets, and thereby constrain optimal portfolio choices? For European corporations, do national accounting and reporting differences limit cross-border issuing or listing decisions? If accounting diversity does harbour potentially detrimental effects, are market participants capable of coping effectively with these differences? Or are politically mandated initiatives to eliminate accounting barriers to market integration the ultimate remedy?

II. MOTIVATION

The Single European Act of 1987 seeks the free movement among EC member countries of goods, people, services, and financial capital. To the extent that capital flows – i.e. investment decisions – are influenced by accounting data, differences in accounting measurements could lead to problems of understanding and interpretation when company accounts are read by investors who are unfamiliar with local accounting and reporting rules. As national accounting and reporting practices are influenced by company/corporation laws, differences in these laws would naturally lead to differences in financial accounting and reporting. Accordingly, EC member countries have agreed to harmonize (but not necessarily to make identical) their respective company laws as a basis for reducing legal disparities that might hinder freedom of capital movements.[1]

European Accounting Requirements Under EC Directives

The instrument that has been used to harmonize company law is the *directive*. Drafted by the European Commission in the first instance, and subsequently revised and agreed by the Council of Ministers, the provisions laid down in a directive are binding on all companies once the directive is written into national law. However, each country is free to choose the form and method of implementation and also to modify options for specific requirements.

It is important to recognize that even after directives have been written into law, the latter must still be interpreted and applied at the level of the Member State. Hence the adoption of a directive by all EC Member States does not guarantee accounting uniformity if directives are not uniformly interpreted.[2]

While several accounting directives have been issued to date, the EC's Fourth Directive (ratified in 1978) was a major accomplishment with regard to EC company law harmonization. Specifying the form and content of annual financial statements, the Fourth Directive represents an important compromise between the legalistic approach to accounting and financial reporting prevalent in continental Europe and the case-precedent approach prevailing in the United Kingdom. While very detailed, the Fourth Directive nevertheless permits many alternative treatments and permits Member States additional options upon implementation.

The following are examples of specific accounting measurements where practice alternatives are permitted:[3]

- Intangible assets such as goodwill, formation and start-up expenses, and research and development costs may be amortized through the income statement over a period of five years, or written off immediately to reserves or amortized through the income statement over its estimated useful life.

[1] KPMG Peat Marwick (1989).
[2] Mueller (1991).
[3] Coopers & Lybrand (1991); Price Waterhouse (1987).

- Inventories may be valued at the lower of cost or market. Member States may allow actual cost, FIFO, LIFO weighted average, or a similar cost method, or a combination of these methods.
- Assets may be valued at historical cost. However, companies are also allowed to revalue assets. Assets may also be adjusted for inflation using the following bases: revaluation of tangible and financial fixed assets; replacement cost for plant, equipment, and inventories; and valuation of all financial statement items by a method 'designed to recognize the effects of inflation'.
- The Fourth Directive is also silent on a number of measurement issues for which authoritative guidance is sorely needed, including: foreign-currency translation, accounting changes, prior period adjustments, related party transactions, leases, long-term contracts, capitalization of interest costs, accounting for deferred taxes, pensions and other post retirement benefits, discontinued operations, and earnings per share.

Financial disclosure options are also a common feature of the Fourth Directive. Consider the following provision with respect to segment and geographic disclosure of sales. While sales revenues must be broken down by (1) product and line of business and (2) geographical area, companies are permitted to omit this information if its nature is deemed to be seriously prejudicial to the company.

European Accounting Principles and Practices

Accounting and reporting options permitted by the European directives suggest that *financial reporting principles and practices in Europe need not be uniform.* That this is indeed the case is illustrated by Exhibit l. As can be seen, accounting principles promulgated by accounting rule-makers in one EC member country are *not* always consistent with those fashioned by another. Variations in corporate measurement practices across Europe have also been documented. One study, conducted two years after ratification of the Fourth Directive, found major reporting differences among reporting entities in Belgium, Denmark, France, Germany, Ireland, Italy, the Netherlands, Norway, Spain, Switzerland, and the United Kingdom. Accounting measurements for which major practice differences were observed included foreign consolidations, business combinations, leases, pensions, defined taxes, use of discretionary reserves, asset revaluations, and foreign-currency translation and transactions.[4]

[4] Choi and Bavishi (1983), pp. 62-8.

Exhibit 1. Differences in Accounting Practices Across European Countries

Accounting principle	UK	Germany	France	Netherlands	Switzerland	Italy
Inventory costed using LIFO	A-	A'	NA	A	A	A
Pooling method used for mergers	A'	A'	NA	A-	A-	NA
Ownership 21-50%-equity method	A'	A	A'	R	R	A
Deferred taxes recognized	A	A-	A'	R	A	A-
Financial leases capitalized	R	A'	NA	R	A	NA
Capitalization of R&D	A'	NA	A'	A'	A'	A'
Pension expense accrued during period of service	R	R	A	R	A	A
Fixed assets may be revalued	` A	NA	A	A'	NA	A'

Key: R= required, A= allowed, A' = allowed in certain circumstances,
A- = allowed but rarely done, NA = not allowed.
Source: Peller and Schwitter (1991).

A decade later, studies continue to report significant practice differences among EC member countries.[5] In a recent simulation of the financial statement effects of European accounting differences, Touche Ross found that a hypothetical European company (with identical economic operations) could report profits as low as 27 million ECU in Germany and as high as 194 million ECU in the United Kingdom.[6]

On the face of it, differences in accounting practices across the European Community would appear to pose a barrier to cross-border investment flows. The German automobile manufacturer Daimler-Benz recently demonstrated quite dramatically how important accounting rules can be to the determination of the public figures which investors ultimately have to work with. Investors in the company were taken aback when the firm reported its results for the first half of 1993. It declared a profit of DM 168 million based on German accounting principles. It simultaneously reported a *loss* of DM 949 million for the same period in

[5] Emenyonu and Gray (1992), pp. 49-58.
[6] Simmons and Azières (1989).

filing for a US listing, which required reconciliation to US Generally Accepted Accounting Principles (GAAP). Which was the more accurate performance measure? This is a question that many analysts are still pondering and debating.

In a more recent development, Daimler-Benz has announced a decision to present all of its financial information in accordance with US GAAP. It will no longer publish a balance sheet following German accounting practice. Daimler's chief financial officer explained that the decision reflected the company's judgment that US accounting practices provide shareholders with a more realistic and detailed picture of the company's financial situation.[7] To the extent that this view is correct, accounting data must influence the public's investment decisions.

Major European companies could presumably follow the Daimler-Benz example in EC national markets, where prospects for increased investor share demand are very positive. Alternatively, reliance could be placed on a set of internationally recognized reporting standards. Whether policy initiatives to harmonize accounting and disclosure norms across Europe are necessary or desirable, however, is ultimately an empirical question.

Accounting Standards and the Social, Legal, and Economic Environment

In addressing the issue of harmonization of accounting norms, an understanding of accounting and disclosure regimes currently operating in Europe may be helpful. The three examples which follow reflect the premise that accounting not only influences its environment, by way of its decision effects, but is, in turn, influenced *by* its environment – social, legal, and economic.

Consider the effect of socio-cultural influences. France operates under a uniform and highly codified system of accounts. Subject to the *Plan Comptable Générale*, social responsibility accounting is mandatory. The legal system in Germany likewise produces a system of accounts that is largely based on statutory law. This is a far cry from UK practices, which reflect a much less rigid approach to accounting and reporting. Private professional initiatives, more than statutory law, drive accounting principles in this setting. Owing to high and socially divisive unemployment during the early postwar years, Swedish accounting reflects social welfare goals.

Differential patterns of business ownership and financing represent another major influence on European accounting systems. In countries such as Germany and France, as well as in Scandinavia, banks are major providers of external capital to firms. In such environments, accounting and financial reporting are characterized by their creditor focus. Accounting measurements that provide a

[7] 'Daimler-Benz to Adopt US Gaap for Good' (1995).

conservative earnings figure are considered prudent, in that more funds are available internally to service debt. In the United Kingdom, greater reliance is placed on equity financing, partly owing to the existence of a reasonably efficient and broadly based market for equity securities. Reported earnings in the United Kingdom tend to be less conservative, as they are relied on for unbiased estimates of a firm's future cash-generating ability.

A third important environmental influence on accounting in Europe is taxes. In contrast to the self-assessment system in the United States, Europe relies more on government assessments and billings. The underlying belief is that the latter minimizes tax evasion and assures an equitable collection of taxes that are due. The consequence of this is that the distinction between accounting for tax and external reporting purposes, a long-standing practice in the United States, is not as evident in continental Europe.

III. CONCEPTUAL FRAMEWORK – LINKAGES BETWEEN ACCOUNTING DIVERSITY AND MARKET BEHAVIOUR[8]

Accounting rules may affect the value of the firm via several channels. First, national accounting rules are typically well integrated with national codes for taxation. Accounting rules for taxation that pertain to the recognition of income and expenses, non-cash items such as depreciation and reserving, and dozens of other rules come together to set the definition of corporate income and, in turn, corporate taxes. As taxes are real cash flows, accounting diversity may have a direct effect on firm valuation. Second, complementing their impact on tax payments, accounting rules may also affect the figures used by managers for decision-making, as well as the figures pertaining to managerial performance evaluation (e.g. compensation). This may have an impact on managerial decisions and, in turn, on corporate cash flows. Third, accounting rules affect the magnitudes of the numbers that are relied on by shareholders and financial analysts in estimating the cash-generating ability of borrowing firms. Fourth, rules on disclosure may alter the categories of information that are released. Variation in this external information base may directly affect analysts' estimates of the market value of the firm – either by affecting the expected value of key variables or through the uncertainty surrounding these estimates. Alternatively, the effect of variation in externally reported information on market value may be indirect, through an effect on the firm's credit rating or credit capacity.

[8] The following discussion is excerpted from Choi and Levich (1991).

Exhibit 2. Accounting Diversity and Economic Environments

		Economic Situations of Two Firms: Similar	Economic Situations of Two Firms: Dissimilar
Accounting Treatment	Similar	Logical practice Results comparable (A)	May or may not be logical Results may or may not be comparable (B)
	Dissimilar	Illogical practice Results not comparable (C)	Logical practice Results may not be comparable (D)

Accounting diversity, therefore, holds the possibility of leading to a *real* economic difference by changing managerial decisions, corporate cash flows, or analysts' evaluations of the firm. But accounting diversity may have only a *nominal* impact (i.e. a change in accounting numbers, but not a change in market values) if the accounting rules affect only non-cash-flow items, or do not affect the variables that managers use for decision-making, or the evaluation of the firm by financial analysts.

The connections between accounting diversity and the firm's economic environment are summarized in Exhibit 2.

If we consider the case of two firms that are similarly situated in economic terms, then clearly it would be logical for those firms to follow similar accounting practices (Box A). And if they did, then the accounting statements of the two firms could be used for comparative analysis.

If these two similarly situated firms were permitted to adopt two dissimilar accounting treatments (Box C), then the firms would be made to appear dissimilar. This hypothetical case could represent a real effect if, for example, one firm used aggressive accounting techniques to gain a real cash-flow advantage. Since the two firms are similarly situated, a variation in accounting treatments would pose an unacceptable competitive result. On the other hand, this hypothetical case could simply represent a nominal effect that financial analysts would 'see through' after spending some additional time and effort.[9] In either case, the combination illus-

[9] The empirical evidence in Ball (1972) strongly suggests that share prices are set as though analysts were able to see through nominal accounting changes.

trated by Box C is an illogical choice, and the accounting reports of the firms would not (by themselves) be suitable for comparative analysis.

The more interesting cases involve firms that are dissimilar in a real economic sense. Accounting harmony in the presence of diverse economic situations (Box B) is sometimes defended on the basis that this facilitates meaningful inter-firm comparisons. For example, an airline that depreciates its aircraft over five years (because these aircraft make thousands of take-offs and landings per year) is not similarly situated to an airline that flies long-haul routes and depreciates its aircraft over 10 years. Use of the same accounting rule (in this case, straight-line depreciation) allows this economic difference to be highlighted.

However, suppose that the dissimilarity between the two firms pertains to the legal definition of income, or the rules available for computing taxes, or the cultural or accounting variables that influence managerial performance measures and compensation. In this case, the adoption of similar accounting treatments will only obscure the dissimilarities between the two firms. As a result, when the economic situation of firms is dissimilar, the adoption of similar accounting treatments (Box B) may or may not be a suitable response.

In cases where our two hypothetical firms are in the same industry, and the same tax laws and business customs apply, then it seems clear that the firms ought to use similar accounting practices, if only to maintain a level competitive playing-field.[10] However, when the source of the dissimilarity relates to national tax rules, national industry practices, or regulations, then, as we have argued elsewhere,[11] dissimilar accounting treatments may be necessary (Box D). In this case, however, direct comparisons between firms may be difficult.

Accounting Diversity and Cash Flows

The treatment of goodwill offers a clear illustration of the potential impact of differences in accounting principles. Suppose that firm A, with a book value (assumed to equal fair market value in this example) of \$5 billion, is purchased for \$6 billion by firm B. In the United States, firm B_{US} would book the excess \$1 billion as an asset (goodwill) and amortize it over a period not to exceed 40 years. At the end of the amortization period, the book value of shareholder equity for firm B_{US} will be lower by \$1 billion. As a result of higher amortization expense, B_{US} will report lower earnings. This might appear to put US firms at a disadvantage. How-

[10] The new supervisory guidelines for banking from the Bank for International Settlements (BIS) are a good case in point. Now that policy-makers have agreed to uniform guidelines for bank supervision (including capital adequacy measures, risk rating measures, etc.), uniform accounting seems to be a natural outgrowth.

[11] Choi and Levich (1990).

ever, since amortization is a non-cash item, cash flows available from the acquisition of firm A will be unaffected.[12]

In the United Kingdom, the excess $1 billion associated with the purchase of Firm A generally would be charged immediately against shareholder equity, leaving reported earnings, taxable earnings, and income taxes for firm B_{UK} unaffected by any amortization charges. However, the write-off of goodwill in the United Kingdom raises the debt to equity ratio for firm B_{UK}. Assuming that this change does not affect the firm's credit rating or cost of borrowed funds, the reported earnings of firm B_{UK} would remain unaffected.[13] If the capital markets (i.e. investors or rating agencies) respond to differences in *reported* earnings rather than to cash flows, then the accounting treatment of goodwill might give bidding firms from the United Kingdom an advantage over firms from the United States.[14]

Other differences in accounting principles can also lead to asymmetric effects. For example, recognition of deferred taxes as a current expense item is permitted in the United States and the United Kingdom, but disallowed in Germany, Switzerland, and Sweden. This accounting difference may exert an upward bias on earnings from these last three countries. Similarly, general purpose or purely discretionary reserves are not allowed in the United States and the United Kingdom. However they are commonplace in Germany, Switzerland, Japan, and elsewhere. As over-reserving is popular, reported earnings from these countries may have a tendency to be 'understated', except during periods of economic downturn, when discretionary reserving is relaxed.

Accounting Diversity and Available Information

Differences in corporate financial disclosure practices are also widespread. Frequency of reporting is perhaps the most basic difference. The United States is alone in requiring quarterly reports of its large, publicly traded firms. Most of the rest of the world requires only semi-annual or annual reporting. As a result, comparison of first, second, and third quarter reports between US firms and other firms is ruled out. When like-dated reports are available, US firms will typically provide more segmental information – the break-down of sales and profits across geographic regions and product lines – than do non-US firms. US firms may also

[12] If amortization of goodwill applied to tax accounting as well, then B_{US} would experience lower taxable earnings and lower corporate income taxes, providing a net *improvement* to real cash flows.

[13] In an empirical study of UK firms in the period 1982-86, Russell *et al.* (1989) conclude that firms with stronger balance sheets tend to write off larger amounts of acquired goodwill to reserves. These firms would incur a smaller impact on their credit ratings. This evidence is largely consistent with the positive accounting framework of Watts and Zimmerman (1986).

[14] For more on the treatment of goodwill in the United Kingdom and comparisons with US practices, see Choi and Lee (1991).

be more forthcoming about their off-balance-sheet transactions, contingencies, and valuation procedures. On the other hand, non-US firms may disclose more about their accounting for tax authorities, if only because their external reports use the same procedures for recognizing income, calculating depreciation, and so forth, as is required by the tax authorities.

The final point reveals a critical difference between the United States and other countries. In the United States, there are accounting principles for external reporting (GAAP), accounting principles for the calculation of taxes (TAP), accounting for regulatory bodies (RAP), and perhaps accounting for managerial decision-making. In other countries – such as Germany, Italy, and Japan – accounting principles are said to be 'tax-driven', as there is no distinction between TAP, RAP, and GAAP. If accounting rule changes would have immediate cash-flow and tax implications, it is easy to understand why firms would resist conforming to some external standard. And, where firms come from a tradition of supplying only one 'correct' accounting statement, it is easy to understand why they would resist preparing a second (potentially confusing) accounting statement even if it had no direct cash-flow implications.

Accounting Diversity and Cross-Country Comparisons

Our analysis of differences in international accounting principles raises doubts as to whether meaningful cross-country comparisons are always possible using publicly reported accounting data.

Consider the case of the acquisition of US-based Pillsbury by UK-based Grand Metropolitan. The accounting and tax treatment that Grand Met enjoys as a UK firm is a non-traded asset. While one could restate the accounts of Grand Met as if it were a US firm (Exhibit 2, Box B) reporting according to US GAAP and TAP, this would be misleading since Grand Met is in fact a UK firm, and able to pass along to shareholders whatever costs and benefits there are in the UK accounting and tax system.[15] As we illustrated earlier, country differences in the treatment of goodwill can affect reported earnings, debt-to-equity ratios, and after-tax income (when amortization of goodwill is treated as a tax item). When managerial decisions (such as those relating to capital budgeting or performance-based management compensation) or corporate tax payments depend on local accounting conventions, restated accounts would offer readers a noisy signal of the accounting figures that actually drive decisions and cash flows.

[15] This suggests a link between the *lack of* accounting harmony across countries and efforts to coordinate trade policies and other macroeconomic policies across countries. To the extent that accounting diversity actually imparts real costs and benefits on firms, it is an additional factor that undermines the notion of a level competitive playing-field in international transactions.

The difficulty of comparative analysis across firms within an international industry corresponds nicely to the 'top-down' investment approach commonly employed by institutional investors. In this approach, investors first select an asset allocation across countries on the basis of macroeconomic variables. The choices of countries may be tempered by market size, liquidity, absence of capital controls, political risk, and so forth. The result is a set of portfolio weights for countries rather than for industries. Given these allocations, investors are led to ask which are the best stocks *within* countries, rather than which are the best within an industry but *across* countries. As a result, comparative analysis of firms across countries (with differing accounting principles) is discouraged.

IV. RESPONSES TO ACCOUNTING DIVERSITY

With the growing openness of global capital markets, market participants are increasingly called upon to make decisions that rely on accounting data prepared according to foreign principles. For investors, this means having to evaluate foreign investment opportunities and allocate an international portfolio between domestic and foreign securities. For corporations, openness implies the ability to issue debt instruments and/or equity in another market, or simply to have existing shares listed and traded outside the domestic market. How can these market participants respond to accounting diversity?

Investor Decisions

In the context of our discussion, the primary decisions facing an investor are how to allocate funds between domestic and foreign securities, and how to select specific securities from the available universe. An international portfolio of securities would appeal to investors following passive or indexation strategies, under the premise that the international portfolio is more broadly diversified than any national portfolio.[16] International investing may also appeal to investors following more active stock-selection strategies. These investors may be attracted by the higher rates of growth outside their home country, as well as by special situations such as the privatization of foreign firms and the development of market-oriented economies in Eastern Europe and Southeast Asia.

Investors often begin by assessing the legal, institutional, and political environment of target countries. Countries that place constraints on capital mobility or foreign ownership are ruled out, as are countries with especially small

[16] See Solnik (1988, Chapter 2) for a discussion of the gains from international portfolio diversification.

markets that would not offer adequate liquidity for large institutional investors.[17] The remaining countries form the universe for international investment.

Institutional investors with a global objective must cope with international accounting diversity. However, certain investment approaches put more or less emphasis on fundamental analysis involving accounting information. At one extreme, investors might adopt a passive or indexation approach to international investing. In this approach, assets are allocated across countries on the basis of market capitalization weights, gross national product (GNP) weights, or an alternative macroeconomic variable. Within each country, assets are selected according to market value weights. The objective of this approach is to match the returns of a market index, rather than to outperform the index. The passive approach is intended to minimize transactions costs while holding a constant market level of risk. The passive approach makes no use at all of accounting data or other fundamental data regarding individual firms.[18]

An intermediate approach is to follow a passive strategy only in those countries or industries where information (specifically accounting information) is not sufficient for active stock selection. Countries that seem suitable for investment because of their growth prospects and open capital markets may appear unsuitable if differences in accounting principles and lack of disclosure make security analysis difficult. Investors could adopt a passive indexation approach in these cases.

Most international investment firms are organized along geographic lines, with an individual analyst (or team of analysts) following a single country or several countries within a region.[19] For institutional investors that elect an active stock selection approach, there are several ways of coping with accounting diversity.

At one extreme, each country or region could be tracked by an analyst who is completely familiar with the accounting principles of that geographic area. The analyst adopts a local perspective when analysing foreign financial statements and gauging the relative value of one security versus another within his market. Large institutional investors with a specialist of this sort in every country or region could be said to have developed a *multiple principles capability* (MPC). The reasoning behind this approach is the belief that international securities markets are still segmented. The practical implication of segmentation is that the securities of country

[17] Restrictions on capital movements are summarized in *The Handbook of Exchange Rate Restrictions* (1994). Information on smaller foreign securities markets is contained in *Emerging Stock Markets Factbook* (1994).

[18] It is important to note that the stimulus for the indexation approach developed in the United States, where the presumed level of capital market efficiency is high and investors find it difficult to use available information to outperform an index. It was *not* a response to the lack of accounting information.

[19] A few industries that are truly global in nature, such as petroleum, may be treated as a group.

X are largely owned and traded by investors from country *X*, who use local accounting principles to guide security valuation. Although a foreign investor might arrive with a different (and hopefully superior) method of valuation, he might be at considerable risk in betting against the local investment community.

In short, the MPC approach copes with accounting diversity by employing specialists who know and understand foreign accounting principles. The manager will very probably be evaluated against the performance of the local stock market index. No attempt is made to compare or rationalize the valuation of individual securities across markets.

At another extreme, the investment manager of a country or region could cope with accounting diversity by restating local accounting statements into a more familiar, or more commonly used, set of principles. The rationale for restatement could be to facilitate comparison with an outside norm or an outside firm. Another rationale is the belief that other accounting principles provide a 'truer and fairer' view of the firm. To have an impact on the local manager's investment decisions, the restatement algorithm must change the ranking of firms relative to that which would occur under local accounting data.[20]

There are many variations between these two extremes of dealing with accounting diversity. For example, an analyst might adopt a dividend discount approach to valuation, rather than a discounted earnings approach, under the assumption that dividends were a real cash flow and freer from accounting distortions. Analysts might also rely on proxy variables to supplement the lack of disclosure in certain countries. For example, an analyst might look at world-wide industry trends to detect whether a particular firm was using reserves to smooth its income. An analyst might consider recent real-estate transactions to gauge the value of real-estate assets that are accounted for using historic values and full depreciation.

Corporation Decisions

Corporate treasurers are concerned with the ready availability of capital in sufficient quantity and at low cost. Increased openness of international capital markets raises the question of whether, in order to reach their goals, treasurers should issue securities in foreign markets or have their existing securities listed for trading elsewhere. Accounting diversity enters the equation if (1) firms are unable to communicate effectively with this wider universe of international investors, or (2) regulations in foreign capital markets require the firms to subscribe to particular accounting principles, or to disclose particular items.

[20] Choi and Hong (1990) examine the usefulness of restating accounting data from one set of accounting principles to another. In a sample of Korean firms, they find no significant change in enterprise rankings after restatement.

The basic dilemma facing the treasurer is that, while the capital markets might respond favourably to an increase in available information, it is costly for the firm to prepare and release new information.[21] One component of this cost is simply administrative: the preparation of new accounting data requires time and resources, and may require the development of new accounting systems. But a greater cost may be the impact of this information on other constituencies of the firm – such as domestic tax authorities, regulatory bodies, and labour unions – and the value of additional information to market competitors.

While classical financial theory assigns to managers the objective of maximizing the value of the firm (which necessarily entails minimizing all costs), our discussion suggests that minimization of the cost of capital should be interpreted in a broad manner. The total cost of raising funds includes (1) financial costs, (2) information preparation costs, and (3) competitive costs. The task of managers is to produce the amount of information that optimizes the trade-off between lowering financial costs and raising preparation and competitive costs.

In order to cope with accounting diversity, the first alternative open to managers is to maintain the status quo regarding accounting principles and disclosure. Managers might be led to this choice if, by law, the firm may submit only one statement of accounts rather than separate statements for external reporting, tax purposes, regulatory authorities, and so forth. A firm that maintains its local accounting practices without modification may complement this strategy with other coping mechanisms.

First, the firm may continue to seek funding in other markets that do not demand additional accounting information or disclosures. The Eurobond market is one such market. In the Eurobond market, there are no rigid information disclosure practices. These are determined on a case-by-case basis and are usually minimal, especially for large, well-known firms.[22] The private placement market offers another alternative for firms to seek funding based on their original accounting reports. Recent changes in US regulations have removed resale restrictions for large institutional investors ($100 million or more under management), thus making the US private placement market somewhat comparable to the Eurobond market.[23]

[21] Empirical evidence suggests that markets respond favourably to increases in information (Choi, 1973) and that firms may be willing to provide additional disclosures over and above those mandated by regulatory authorities (Meek and Gray, 1989). See discussion in Section V.

[22] For further discussion on the operation of the Eurobond market, see Levich (1985).

[23] The regulatory changes are contained in Rule 144A and Regulation S, which were adopted by the Securities and Exchange Commission on 19 April 1990. For further discussion of these changes, see Gurwitz (1989).

Second, a firm could maintain its local accounting practices and meet with analysts directly or on road shows to provide supplementary information or interpretations of local accounting data. Information provided in these ways may be 'off the record' or unofficial.

Finally, a firm could maintain its local accounting practices and encourage institutional investors to purchase existing shares or new issues directly on the local market. As barriers to international capital mobility break down, firms may find the expense of attracting large institutional investors to their home market preferable to the expense of public offerings in foreign markets, especially if the latter require modifications to the firm's accounting practices. This strategy has further appeal if large institutional investors are viewed as 'long-term' investors, and if foreign public offerings attract a proportionately greater number of smaller, retail investors who may be unpredictable.[24]

The firm may elect to cope with accounting diversity by supplying additional accounting information beyond local requirements (e.g. providing secondary statements based on some internationally accepted reporting norm). In this case, other capital markets may be open to the firm. A public security offering and exchange listing in the United States is often regarded as the most demanding among international securities markets. The United States Securities and Exchange Commission (SEC) enforces a level playing-field by requiring all firms raising new capital to prepare accounting statements according to US GAAP, and to provide disclosures on a par with US firms. Those listing existing shares on a major US exchange may continue to report their earnings based on home-country accounting standards, but must provide reconciliations of reported earnings to US GAAP in footnotes to the financial statements. As discussed earlier, some non-US firms may view this requirement as onerous. Other non-US firms may view it in an opportunistic way – for instance, a non-US firm may 'look better' under US GAAP, and so elect to produce US GAAP statements.[25] However, in some cases the size of a transaction (e.g. the privatizations of British Gas and British Telecom) is such that the deal cannot be concluded without a tranche targeted at the US capital market. In that case, conformity with US accounting and disclosure requirements in the form of 'secondary statements' is incumbent on the firm.

[24] The specific problem is that small investors may sell their shares after the initial public offering. If there are no foreign buyers, arbitrage will cause the shares to flow back to the home securities market, thus defeating the purpose of the foreign public offering. For further discussion of the 'flow-back' problem, see Stonehill and Dullum (1982).

[25] This behaviour conforms to the predictions of positive accounting theory as in Watts and Zimmerman (1986).

Other securities markets are more flexible, and usually permit the foreign firm to enter the local market without restating to local accounting principles. Additional disclosures may be required; however, these tend to be treated on a case-by-case basis.[26]

V. PRIOR RESEARCH

To date, empirical evidence on the relationship between international accounting diversity and capital market decisions has been limited. There is, however, a vast literature on the subject of stock market data and accounting information that indirectly bears on the question at hand. This literature can be divided into three categories. First are studies that test whether accounting information is indeed reflected in market prices. If favourable accounting results are correlated with favourable stock market or economic performance, then this suggests that accounting measures, however generated, provide useful information. The evidence thus far supports the conclusion that earnings announcements (current, quarterly, and annual) are associated with changes in the distribution of stock prices.[27] This, in turn, is consistent with the contention that earnings announcements (*including* those generated under US GAAP, UK GAAP, Australian GAAP, Swedish GAAP, and so forth) provide timely and relevant information to the marketplace. These results, however, beg the question of whether some other accounting system would provide still more useful information.

The second strand of research examines whether differences in discretionary accounting techniques have an impact on investors, managers, and firms. If discretionary changes do not have an impact on market decisions, this would suggest that markets are able to 'see through' the diverse accounting information being presented, and to set share prices fairly. Studies of cross-sectional differences in accounting practices seem to suggest that investors are not fooled by accounting changes; yet some anomalies have been reported.

As one example, during the 1970s the US Financial Accounting Standards Board (FASB) issued a controversial foreign-currency translation pronouncement (Financial Accounting Statement [FAS] No. 8) that required current recognition of translation gains and losses (paper gains and losses resulting from the consolidation of foreign accounts). Prior pronouncements had permitted deferral. Despite

[26] For a discussion of the requirements of the London International Stock Exchange, see Meek and Gray (1989).

[27] Ball and Brown (1968); Patell (1976); Gonedes (1974); Brown and Kennely (1972); Firth (1976); Deakin, Norwood and Smith (1974); Ooghe, Begin and Verbaere (1981); Korhonen (1975); Coenenberg and Brandi (1976); and Forsgardh and Hertzen (1975).

academic evidence to the contrary, the statement had a significant effect on corporate management practices.[28] Studies on the economic impact of FAS No. 8 by the FASB,[29] Financial Executives Research Foundation[30] and others,[31] found management, in many instances, incurring current and/or potential cash costs to minimize non-cash (translation) adjustments, including the opportunity costs of management time diverted away from mainstream operating problems.

Evidence also suggests that investors have some ability to discern non-substantive accounting changes; but here too, the evidence is not without surprises. On the whole, the evidence is consistent with a variety of hypotheses, none of which can be ruled out at this stage of our knowledge.[32] Moreover, the evidence on this aspect of accounting diversity does not address the questions of how costly it is for investors to process diverse accounting information, and of whether, based on their analyses, foreign investors are confident enough to participate in international markets to the extent required to hold well-diversified portfolios.

The third strand considers how capital markets respond to increases in (deviations from) a standard reporting level. If they respond favourably to an increase in accounting information, this suggests that such information has value and that firms must decide on the optimal amount and type of information to release. Choi (1973a) has adapted this argument to the case of firms operating in global capital markets. He describes the case for more standardized and complete disclosure as follows:

> Increased firm disclosure tends to improve the subjective probability distributions of a security's expected return streams in the mind of an individual investor by reducing the uncertainty associated with the return stream. For firms which generally outperform the industry average, it is also argued that improved financial disclosure will tend to increase the relative weighting which an investor will place on favorable firm statistics relative to other information vectors which he utilizes in making judgements with respect to the firm. Both of the foregoing effects will entice an individual to pay a larger amount for a given security than otherwise, thus lowering a firm's cost of capital. (pp. 282-92)

[28] Dukes (1978).
[29] Evans, Folks, and Jilling (1978).
[30] Shank, Dillard, and Murdock (1979).
[31] Choi, Lowe, and Worthley (1978).
[32] Lev and Ohlson (1982).

The hypothesis that a firm would tailor its provision of accounting information in order to achieve a financial objective can be subjected to empirical testing. In a study of European firms, mostly multinationals, that were preparing to issue bonds on the Eurobond market, Choi (1973b) concluded that the majority of firms preceded their offering by an increase in the volume and quality of their financial disclosures. The results suggest that these actions were taken to lower the cost of funds and to increase the chances for a successful offering. And during the study period, the Eurobond market was indeed the low cost source for corporate funding.

A recent study by Meek and Gray (1989) reaches much the same conclusion, but in the context of the equity market. The authors examine 28 continental European firms with shares listed on the London Stock Exchange. They find that the companies have exceeded Exchange requirements through a wide range of voluntary disclosures. In some cases, the authors conclude, the additional voluntary disclosures were 'substantial'. These results suggest that firms have found it in their interest to provide additional accounting disclosures in the hope of improving their share prices, reducing their cost of funds, and competing with other firms for capital in the international market.

While the foregoing research is relevant in assessing the market effects of accounting differences, most have examined the effects of accounting diversity within the context of a single country. From a policy standpoint, the evidence marshalled to date begs the question of whether diverse national accounting systems act as a non-tariff barrier affecting the capital market decisions of investors and issuers.

The following studies address more directly the capital market effects of international accounting and reporting differences.

Choi and Levich: Survey of Market Participants

The first study, conducted by Choi and Levich,[33] sought to find out directly from market participants whether, and to what extent, differences in accounting principles, financial disclosure, and auditing practices affected the measurement of their decision variables and, ultimately, their financial decisions. Interviews were conducted with 52 institutional investors, corporate issuers, investment underwriters, and market regulators in Germany, Japan, Switzerland, the United Kingdom, and the United States. Those interviewed had to have direct decision responsibility – i.e. actually make international investment, funding, underwriting, regulatory, and rating decisions. The findings are summarized in Exhibit 3.

[33] Choi and Levich (1990).

Exhibit 3. Responses to the Survey Question: 'Does Accounting Diversity Affect Your Capital Market Decisions?'

	Yes	No	N.A.	Total
Investors	9	7	1	17
Issuers	6	9		15
Underwriters	7	1		8
Regulators	0	8		8
Raters and others	2	1		3
Total	24	26	1	51

Source: Choi and Levich (1990), p. 127.

Overall, half of those interviewed declared that their capital market decisions were affected by accounting diversity. This finding understates the proportion of respondents who felt that accounting differences mattered, as it ignored second-order behavioural effects – e.g. users who changed the way in which they analysed investments in foreign markets. For those whose decisions were affected by accounting differences, diversity was often associated with capital market effects, including the geographic location of market activity, the types of companies invested in, types of securities issued, security valuation or expected returns, and, and to a lesser extent, information processing costs.

As can be seen in Exhibit 3, response patterns were not uniform among respondent categories. More than one-half of the institutional investors interviewed felt that accounting differences hindered the measurement of their decision variables and ultimately affected their investment decisions. Comparisons between Japanese and non-Japanese companies were cited as especially difficult.

A significant number of investors coped with accounting diversity by restating foreign accounting numbers to the reporting principles of the investor's country of domicile, or to a set of internationally recognized standards. Restatement, however, did not appear sufficient to remove the problem of accounting diversity. This suggests that existing restatement algorithms may not be optimal, are not being applied effectively, or are incapable of producing meaningful information.

Some investors coped by developing a multiple principles capability, relying on foreign financial statements in their original form, together with an intimate knowledge of foreign accounting practices and financial market conditions. These investors, though few in number, reported no decision problems or capital market effects associated with accounting differences.

Investors were evenly divided as to the necessity or utility of international accounting standards. Those in favour felt that harmonization would not only make analysts' lives easier, but would enlarge investor interest in international markets.

Most corporate issuers did not feel that differences in accounting measurement rules affected their decisions. Reasons for the absence of an effect include company funding strategies that insulate a company from having to report to foreign investors (e.g. reliance on internal funding, bank borrowing, and private placements), management's focus on economic fundamentals, management's confidence in investors' abilities to deal with accounting differences, the value of name recognition, and various coping strategies that have proved effective. On the other hand, financial disclosure differences did have an impact on their funding decisions, especially for issuers domiciled in Japan and Germany, suggesting that accounting diversity and regulatory diversity are closely related issues.

Size and nationality had a bearing on issuer responses. Large firms, especially those from the United States and the United Kingdom, whose standards of accounting and financial disclosure tend to be relatively high, appeared to have greater flexibility in accessing international capital markets. In contrast, German, Japanese, and Swiss firms appeared to have less flexibility.

Corporate issuers who said that accounting differences did affect their behaviour attempted to cope with such differences. In some cases, these attempts took the form of GAAP restatements. In others, it took the form of road shows or hosting meetings with analyst groups. All coped in a financial sense; that is, all avoided raising funds in the United States by either (1) bypassing the US market for the Eurobond market, (2) relying on domestic bank financing, (3) encouraging foreign investors to come to their financial market to buy their shares, (4) offering sponsored but unlisted American Depository Receipts (ADRs) in the United States, or (5) undertaking a private placement.

Demand for international standards was not voiced unanimously by the corporate sector. In view of the multiple constituencies with which a company must cope, compliance with international standards would impose an added variable to the decision calculus of financial managers.

Saudagaran and Biddle: Corporate Listing Decisions

In a study on corporate listing decisions, Saudagaran and Biddle[34] examine whether differential disclosure requirements affect firms' choices regarding alternative foreign stock exchange listings. To answer this research question, they examined the listings of 302 internationally traded firms with at least one foreign

[34] Saudagaran and Biddle (1992).

Exhibit 4. Contingency Tests of Association Between Foreign Listings in 1987 and Financial Disclosure Standards of Domicile Relative to Exchange[a]

	NYSE/AMEX		Toronto		London		Amsterdam	
Domicile disclosures	Listed	Not listed	Listed	Not listed	Listed	Not listed	Listed	Not listed
More stringent	0	0	31	127	110	78	97	120
Less stringent	42	102	5	109	18	67	26	52
Supports hypothesis 1	N/A[b]		Yes		Yes		Yes	
Chi-square (*p*-value)	N/A		12.09 (0.000)		31.28 (0.000)		2.60 (0.053)	
Fisher *p*-value	N/A		(0.000)		(0.000)		(0.053)	

	Paris		Tokyo		Frankfurt		Zurich	
Domicile disclosures	Listed	Not listed	Listed	Not listed	Listed	Not listed	Listed	Not listed
More stringent	65	159	29	204	110	169	129	168
Less stringent	23	46	0	23	3	2	0	0
Supports hypothesis 1	No		Yes		No		N/A	
Chi-square (*p*-value)	0.285 (0.297)		2.11 (0.073)		N/A		N/A	
Fisher *p*-value	(0.294)		(0.055)		(0.313)		N/A	

[a] Based on financial disclosure levels. *p*-values are for one-tailed tests.
[b] N/A indicates not applicable
Source: Saudagaran and Biddle (1992), pp. 127.

listing on one of nine major exchanges as of year-end 1987. They also examined changes in listings between 1981 and 1987 – an important design feature, since these changes were more likely to have been influenced by differences across countries in financial disclosure levels during the observation period. Financial disclosure levels were measured by the construction of a disclosure index obtained by surveying 142 experts actively involved in the foreign listing process.

Exhibit 4 presents the results of univariate tests of association between foreign-exchange listings in 1987 and firms' financial disclosure levels. Two-by-two contingency tables indicate the numbers of foreign firms with more/less stringent disclosure standards listing/not listing on each of the exchanges.

The evidence is consistent with the hypothesis that the probability that a firm will list on a given exchange is inversely related to the extent of the exchange's disclosure requirements. This finding is supported by both univariate and multivariate tests. It is also supported by tests which examine changes in foreign listings between 1981 and 1987, which controlled for possible differences across domiciles in the frequency of listings.

McQueen: Information Content of US GAAP Reports

Given that accounting and reporting practices vary from country to country, a key question is whether or not these differences matter, in terms of actually affecting some decision process. In other words, do international GAAP differences have an impact on investor decisions and, ultimately, market prices? McQueen,[35] in her recently completed PhD dissertation, examines whether US market participants rely on foreign accounting numbers that have been reconciled to US GAAP. Under current US SEC regulations, foreign private issuers of securities in the United States are permitted to use foreign GAAP to fulfil the registration requirements of Form 20-F. If they do, however, they must provide footnote disclosure of quantitative reconciliations of material variations between both earnings and balance-sheet items as reported under foreign versus US GAAP.

A major difficulty in assessing the use of footnote disclosures is determining when such information becomes available to the market. Foreign GAAP earnings generally become available through earnings announcements at or near fiscal year end. US GAAP information may also become available to the market before Form 20-F is filed, either through earnings announcements or through disclosure in the annual report to shareholders. Even if this information is not formally disclosed, US investors may use their own *ad hoc* US GAAP reconciliations or estimates.

To determine if and when US GAAP information is used by the market, McQueen tested for the information content of both reported earnings and book values and the respective US GAAP reconciliations during three contiguous time intervals. The first observation interval (or window) began 7 days before and ended 2 days after the filing date. The second window began 2 days after and ended 7 days after the filing date. The third window began at fiscal year-end and ended 7 days before the filing date. These windows were selected to capture possible differences in the timing of the market's use of information found in footnote disclosures. Cross-sectional regression analyses suggest that levels of both reported earnings and foreign earnings reconciled to a US GAAP basis are significantly associated with securities returns in the long window. This supports the hypothesis either that information about US GAAP earnings is available early, or that investors develop their own estimates and find these estimates useful in pricing foreign securities.

[35] McQueen (1993).

Choi and Lee: Merger Premia and Goodwill Accounting Differences

In an acquisition accounted for as a purchase, any difference between the purchase price and the fair value (generally market value) of the net assets that are acquired is usually recognized as an intangible asset: goodwill. In the United States, this merger premium must be capitalized and amortized to expense over a period not exceeding 40 years. While a similar methodology can also be employed in the United Kingdom, the accounting treatment preferred by UK managers is to write off goodwill immediately against reserves. This allows British companies to report higher earnings than would be the case if US GAAP were used.[36]

Conventional wisdom says that differences in accounting treatment for goodwill provide an incentive for British companies to offer more than US acquirers for a US target, because future earnings need not be reduced by the higher price paid.[37] However, except for reasons associated with management compensation, the notion that merger premia are affected by an accounting measure is unsupported. Goodwill is not deductible for tax purposes in the United Kingdom or the United States. Hence, it does not appear likely that differences in the treatment of goodwill will be economically substantive in their effect. Furthermore, even if differing goodwill treatments gave UK acquirers a bidding advantage, they need not pass on these benefits to target shareholders in the absence of competition from other non-US bidders.

To ascertain whether conventional wisdom is supported empirically, Choi and Lee[38] sought answers to the following questions:

1. Do UK acquirers pay higher premiums on average than their US counterparts when bidding for US targets?
2. Are premium differentials paid by UK acquirers associated with not having to amortize goodwill to earnings?

Choi and Lee first compared average premiums paid by US acquirers with those paid by UK acquirers of US target companies.[39] They next performed regres-

[36] Weetman and Gray (1990).

[37] See, for example, 'An Edge to Foreign Buyers?' (1988).

[38] Choi and Lee (1991).

[39] Their sample consisted of 1,160 deals in which the target is a US company and the acquirer either a US or a UK company, as reported by Automatic Data Processing, Inc. It includes 1,056 US and 104 UK deals announced between 1985 and 1989.

sion analyses to see whether goodwill, in addition to other variables identified in the literature, explained cross-sectional variations in merger premia offered by UK acquirers. To control for other variables found to be associated with merger premia, Choi and Lee matched UK with US acquirers on the basis of explanatory variables identified in the previous regression. For each matched pair, they regressed observed premium differences against goodwill differences and a proxy variable for the effect of differing national accounting treatments for goodwill.

Choi and Lee found merger premia associated with UK acquisitions to be consistently higher, on average, than those for US acquisitions. Moreover, premiums paid by UK acquirers were associated with goodwill, and higher premiums paid by UK acquirers do appear to be associated with not having to amortize goodwill to earnings. This finding suggests that national differences in accounting do have an impact on managerial behaviour in the market for corporate control.

As German and Japanese companies have also been active acquirers of US companies, Choi and Lee recently replicated their goodwill study,[40] this time including Japanese and German acquirers of US targets, but there was one significant difference from the previous study: whereas goodwill is not deductible for taxes in either the United States or the United Kingdom, it is deductible for taxes in Germany and Japan.

Choi and Lee found that merger premia offered by German and Japanese acquirers, who enjoy advantageous accounting or tax treatments relative to US acquirers, were higher, on average, than those offered by the latter. Premia offered by German companies were the highest. Regression analyses again showed that goodwill accounting does explain merger premia. The higher regression coefficient on Choi and Lee's goodwill measure for German acquisitions, relative to Japanese acquisitions, indicates that merger premia are associated with accounting diversity among countries in the sense that, although tax benefits are available in both Japan and Germany, more favourable accounting treatments are operative in the latter.

In addition to providing further evidence on the market effects of international accounting differences, a major implication of Choi and Lee's findings is that although international accounting standards are increasingly viewed as a *necessary* ingredient for the creation of a level merger and acquisition playing-field, they may not be *sufficient* in a world characterized by international tax differences.

[40] Lee and Choi (1992).

VI. SURVEY DESIGN

Although information on the capital market effects of international accounting diversity is increasing, data with regard to Europe have largely been of the anecdotal variety, based on small samples, and narrow in geographic coverage. To provide a markets-based response to the question of whether differences in European accounting and disclosure standards present a serious barrier to European secondary market integration, we designed a survey questionnaire to poll corporate issuers and institutional investors across Europe directly. The survey instrument included both factual and behavioural questions relating to investment and funding practices, the location of market activity, and methods of dealing with accounting and reporting differences. Most questions were left open-ended to provide additional information as to the reason for a particular response and the nature of the response.

The questionnaire was tested for clarity, relevance, and comprehensiveness by way of personal interviews with representatives of reporting entities and institutional investors in France, Germany, the Netherlands, and the United Kingdom. A copy of the questionnaires used for investors and issuers is included as Appendix A.

The questionnaire tailored to European investors and fund managers was sent to 400 of the largest institutional investment firms across Europe. We received 97 completed questionnaires, a response rate of 24 percent. The questionnaire designed for the European corporate side was mailed to chief financial officers of all non-financial corporations listed in the *Financial Times* 500 Index. Of the 487 questionnaires mailed, 88 were returned, a response rate of 18 percent.[41]

Before examining the data more closely, it is important to verify that the response rates are fairly uniform across the major sub-groups of the sample population. Our primary concern is a bias in responses from English-speaking countries (the UK and Ireland). In Table B1 (in Appendix B), we see that the response rate from the UK (27.6 percent), Swiss (29.6 percent), and Spanish investors (33.3 percent) is slightly higher than the overall average of 24.2 percent. Among the more highly sampled countries, French, Dutch, German, Austrian and Belgian investors produced a relatively low response rate. For corporate issuers (in Table B2), the response rate for the largest sub-group of UK firms (14.4 percent) is slightly less that the overall response rate (18.3 percent). The response rate from French and Italian firms is lower than the average, while the German corporate response rate is fairly close to average.

[41] A complete tabulation of the responses for investors and corporate issuers is available on request from the authors.

Overall, the response rates vary across countries, but there is no significant over-representation of English-speaking countries. At the 5 percent level based on a chi-square test, we cannot reject the hypothesis that the sample responses are distributed uniformly and independently across countries.[42]

VII. SURVEY RESPONSES: INVESTORS

Investor Characteristics

Characteristics of Investors Who Answered the Survey

Country Characteristics

Investors responding to the questionnaire were from 13 countries, as shown in Table 1. Of the 97 respondents, the largest number (42) were from the United Kingdom, followed by France (14).

Job and Organization Characteristics

By far the largest number of investors responding to the questionnaire were portfolio managers (71 percent). The remainder filled various high-level positions such as head of research, chief investment officer, and chief strategist. Most respondents (76 percent) take a centralized approach to asset allocation across countries and industries, and the majority (66 percent) follow a decentralized approach to the selection of individual stocks.

Firm Size, Scale of Investment Activity, and Investment Experience

Figure 1 shows the value of funds under management by the investors in our sample. Most investors (62 percent of 92 cases) worked for larger firms with more than $5 billion under management. The assets under management ranged from under $1 million to as much as $150 billion, with a median value of $8 billion. A large number of individual respondents (34 per cent of 68 cases) were 'high-powered' managers, who personally managed more than $1 billion in assets.

The median age of the investment firms was 60 years, varying from one year to 275 years of experience across the sample. A large number of individual respondents (26 percent) claimed 20 years or more of personal experience in investment analysis or portfolio management.

Investment Practices of European Institutional Investors

Scope of International Investment

Investors were asked to report the percentage of their investments in foreign equity shares. A summary of all 91 responses is shown in Figure 2. All but five

[42] The Chi-square for the issuer sample is significant at the 10 percent level, because of the unusually large response from Austrian, Belgian, Irish, and Spanish firms. See Appendix B for details.

Table 1. Investor Responses by Country

Austria	5	Ireland	1	Sweden	1
Belgium	2	Italy	2	Switzerland	8
Denmark	4	Netherlands	6	UK	42
France	14	Norway	1		
Germany	4	Spain	7	TOTAL	97

Figure 1. Investment Funds Under Management (Number of Respondents)

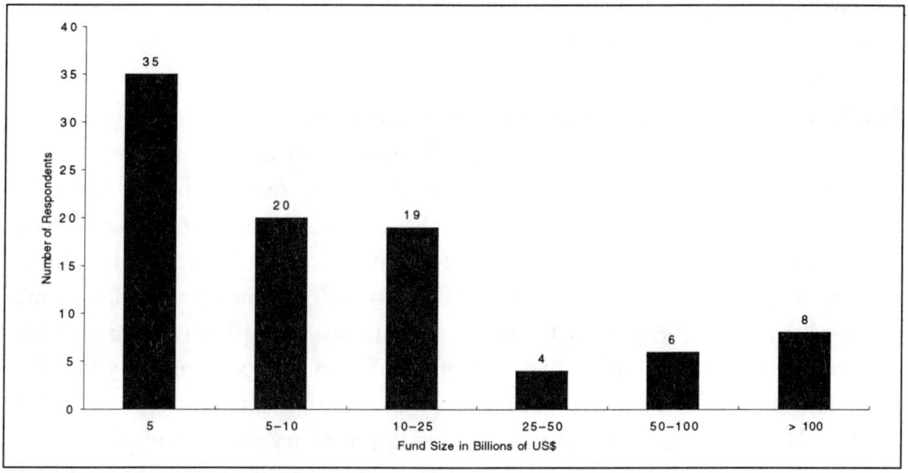

Note: Based on N=92 responses.

Figure 2. Scope of Investments in Foreign Equity (Number of Respondents)

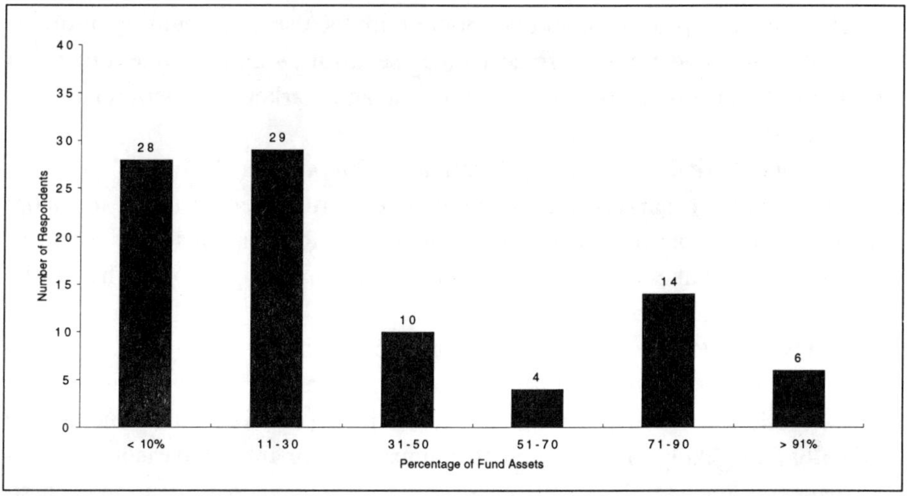

Note: Based on N=91 responses.

respondents had some fraction of their portfolio in foreign securities, ranging from one to 100 hundred percent. The median fraction held in foreign securities was 25 percent.

Overall Approach to Investment

Investors were asked to report their general investment approach. The answers are summarized in Table 2.

While investment approaches varied, most respondents (72 percent) draw primarily on fundamentals, emphasizing either a value- or a growth-oriented approach to security investments.

The Role of Accounting Information for Investors

Is Accounting Information Important for Selecting Stocks?

Respondents were asked to assess how important accounting information was for the selection of individual *foreign* stocks. The results are summarized in Table 3, and broken down by the size, experience, scope of foreign investment activity, and organizational structure of the respondent. The overwhelming majority of investors (96 percent) agree that company-specific information is important when selecting individual foreign stocks, and 66 percent reply that it is 'very important'. In the cross-tabulation by size, it appears that 'large' investors are more likely to rate accounting information as 'very important'. And in the cross-tabulation by scope of foreign investment activity, it appears that investors with 'extensive' foreign investment are also more likely to rate accounting information as 'very important'.

The four respondents not relying on accounting information explain that their investment approach either does not require the use of accounting information or that they invest only in fixed-income securities – an investment medium that is dependent primarily on macroeconomic and market considerations.

Do Investors Make Cross-Country Investment Comparisons?

In order for capital markets to be integrated, it is often presumed that investors must make cross-country investment comparisons. Respondents were asked if, indeed, they do make such cross-country investment comparisons. The results are summarized in Table 4.

Overall, 85 percent of responding investors make cross-country investment comparisons. In the cross-tabulation data, it appears that investors with 'long' experience and investors with a 'centralized' organizational structure are especially more likely to attempt cross-country investment comparisons. We expect that experience facilitates the job of comparison, and centralization necessitates comparisons across countries.

Table 2. Investment Approaches

	Primary approach	Secondary approach
Value oriented	43	25
Growth oriented	24	31
Quantitative-driven active	9	10
Asset allocation	18	15
Indexation	7	5
No answer	4	7

Table 3. Importance of Company-Specific Information When Selecting Individual Foreign Stocks

	Very important	Somewhat important	Not important	Total
Total	64	29	4	97
Size				
Large	41	14	2	57
Less large	20	14	1	35
N.A.	3	1	1	5
Total	64	29	4	97
Experience				
Long	25	12	0	37
Short	35	14	4	53
N.A.	4	3	0	7
Total	64	29	4	97
Scope of activity				
Limited	42	21	2	65
Extensive	20	6	0	26
N.A.	2	2	2	6
Total	64	29	4	97
Organizational structure				
Centralized	19	9	0	28
Decentralized	42	18	4	64
N.A.	3	2	0	5
Total	64	29	4	97

Notes: *Size:* 'Large' is greater than $5 billion under management.
Experience: 'Long' is more than 100 years of firm experience.
Scope of activity: 'Limited' is less than 50% foreign investments.
Organizational structure: refers to the selection of individual stocks.

Table 4. Do You Compare Investment Opportunities Across Countries?

Country	Yes	No	Other	Total
Total	82	13	2	97
Size				
Large	50	7	0	57
Less large	27	6	2	35
N.A.	5	0	0	5
Total	82	13	2	97
Experience				
Long	34	3	0	37
Short	42	9	2	53
N.A.	6	1	0	7
Total	82	13	2	97
Scope of activity				
Limited	54	9	2	65
Extensive	22	4	0	26
N.A.	6	0	0	6
Total	82	13	2	97
Organizational structure				
Centralized	25	3	0	28
Decentralized	52	10	2	64
N.A.	5	0	0	5
Total	82	13	2	97

Notes: 1. 'Other' reply: I only do so in certain sectors, e.g. commodities, chemicals.
2. For description of size, experience, scope, and organizational structure variables, see note to Table 3.

For those who do not make cross-country comparisons, all said that their investment approach did not require it. In addition, some accounting measurement differences related to multinational consolidations, the use of discretionary reserves, accounting for goodwill, provisioning, and accounting for pension costs were said to complicate the task of comparing reports. Lack of financial disclosures on segmental information, the use of hidden reserves, and non-disclosure of asset valuation methods were also reported to make cross-country comparisons more difficult.

Opinions Regarding Barriers and Inducements to Investments Across Europe

As the major purpose of this study was to determine the extent to which financial reporting considerations impede cross-border investing, investors were asked their opinions on the major factors inhibiting their security investments across Europe. Survey responses on this point are listed in Table 5, in decreasing order of importance.

Table 5. Reasons to Limit Investment Across Europe

Most important reasons to limit investments across Europe	Percentage of investors responding
Liquidity risks	55
Currency risks	47
Market risks	40
Country risks	32
Quality of financial reporting	23
European accounting differences	14
Settlement procedures	14
Access to corporate management	13
Regulatory barriers	8
Other	16

Perhaps not surprisingly, investors feel that the most important impediments to pan-European investment pertain to macroeconomic and market considerations such as liquidity, currency, market, and country risks. Accounting differences and quality of financial reporting are mentioned, but they do not appear to be the primary obstacles.

We then asked whether a common set of accounting and reporting standards would (at the margin) act to encourage respondents to increase their pan-European investments. These results are summarized in Table 6.

The results in Table 6 suggest that a minority of respondents (42.3 percent) would be encouraged to increase their investments across Europe if common accounting and reporting standards prevailed. More than half of the respondents (57.7 percent) are not persuaded that some form of accounting harmonization is a precondition for expanding their pan-European investment. These results are fairly consistent in the cross-tabulated results for size, experience, scope of foreign investment activity, and organizational structure. In the words of one investor:

> If accounting standards were uniform across Europe but national currencies continue to vary as they do today, you will still see enormous disparities in equity valuations across markets. So if market integration is the cornerstone of accounting harmonization, you won't achieve it. Or, to put it another way, if we have differences in accounting principles but a common currency in Europe, we will see a lot of valuation discrepancies disappear irrespective of accounting.

Additional reasons underlying this difference in opinion are detailed in Exhibit 5. The testimonials imply that some investors are comfortable analysing foreign accounting statements or feel that they have developed other methods for coping with accounting diversity. Yet other investors feel that common accounting

Table 6. Would a Common Set of Accounting and Reporting Standards Encourage You to Increase Your Investment Across Europe?

	Yes	No	Don't know	Total
Total	41	33	23	97
Size				
Large	24	18	15	57
Less large	15	13	7	35
N.A.	2	2	1	5
Total	41	33	23	97
Experience				
Long	16	11	10	37
Short	22	20	11	53
N.A.	3	2	2	7
Total	41	33	23	97
Scope of activity				
Limited	27	20	18	65
Extensive	13	9	4	26
N.A.	1	4	1	6
Total	41	33	23	97
Organizational structure				
Centralized	14	8	6	28
Decentralized	25	23	16	64
N.A.	2	2	1	5
Total	41	33	23	97

Note: For description of size, experience, scope, and organizational structure variables, see note to Table 3.

and reporting standards would allow for better comparisons and possibly 'unlock' values in European equities. One analyst offered the following perspective:

> If the aim of international accounting standards is to develop more integrated capital markets, then the absence of accounting harmony is not the main obstacle. Having said this, the work of a sector analyst is facilitated by more harmonized GAAP in that: 1) it helps to a limited extent, 2) it improves shareholder relations for a European company, and 3) if a company goes to US GAAP this signals that the company is adopting more of a shareholder focus.

As a follow-up question, we asked those in favour of harmonization to indicate the form of harmonization they preferred. The 41 respondents were evenly divided between international accounting standards of the International Accounting Standards Committee (IASC) variety and Anglo-American norms. Interviews with market participants, however, suggest that the distinction between international accounting standards and US accounting standards is often blurred. According to one European investment adviser:

> Several companies listed on the Paris Bourse say they are following IASC standards for political reasons but are really following US GAAP.

When pressed for an explanation, his response was:

> Harmonization, in my opinion, has to take place around US GAAP. IASC standards are unsatisfactory because: (1) there is a clear contradiction between the UK/US versus the French/German approach to promulgating accounting rules, (2) the IASC takes too long to respond to emerging issues and has no mechanism in place to respond to such, and (3) the IASC is subject to too much in the way of political compromise.

Conclusions on Investors

Is Accounting Diversity An Important Barrier to International Investment?

We asked investors to report on those European countries where they had *not* invested and to indicate the reasons for not investing. The responses to this question are summarized in Table 7.

As Table 7 reveals, of our 97 investor respondents, nearly all have investments in the four major European equity markets: France, Germany, the Netherlands, and the United Kingdom. A larger number of respondents have not made investments in the smaller European markets. The most common reason for not investing in these markets is their small size and lack of liquidity. Difficulty of understanding company accounts either because of accounting or disclosure is not cited often as a major barrier in pan-European investing. Accounting issues are mentioned sporadically; and *not at all* for France, Germany, Spain, and the United Kingdom, and only *once* (out of 97 respondents) for Belgium, Luxembourg, the Netherlands, and Sweden.

How Do European Investors Cope With European Accounting Diversity?

Investors in our survey acknowledge that they experience some difficulty in reading financial statements in almost all of the European countries *where they currently invest*. The degree of difficulty varies, as shown in Table 8. Our sample of investors regards financial statements from the Netherlands and the United Kingdom as the easiest to analyse, and those from Greece, Italy, Portugal, and Spain as the most difficult.[43] For the sake of comparison, we also asked them to rate the

[43] Note that if the 42 respondents from the United Kingdom are removed, the UK mean score rises to 2.00.

Exhibit 5. Would Common Accounting and Reporting Standards Encourage You to Increase Your Investment Activity Across Europe?

YES:

It would provide better comparison of key figures.

It would improve disclosure.

I would have greater confidence when I read reports from companies located in areas where reporting standards are less rigorous.

A common set of accounting standards would help to unlock value and standardize cross country/sector comparisons. I think this would encourage investors to take longer-term views in certain areas.

As a quantitative stock selection specialist, anything that improves the quality of our data or standardizes it is helpful to our business.

This would get more countries into our scope.

Marginally. But only marginally. Investment activity is primarily determined by macro criteria and asset allocation may then be restricted by problems of accounting standards.

It would help estimating near-term earning prospects.

Would like the transparency seen in UK reporting standards across Europe.

It would assist our modelling.

NO:

Common standards would increase the comfort zone, but practically speaking, we already take the exposure we want/need without too much hesitation.

I already possess good knowledge of different accounting approaches.

It would make no difference in our general asset allocation strategies.

We have the in-house expertise to compare different national GAAPs.

Common accounting standards would improve our decision-making process provided they are set at a sufficiently high level.

I am already used to regularly dealing with accounting handicaps and, to an extent, inefficiencies create opportunities. Dishonesty is more of a problem than lack of common accounting standards.

We only invest in the major European markets, i.e., where accounting standards are reliable.

The standards of reporting are high in most European countries, regardless of accounting standards.

We already have a high allocation relative to benchmark.

We feel comfortable with the different existing rules and try to overcome the difficulty with the help of the analysts and the brokers.

We have to invest in Europe anyway regardless of accounting practices. Besides, our investment analysts will adapt to different accounting and reporting standards.

It is obviously more difficult to compare stocks in different markets, but these obstacles can be overcome through an analysis of cash flows rather than reported earnings.

The most important obstacles regarding European opportunities are due to unstable currency conditions.

Accounting data are only a point estimate of a company's health.

It would be beneficial but would not increase the overall size of the investments in Europe.

We apply a strict trend-following discipline and we are not interested in fundamentals.

Table 7. European Countries Where You Have *NOT* Invested and the Reasons Why

	We are not allowed to invest there	Market too small, not liquid	Company accounts difficult to understand	Company accounts do not contain enough details	Lack of economic growth prospects	Other reasons	Total
Austria	7	22	3		2	8	36
Belgium	6	9	1	1	5	4	19
Denmark	4	14	2		1	5	23
Finland	4	18	2		1	7	23
France	1						1
Germany	1					1	2
Greece	13	52	10	6	6	9	71
Ireland	8	20	2	1	3	5	31
Italy	4		2	2		2	12
Luxembourg	7	35	1		2	9	48
Netherlands	3		1			1	3
Norway	5	13	2			6	24
Portugal	8	28	4	2	3	9	44
Spain	3	1				2	8
Sweden	4	4	1			7	18
UK	2				1	1	4

Note: The number in the column labelled 'Total' is the number of respondents who listed *any* reason for not investing in a country. Respondents were also given other answers to tick such as currency risk, country risk, costly transaction fees and taxes, and limits on foreign ownership. These responses are omitted here.

difficulty of interpreting financial statements from Japan, Switzerland, and the United States. The US statements were regarded as the easiest to analyse across all countries in the sample, Switzerland was near the average of EC countries, and Japan rated among the most difficult – second only to Greece.

Given how widespread international investing is among our respondents, it is reasonable to presume that investors make use of various coping mechanisms to deal with difficulties related to accounting diversity. We asked respondents to indicate what approaches they found helpful for dealing with differences in international accounting principles. Their answers are summarized in Table 9.

When making cross-country investments, our respondents report several approaches for dealing with differing national accounting principles (Table 9). Two-thirds of those responding place a higher weight on other information, including industry information, non-accounting information such as cash flows, or macroeconomic information. Over half restate foreign accounts to another accounting framework. These GAAP restatements are divided fairly evenly between home-country standards, those of the IASC, and US accounting standards. Some respond-

Table 8. How Easy or Difficult is it to Analyse Company Financial Accounts for the Following Countries in Which You DO Invest?

	1	2	3	4	5	Don't know/ not sure	Total	Mean score
Austria	4	9	18	9	4	9	53	3.00
Belgium	5	16	29	6	3	13	72	2.76
Denmark	6	17	26	10	2	10	71	2.75
Finland	5	15	25	9	1	13	68	2.75
France	16	32	24	8	1	3	84	2.33
Germany	16	14	22	23	6	3	84	2.86
Greece	0	0	3	12	13	25	53	4.36
Ireland	21	17	7	9	1	10	65	2.13
Italy	3	11	20	21	12	8	75	3.42
Luxembourg	10	8	9	3	5	22	57	2.57
Netherlands	28	31	16	0	0	2	77	1.84
Norway	6	19	22	8	1	11	67	2.67
Portugal	2	3	20	15	3	17	60	3.33
Spain	5	12	18	25	6	8	74	3.23
Sweden	15	25	18	6	0	10	74	2.23
UK	48	22	5	0	1	3	79	1.47
Japan	6	8	8	17	18	10	67	3.58
Switzerland	17	15	21	20	0	3	76	2.60
US	44	16	3	0	1	5	69	1.41

Notes:
1. The degree of difficulty ranges from 1 to 5, with 1 being the easiest.
2. Some investors did not answer about certain countries because they do not have investing experiences in those countries.

Table 9. Approaches for Dealing with Differences in National Accounting Principles

	Number of responses (out of N=97)	Percentage
Placing a higher weight or greater importance on other information	64	66.0
Restating foreign accounts to other accounting standards	49	50.5
Rely on information and analyses from investment advisory services	41	42.3
Attach a low weight to accounting information	10	10.3

ents calculate more than one restatement. Others (42.3 percent) rely on financial information or analyses supplied by one or more investment advisory services. Two investors reduce their investment allocations to foreign firms, indicating that accounting diversity could lead to a pricing or efficiency effect.

Table 10. Approaches for Dealing with Differences in National Accounting Disclosure Practices

	Number of responses (out of N=97)	Percentage
Visiting the company to collect information	46	47.4
Assigning a higher risk rating to the company	44	45.4
Attending company road shows	42	43.3
Avoiding investment in companies with less disclosure	34	35.1
Requiring higher expected returns from companies with less disclosure	26	26.8
No answer	13	13.4

Another part of accounting diversity is the lack of uniform financial disclosures. We asked investors in our sample to indicate which coping mechanisms they have found useful in dealing with problems of insufficient disclosures. Their answers are summarized in Table 10.

To compensate for insufficient financial disclosures, many respondents (47.4 percent) visit prospective companies to seek additional information. Attendance at company road shows is also mentioned by 43.3 percent of our respondents. Even when additional information is collected, investors appear to treat firms with insufficient disclosures in different ways. For example, many respondents (45.4 percent) say that they attach a higher risk rating to companies with less disclosure, and some investors (26.8 percent) require higher returns from low-disclosure companies. And a sizeable number (35.1 percent) reply that they avoid investing in low-disclosure companies altogether. These responses suggest that insufficient disclosures could deter a sizeable block of investors from investing in a company, and result in a negative impact on pricing or availability of financial resources.

We postpone any further summary of the results for investors until we have reviewed the results from the corporate issuer survey.

VIII. SURVEY RESPONSES: CORPORATE ISSUERS

Corporate Issuer Characteristics

Characteristics of Corporate Issuers Who Answered This Survey

Country Characteristics

Corporate issuers responding to the questionnaire were from 13 countries, as shown in Table 11. Of the 88 respondents, the largest number were from the United Kingdom (26), followed by France (11) and Germany (10).

Table 11. Corporate Issuer Responses by Country

Austria	3	Ireland	3	Sweden	6
Belgium	6	Italy	2	Switzerland	6
Denmark	2	Netherlands	3	UK	26
France	11	Norway	3		
Germany	10	Spain	7	TOTAL	88

Job and Organization Characteristics

Most respondents to the corporate issuer questionnaire were either the firm's chief financial officer (42.0 percent) or the firm's treasurer (29.5 percent). The remainder of the respondents filled various high level positions such as financial director, vice president for finance, or head of capital markets. The vast majority of respondents (88.5 percent) indicated that funding activities at their firm are centralized.

Firm Size and Financial Experience

As our sample population is non-financial firms in the FT 500, all firms are 'large', ranging from a market capitalization (at year-end 1994) of $94 billion for Royal Dutch/Shell to $1.1 billion for Baer Holdings. Most of the firms on the FT 500 list are long-established companies. In our sample, 43.2 percent of the firms had been in operation for more than 100 years. As for personal experience in financial markets, 54.3 percent of respondents have more than 20 years of experience in funding activities in international markets.

Debt and Equity Capital Raising Practices

Debt Capital Practices

Most firms in our sample rely on several sources for their long-term debt. The most common sources are bank financing, mentioned by 75.0 percent of all respondents, local bond markets (59.1 percent), and private placements (48.9 percent). A smaller number of respondents mention access to the Eurobond or Euronote markets (46.6 percent), or access to foreign bond markets (37.5 percent).

We also asked respondents to report on their parent firm's long-term senior debt rating. A rating in the 'A' range was reported by 37 respondents (42.0 percent) and a rating in the 'B' range by 4 respondents (4.5 percent). The remaining 47 respondents offered no answer, which suggests that more than half of the responding firms have no senior debt rating from a rating agency. This is consistent with a funding strategy that de-emphasizes access to foreign bond markets.

Lack of access to foreign bond markets, however, need not mean lack of access to foreign-currency financing. We asked if firms make use of currency

Figure 3. Ownership of Equity Shares (Percentage Held by Domestic Investors)

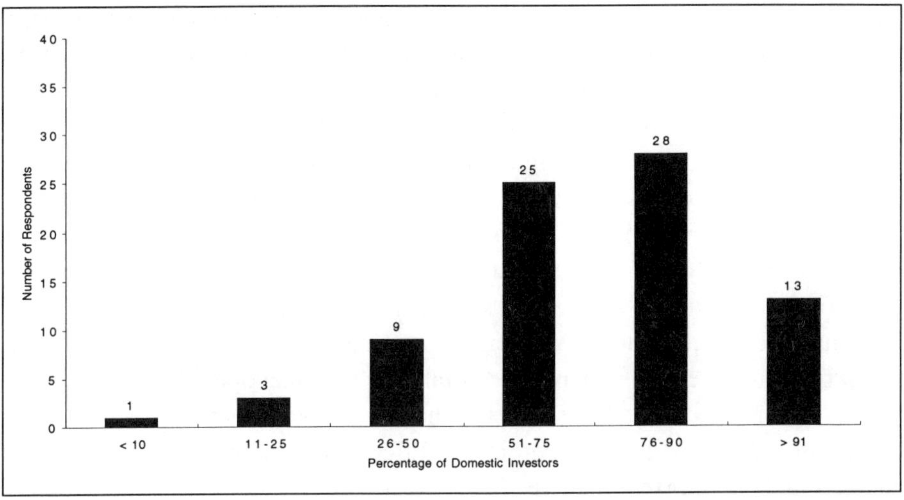

Note: Based on N=79 responses.

futures, forwards, options, swaps, or other derivatives to manage the currency composition of their debt. Most firms (78.4 percent) replied that they use derivatives 'sometimes' (28.4 percent), 'regularly' (21.6 percent), or 'frequently' (28.4 percent) to manage the currency composition of their debt.

Equity Capital Practices

In terms of equity capital, only 38.6 percent of the respondents report issuing equity abroad. And only 18.2 percent report a global equity offering. Most equity capital raising appears to take place in the domestic market.

Most of our respondents have not issued equity or listed their shares across a broad spectrum of European countries. The United Kingdom is an exception. Two-thirds of the non-UK firms have either issued or listed shares in the United Kingdom. The next most popular location is Germany, where 39.1 percent of the non-German firms have either issued or listed shares. Roughly 80 percent of our sample firms have not listed or issued their shares in the remaining EC sample countries.

By the same token, most corporate respondents report that the bulk of their equity ownership is in the hands of domestic investors. A chart illustrating the range of domestic ownership is shown in Figure 3. Of the 79 firms responding on this question, estimates range from 10 percent to 100 percent domestic ownership, with a median value of 78 percent.

The Role of Accounting Information for Issuers

Would You Prepare Additional Data According to Different Principles?

Although investors may not rank accounting practices as a primary barrier to the purchase of foreign equity shares, at the margin additional information that clarifies the condition of the firm or reduces uncertainty about it could attract additional investors. We asked respondents to report on how often they prepare additional accounting data, according to different accounting principles, in order to improve the success of an equity issue. The results are summarized in Table 12.

Of the 67 respondents to this question, 48 (or 71.6 percent) say that they would never supply additional accounting data in this situation. Note that among those firms that would 'very often' supply additional accounting data, most of these have relatively 'short' experience in business, and an 'extensive' international funding base, and all have a 'centralized' financial operation.

We asked corporate issuers why they *do not* provide investors with additional information prepared according to different accounting principles. These answers are summarized in Table 13.

Firms may recognize the highly institutional nature of European equity markets. In this setting, firms may calculate that their regular accounting statements are sufficient for informing and attracting institutional investors. Those with a longer history of operation and name recognition also have an edge in attracting investors. Ten firms list private placements as an alternative to further data preparation. Six cite preparation of US GAAP statements as justifying no additional accounting information.

Would You Prepare Additional Data Disclosure Items?

We also asked respondents to report on how often they prepare additional accounting information in order to improve the success of an equity issue.[44] The results are summarized in Table 14.

Our corporate respondents seem more willing to provide additional accounting information in order to benefit an equity offering. In total, 25 reply 'very often' or 'sometimes' to the question of how often they provide additional information. However, most of those who responded (33, or 56.9 percent) would 'never' provide additional accounting information disclosures. In the cross-tabulations, it appears that firms we classify as 'less large', with 'short' experience, and a 'centralized' financial structure, are more likely than average to provide additional accounting information.

[44] This question was intended to solicit answers regarding disclosure items, although the word 'disclosure' itself was not used in the question.

Table 12. How Often Do You Prepare Additional Accounting Data (Prepared According to Different Accounting Principles) in Order to Improve the Success of an Equity Issue?

Country	Very often	Sometimes	Never	Don't know	No answer	Total
Total	7	11	48	1	21	88
Size						
Large	3	4	17	1	3	28
Less large	4	5	28	0	17	54
N.A.	0	2	3	0	1	6
Total	7	11	48	1	21	88
Experience						
Long	2	5	22	1	8	38
Short	4	3	18	0	7	32
N.A.	1	3	8	0	6	18
Total	7	11	48	1	21	88
Scope of activity						
Limited	2	2	26	0	16	46
Extensive	5	7	16	1	4	33
N.A.	0	2	6	0	1	9
Total	7	11	48	1	21	88
Organizational structure						
Centralized	7	11	42	1	17	78
Decentralized	0	0	4	0	2	6
N.A.	0	0	2	0	2	4
Total	7	11	48	1	21	88

Notes: *Size:* 'Large' is greater than $5 billion market value of equity; *Experience:* 'Long' is more than 100 years of firm experience; *Scope of activity:* 'Extensive' is more than 25% foreign investors; *Organizational structure:* refers to the firm's funding activities.

Table 13. Reasons for NOT Providing Investors with Additional Accounting Data Prepared According to Different Accounting Principles

	Number of responses	Percentage (out of N=56)
Target foreign investor groups that are familiar with firm and its operations	26	46.4
The firm's name is well known in foreign financial markets	16	28.6
Make use of private placements for funding	10	17.9
Firm's credit rating is high	9	16.1
Accounting statements prepared according to US accounting principles	6	10.7
Other answers	23	41.1
No answer	32	–.–

Table 14. How Often Do You Provide Additional Accounting Information About the Firm in Order to Improve the Success of an Equity Issue?

Country	Very often	Sometimes	Never	No answer	Total
Total	10	15	33	30	88
Size					
Large	2	4	16	6	28
Less large	7	9	17	21	54
N.A.	1	2	0	3	6
Total	10	15	33	30	88
Experience					
Long	4	9	14	11	38
Short	5	4	12	11	32
N.A.	1	2	7	8	18
Total	10	15	33	30	88
Scope of activity					
Limited	5	5	17	19	46
Extensive	4	8	13	8	33
N.A.	1	2	3	3	9
Total	10	15	33	30	88
Organizational structure					
Centralized	10	15	27	26	78
Decentralized	0	0	2	4	6
N.A.	0	0	4	0	4
Total	10	15	33	30	88

Note: For description of size, experience, scope, and organizational structure variables, see note to Table 12.

Again, we asked issuers why they would not provide additional accounting information to benefit an equity issue. The reasons given were essentially identical to those reported in Table 13.

Communicating with Investors

In light of the diversity in accounting principles and disclosure practices across Europe, we asked several questions to probe whether corporate issuers find it difficult to communicate with investors. We asked specifically about differences in principles and disclosure.

Do Issuers Find it Difficult to Communicate with Investors?

The results for this question are summarized in Table 15. More than half of the respondents (59.1 percent) admit that principles differences make communicat-

Table 15. Do Accounting Principle Differences and Disclosure Differences Make it Difficult to Communicate with Investors?

	Principle differences – number of responses	Principle differences – percentage	Disclosure differences – number of responses	Disclosure differences – percentage
Yes, very difficult	6	6.8	2	2.3
Somewhat difficult	46	52.3	39	44.3
Not difficult at all	29	33.0	32	36.4
Don't know	0	0.0	5	5.7
No answer	7	8.0	10	11.4
Total	88	100.0	88	100.0

ing with foreign readers either 'very difficult' or 'somewhat difficult'. Only 33.0 percent reply that there are no difficulties at all. With disclosure differences, the results are somewhat more encouraging, as only 46.6 percent of the respondents reply that disclosure differences make communicating with foreign readers either 'very difficult' or 'somewhat difficult'. These answers conform to our earlier finding that issuers were more likely to provide additional disclosures than they were to provide additional information according to alternative accounting principles.

What Makes Communications with Investors Difficult?

As a follow-up question, we asked respondents what specific accounting issues made it difficult to communicate with investors. The results from this question are summarized in Table 16. The results show that principles differences are mentioned more frequently than disclosure differences. Among principles differences, respondents mention goodwill and intangibles, deferred taxes, and pension costs most often. Among disclosure differences, quarterly accounting information is mentioned most frequently, but only by 14 respondents (15.9 percent of the sample).

Conclusions on Corporate Issuers

Is Accounting Diversity an Important Barrier for European Corporate Issuers?

We asked corporate issuers to report on those EC countries where they have *not* listed or issued their equity shares and to indicate the reasons for this decision. For comparison, we also included Japan, Switzerland, and the United States as alternative markets for listing and issuing equity shares. The responses to this question are summarized in Table 17.

Table 16. Most Frequently Reported Reasons Why Accounting Differences Make it Difficult to Communicate With Investors

Reasons pertaining to accounting principles differences	Number of responses (Out of N=88)	Reasons pertaining to accounting disclosure differences	Number of responses (Out of N=88)
Goodwill, intangibles	29	Quarterly information	14
Deferred taxes	22	Off-balance-sheet items	11
Pension costs	20	Segment information: on products	10
Provisioning	19	Methods of asset valuation	10
Depreciation/valuing fixed assets	16	Hidden reserves	9
Discretionary reserves	15	Foreign operations: geographic	3
Foreign currency transactions	14	Description of capital expenditures	1
Multinational consolidations	11		
Financial instruments	6		
Inventory valuation	3		
No answer	33	No answer	53

As we noted earlier, most of our respondents have not issued equity or listed shares across a broad spectrum of European countries. The United Kingdom is the exception: nearly two-thirds of non-UK firms have either issued or listed their shares there. Germany is the next most popular market: 39.1 percent of non-German firms have either issued or listed shares there. In our sample, the equity markets in other countries have been used, on average, by only 21.8 percent of the foreign firms. What accounts for this limited use of other European equity markets?

Respondents were asked to indicate *any* reasons that apply to their decision not to list or issue securities in a particular market. In Table 17, we see that accounting issues – specifically, costs of conforming with accounting principles rules, or costs of conforming with accounting disclosure rules – were mentioned rarely, and only for four European countries. The limited importance of accounting diversity is not surprising, given the broad practice of reciprocity among European countries with regard to accounting statements.[45] Note that respondents mention accounting issues more often as a reason for not listing or issuing equity in the United States.

The results in Table 17 suggest that European firms do not widely cross-list or issue their shares throughout Europe because most of the market-places are small, and investors from those markets are willing to buy the firm's shares in

[45] See Choi and Levich (1990: 74-5 and 94-5) for a discussion of reciprocity versus national treatment for accounting rules.

Table 17. European Countries and Other Countries Where You Have NOT Issued or Listed Your Firm's Equity Shares

	Small size of market	Issuing costs too high	Costly to conform with accounting rules	Costly to conform with disclosure rules	Investors not familiar with our firm	Investors are willing to buy our shares in home market	Other reasons	Total
Austria	31	3			14	30	12	63
Belgium	29	3			12	29	10	63
Denmark	35	2			14	30	13	71
Finland	37	2			16	30	12	72
France	9	3		2	8	34	11	51
Germany	8	4		1	9	28	9	47
Greece	38	2			18	27	12	73
Ireland	36	2			14	29	11	71
Italy	20	4	1	3	10	33	12	65
Luxembourg	28	1			10	31	10	65
Netherlands	23	2			9	30	10	64
Norway	32	2			15	29	12	69
Portugal	35	2		1	13	29	13	73
Spain	26	2			11	27	11	63
Sweden	26	2			15	30	11	66
UK	3	1			3	14	2	21
Japan	3	11	3	4	16	27	14	64
Switzerland	12	2			8	28	11	52
US	3	9	18	12	8	29	6	48

Note: The number in the column labelled 'Total' is the number of respondents who listed *any* reason for not issuing or listing share in a country. Respondents were also given other answers to tick such as currency risk, and specific instructions from management not to list. These responses are omitted here.

the home market. As investment across Europe is dominated by large institutions, corporate issuers may calculate that foreign issues and listings are unnecessary or not cost-effective.

How Do European Issuers Cope with European Accounting Diversity?

As we have seen, corporate issuers experience some difficulties in communicating their company's performance to foreign investors. We asked respondents to indicate what coping mechanisms they used to overcome differences in accounting principles differences and in accounting disclosure requirements. These results are summarized in Table 18.

'Road shows' and analysts' visits to headquarters are by far the most common coping mechanisms for dealing with both principle differences and disclosure differences, having been mentioned by more than 60 percent of those respondents who report any coping mechanism.

Table 18. Coping Methods Adopted by European Corporations for Dealing with Diversity in Accounting Principles and Disclosure Requirements

Methods for dealing with accounting principles differences	Number of responses (out of N=88)	Methods for dealing with accounting disclosure differences	Number of responses (out of N=88)
'Road shows' to meet with foreign analysts	44	'Road shows' to meet with foreign analysts	41
Invite foreign analyst to corporate headquarters	44	Invite foreign analyst to corporate headquarters	37
Translate reporting language to that of foreign reader	21	Increase financial disclosures in external reports to markets	17
Restate to US GAAP	17	Comply with disclosure requirements of International Accounting Standards	12
Translate reporting currency to that of foreign reader	12	Comply with disclosure requirements of US GAAP	9
Restate to International Accounting Standards	9	Comply with disclosure requirements of EC Accounting Directives	8
Restate to EC Accounting Directives	9	Reduce our foreign funding objective	4
Reduce our foreign funding objective	2	Do nothing	4
Other	5	Seek an accommodation from market regulators	3
		Other	3
No answers	18	No answers	25

Other methods for dealing with principle differences include both nominal and substantive financial statement translations. The former take the form of 'convenience' translations, comprising either language translations (21 respondents) or currency translations of accounting statements (12). At a more substantive level, restatement of financial accounts to US GAAP (17 mentions), International Accounting Standards (9), or EC Directives (9) are listed and together comprise 40 percent of the methods of respondents.

To deal with disclosure differences, our respondents report, in addition to the most popular methods, making additional (voluntary) disclosures along the lines of International Accounting Standards (12 mentions), US GAAP (9), or EC Directives (8). A larger number (17) report making additional disclosures in their external reports.

IX. CONCLUSIONS

Theory and Prior Research

In this chapter, we have documented the scope allowed by the EC Directives for diversity in the presentation of accounting reports. Prior research shows that, indeed, companies across Europe avail themselves of different accounting practices (Exhibit 1). A company with a given set of economic operations could report vastly different profit and loss figures, depending on the accident (or choice) of where the firm is headquartered and what accounting principles are used there. This licence for accounting diversity creates a *potential* barrier to international capital flows.

At a conceptual level, we showed (Exhibit 2) that accounting diversity may be a logical or illogical response for the measurement of a firm's economic condition. If two firms are similarly situated, then logically they should use similar accounting procedures and report similar economic results. But if two firms are not similarly situated, then the use of a standardized accounting system may distort comparisons between them.

Our example of (UK-based) Grand Metropolitan's takeover of (US-based) Pillsbury supported the view that the accounting treatment (of goodwill) afforded to Grand Met was similar to a non-traded asset. To prepare new US accounting statements for Grand Met as if it did not have access to favourable UK accounting and tax treatment would be misleading. Harmonization in cases like this would obfuscate rather than facilitate cross-country firm comparisons. Harmonization on the treatment of goodwill, for example, would be superficial unless all firms had access to the same tax treatment on the cash flows related to goodwill.

The Grand Met example also shows the connection between tax reporting and external reporting, which is common in Europe but not practised in the United States. Fundamental stock analysis requires an examination of a firm's performance in the social, legal, economic, and tax environment in which it operates. Accounting diversity may help to highlight these country-specific differences. Accounting policy appears then to be the 'tail' wagged by the dog of social, legal, economic, and tax diversity. Once these parameters are suitably harmonized, accounting harmonization might logically follow.

The case for expediting accounting harmonization might improve if it were observed that accounting diversity were a great burden to issuers and investors. Prior research has addressed this point to some extent. Basically, the research suggests that market participants have developed a variety of coping mechanisms to deal with accounting diversity. Investors may adopt strategies that de-emphasize accounting data (such as indexation, or reliance on cash flow or dividend payments), or go to the opposite extreme and hire individuals with expertise in diverse accounting practices ('multiple principles capability'). Issuers also often take steps to address any loss of financial market access that comes with accounting diversity. Some corporate issuers voluntarily provide additional accounting information over and above the narrow requirements of their national rules. These measures may be as simple as translating reports into a foreign language and/or currency, or as complex as preparing new statements following US GAAP. Firms face market incentives which encourage them to weigh the costs of providing additional accounting information properly against the additional benefits that might be achieved if indeed accounting diversity were a critical financial barrier.

The Survey of European Investors and Issuers

We know that accounting diversity is one factor in a sea of factors affecting capital flows, and prior research has shown that both investors and issuers adopt coping mechanisms to overcome the costs of accounting differences. Our research has attempted to shed light on whether accounting diversity is a *substantial* barrier to European capital movements. Put differently, we are asking whether the coping mechanisms are *effective* in reducing the costs of accounting differences. Once this question is answered, we can consider whether an externally imposed harmonization of accounting principles will be a necessary or an effective solution to the problem of accounting diversity.

In our present survey of European institutional investors and corporate issuers, we have confirmed that accounting diversity plays a relatively small part as a barrier keeping European investors and issuers apart. Investors are more concerned about markets that are small, illiquid, and subject to currency risks. Investors have numerous ways to cope with accounting diversity, but market size, lack of liquidity, and currency risk are more fundamental, and the first two are certainly beyond the power of investors to overcome.

The present survey suggests that a typical European institutional investor adopts a value- or growth-oriented investment approach, feels that accounting information is very important to his or her analysis, and strives to make cross-country investment comparisons. The median investor in our sample holds 25 percent of the portfolio in foreign securities, and most investors include most (or all) EC countries within their investment opportunity set.

In this survey, no attempt was made to quantify the impact of accounting diversity in Europe on equity pricing or market efficiency. Responses regarding approaches taken to deal with differences in European accounting and disclosure practices are, nevertheless, suggestive.

Forty-five percent of investors say they assign a higher risk rating to companies which are less forthcoming than desired; 35 percent avoid investing in low-disclosure firms altogether, while 26 percent demand higher returns. Corporate issuers are less vocal in this regard, although four respondents report reduced funding objectives when disclosure requirements are burdensome. Only two companies report similar behaviour with respect to GAAP differences.

On the matter of differences in accounting principles, we examined whether greater investment flows might follow a move towards greater account-

Table 19. If Company X Were to Change its Method for Preparing Accounting Reports, Would This Make You More Likely to Consider Investing in Company X?

Change to	Much more likely	Somewhat more likely	Not more likely	Don't know	No answer	Total
Home country accounting principles	18	36	21	8	14	97
IAS	12	44	19	6	16	97
US GAAP	13	30	32	6	16	97

ing harmonization. Specifically, we asked whether greater harmonization would make investors more likely to consider investment in a foreign company. The results are summarized in Table 19.

More than half (55.7 percent) of the investor respondents say they would be more likely to consider investing in a foreign company if that company prepared its annual accounts according to the accounting principles of the investor's country of domicile. Virtually the same number (57.7 percent) say they would be more likely to consider investing in a foreign company if the accounts were prepared according to International Accounting Standards, while 44.3 percent say they would be more inclined to invest abroad if companies reported in accordance with US GAAP.

A desire on the part of investors for more information about a firm is natural – the information may be useful, and from their standpoint it is essentially a free good. One testimonial from our face-to-face interviews may provide some insight into the results in Table 19:

> The real question for a portfolio manager is the prediction of earnings and stock prices 6–12 months in the future. All analysts recognize that earnings figures are manipulated, so they will conduct their fundamental analysis on a 'relative' basis: either relative to earlier years, or relative to other firms in the same country. The desire for accounting standardization is 'computer driven', growing from a desire to mechanize the analysis of firms.

One significant factor fuelling the desire for greater harmonization of accounting reports would appear to be the desire to speed up the analysis of investment targets. The underlying hope is that the numbers going into the analysis are sufficiently comparable for the findings to make sense. Full comparability may be in doubt, but as one investor told us in an earlier study:

> You don't have to be that precise for those comparisons. Absolute precision doesn't help you very much. Getting to the third decimal point is not going to make a difference in your views.[46]

Another investor offered a very different interpretation as to why accounting changes might matter for investors:

> Again, [the impact of accounting harmonization] depends on the firm. If Nestlé decides to issue in US GAAP, it will not affect us, since we feel we already know a great deal about Nestlé and the outlook for the firm. On the other hand, if a smaller firm makes an accounting change, it could be a signal of a 'cultural change' within the firm. For small and mid-cap firms, this accounting change could be important as a signal.

This investor is interested in accounting changes for what they might signal about the firm – whether it is managed for shareholders or debt-holders, for profit maximization and wealth maximization, or for some other less transparent target.

While firms might like to signal their more favourable intentions towards shareholders and wealth maximization, they cannot alter their accounting reporting practices for free. For many European firms, there is no tradition of external reporting as distinct from tax reporting. The cost of imposing another layer of accounting requirements would fall directly on issuers, while the benefit is fairly uncertain – especially when firms can voluntarily take interim steps on their own.

In our survey, corporate issuers express great reluctance towards supplying additional accounting information prepared according to different accounting principles, but somewhat less reluctance towards supplying additional disclosures. This is consistent with our finding (Table 16) that differences in accounting principles are more frequently cited than disclosure differences as a source of communication difficulties. Most corporate issuers in our sample conduct road shows and meetings with institutional investors, which may be an effective coping mechanism.

Overall, it appears that the majority of European investors and corporate issuers in our sample have found ways of coping with accounting diversity. In the absence of quantitative data, we cannot conclude whether their coping mechanisms are optimal. We do observe, however, that five years ago approximately one-half of the respondents to our earlier capital markets survey[47] said that

[46] See Choi and Levich (1990: 86).
[47] See Choi and Levich (1990).

accounting differences were a problem despite efforts to cope with such differences; these differences are less of a problem today. Accordingly, the gains from imposing harmonized accounting practices across Europe would also seem to be decreasing. European market participants, in moving up the learning curve, have been developing their own market-driven coping mechanisms to the problems created by accounting diversity. These market-driven mechanisms are continually evolving.

True and beneficial European accounting harmonization – whether towards IASC, US GAAP, or new EC standards – would first require harmonization of important components of the legal, tax, and social environment. Unless these preconditions are met, accounting harmonization is likely to be superficial at best and detrimental at worst. For this reason, a cautious stance on imposed policy prescriptions is in order. An externally imposed accounting system which fails to communicate material cross-country differences in the underlying economic environment would be unlikely to facilitate European equity market integration.

References

'An Edge to Foreign Buyers?', 1988. *Mergers and Acquisitions*, No. 22 (March/April), 7–8.

Ball, R., 1972. 'Changes in Accounting Techniques and Stock Prices', *Empirical Research in Accounting, Selected Studies, 1972* (supplement), *Journal of Accounting Research*, No. 10, Spring, 1–38.

Ball, R. and P. Brown, 1968. 'The Empirical Evaluation of Accounting Income Numbers', *Journal of Accounting Research*, Autumn, 159–77.

Brown, P. and J.W. Kennely, 1972. 'The Information Content of Quarterly Earnings: An Extension and Further Evidence', *Journal of Business*, July, 403–15.

Choi, F.D.S., 1973a. 'Financial Disclosure in Relation to a Firm's Capital Costs', *Accounting and Business Research*, Autumn, 282–92.

Choi, F.D.S., 1973b. 'Financial Disclosure and Entry to the European Capital Market', *Journal of Accounting Research*, Autumn, 159–75.

Choi, F.D.S. and Vinod Bavishi, 1983. 'International Accounting Standards: Issues Needing Attention', *Journal of Accountancy*, March, 62–8.

Choi, F.D.S. and S.B. Hong, 1990. 'The Decision Utility of Restating Accounting Information Sets: Korea', in Raj Aggarwal (ed.), *Advances in Financial Planning and Forecasting*.

Choi, F.D.S. and Changwoo Lee, 1991. 'Merger Premia and National Differences in Accounting for Goodwill', *Journal of International Financial Management and Accounting*, Autumn, 219–40.

Choi, F.D.S. and Richard M. Levich, 1990. *The Capital Market Effects of International Accounting Diversity,* Dow Jones-Irwin Publishing Company, Chicago.

Choi, F.D.S. and Richard M. Levich, 1991. 'Accounting Diversity and Capital Market Decisions', in Frederick D.S. Choi (ed.), *Handbook of International Accounting* John Wiley & Sons, Inc., New York, 7.3–7.11.

Choi, F.D.S., H.D. Lowe and R.G. Worthley, 1978. 'Accountors, Accountants and Standard No. 8', *Journal of International Business Studies*, Fall.

Coenenberg, A. and E. Brandi, 1976. 'The Information Content of Annual Accounting Income Numbers of German Corporations: A Review of German Accounting Standards and Some Preliminary Empirical Results', *Internationale Arbeitsberichte zur Betriebswirtschaftslehre der Universität Augsburg*, No. 7.

Coopers & Lybrand, 1991. *1991 International Accounting Summaries,* John Wiley & Sons, Inc., New York.

'Daimler-Benz to Adopt US Gaap for Good', 1995. *Global Investment Technology*, 18 September, 9.

Deakin, Edward, Gyles Norwood and Charles Smith, 1974. *International Journal of Accounting*, Fall, 123–36.

Dukes, Roland, 1978. *An Empirical Investigation of the Effects of Statement of Financial Accounting Standards No. 8 on Security Return Behavior,* Financial Accounting Standards Board, December, Stamford, CT.

Emenyonu, Emmanuel N. and Sidney J. Gray, 1992. 'EC Accounting Harmonization: An Empirical Study of Measurement Practices in France, Germany and the UK', *Accounting and Business Research*, Winter, 49–58.

Evans, T.G., W.R. Folks and M. Jilling, 1978. *The Impact of Financial Accounting Standards No. 8 on the Foreign Exchange Risk Management Practices of American Multinationals: An Economic Impact Study*, Financial Accounting Standards Board, Stamford, CT.

Firth, M., 1976. 'The Impact of Earnings Announcements on the Share Price Behavior of Similar Type Firms', *The Economic Journal*, June, 296–306.

Forsgardh, L.E., and K. Hertzen, 1975. 'The Adjustment of Stock Prices to New Earnings Information: A Study of the Efficiency of the Swedish Stock Market', in E. Elton and M. Gruber (eds), *International Capital Markets,* North-Holland Publishing Company, Amsterdam.

Gonedes, N., 1974. 'Capital Market Equilibrium and Annual Accounting Numbers: Empirical Evidence', *Journal of Accounting Research*, Spring, 26–62.

Gurwitz, Aaron S., 1989. 'SEC Rule 144A and Regulation S: Impact on Global Fixed Income Markets', Fixed Income Research Series, September, Goldman Sachs, New York.

International Monetary Fund, 1994. *Handbook on Exchange Rate Restrictions,* IMF, Washington, DC.

KPMG Peat Marwick, 1989. *KPMG World*, No. 3.

Korhonen, A., 1975. 'Accounting Income Numbers, Information and Stock Prices: A Test of Market Efficiency', *The Finnish Journal of Business Economics*, 24: 306–22.

Lee, Changwoo and Frederick D.S. Choi, 1992. 'Effects of Alternative Goodwill Treatments on Merger Premia: Further Empirical Evidence', *Journal of International Financial Management and Accounting*, Autumn, 220–36.

Lev, B. and J.A. Ohlson, 1982. 'Market-Based Empirical Research in Accounting: A Review, Interpretation, and Extension', *Empirical Research in Accounting: Selected Studies.* Supplement to *Journal of Accounting Research*, 20: 249–322.

Levich, Richard M., 1985. 'Empirical Studies of Exchange Rates: Price Behavior, Rate Determination and Market Efficiency', in R. Jones and P. Kenen (eds), *Handbook of International Economics*, North-Holland Publishing, Amsterdam.

McQueen, Patricia D., 1993. 'The Information Content of International Differences in Accounting', unpublished Ph.D. dissertation, New York University.

Meek, G.K. and S.J. Gray, 1989. 'Globalization of Stock Markets and Foreign Listing Requirements: Voluntary Disclosures by Continental European Companies Listed on the London Stock Exchange', *Journal of International Business Studies*, 20 (2), Summer, 315–36.

Mueller, Gerald G., 1991. '1992 and Harmonization Efforts in the EC', in Frederick D.S. Choi (ed.), *Handbook of International Accounting,* John Wiley & Sons, Inc., New York.

Ooghe, H., P. Beghin and V. Verbaere, 1981. 'The Efficiency of Capital Markets: A "Semi-Strong Form" Test', *Tijdschrift voor Economie en Management,* 26: 421–40.

Patell, J.M., 1976. 'Corporate Forecasts of Earnings Per Share and Stock Price Behavior: Empirical Tests', *Journal of Accounting Research,* Autumn, 246–76.

Peller, R. and Frank J. Schwitter, 1991. 'A Summary of Accounting Principle Differences Around the World', in Frederick D.S. Choi (ed.), *Handbook of International Accounting,* John Wiley & Sons, Inc., New York.

Price Waterhouse, 1987. *EC Bulletin,* Special Issue, 'Fourth EC Directive – Analysis of its Implementation in the EC Member States', Price Waterhouse, Brussels.

Russell, A., J.R. Grinyer, M. Walker, and P.A. Malton (1989). *Accounting for Goodwill,* Research Report No. 13, June, Certified Accountant Publications Limited, London.

Saudagaran, Shahrokh M. and Gary C. Biddle., 1992. 'Financial Disclosure Levels and Foreign Stock Exchange Listing Decisions', *Journal of International Financial Management and Accounting*, Summer, 106–48.

Shank, J.K., J.F. Dillard and R.J. Murdock, 1979. *Assessing the Economic Impact of FASB 8,* Financial Executives Research Foundation, New York.

Simmons, Andy and Olivier Azières (1989). *Accounting for Europe – Success by 2000 AD?,* Touche Ross, London.

Solnik, Bruno, 1988. *International Investments*, June, Addison-Wesley Publishing, Reading, MA.

Stonehill, Arthur I. and Kare B. Dullum, 1982. *Internationalizing the Cost of Capital* John Wiley and Sons, Inc., New York.

Watts, R.L. and J.L. Zimmerman, 1986. *Positive Accounting Theory,* Prentice Hall, Englewood Cliffs, NJ.

Weetman, P. and S.J. Gray, 1990. 'International Financial Analysis and Comparative Corporate Performance: The Impact of U.K. versus U.S. Accounting Principles on Earnings', *Journal of International Financial Management and Accounting,* Summer and Autumn, 111-30.

World Bank, 1994. *Emerging Stock Markets Factbook,* International Finance Corporation, Washington, DC.

APPENDIX A

EUROPEAN CAPITAL MARKETS INSTITUTE RESEARCH PROJECT

Questionnaire for Investors/Funds Managers

A. BACKGROUND INFORMATION

1. In what country is your office located? ______________________

2. Which of the following best describes your job responsibilities? Please tick (√) the appropriate response.

___ a. Portfolio manager

___ b. Security analyst

___ c. Country analyst

___ d. Industry analyst

___ e. Other. Please explain ______________________

3. Organization of Investment Activity

a. In your firm, is decision making regarding the allocation of assets across countries and industries centralized or decentralized?

___ 1. Centralized

___ 2. Decentralized

___ 3. Other: Please describe ______________________

____

b. In your firm, is decision making regarding the selection of individual stocks centralized or decentralized?

___ 1. Centralized

___ 2. Decentralized

___ 3. Other: Please describe ______________________

____

4. Size of Firm and Investment Activity

a. As of December 31, 1994 what was the total value of funds under management at your firm?

Currency (e.g. $) ________ Amount ______________________

b. As of December 31, 1994 what was the total value of funds that you personally managed?

Currency (e.g. $) ________ Amount ______________________

5. Age of Firm

a. How old is your firm?

____

b. How long have you personally been in the investment analysis or portfolio management business?

____

B. INVESTMENT PRACTICES

6. Scope of Investment Activity

a. What percentage of your investments is in equity securities?

Please enter a percentage (%) amount. ____________

b. What percentage of your investments is in equities of FOREIGN companies (that is, a company whose headquarters is not in the country where your office is located)?

Please enter a percentage (%) amount. ____________

7. General Investment Approach

Which of the following best describes your general investment approach? Please indicate your primary investment approach and, if appropriate, your secondary approach.

	Primary Investment Approach (Tick [√] only one in this column)	Secondary Investment Approach (Tick [√] only one in this column)
a. Value oriented	☐	☐
b. Growth oriented	☐	☐
c. Quant-driven active	☐	☐
d. Asset allocation (e.g. country fund)	☐	☐
e. Indexation	☐	☐
f. Other, please specify	☐	☐

____

8. Opinions Regarding European Investing and Accounting Practices

a. What do you feel are the most important reasons that limit your investments across Europe? Tick (√) all that apply.

___ 1. Currency risks
___ 2. Country risks
___ 3. Market risks
___ 4. Regulatory barriers
___ 5. Accounting differences across EC countries
___ 6. Quality of financial reporting
___ 7. Settlement procedures
___ 8. Liquidity considerations
___ 9. Access to corporate management
___ 10. Other, please explain ______________________________

b. Would a common set of accounting and reporting standards encourage you to increase your investment activity across Europe? Tick (√) one answer.

___ 1. Yes (please explain)______________________________

___ 2. No (please explain)______________________________

___ 3. Don't know / Not sure.

c. If you answered "Yes" to the above question, please tell us your preference for a model of accounting and reporting harmonization. Tick (√) one answer.

___ 1. European Community directives
___ 2. Standards promulgated by the International Accounting Standards Committee
___ 3. United States accounting and reporting standards
___ 4. United Kingdom accounting and reporting standards
___ 5. Other, please explain______________________________

9. Identify those European Community (EC) countries where you have <u>NOT</u> invested and tick (√) all of the reasons that describe why your firm would not consider buying equity shares in a firm headquartered in that country (Tick [√] all boxes that apply).

	a	b	c	d	e	f	g	h	i	j
	We are not allowed to invest there	Limits on foreign owners	Market too small, not liquid	Currency risk too high	Country risk too high	Cost of invest: fees, taxes, delivery	Company accounts difficult to understand	Company accounts do not contain enough details	Lack of economic growth prospects	Other reasons Describe at bottom of table
Austria										
Belgium										
Denmark										
Finland										
France										
Germany										
Greece										
Ireland										
Italy										
Luxembourg										
Netherlands										
Norway										
Portugal										
Spain										
Sweden										
U.K.										

j. Other Reasons______________________________

10. For the following countries in which you **DO** invest, how easy or difficult is it to analyze company financial accounts (e.g. profit and loss accounts, balance sheets)? Please tick (√) the appropriate response for each country.

	Very Easy to Analyze				Very Difficult to Analyze	Don't know/ not sure
Austria	❑	❑	❑	❑	❑	❑
Belgium	❑	❑	❑	❑	❑	❑
Denmark	❑	❑	❑	❑	❑	❑
Finland	❑	❑	❑	❑	❑	❑
France	❑	❑	❑	❑	❑	❑
Germany	❑	❑	❑	❑	❑	❑
Greece	❑	❑	❑	❑	❑	❑
Ireland	❑	❑	❑	❑	❑	❑
Italy	❑	❑	❑	❑	❑	❑
Luxembourg	❑	❑	❑	❑	❑	❑
Netherlands	❑	❑	❑	❑	❑	❑
Norway	❑	❑	❑	❑	❑	❑
Portugal	❑	❑	❑	❑	❑	❑
Spain	❑	❑	❑	❑	❑	❑
Sweden	❑	❑	❑	❑	❑	❑
U.K.	❑	❑	❑	❑	❑	❑
Japan	❑	❑	❑	❑	❑	❑
Switzerland	❑	❑	❑	❑	❑	❑
U.S.	❑	❑	❑	❑	❑	❑

C. ROLE OF ACCOUNTING INFORMATION

11. How important is company-specific financial information (e.g. profit and loss accounts and balance sheets) when selecting individual FOREIGN stocks? (Tick [ ] one)

Very important		Somewhat important		Not at All important	Don't know/ not sure
❑	❑	❑	❑	❑	❑

If you answered "Not at All Important" to Question 11, then go to Question 12
Otherwise, go to Question 13

12. The reason I do <u>NOT</u> rely on company-specific financial information (e.g. profit and loss accounts and balance sheets) when investing in foreign stocks is because (Tick [√] all that apply)

___ a. My investment approach does not require the use of company-specific financial information.

___ b. I believe that company-specific financial information is difficult to interpret because unfamiliar accounting principles are used.

___ c. Reporting companies do not provide sufficient information for me to properly interpret accounting numbers.

___ d. I rely on information about the firm which is less sensitive to differences in generally accepted accounting principles (GAAP).

___ e. Other reason: Please explain ______________________________

____

____

____

13. Do you compare investment opportunities in one country with investment opportunities in other countries?

___ a. Yes.

___ b. No.

___ c. Other ______________________________

If you answered "No" to Question 13, then go to Question 14
If you answered "Yes" to Question 13, then go to Question 15

14. I do <u>NOT</u> compare investment opportunities between countries because (please tick [√] all that apply):

___ a. My investment approach does not require cross-country comparisons.

___ b. The following accounting items make it difficult for me to compare accounts between countries (Tick [√] all accounting principles that apply)

___ Multinational Consolidations	___ Provisioning
___ Discretionary Reserves	___ Financial Instruments
___ Inventory Valuation	___ Depreciation/Valuing Fixed Assets
___ Goodwill, Intangibles	___ Deferred Taxes
___ Pension Costs	___ Foreign Currency Transactions
___ Other items: Please list	

___ c. Lack of information on the following topics makes it difficult for me to compare accounts between countries (Tick [√] all accounting items that apply)

___ Segment Information: on products	___ Foreign Operations: Geographic
___ Quarterly Accounting Information	___ Hidden Reserves
___ Off-balance Sheet Items	___ Methods of Asset Valuation
___ Description of Capital Expenditures	
___ Other items: Please list	

___ d. Other ___

STOP. End of Questionnaire.

15. When making cross-country investment comparisons, I find that the following approaches are helpful in dealing with national accounting principles: (Tick [√] all that apply)

___ a. Re-stating foreign accounts to my home country accounting standards.
___ b. Re-stating foreign accounts to International Accounting Standards.
___ c. Re-stating foreign accounts to accounting standards consistent with EC accounting directives.
___ d. Re-stating foreign accounts to United States accounting standards.
___ e. Relying on financial information or analysis supplied by one or more investment advisory services.
___ f. Attaching a low weight or lesser importance to accounting information.
___ g. Placing a higher weight or greater importance on non-accounting information (such as cash flows).
___ h. Placing a higher weight or greater importance on industry information.
___ i. Placing a higher weight or greater importance on macroeconomic information.
___ j. Reducing the investment allocation on foreign firms.
___ k. Other: Please explain.___

16. When making cross-country investment comparisons, I find that the following approaches are helpful for analyzing companies that do not provide sufficient financial information: (Tick [√] all that apply)

___ a. Visiting the company to collect information.
___ b. Attending company "road shows" to collect additional information.
___ c. Assigning a higher risk rating to companies with less disclosure.
___ d. Requiring higher expected returns from companies with less disclosure .
___ e. Avoiding investments in companies with less disclosure.
___ f. Other: Please explain___

17. Suppose that *Company X* -- A foreign company -- decides to prepare its 1995 accounting statements according to *the accounting principles of your home country.*

Would this change in financial reporting make you more likely to consider investing in Company X?

Much more likely		Somewhat more likely		No more likely	Don't know/ not sure
❑	❑	❑	❑	❑	❑

18. Suppose that *Company X* -- A foreign company -- decides to prepare its 1995 accounting statements according to *International Accounting Standards.*

Would this change in financial reporting make you more likely to consider investing in Company X?

Much more likely		Somewhat more likely		No more likely	Don't know/ not sure
❑	❑	❑	❑	❑	❑

19. Suppose that *Company X* -- A foreign company -- decides to prepare its 1995 accounting statements according to *United States accounting standards.*

Would this change in financial reporting make you more likely to consider investing in Company X?

Much more likely		Somewhat more likely		No more likely	Don't know/ not sure
❑	❑	❑	❑	❑	❑

*** END *** END *** END *** END *** END *** END *** END *** END *** END *** END ***

EUROPEAN CAPITAL MARKETS INSTITUTE RESEARCH PROJECT

Questionnaire for Issuers/Corporate Treasurers

A. BACKGROUND INFORMATION

1. In which country is your office located?____________________

2. Which of the following best describes your job responsibilities? Please tick (√) the appropriate response.

   ___ a. Chief Financial Officer
   ___ b. Treasurer
   ___ c. Other, Please specify.____________________

3. Organization of Firm
   Are the funding activities at your firm centralized (so that funding decisions are made at corporate headquarters) or decentralized (so that funding decisions are made at the regional or subsidiary level) ?

   ___ a. Centralized
   ___ b. Decentralized
   ___ c. Other: Please describe. ____________________

4. Size of the Firm's Funding Activities
   As of December 31, 1994 what was the

   Market value of equity outstanding Currency (e.g. $): _____ Amount:__________
   Face value of the firm's long term-debt Currency (e.g. $): _____ Amount:__________

   Credit rating for parent's long-term senior debt ____________________

5. Age of Firm

   a. How old is your firm? ____________________

   b. How long have you been involved in funding activities in

      1. Domestic markets ____________________
      2. Foreign (international) markets ____________________
      3. Other, please explain ____________________

6. Scope of Funding Activities

   a. What are the sources of your firm's outstanding long-term debt. Please tick (√) all that apply.

	Long Term Debt
Local bond market	
Foreign bond markets (Note countries)	
Eurobond or Euronote markets	
Private Placements	
Bank Financing	
Other	

   b. To what extent does your firm make use of currency futures, currency forwards, currency options, currency swaps or other currency derivatives to manage the currency composition of its debt? Please tick (√) one response.

Frequently	Regularly	Sometimes	Rarely	Never	Don't know/ not sure
❑	❑	❑	❑	❑	❑

   c. What are the sources of your firm's equity capital? Please tick (√) all that apply.

   ____ 1. Domestic primary equity
   ____ 2. Foreign primary equity
   ____ 3. Global primary offering
   ____ 4. Other, please explain ____________________

   d. What proportion of your firm's equity shares are held by investors who reside in the following countries? Also tick (√) those countries where your shares are either listed or traded.

Date: as of 31/12/94 or most recent date / /	Estimated Percentage of Equity Shareholders	Tick (√) if Equity Shares Are Listed or Traded on Local Exchange
Austria		
Belgium		
Denmark		
Finland		
France		
Germany		
Greece		
Ireland		
Italy		
Luxembourg		
Netherlands		
Portugal		
Spain		
Sweden		
United Kingdom		
Switzerland		
United States		
Japan		
Other or % not allocated		
TOTAL	100%	

B. EQUITY CAPITAL RAISING PRACTICES

7. Please identify those countries listed below in which you have **NOT** issued or listed your stock. Tick (√) all of the reasons why.

	a	b	c	d	e	f	g	h	i
	Small size of market	Currency risk too high	Issuing costs too high	Costly to conform with accounting rules	costly to conform with disclosure rules	Investors not familiar with our firm	Investors are willing to buy our shares in home market	I was instructed not to pursue a foreign listing	Other reasons Describe at bottom of table
Austria									
Belgium									
Denmark									
Finland									
France									
Germany									
Greece									
Ireland									
Italy									
Luxembourg									
Netherlands									
Norway									
Portugal									
Spain									
Sweden									
U.K.									
Japan									
Switzerland									
US									

j. Other Reasons ____

____

____

8. For the following countries in which you **DO** *issue* securities or *list* your securities, please indicate how easy or difficult it is for you to satisfy investors' demand for financial information about your firm:

	Very Easy to Satisty				Very Difficult to Satisfy	Don't know/ not sure
Austria	❑	❑	❑	❑	❑	❑
Belgium	❑	❑	❑	❑	❑	❑
Denmark	❑	❑	❑	❑	❑	❑
Finland	❑	❑	❑	❑	❑	❑
France	❑	❑	❑	❑	❑	❑
Germany	❑	❑	❑	❑	❑	❑
Greece	❑	❑	❑	❑	❑	❑
Ireland	❑	❑	❑	❑	❑	❑
Italy	❑	❑	❑	❑	❑	❑
Luxembourg	❑	❑	❑	❑	❑	❑
Netherlands	❑	❑	❑	❑	❑	❑
Norway	❑	❑	❑	❑	❑	❑
Portugal	❑	❑	❑	❑	❑	❑
Spain	❑	❑	❑	❑	❑	❑
Sweden	❑	❑	❑	❑	❑	❑
U.K.	❑	❑	❑	❑	❑	❑
Japan	❑	❑	❑	❑	❑	❑
Switzerland	❑	❑	❑	❑	❑	❑
U.S.	❑	❑	❑	❑	❑	❑

C. ROLE OF ACCOUNTING INFORMATION

9. For your foreign share issuing and/or listing decisions, how often do you prepare additional accounting data -- **prepared according to different accounting principles** -- in order to improve the success of an equity issue?

Very often		Sometimes		Never	Don't know/ not sure
❑	❑	❑	❑	❑	❑

If you answered "Never" to Question 9, then go to Question 10
Otherwise, go to Question 11

10. The reason that we **DO NOT** provide investors with additional accounting data **prepared according to different accounting principles** is (tick [√] all that apply):

____ a. Our investors make their decisions on the basis of macro-economic conditions (such as income growth, interest rates, and foreign exchange rates) rather than on the basis of accounting information about our company
____ b. Our firm's name is well-known in foreign financial markets
____ c. Our firm's credit rating is very high
____ d. We target foreign investor groups that are familiar with our firm and its operations
____ e. We make use of private placements for funding
____ f. We prepare our accounting statements according to U.S. accounting principles
____ g. Other reason, please explain ______________________________

____

11. For your foreign share issuing and/or listing decisions, how often do you provide **additional accounting information** about the firm in order to improve the success of an equity issue?

Very often		Sometimes		Never	Don't know/ not sure
❑	❑	❑	❑	❑	❑

If you answered "Never" to Question 11, then go to Question 12
Otherwise, go to Question 13

12. The reason that we **DO NOT** provide **additional accounting information** for investors is (tick [√] all that apply):

____ a. Our investors make their decisions on the basis of macro-economic conditions (such as income growth, interest rates, and foreign exchange rates) rather than on the basis of accounting information about our company
____ b. Our firm's name is well-known in foreign financial markets
____ c. Our firm's credit rating is very high
____ d. We target foreign investor groups that are familiar with our firm and its operations
____ e. We make use of private placements for funding
____ f. We prepare our accounting statements according to U.S. accounting principles
____ g. Other reason, please explain ____________________

13. Do differences in accounting principles from country to country make it difficult for you communicate with foreign investors?

Yes, very difficult		Somewhat difficult		Not difficult at all	Don't know/ not sure
❑	❑	❑	❑	❑	❑

14. Which of the following accounting principles make it difficult for you to communicate clearly with investors in other EC countries? Tick [√] all that apply.

____ Multinational Consolidations
____ Discretionary Reserves
____ Inventory Valuation
____ Goodwill, Intangibles
____ Pension Costs
____ Other items: Please list
____ Provisioning
____ Financial Instruments
____ Depreciation/Valuing Fixed Assets
____ Deferred Taxes
____ Foreign Currency Transactions

15. When I encounter differences in local accounting principles across investor countries, I react by (tick [√] all that apply):

____ a. Re-stating to the foreign investor's accounting standards.
____ b. Re-stating to International Accounting Standards.
____ c. Re-stating to accounting standards consistent with EC accounting directives.
____ d. Re-stating to United States accounting standards.
____ e. Going on "road shows" to meet with foreign stock analysts
____ f. Hosting meetings with analysts at our firm's headquarters
____ g. Translating reporting currency to that of the reader's country of domicile
____ h. Translating reporting language to that of the reader's country of domicile

____ i. Reducing our funding objectives in foreign capital markets
____ j. Do nothing
____ k. Other: Please explain. ____________________

16. Do differences in investor information requirements (disclosure requirements) from country to country make it difficult for you communicate with foreign investors?

Yes, very difficult		Somewhat difficult		Not difficult at all	Don't know/ not sure
❑	❑	❑	❑	❑	❑

17. Which of the following accounting disclosure items make it difficult for you to communicate clearly with investors in other EC countries? Tick [√] all that apply.

____ Segment Information: on products
____ Quarterly Information
____ Off-balance Sheet Items
____ Description of Capital Expenditures
____ Other items: Please list
____ Foreign Operations: Geographic
____ Hidden Reserves
____ Methods of Asset Valuation

18. When I encounter differences in disclosure requirements across other EC national markets, I react by (tick [√] all that apply):

____ a. Complying with disclosure requirements in International Accounting Standards
____ b. Complying with disclosure requirements in EC accounting directives
____ c. Complying with disclosure requirements in United States accounting standards
____ d. Inviting foreign stock analysts to visit corporate headquarters
____ e. Going on "road shows" to meet with foreign stock analysts
____ f. Increasing financial disclosures in my external reports to the market
____ g. Seeking a listing in a market with less burdensome requirements
____ h. Seeking some form of accommodation from market regulators
____ i. Reducing our funding objectives in foreign capital markets.
____ j. Do nothing
____ k. Other: Please explain. ____________________

*** END *** END *** END *** END *** END *** END *** END *** END *** END *** END ***

Appendix B

ADDITIONAL TABLES

Table B1. Response Rates for Investors

	Questionnaires mailed	Questionnaires answered	Questionnaires returned (undeliverable)	Response rate (%)
Austria	23	5	0	21.74
Belgium	23	2	0	8.70
Denmark	7	4	0	57.14
France	71	14	0	19.72
Germany	25	4	0	16.00
Ireland	5	1	0	20.00
Italy	6	2	0	33.33
Monaco	1	0	0	0.00
Netherlands	31	6	0	19.35
Norway	4	1	0	25.00
Portugal	3	0	0	0.00
Spain	21	7	0	33.33
Sweden	1	1	0	100.00
Switzerland	27	8	0	29.63
UK	152	42	0	27.63
TOTAL	400	97	0	24.25

Note: Chi-square = Σ_i (Expected number – Actual number)^2/Expected number, for i=1,...15 categories. Chi-square = 12.419 for these data. P-values for the chi-square distribution on 14 degrees of freedom are 21.064 (0.10 level) and 23.685 (0.05 level). Thus we cannot reject that the responses are drawn independently across the categories.

Table B2. Response Rates for Corporate Issuers

	Questionnaires mailed	Questionnaires answered	Questionnaires returned (undeliverable)	Response rate (%)
Austria	7	3	1	50.00
Belgium	16	6	0	37.50
Denmark	7	2	0	28.57
Finland	7	0	0	0.00
France	79	11	0	13.92
Germany	60	10	3	17.54
Ireland	7	3	0	42.86
Italy	28	2	0	7.14
Netherlands	19	3	1	16.67
Norway	7	3	0	42.86
Portugal	1	0	0	0.00
Spain	21	7	0	33.33
Sweden	21	6	0	28.57
Switzerland	26	6	1	24.00
UK	181	26	1	14.44
TOTAL	487	88	7	18.33

Note: Chi-square = Σ_i (Expected number – Actual number)^2/Expected number, for i=1,...15 categories. Chi-square = 21.445 for these data. P-values for the chi-square distribution on 14 degrees of freedom are 21.064 (0.10 level) and 23.685 (0.05 level). Thus, at the 5% level we cannot reject that the responses are drawn independently across the categories, but we can reject at the 10% level.

Chapter 9

CLEARANCE AND SETTLEMENT

I. INTRODUCTION

In this chapter, we examine the barriers to European equity market integration posed by imperfections and frictions relating to the clearance and settlement of equity trades. Clearance and settlement costs can be viewed as a subset of the total transaction costs facing an investor in effecting an equity trade. To date, their effect on the structure of equity trading has been largely ignored by researchers. Yet in the European context, where equity trading is still largely fragmented along national lines, such costs merit particular attention.

In recent years, there has been considerable focus on the potential gains from international portfolio diversification (IPD). Specifically, by buying a wide array of international equities (and other securities) investors can potentially improve returns while reducing their exposures to both local market risk and local currency risk. This has resulted in a rapid growth of specialized mutual and investment funds (and managers) seeking to maximize the gains from IPD to institutional and individual investors.[1]

Reflecting this growth in interest in the potential gains from IPD has been the expansion in cross-border trading in equities. For example, in 1994, reported turnover on the London Stock Exchange (SEAQ International) in foreign shares was £671 billion – an increase of 83 percent over 1992. Moreover, European equities accounted for £428 billion, with trading in the French equity sector of £114 billion and in the German sector of £95 billion. This compares to turnover of £612 billion in the domestic UK share market.[2] While liquidity in continental European equity trading has undoubtedly been flowing back to continental bourses in recent years, this largely reflects significant improvements in trading structures, rather than a diminished appetite for foreign share trading.

[1] In recent years, however, a growing body of evidence has pointed to an erosion of IPD benefits with increasing foreign ownership of local equities. Periods of high volatility have shown sharp increases in correlations across equity markets (Solnik 1993). The impact of the 1994–5 Mexico crisis is one example.

[2] Turnover figures are provided for illustrative purposes, but the actual numbers must be treated with some caution for reasons such as 'double-counting' (see Chapter 1).

Table 1. Cross-Border Trading of Bonds and Equities[a] (as a Percentage of GDP)

Country	1970	1975	1980	1985	1990	1993
United States	2.8	4.2	9.3	36.4	92.1	134.9
Japan	n.a.	1.5	7.0	62.8	120.7	78.7
Germany	3.3	5.1	7.5	33.9	61.1	169.6
France	n.a.	n.a.	8.4[b]	21.4	53.6	196.0
Italy	n.a.	0.9	1.1	4.0	26.6	274.6
United Kingdom	n.a.	n.a.	n.a.	366.1	689.0	1,015.8[c]
Canada	5.7	3.3	9.6	26.7	64.1	152.7

Note: n.a. = not available.[a] Gross purchases and sales of securities between residents and non-residents. [b] 1982. [c] 1991. The series has since been discontinued.
Source: National balance-of-payments statistics; BIS (1995).

Table 1 shows that the growth of cross-border trading in the G-7 countries has far exceeded GDP growth over the past two decades, and particularly during the past several years. These data highlight the rapidly growing importance of safe and efficient cross-border clearance and settlement services.

Much of the focus of IPD (and the asset allocation models underlying investment portfolio decisions) is on the *gross* portfolio return/risk trade-off. As a result, some important costs that affect both the actual return and the risk of an equity investment are either implicitly or explicitly ignored. Potentially important costs that impact the return/risk matrix – and that can drive a wedge between gross and net returns (and risks) – are clearance and settlement costs. In general, the higher such costs, the more constrained investors are in achieving their optimum portfolios. Moreover, such costs impose an explicit and implicit tax on trading, and can inhibit both the growth of domestic equity markets and the international or cross-border trade in equities. Potentially at least, costly and inefficient clearance and settlement services could hinder progress towards an effective market-driven integration of the European equity markets. In a recent paper focusing on the effects of US discount brokerage cost functions on investors' ability to diversify, it was found that the cost functions facing large investors caused a parallel downward shift in the efficient frontier,[3] while those facing small investors sharply reduced the benefits from diversification.[4]

In this chapter we first examine the organizational structure of clearance and settlement systems (Section II). We discuss five different models or channels for settlement of international securities transactions, and outline the economies

[3] That is, returns were reduced uniformly across all classes of risky securities.
[4] Levy and Livingston (1995).

of consolidated settlement. Where relevant, we will use examples from the clearance and settlement industry in the European equity markets. Sections III and IV consider national barriers to consolidation, including those arising from the competitive structure of the European clearance and settlement industry and specific frictions that pose 'hidden costs' to cross-border trading. Section V examines the important role of global custodians in promoting European securities market integration. Section VI presents some empirical evidence on the links between clearance and settlement efficiency and trading volume. Section VII provides a summary and conclusion.

II. THE ECONOMICS OF CLEARANCE AND SETTLEMENT

Clearance and settlement are necessary services that arise from securities trading. *Clearance* involves the determination of what each party owes and is due to receive. *Settlement* involves the actual transfer of securities from the seller to the buyer, with an offsetting payment of cash by the buyer to the seller. In most cases, the settlements organization, or *central securities depository* (hereafter 'CSD'), directly handles the bookkeeping-type clearance function and the securities side of the settlement, while the cash side of settlement is usually effected through the banking/payment system. In many cases, CSDs also provide ancillary services such as custody, corporate dividend processing, and transactions related to corporate events, such as mergers.

A Chain of Services

The demand for CSD services is a derived demand. That is, as the demand for equities rises or falls, so does the demand for the underlying CSD services. However, high-cost or inefficient CSD services increase the cost of equity trades, and can thus inhibit the demand for the equities themselves. There is therefore a 'feedback' effect from CSD efficiency to investor demand for equities, inducing a complementarity between the demand for underlying tradable assets and the demand for CSD services.

The key feature of the clearance-and-settlement value chain is that it involves a sequence of related services of which clearance and settlement is but one element. That is, CSDs rarely handle a single class of securities or provide a single type of service, but rather offer a range of ancillary services that create potential economies of scope and scale. Thus, most CSDs are properly viewed as multi-product enterprises, which adds to the complexity of assessing the full costs of clearance and settlement and the efficiency of CSDs. Moreover, since investors, banks, broker-dealers, and custodians may utilize different subsets of this chain of services, the costs of using any particular CSD (and its particular chain of services) will tend to differ across users. For example, local broker-dealers may have *direct* access to CSDs, while foreign institutional investors may only have *indirect* access through local agents and custodians (including global custodians). Indeed, reliance on custodians (both local and global) has placed them in a key role in effecting cross-border institutional trades.[5]

The chain of services offered by CSDs is illustrated in Box 1. We can divide these services into three groups which follow one another in roughly chronological order.

- The first group comprises pre-settlement services arising from information-gathering and dealing.
- The second group consists of settlement-type services, as currently provided by national CSDs, as well as ICSDs such as Euroclear and Cedel. National CSDs, form the core of the current European clearance and settlement industry.
- The third group includes agency and other ancillary services closely related to the settlement and payments process. In many ways the third group is the most interesting, for it represents the prime investor interface and as such offers the greatest scope for inhibiting or enhancing European financial integration.

Although we find it useful for analytical purposes to divide the transactions sequence into a number of sub-categories, this is in a sense artificial – the driver wants a car, not a set of wheels, an engine, and a body. Since investors ideally want a seamless *transactions service* that allows them to buy or sell without excessive costs or complications, one could imagine that the most successful provider of securities clearance and settlement services in the future will be the one who integrates all the above services under one roof. Indeed, this is what some of the settlement services competitors or potential competitors seek to do. A good example is the Chicago Mercantile Exchange, where participants executing a futures or options transaction need not concern themselves with confirmation, delivery, payments, clearance, marking-to-market, or custodial issues. Some of the major domestic stock exchanges also seek to offer a vertically integrated set of transactions services from quotation to settlement, although this is more difficult to do than in derivatives markets, which only require simple cash settlement (i.e., no exchange of the underlying asset).

[5] For more details, see BIS (1995), which drew on a February 1991 study by the International Stock Exchange and Price Waterhouse.

Box 1. Key Services in the Securities Transaction Value Chain

Pre-settlement services

1. Information and analytical services – e.g. Reuters, Bloomberg, Extel
2. Trading systems and services – e.g. SEAQ, CAC, IBIS

Settlement-type services

3. Trade information processing:
   - trade communication
   - matching
   - verification
   - regulatory reporting
4. Clearance and netting
5. Settlement: delivery of good title to securities, whether material or non-material
6. Payment: transfer of final funds
7. No-frills cash and securities depository services

Agency and ancillary services

8. Essential custodial services including: coupon collection, redemption, global certificate exchanges, tax reporting and withholding, tax-relief processing, and acting on client instructions on exercise of rights and voting
9. Extended custodial services including: accounting and reporting, foreign exchange, sale of rights, information provision on redemption payments, interest-rate resets, and corporate events
10. Credit and other services ancillary to settlement including: money transfer, providing participants with cash or securities lending in order to facilitate failure-free settlement, guarantees of performance, and collateralized lending
11. Fiduciary services including: making discretionary decisions as a trustee, portfolio management, cash management, discretionary short selling, and securities lending services for institutional investors
12. Analytical service including: performance measurement and comparisons, trend analysis, and on-line access to portfolio valuation and analytics
13. Agent services provided to the issuer including: indenture trustees, registrars or ADR issuers, corporate events reporting, and payment, conversion, and warrant agent services unique to the security concerned
14. Securities lending services for trading purposes, to meet the needs of broker-dealers implementing short-selling trading strategies.

It is thus tempting to think of increased vertical integration as the most logical and economical way for the future development of CSD services. Yet the economics of industrial structure may suggest the contrary. Most vertically integrated industries do not make sense on pure cost grounds. The firm and the consumer are typically best served if the firm buys from competing suppliers and sells to competing distributors. The chief exceptions are when vertical integration is necessary to wrest control from a monopolistic supplier or monopsonistic buyer, or when economies of scope are compelling. To help clarify this, we first explain the channels currently used by international investors to consummate cross-border trades.

Channels for Settling International Securities Transactions

As illustrated in Figure 1, non-residents can currently settle trades in domestic securities of another country in as many as five different ways; in other words, there are five different 'models' of effecting cross-border trades. These are:

(1) through *direct access* to the CSD in the security's country of issue. This is seldom used, partly because it is cumbersome, but also partly because it would require the non-resident to have membership in the domestic CSD, which is seldom permitted.

(2) through a *local bank* or broker-dealer that is a member of the domestic CSD. This method is more common.

(3) through *global custodians*: i.e. international banks that consolidate and coordinate cross-border transactions for investors. Although such banks normally have to go through local agents (because they do not have direct membership in local CSDs), this is increasingly the channel of choice for institutional investors.

(4) through *ICSDs*. Securities dealers, as well as global custodians, have also turned to ICSDs to settle trades in Eurobonds, European government securities, and, to a limited extent, equities.

(5) through *CSD-to-CSD* links. Although much effort has been expended on the development of local-CSD-to-local-CSD links (the so-called 'spaghetti model'), this channel is currently not heavily utilized.[6] In the spaghetti link (or CSD-to-CSD) model, investors access all local markets via their national CSDs. In turn, the national CSD is bi-directionally linked to other national CSDs. If n CSDs form such bilateral links, there would be $n(n-1)$ inter-CSD connections.

[6] See BIS (1995).

Figure 1. Alternative Channels for Settling Cross-Border Securities Trade

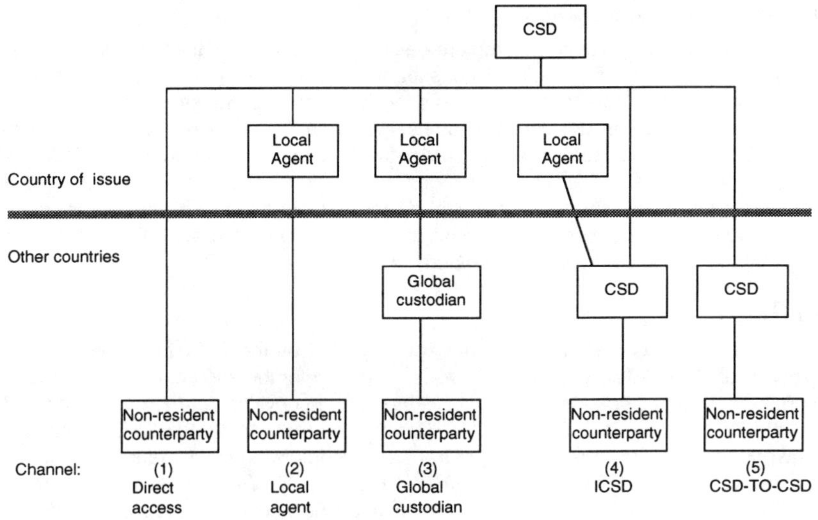

Source: BIS (1995)

CSD Structures for European Equities

National-based CSDs, such as the French Sicovam and the German Deutscher Kassenverein (DKV), usually linked to a local agent or global custodian (models 2 and 3 above), currently dominate the clearance and settlement of cross-border European equity trades. Box 2 offers brief descriptions of the German and French clearing systems.

Both the German and French CSDs clear the vast majority of both domestic and international trades in their home equities. For example, it was noted earlier that reported trading in French and German stocks on the London Stock Exchange amounted to £114 billion and £95 billion respectively in 1994. However, while these trades take place in London, clearance and settlement takes place on the local CSDs (in this case Sicovam and the DKV). Hence, internationalization of equity trading has *not* been mirrored by a general internationalization of the clearance and settlement process in Europe. That is, CSD services have remained predominantly national-based.

Comparing the cost of clearance and settlement in the French and German markets, Figure 2 suggests that the cost of settling trades is greater in France than in Germany. Cross-border trades cost significantly more than domestic ones, even when executed via an ICSD (in this case Euroclear), particularly in France.

Box 2. Profiles of the German and French Clearing Systems

The German Clearing System

Deutscher Kassenverein (DKV) is structured as a cooperative, with the owners being system users, and has a close link to the Bundesbank. Its focus has been to maintain state-of-the-art technology and speed* and low costs for users, while at the same time minimizing operational risks. DKV has developed a number of international link-ups, beginning with the Dutch CSD and expanding to include those of Austria, France (Sicovam), Switzerland (SEGA), and the United States (DTC). These linkages have required reconciling legal as well as operational differences among the national systems. German stocks are held in bearer form. For legal reasons, cross-border trades in equities in Germany are handled by a subsidiary of the DKV called *Deutscher Auslandskassenverein.*

The French Clearing System

The French system dates back to work begun in 1942 by the *Caisse de Dépôts et de Virements de Titres* (CCDVT); two milestones were implementation of dematerialization (securities issued as book-keeping entries rather than in physical form) in 1984 and DVP under the Relit system in 1991. The CCDVT reforms created both the CSD institutional framework and book-entry accounting of transactions following stock market trades, and was followed by the formation of Sicovam in 1949 as a *société anonyme* under French corporate law, with shareholders being the major financial institutions and stock-brokerage firms. Both the Banque de France and the national stock exchange association are represented on its board. Its mandate is to 'facilitate the circulation of shares among member institutions'.† The ownership structure of Sicovam means close ownership and board linkages to both the major domestic intermediaries using the system and the principal regulators.

The evolution of Sicovam has meant steady progress towards dematerialization in order to achieve greater accuracy and cost reductions for its members, ultimately resulting in the disappearance of bearer securities. Sicovam has also broadened its range of activities to include oil shares (1957), convertible bonds (1964), open-end mutual fund shares and unlisted shares (1957), and bonds redeemable by lottery (1977).

A distinguishing feature of the French approach has been the balanced development of front-office and back-office functions, with back-office reform (dematerialization) followed by front-office reform (creation of Monep and Matif in the derivatives sector, and implementation of computerized continuous trading), followed in turn by the Relit initiative involving settlement via simultaneous delivery and payment, adherence to T+5 for all market transactions, and simultaneous processing of securities transactions by Sicovam and payments transactions by the Banque de France. By 1990, therefore, the French clearance and settlement system was already broadly in conformity with the Group of Thirty recommendations, with the T+3 DVP deadline being implemented in March 1992. All systems for order routing, trading, settlements, delivery versus payment, and management of securities operations are now fully automated and operate virtually in real time.**

The Sicovam approach to operating a CSD means that it has an effective monopoly on clearance, settlement, and payments (via the Banque de France) regarding French stock transactions. It is, however, an open system: any firm certified as a credit institution or broker-dealer – foreign or domestic – may participate in Sicovam.

*Settlement occurs in 'T+2'; that is, two business days after the trade is agreed upon.

†Sicovam , *History of France's Depository Institution* (Paris: Editions les Djinns, 1992), p. 9.

**Ibid., p. 21.

Figure 2. Comparison of Costs per Trade of Domestic and Cross-Border Settlement (ECUs)*

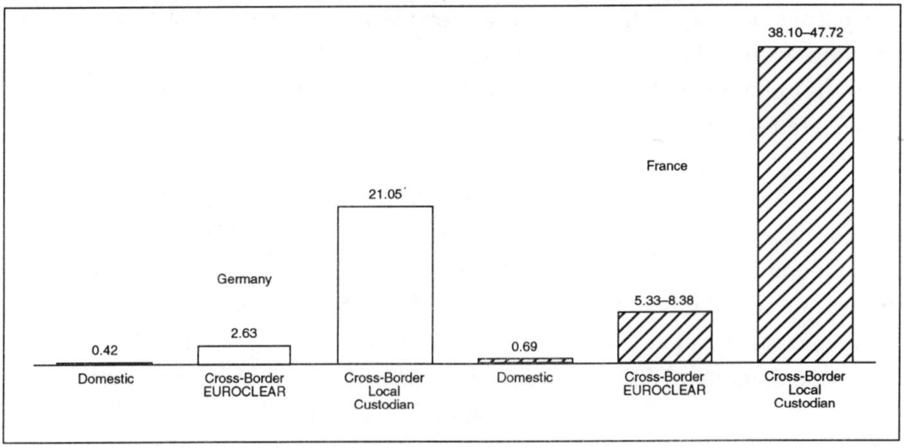

* Using Deutsche Mark and French Franc exchange rates as of end-1994.
Source: *Financial Times* (1994).

Settling a cross-border trade via a local custodian (such as a bank) is by far the most expensive in both cases.

In recent years, some limited and tentative moves have been made towards the internationalization of CSD services. One has been the development of bilateral links (or bridges) between national CSDs (model 5, the so-called 'spaghetti model').[7] This has allowed some international trades to settle outside their domestic CSD. Two examples of this development are the links between the German DKV and the French Sicovam, and the links between the DKV and the Austrian CSD. A second has been the attempted move by both Euroclear and Cedel into equity clearance and settlement (model 4). Both of these ICSDs have developed expertise and customer networks through clearing Eurobonds. They have attempted to piggy-back on this expertise by offering to settle cross-border European equity trades for their customers as well. Yet despite the fact that both Euroclear and Cedel can settle trades in over twenty equity markets, their share of business in cross-border equity settlement remains small (in the 1-2 percent range).

Two immediate questions arise. First, is European capital market in-tegration and cross-border trading best served by the current system (models [illegible] and 3); national CSDs with bilateral links (an enhanced spaghetti model – model 5); or a single (or a few) European ICSD(s) or hub(s) – e.g. a Euroclear or Cedel (model 4)? Second, if a centralized European CSD hub is to be preferred, what

[7] ICSDs such as Cedel and Euroclear have also improved their bridge.

are the current barriers to achieving it? In particular, is the major barrier the fact that many European CSDs are owned directly by the local stock exchange (as in Spain, for example), or that they have strong links to the national central bank (as with Sicovam and the Banque de France)? To date, the ability of foreign institutions to become members of local CSDs has generally been limited.

In Figure 3, we illustrate the structure of a potential centralized Euro-hub (ICSD) for equities.

Note that initially all national CSDs are linked via the ICSD, with institutional investors settling cross-border trades via national CSDs and the ICSD hub. One potential outcome of such a model (in the long term) is that both domestic and international trades might eventually be routed via the ICSD by brokers/dealers/investors, with national CSDs eventually disappearing. This would leave one dominant CSD for all European equities (i.e. a true Euro-hub).

To address the question of the optimality of a Euro-hub for CSD services, we have to look at the fundamental industrial economics of CSDs. In particular, as will be argued below, the basic economics of CSDs seem to favour centralization of services over competition in 'like products'. That is, if UK, French, and German equities (including their underlying clearing and settlement arrangements) are 'like products' – i.e. sufficiently homogeneous financial contracts – a strong economic welfare case can be made for a single (or a few) large ICSD(s) for European equities.[8] If European stocks are viewed as heterogeneous or nationally distinct products – for legal, regulatory, institutional, or currency reasons – then nationally based CSDs will generally be preferred to a single Euro-hub for clearance and settlement. This assumes, of course, that the causes of European stocks being 'distinct' are immutable. If they are not, there may indeed be benefits in eliminating them. Such a possibility, however, is generally beyond the scope of this chapter.

The relative homogeneity/heterogeneity of European stocks will be examined in detail in the next section. Here we will assume that European equities are relatively homogeneous financial contracts (e.g. they have similar priority, delivery, payment, and settlement rules). We can then examine the advantages of a centralized Euro-hub (single ICSD) over smaller, nationally specialized CSDs. However, it will be argued later that as the number and type of clearance/settle-

[8] Intersettle is a further development of the Swiss SEGA system intended to create a third ICSD. It involves a cooperative effort among the three large Swiss banks (Crédit Suisse, Swiss Bank Corporation, and Union Bank of Switzerland), although each has its own interests and historical ties to either Euroclear or Cedel. While these divergences may pose some problems, Intersettle may have a systems advantage, being of more recent vintage than the competing systems, and having real-time settlement with the Swiss National Bank. Moreover, there will be no borrowing/netting facilities for securities because the positions of the beneficiaries are unknown. On the other hand, there will be 2-day settlement in spot foreign exchange.

Figure 3. Euro-Hub Model

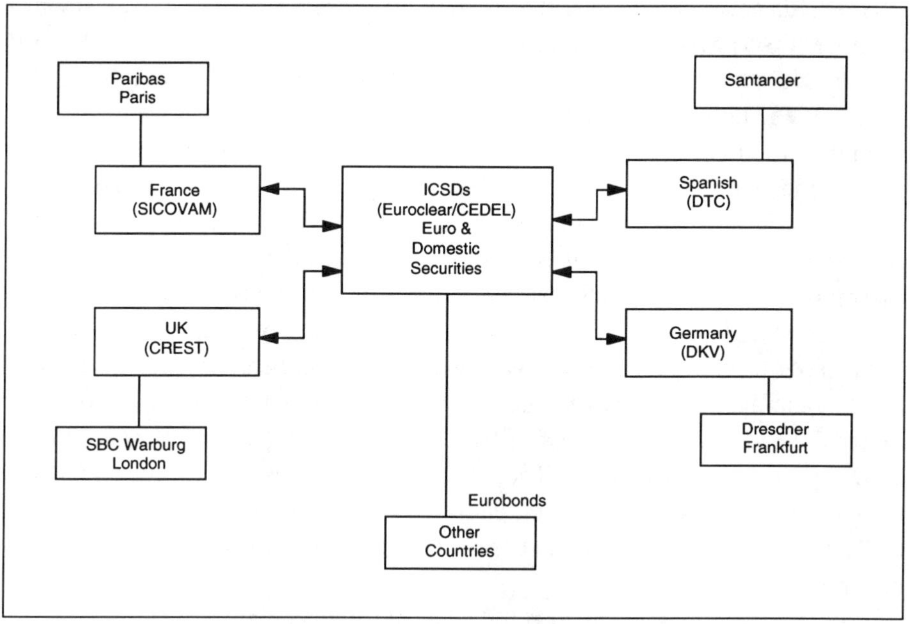

ment and other frictions to Euro-equity trading increase, any relative advantages of a centralized ICSD over national CSDs will fall. This implies that one cannot examine the efficiency of CSD arrangements independently of the legal, regulatory, institutional, and currency environment for trading equities across borders.

Economic Advantages of a Euro-Hub for Clearing and Settlement

There are at least three economic reasons for centralizing CSD services as much as possible. These have been identified by Kyle and Marsh (1993); Giddy, Saunders, and Walter (1992); and Economides (1993); among others. Indeed, under certain conditions a centralized (and monopoly) CSD can be shown to be preferable to (smaller) competitive CSDs. Specifically, while a monopolist generally has an incentive to restrict output and raise prices, the benefits of a centralized CSD to the consumer can still dominate the amount that the monopolist CSD operator can expropriate.[9]

The major reason for this relates to the economics of centralized networks and the 'critical mass' services they provide. As has been shown for airline networks,[10] a network system with a central hub can provide consumers with

[9] See Economides (1993) and Economides and Himmelberg (1993).
[10] Brueckner and Spiller (1991).

considerable *positive externalities*. To see the favourable externalities created by a large CSD network, consider the addition of an extra member to an existing n-member (CSD) network. The addition of an extra member (network node) creates $2n$ additional bi-directional (in- and out-bound) connections to other CSDs via the ICSD hub. As a result, each member has received a positive externality from the addition of that extra member without paying for it. Moreover, only n links to the centralized ICSD are needed, compared with $n(n-1)$ inter-CSD links under the CSD-CSD (spaghetti link) model (model 5). Note that private marginal cost pricing would ignore this benefit, since it takes the form of an 'unpriced' externality. Indeed, marginal cost pricing, as under pure competition, would not produce the first-best outcome in this case. While the above example relates to a network connection cost reduction, the critical mass benefits extend to many areas of ancillary CSD services, such as securities lending. Since the size of these externalities depends on the law of large numbers and the 'critical mass' of the CSD, a monopoly CSD may well dominate a system of smaller CSDs, even when the monopolist seeks to restrict output by raising prices (i.e. fees). This is especially so if the CSD has sufficient critical mass to attract increasing numbers of new members.

A second reason why a centralized CSD may dominate smaller competing CSDs concerns the efficient use of collateral. While members of a CSD want efficient settlement with minimal risk, they each face private incentives to pledge the minimum amount of collateral to back their clearance and settlement activities. The advantage of a centralized CSD is that collateral is potentially never wasted (i.e. there is an efficiency gain). For example, with two competitive CSDs, a member of both with excess collateral in one and deficient collateral in the other will generally be unable to cross-collateralize or cross-margin, unless special arrangements or links are made between the CSDs. If the CSDs are competitive (or non-cooperative), the member would end up holding more collateral than in a centralized CSD. Excess collateral limits the members' leverage, and thus the ability to trade to the maximum extent possible. Further, if a centralized CSD also allows netting of trades (either bilateral or multilateral, within or across security types), a further conservation of collateral becomes possible. Thus netting tends to add to the potential advantages of a centralized CSD in conserving collateral as well as reducing settlement risk. This requires the ICSD to act as delegated monitor *vis-à-vis* the credit risks of the national CSDs (and ultimately the traders).

The third set of advantages relates to potential economies of scope and scale. Revenue economies of scope may exist if there are savings from vertical integration in the CSD service value chain (Box 1). That is, large ICSDs offer the potential benefits of 'one-stop' shopping, and thus reduce investor search costs across an array of vendors. However, as with universal banking, these benefits may be mitigated if a powerful ICSD pursues monopoly pricing.[11] Kyle and Marsh (1993) also show that there are potential economy-of-scale benefits resulting from centralization, using the example of the centralization of the clearing activities in the five US options exchanges into one facility: the Options Clearing Corporation.

Given that there appear to be potential benefits to investors from a centralized CSD, why have we not yet seen the emergence of a dominant, centralized Euro-equity ICSD?[12] There are at least three possible reasons:

(1) Concerns that such a powerful 'public utility' would pursue monopoly power and pricing. This could lead to regulatory obstacles being placed in front of efforts by the existing ICSDs to integrate European clearing and settlement. To the best of our knowledge this has not happened, nor have any formal efforts been launched at the national or European level specifically to prevent such a hub from emerging.

(2) A second reason could be efforts by national exchanges to preserve their monopoly power over the stocks they trade by restricting access to national CSDs (for instance, restricting the direct access of foreign investors and ICSDs, and limiting cross-exchange linkages of the Sicovam-DKV type). This possibility is addressed in section III.

(3) A third reason could be that there are other CSD barriers and frictions which are so large as to offset the potential gains from conglomeration of equity clearance and settlement at the ICSD level, making national CSDs a more economically efficient structure. That is, the costs of Euro-equity heterogeneity (legal, regulatory, tax, etc.) offset the potential benefits of network externalities, economies of collateral conservation, and economies of scope and scale from centralization. We examine these frictions in section IV.

III. STOCK-EXCHANGE CONTROL OF CSDs AS A BARRIER

Is national stock-exchange control of CSDs a major barrier to European equity market integration? At first glance, such an argument seems plausible. The stocks traded on a national exchange are a valuable franchise: by restricting access to a

[11] There are a number of possible ownership options for a Euro-hub ICSD, from full 'nationalization' (by the EU), to control by the national CSDs, to full private-sector control. Each would tend to have different pricing implications.

[12] As noted earlier, both Euroclear and Cedel have very small market shares of existing cross-border trades in European equities.

national CSD facility to local members, an exchange can endeavour to keep a degree of control and monopoly power over its franchise.[13] However, in the context of *major* European market CSDs, only the UK's Talisman is directly controlled and operated by an exchange (the London Stock Exchange).[14] Even in this case, however, a new UK CSD called CREST will become operational in 1996. This system has been sponsored (not owned) by the Bank of England, and provides for open access, in the sense that any recognized agent (e.g. an ICSD) – subject to certain (as yet unspecified) criteria – can become a member. Of particular importance, the London Stock Exchange's ownership share of CREST is limited to 3 percent (with some 60 other financial institutions also having initial ownership claims in the CSD). In both France (Sicovam) and Germany (DKV), the ownership of the CSD is largely divorced from the exchange(s). As noted earlier, the German DKV is largely owned by German banks, while the French Sicovam has strong links to the Banque de France, with its shares owned mostly by banks and brokers.[15]

Further, even where a national exchange owns a CSD, it is becoming increasingly doubtful that this can protect its franchise over shares traded. In the UK, a new proprietary trading system competing with the London Stock Exchange, Tradepoint, began operations as a 'Recognized Investment Exchange' in September 1995. Not only is its trading system different from that of the London Stock Exchange (Tradepoint operates an electronic order-driven market, with both continuous and periodic call trading), but it also clears and settles trades through the London Clearing House (rather than through Talisman). While it is difficult to say at this point in time how successful Tradepoint might be, it is clear that national stock exchange franchises, as well as their control over local CSDs, are becoming increasingly contestable.

Finally, it is worth noting market trends pushing exchanges to *divest* themselves of ancillary services, rather than fighting to maintain them. As we pointed out in Chapter 1, increasing inter-exchange competition is putting pressure on exchanges to reduce costs and increase efficiency in order to retain and attract members. To this end, the Chicago Stock Exchange announced in September 1995 that it would begin shedding all its clearance, settlement, and depository services businesses, and subcontract the work instead.

[13] For example, this would raise the costs of settling a trade through an ICSD, since an investor would have to bear settlement costs at the ICSD level which would have to be high enough to cover the ICSD's direct settlement costs, plus the costs to the ICSD of settling with the national CSD through a local agent.

[14] The Spanish CSD and Exchange are also directly connected.

[15] Member control of CSDs may be even more relevant in terms, for example, of blocking access by major investors.

IV. BARRIERS TO CENTRALIZATION OF CSD SERVICES FOR EUROPEAN EQUITIES

If monopoly power of local exchanges and their members over national CSDs is not the real barrier to a centralized Euro-hub (ICSD) for equity clearance and settlement, what is? In this section we consider a wide number of other frictions and barriers in the Euro-equity clearance and settlement environment that appear, at present, to be sufficiently strong to militate against the imminent emergence of a centralized Euro-hub. These frictions and barriers largely relate to legal, contractual, payment, institutional, and regulatory differences across EU members' equity markets, all of which appear to add costs to centralizing CSD arrangements at the Euro-hub level sufficient to offset potential benefits from centralization. Specifically, the full benefits of a centralized hub are unlikely to be achieved without similar priority, delivery, settlement, payment, and custody rules and procedures across the national markets linked to the ICSD hub.

A 1989 report by the Group of Thirty laid down nine benchmarks for CSD efficiency – benchmarks which set the standard aimed at by most European and other major securities markets. Indeed, most European countries claim that they have either achieved or, in some cases, gone beyond the Group of Thirty recommendations. Regardless of the merits of these claims (many practitioners dispute them), there remain wide variations across European markets with respect to institutional, legal, payment, and regulatory practices. It is arguably these differences, rather than any explicit barriers created by national CSDs, that pose the greatest barriers to European equity market integration. Differences in settlement cycles, paper versus book-entry settlement, bearer versus registered shares, differences in tax treatment, multiple currencies, and access to national payment systems are the principal issues.[16]

Settlement Cycles

Although the Group of Thirty task force advocated moving towards settlement three days after the trade (T+3) as the target for equity trades, a wide variety of settlement cycles still exists in European markets, and this poses significant problems for cross-border investors. In the three major European equity markets,

[16] In addition, accounting and bankruptcy systems still differ widely across EU countries. Differences in accounting systems impose internal or back-office network costs on participants in cross-border trading. Harmonization of EU accounting standards could have an important positive externality in saving resources in back-office settlement of cross-border trades. Similarly, harmonization of bankruptcy rules with regard to netting by novation, unwinding of trades, and the like, could also generate important efficiency gains for cross-border equity investors by potentially conserving collateral.

Germany now settles at T+2, France at T+3, and the UK at T+5 (having moved from T+10 in July 1995).[17]

As a result, an investor selling UK stocks (T+5 settlement) and buying German stocks (T+2) would have to borrow money for 3 days to bridge the settlement date differences. This imposes additional transaction costs on active investors. In addition, as shown by Ireland and Ryan (1993), the number of settlement failures is higher in Germany than in the UK. In general, the shorter the settlement cycle, the greater the probability of failures; and settlement failures impose costs on investors, especially in the absence of an efficient securities lending market. In France, moreover, despite the official existence of T+3, many trades are still settled on the old monthly account cycle (effectively T+20). Italy also uses the one-month settlement account, although this is scheduled to switch to T+5 rolling settlement from 16 February 1996.

All this suggests that there is a considerable degree of heterogeneity in settlement cycles which interferes with international equity investment and trading efficiency, and makes it difficult to attain the critical mass necessary to produce efficiency gains from a centralized Euro-hub. What is clearly required is a move by European national authorities, perhaps coordinated by the European Commission, to produce greater harmonization in settlement cycles. While shorter settlement cycles are a worthwhile objective, *harmonization* of settlement cycles should be the primary objective, even if this means a somewhat longer cycle.

Paper versus Book-Entry Settlement

Not only do settlement cycles differ across countries, but so does the degree to which countries have dematerialized their equities. In France, for example, equities have long been completely dematerialized in Sicovam. By contrast, the UK only implemented paperless dematerialized stock lending services in September 1995. The Talisman system was paper-based, moving millions of pieces of paper a week as ownership to equities was transferred. This archaic system posed a barrier to entry to both Euroclear and Cedel (the existing ICSDs) acting as CSDs in the UK equity market. However, with the advent of CREST and its centralized book-entry system in 1996, both Euroclear and Cedel are likely to form links to the new system and to start clearing UK equities.[18]

[17] In December 1995, the board of Euroclear approved the development of a technology platform that would enable it to process and settle transactions on a real-time basis. The first stage of the project is scheduled for completion in 1997.

[18] Even post-CREST, the UK will still allow those investors who so choose to continue to hold physical certificates. This contrasts with the public burning of share certificates by Sicovam in 1989 and their replacement by electronic records.

The difference in approach and timing of dematerialization between France and the UK accentuates another key difference in the regulatory and legal CSD environment. Specifically, since the establishment of Sicovam in 1949 the French government has issued a variety of rules and orders moving it towards full dematerialization (this might be viewed as the 'regulatory approach' to CSD development). By contrast, the UK approach has been largely free-market based, and it was only the failure of the Stock Exchange TAURUS project in 1993 that prompted the Bank of England to endorse the development of the new CREST system.

Bearer versus Registered Shares

A further barrier to CSD integration across European markets relates to the legal form of ownership of shares. In the UK (and Italy), shares are still predominantly held in registered form, often at the individual investor level.[19] This means that following each trade, company registrars have to update records of individual share ownership. Under the CREST system, an electronic interface with major company registrars should update these records in a matter of hours (two hours is the target). Under the Talisman (paper-based) system, such updating involved considerable delays, often extending to weeks. By contrast, in France and Germany shares are in bearer form (even if dematerialized), with many held by large institutional nominees, such as the German universal banks. While the purpose of bearer shares has traditionally been tax avoidance and owner anonymity, the centralization of shares around a few nominees has a potential CSD transactions cost advantage over the individual investor registration system. It might also be noted that Euroclear and Cedel's expertise in the CSD area has arisen with clearing and settling bearer-form Eurobonds.

Taxation

Another hidden cost of clearing and settling cross-border equity trades, and, in particular, cross-border trades in UK equities, relates to taxation. Specifically, in the UK a stamp duty of 0.5 percent is imposed on domestic trades in UK shares. However, in the case of cross-border trades the stamp duty rises to 1.5 percent. The UK government's logic is that once a share trades outside the country it cannot levy further stamp duties – hence the 1.5 percent. However, for ICSDs such as Euroclear and Cedel such a tax – which their customers directly bear – is viewed as a direct barrier to providing CSD services for their clients trading UK equities. This is given as another reason – over and above the paper form of

[19] Although there is a nominee system for institutional trades called SETON.

certificates – why neither Cedel nor Euroclear currently clears UK equities. The UK is virtually alone in Europe in imposing this type of stamp duty on cross-border transactions, but it will be difficult to persuade the current or any future government to abandon a politically 'quiet' source of over £1 billion per year in tax revenues.[20]

Multiple Currencies

On the face of it, the existence of a national currency backing each national equity market imposes an additional cost in cross-border equity trading and hinders market integration. As a simple illustration, a German investor, on selling German shares to buy UK shares (ignoring settlement cycle differences), must convert his DM proceeds into sterling. The potential cost of doing this depends on: (i) the degree of intra-European exchange-rate volatility; and (ii) the depth and liquidity of the markets in which European currencies trade.

The markets in European currencies are among the deepest and most liquid in the world, with extremely small transaction costs, relative to other tradable assets. Further, whether or not full currency integration is achieved, increasing fixity of European exchange rates lowers currency risk – although major Euro-currency realignments cannot be discounted (as already occurred in 1992, 1993, and 1995).

Thus multiple European currencies may be barriers, but need not be decisive barriers, to efficient Euro-equity trading and market integration. This view is reinforced by the fact that existing ICSDs, such as Euroclear and Cedel, allow for payment in over two dozen currencies, including the ECU basket. Further, there has been a rapid growth in the ECU wire-payment system, largely as a result of the growth of the Euro-commercial paper market. This wholesale wire-transfer system (based in Brussels) clears over 7,000 ECU transactions a day among over 40 member banks. Indeed, the increasing use of the ECU, as well as any increasing fixity of exchange rates, is likely to make the gains from a single currency of relatively small order in terms of the probable impact on ICSD development.

Payment Systems

In the absence of monetary unification, payment systems in the EU will continue to be national in nature, generally under the auspices of the national central bank. One can envisage short-term as well as longer-term effects of monetary union on payment systems – with the short term being defined as the period 1995-9 and the long term the post-1999 period (assuming, at least for illustrative purposes,

[20] Ireland imposes a similar stamp duty.

that the 1999 deadline for EMU is met). In the pre-1999 period, one might see some changes in the formal structure of domestic payment systems with respect to real-time gross settlement (RTGS) implementation. Basically, the individual country wire-transfer/payment systems may be expected to continue much as before, except that each EU central bank is likely to encourage private payments netting and settlement services in ECUs, and eventually to provide settlement services themselves.

The need for ECU payment-related services is likely to grow as inter- and intra-European commercial and financial flows are increasingly conducted in ECUs rather than in the domestic currencies, and the proportions of domestic securities denominated in ECUs rise relative to those denominated in domestic EU currencies. The role and importance of the ECU in this period will depend on whether central-bank policies provide conditions for public confidence and acceptability of the unit, both as a medium of exchange and as a store of value, and whether or not final settlement services are provided by the central banks themselves or by private organizations.

A lender of last resort is important, since the ECU is an artificial currency and can only be created (in the absence of a lender of last resort) by banks bundling or unbundling currencies. That is, an imbalance between a bank's ECU liabilities and assets can be covered only by the potentially costly and difficult procedure of buying and selling the basket components in return for ECUs. Currently, lender-of-last-resort facilities for ECU transactions are principally provided by the Bank for International Settlements (BIS). Since August 1991, if a bank fails to meet its ECU payment commitments it can get temporary help from the BIS, which operates an existing ECU clearing system on behalf of the ECU Banking Association. After 24 hours, if the bank is unable to meet its liabilities the burden has to be shared among all other ECU clearing banks in the Association. Private-sector or quasi-governmental backing is not as credible as full central-bank backing through lender-of-last-resort facilities, so that residual liquidity, credit risk, and systemic risk concerns will remain until full central-bank lender-of-last-resort backing of an ECU system (or its successor) becomes operational.

While there have been no systematic moves by central banks in the direction of collective backing, the Banque de France has launched a scheme to give lender-of-last-resort backing to French banks involved in clearing ECU transactions – using bank reserves as collateral. In 1992 the Bank of England introduced a similar scheme based on ECU bonds, T-bills, and deposits as collateral. The Bank of Portugal committed itself to a similar plan. However, it is far from clear that such an uncoordinated set of policies will give sufficient credibility to the safety of ECU-denominated trades and instruments relative to the individual currencies of the EU. Indeed, the BIS clearing house appears similar to the type of clearing house that existed in the United States prior to the establishment of a single currency and the Federal Reserve System in 1914. The European counterpart would be a trans-European RTGS system when and if a single currency emerges among some or all EU members.

A credible low-cost single currency is likely to emerge only when the five following policies and practices emerge:

- exchange rates are unambiguously fixed;
- central banks allow domestic economic agents to make payments by cheque or wire-transfer in any EU currency;
- EU private banks start clearing cheques or payments at par, independent of origin or denomination of the EU currency;
- a central-bank organized and operated inter-EU cheque/payment clearing system is established;
- a credible central-bank lender-of-last-resort facility denominated in ECUs is established.

In the presence of full monetary unification, the payment system is likely to be centralized under a new European central bank, with the sole right to create money, while the national central banks play a role similar to the US regional Federal Reserve banks under Fedwire. However, using the US and the Federal Reserve as an example, the implications of a single currency and central bank for the EU's CSD structure are far from clear. In particular, in the United States the emergence of the Depository Trust Company (DTC) as the dominant CSD occurred only many years after the Federal Reserve was created and a single national currency adopted. Thus, the links between the creation of a single US currency, the creation of the Fed, and the gradual dominance of the DTC in domestic securities clearance and settlement are tenuous at best. The most that can be said is that a single currency adds to the potential efficiency of a single CSD, but its absence is not an overwhelming barrier, particularly where multi-currency ICSDs (e.g. Euroclear and Cedel) as well as national CSDs (e.g. UK CREST) are operating.

National Payment System Access and Competition

An additional issue is the degree of competition among domestic payment systems. In particular, do barriers to entry in the payment systems 'industry' inhibit the integration of clearance and settlement systems and the growth of cross-border trading? In some countries the payment system is run or operated by the private sector (e.g. APACS in the UK), while in others (e.g. France and Germany) it is owned and operated by the central bank. Concerns have been widely raised about limits to and costs of access with respect to both private and public payment systems. While the Second Banking Coordination Directive requires freedom of establishment and operation for private systems, this has not generally occurred.[21] However, the overwhelming barrier to competing private systems is the explicit and implicit guarantees against credit risk provided by public-system operators such as central banks.

Where private systems do operate (as in the UK), the EU's competition rules apply.[22] As a general rule, a payment system that constitutes an essential facility must be open to further membership according to criteria similar to that applying to existing members. The EU has proposed making membership exclusion subject to an independent review procedure. Moreover, discriminatory pricing, such as double charging of non-national users,[23] is also discouraged by the EU's competition rules. Under the rules, extra fees are not permitted except where genuine additional costs are incurred, such as when:

- a cross-border transfer may need to be reported to the balance of payments authorities as an incoming payment;
- the payment may need to be converted into the currency of the beneficiary;
- the beneficiary may require more information (e.g. details relating to the payment order) than is normally given for domestic payments;
- the details of the beneficiary, his or her account number, and the bank sort code need to be verified, since this information is often incomplete or incorrect; and
- the payment order needs to be reformatted if it is to be processed by the clearing circuit in the destination country.[24]

In such circumstances, the EU competition rules require that there should be complete transparency in setting these fees – that is, they should be explicitly related to the marginal costs.

While the Commission's 'Notice on the Application of EU Competition Rules' regarding accessibility and pricing of private payment systems is useful in harmonizing the rules and reducing the costs of access, there remains the important issue of direct access to national *public* payment systems – especially those

[21] It might be noted that private US wholesale payment systems (such as CHESS) have failed in the face of competition from Fedwire.

[22] See CEC, 1994.

[23] For example, charging a foreign user an interchange fee and then deducting another fee from the gross funds before transferring them to the ultimate funds receiver.

[24] See 'Notice on the Application of the EU Competition Rules to Cross-Border Transfer System', (Annex 2) *Commission of the European Communities*, Brussels, 1994.

run by national central banks – by non-domestic market participants. Recent proposals to interlink or network national European payment systems as a move in anticipation of a single currency may go some way towards resolving the problem of cross-border access to national publicly owned and operated payment systems.

A 1995 study of the payment system environment[25] has suggested that private-sector initiatives in response to growing international capital flows and exclusionary practices by national payment systems are focused on bilateral netting systems, including electronic data interchange (EDI). This is in addition to various national initiatives to institute real-time gross settlement (RTGS) services, collateralization of intra-day settlement credit extended by central banks, formalization of minimum standards for private-sector multilateral netting systems, expansion of operating hours, and the introduction of daylight overdraft facilities. The major problems that need to be addressed are intra-day risk on central-bank-operated RTGS systems, finality-of-settlement risk on private-sector net settlement systems, and time-zone risk associated with multi-currency settlement (so-called 'Herstatt risk').

Other Areas of CSD Non-Harmonization

At least two other areas of non-harmonization across national CSDs are important. The first concerns delivery versus payment (DVP). Virtually all European equity markets claim to have some form of DVP, although in reality no country has achieved exact simultaneity in real time.[26] For example, in the UK under Talisman, settlement of equity trades is made on the evening before the day of payment. Further, CREST share settlement will be in real time (up to some trade cap limits), but with a single net payment in cash among member accounts at settlement banks at the end of the day. As with settlement cycles, there would appear to be a clear market benefit to harmonizing DVP standards across European markets; that is, market participants could evolve a single set of internal systems and procedures consistent with a common Europe-wide DVP standard. Of course, this would ideally involve simultaneous real-time settlement.

The second issue concerns the equity settlement system itself. On some national CSDs (e.g. Sicovam and DKV), trades are *netted* for settlement, while on others (e.g. CREST) the system involves trade-by-trade *gross* settlement.

[25] New York Clearing House Association (1995).

[26] Although arguably the US Federal Reserve has achieved this for bond transactions on Fedwire.

V. GLOBAL CUSTODIANS: AN ALTERNATIVE TO CSD UNIFICATION

Whether a centralized ICSD for European equity trades will emerge is also likely to be profoundly affected by the degree of competition from global custodians. While in general most broker-dealers have direct access to CSDs and ICSDs, many institutional investors only have indirect access through global custodians (see channel 3 in Figure 1). While a case can be made for any future Euro-ICSD to allow open access to all agents, as with the new UK CREST, in the absence of open access global custodians will play an increasingly important role. Thus, the competitive structure of the global custodian segment of the clearance and settlement industry is important in defining the future growth path of cross-border trading in European equities.

Custody of securities comprises a more or less elaborate cluster of services, including:

- Basic cash and securities *depository services*;
- *Essential custody services* – including coupon collection, redemption, global certificate exchanges, tax reporting and withholding, tax-relief processing, acting on client instructions on exercise of rights, and voting;
- *Extended custody services* – including accounting and reporting, foreign exchange, sale of client rights, and provision of information with respect to redemption payments, interest-rate resets, and corporate events; and
- *Securities lending services* for trading purposes, to meet the needs of traders implementing short-selling strategies.

Global custody is a highly competitive business, in part because of its comparatively low credit risk, low regulatory capital demands, relatively long-lived relationships, and links to other financial services such as banking, accounting, cash management and foreign-exchange facilities, and enhanced fee-based services. Table 2 shows the 1995 rankings of global custodians by total assets.

Custody services need to be distinguished from fiduciary services where the custodian undertakes not only to carry out instructions as a pure agent, but also to take decisions as a trustee or investment manager with respect to activities such as investments, cash management, and securities lending. For example, activities such as reporting of income payments, corporate actions taken and securities lending results may be looked upon as part of custody or fiduciary services, or as a separate function. Trust services to issuers performed by banks as indenture trustees, registrars, issuers of American Depository Receipts (ADRs) – or as fiscal, paying, conversion, and warrant agents – are related but need to be distinguished from custody functions. These services are provided by banks acting as issuers' agents, not as security holders' agents. The market for basic depository

Table 2. Global Custody Assets, 1995

Bank	Total assets ($ millions)
Chase Manhattan Bank	634,000
Citibank	495,000
Bankers Trust Co.	312,000
State Street Bank & Trust Co.	237,900
ABN Amro Bank	170,000
Brown Brothers Harriman	163,000
Bank of New York	150,000
Chemical Bank	150,000
Barclays Bank	149,119
Royal Trust Corp. of Canada	104,723
Morgan Stanley Global Securities Services	90,100
Northern Trust Co.	75,900
Skandinaviska Enskilda Banken	62,000
Mellon Trust	60,000
Bank of Tokyo	59,383
Sumitomo Trust & Banking Co. (USA)	57,124
Midland Securities Services	55,173
Lloyds Bank	54,219
Royal Bank of Scotland	49,600
Bank of Bermuda	41,200
S.G. Warburg & Co.	40,350
Bank of Montreal/Harris Trust & Savings	35,492
First Chicago Corp.	20,000
Banque Indosuez Luxembourg	16,777
Toronto Dominion Bank	11,583

Source: *Institutional Investor*, September 1995.

services is highly competitive. Moreover, this type of service is becoming marginalized with the spread of dematerialized securities and competition in core safekeeping from centralized depositories (such as ICSDs).

Most institutions providing safekeeping will also offer the next level, 'essential' custody services, where there are again few barriers to entry (although there may be some economies of scale in processing securities information). Some international banks have earned significant returns by offering these services in a far more efficient fashion than local competitors, but in most of the mature financial markets they constitute a low-return industry segment. Extended custody services command somewhat higher returns because they are differentiated products. The type and quality of service can vary significantly from institution to institution, making price competition less significant than for basic and essential custody services.

All custody-type services can, in principle, be dispersed geographically and by institution. Nevertheless, from the investor's viewpoint there are potential economies of scope and scale involved in the consolidation of custody of different securities in a portfolio in one entity or location, for instance with a global custodian, or an ICSD that provides a similar range of services. Consequently, custody represents a category of services that exhibits some potential economies of scope, but not to the extent inherent in information, trading, or clearing and settlement services. On the one hand, there are probably gains from proximity of the custody function to the location where issuer-related services – such as corporate events reporting – must be carried out. On the other hand, there may be gains from the consolidation of the investor-related services in the custody cluster, such as management of the information associated with a geographically diversified portfolio, as in global custody.

Global custodians, if permitted to compete freely, may serve both to remove some of the barriers listed in Section IV and to encourage harmonization among the national clearing and settlement systems of Europe. In doing so, they may remove some of the economic incentive to replace national CSDs with a Euro-CSD.

National and Cultural Interests

Even if a good deal of settlement and payment harmonization across national CSDs could be achieved, a number of significant 'national interest' and cultural barriers to the emergence of a dominant centralized CSD hub will remain, and will be very difficult to remove in the near future.

The first relates to the fact that equities, unlike bonds, are claims to corporate control. In many countries there are national security concerns regarding excessive foreign ownership of defence industry stocks and stocks in other sensitive industries, such as banking. This has resulted in legal caps being placed on foreign ownership of such shares. Such legal impediments limit cross-border merger and acquisition activity and thus cross-border equity trading.

Second, politicians do not tend to look at CSDs in terms of the classical tenets of cost-benefit analysis. This implies a preference towards tampering with existing national CSDs rather than facing the once and for all costs of switching to a centralized Euro-CSD hub (whether publicly or privately owned), even if the economic case for such a hub is strong. This is likely to be especially true when a significant proportion of the one-time switching costs are likely to be borne by customers of national CSDs and their employees, many of whom are also voters and party contributors. This is likely to result in politicians taking the view that a domestic CSD is in the national interest. It is clear that it will take a considerable cultural change, involving a relaxation of dubious national interest concerns, for these barriers to be removed. Moreover, one can envisage a major battle over where such a Euro-hub should be located (and jobs created), and whether it should be run as a private-sector cooperative (similar to Euroclear or Cedel) or whether more direct EU or national governmental controls would be required.

VI. EMPIRICAL EVIDENCE

There is very little empirical evidence on the costs and efficiency of CSD services. Probably the major reason for this is that these costs – both direct and indirect – are very difficult to measure, especially the back-office component of these costs.

In recent years, Global Securities Consulting Services (GSCS) has published benchmark measures on settlement efficiency, safekeeping efficiency, and operational risk across 20 equity markets.[27] A detailed description of the methodology underlying each of these indices is to be found in the chapter Appendix. The 1994 indices are based on over 870,000 equity trades as reported by ABN-AMRO, Barclays, Midland, State Street, Bank of New York, Mellon Trust, Northern Trust, Bankers Trust, Chase Manhattan, and the Royal Bank of Scotland. Of these trades, the US, Japan, and the UK accounted for nearly 60 percent of cross-border transactions.

The settlement benchmarks for 1994 are shown in Appendix Table 1. In terms of settlement efficiency, the US dominates with an index of 96.7 (out of 100). Among EU members, Denmark (94.3) was the most efficient. The book-entry/shorter-settlement CSD systems of France (92.8) and Germany (91.1) were more efficient than the paper-based/longer-settlement CSD of the UK (86.4). The least efficient EU country covered by the benchmarks was Spain (77.8).

With respect to safekeeping rankings (Appendix Table 2) – reflecting the efficiency of dividend collection, reclamation of withheld taxes, and protection of rights in the event of corporate actions – the US was again rated most efficient, with a score of 95.5. The UK (95.1), Germany (91.4), and France (90.1) were all rated highly efficient, and Italy received the lowest efficiency rating (77.8), based on its poor performance in crediting dividends.

The third benchmark concerns operational risk – which incorporates the settlement and safekeeping benchmarks, as well as taking into account compliance with the Group of Thirty recommendations and the complexity and effectiveness of the legal and regulatory structure of the market. As shown in Appendix Table 3, the US is once again the most efficient (86.5), with France (82.3) and Germany (83.2) more efficient than the UK (79.3).

An interesting question is what the GSCS database tells us regarding the correlation between improvements in settlement efficiency and the volume of

[27] See GSCS (1995).

cross-border equity trading. In particular, do we find a strong positive correlation between changes in volume and changes in settlement efficiency? Appendix Table 4 shows the 1993 to 1994 changes in equity trading volume (ΔV) and change in the settlement benchmark (ΔS) across the 20 equity markets followed by GSCS. The correlation coefficient between ΔV and ΔS is -0.041, which is, statistically, not significantly different from zero. That is, there is no statistically significant positive link between improvements in CSD settlement efficiency and cross-border trading volumes. Of course, such a result depends very much on the accuracy of the GSCS settlement index as a measure of all-in settlement costs. Yet the result reinforces the arguments of Section IV that it is not settlement efficiency (or inefficiency) in itself that is, at present, significantly encouraging (or inhibiting) cross-border trades, but rather the whole spectrum of national legal, regulatory, tax, and other macro-structural issues which create the economic framework in which European settlement systems must operate. The removal of damaging distortions in these areas will be important for reaping the full benefits of improvements in settlements systems.

VII. SUMMARY AND CONCLUSIONS

In this chapter, we have evaluated the efficiency case for a centralized Euro-equity CSD or hub. The economic arguments favouring centralization are quite strong. They relate to potential network externalities, economies deriving from collateral conservation, and economies of scale and scope. We then investigated the reasons why the movement towards a centralized Euro-hub for clearing cross-border equity trades – for example, through existing ICSDs such as Euroclear and Cedel – has been very slow. One possibility is the potential monopoly power of local CSDs. However, it was argued that the power of national CSDs to stop a Euro-hub emerging is not very great, and will probably decline with the growth of new competitive trading platforms. The key barriers appear to relate to direct and indirect transactions costs, arising in part from the lack of harmonization of European clearance and settlement standards and procedures, broadly defined. Barriers include different settlement cycles, taxation of trades, forms of securities (book-entry versus paper-based), and payment systems operations and access. It was also argued that multiple European currencies are probably a less important barrier to cross-border trading than are restrictions on access to national payment systems.

Some of these obstacles can be overcome by allowing competition and innovation by global custodians, which offer investors a seamless cross-border front-end investment. Even so, someone has to bear the costs, and unless the EU seeks to harmonize the institutional environment relating to clearance, settlement, and payment of equity trades across different European markets, the environment will continue to inhibit cross-border trading, making the emergence of a critical-mass supranational clearance and settlement system more distant. Indeed, without harmonization, European clearance and settlement is likely to continue along the current national-CSD model lines, perhaps with enhanced inter-CSD links of the type already created by the French Sicovam and the German DKV. Neither the multiple-link global custodian nor the so-called spaghetti model, however, can truly substitute for a unified CSD that promotes the development of a large, liquid, and dynamic market for equities.

References

Bank for International Security, 1992. 'Delivery Versus Payment in Securities Settlement Systems', September, Basle.

BIS, 1993. 'Central Bank Payment and Settlement Services with Respect to Cross-Border and Multi-Currency Transactions', September, Basle.

BIS, 1995. 'Cross-Border Securities Settlement', September, Basle.

Bank of England, 1994a. 'The Paper Interface',Working Paper of CREST project team, December.

BoE, 1994b. 'Corporate Actions', Working Paper of CREST project team, December.

BoE, 1994c. 'The Business Description', Working Paper of CREST project team, December.

BoE, 1994d. 'The Claims Processing Unit',Working Paper of CREST project team, December.

Bolton, P. and M. Dewatripont, 1994. 'The Firm as a Communication Network', *Quarterly Journal of Economics*, Vol. CIX, Issue 4, 809–39.

Brueckner, J.K. and P.T. Spiller, 1991. 'Competition and Mergers in Airline Networks', *International Journal of Industrial Organization* 9, 323–42.

Commission of the European Communities, 1994. 'Notice on the Application of the EU Competition Rules to Cross-Border Transfer System', (Annex 2), Brussels.

CEC, 1995. 'Draft – Notice on the application of the EU Competition rules to cross-border transfer systems', Brussels, 49–55.

Deutscher Kassenverein AG – Wertpapiersammelbank, 1992. 'Faster, Higher and Stronger!', July.

DK, 1994. 'Central Securities Depository', February.

Dobson, G. and P. J. Lederer, 1995. 'Airline Scheduling and Routing in a Hub and Spoke System', forthcoming in *Transportation Science*.

Earle, D. M. and J. F. Fried, 1992. 'Twenty-Four Hour Trading, Clearance, and Settlement: The Role of Banks', in Franklin R. Edwards and Hugh Patrick (eds), *Regulating International Financial Market: Issues and Policies*, Kluwer, Boston.

Economides, N., 1993. 'Network Economics with Application to Finance', *Financial Markets, Institutions & Instruments*, 2 (5): 89–97.

Economides and Himmelberg, 1993. 'Critical Mass and Network Size', New York University Working Paper, No. 95–11.

Giddy, I., A. Saunders and I. Walter, 1992. 'Securities Clearance and Settlement: Prospects for Convergent Markets', J.P. Morgan, Brussels.

Global Securities Consulting Services, 1995. 'GSCS Benchmarks – Measures for the International Securities Industry', *The 1995 Review of Major Markets*.

Ireland, J and T. Ryan, 1993. 'Equity Settlement in London – Its Importance to London as a Financial Centre', London Business School, The City Research Project, Subject Report V, September.

Kyle, A.S. and T.A. Marsh, 1993. 'On the Economics of Securities Clearance and Settlement', Working Paper, Duke University and U.C. Berkeley.

London Clearance House, 1993. 'Statistics – 1993'.

Levy, Aariel and Miles Livingston, 1995. 'The Gains From Diversification Reconsidered: Transaction Costs and Superior Information', *Financial Markets, Institutions and Investments*, 4 (3): 1–59.

London Stock Exchange, 1992. 'Institutional Net Settlement – Outline Service Description for Institutions and Member Firms', February.

LSE, 1993a. 'Rolling Settlement – Detailed Service Description', November.

LSE, 1993b. 'Guide to the International Equity Market 1994', December.

LSE, 1994a. 'Fact Book 1994 – Information at 31 December 1993', February.

LSE, 1994b. '1994/95 Settlement Services Prices for Member Firms', August.

LSE, 1994c. 'UK Securities Industry Equity Settlement – Code of Good Practice', December.

LSE, 1994d, 'T+5 Rolling Settlement', London Stock Exchange, November.

New York Clearance House Association, 1995. 'Risk Reduction and Enhanced Efficiency in Large-Value Payment Systems: A Private-Sector Response', New York.

Parkinson, P. *et al.*, 1992. 'Clearance and Settlement in US Securities Markets', Board of Governors of the Federal Reserve System, March, Washington, DC.

Paul-Choudhury, Sumit, 1995. 'Only Connect', *Risk*, 8 (3), March.

PSW, 1993. *Payment Systems Worldwide*, 3 (4), Winter 1992–3.

Schoenmaker, D., 1993. 'Externalities in Payment Systems: Issues for Europe', Special Paper No. 55, LSE Financial Markets Group, September.

Securities and Investments Board, 1995. 'Management Plan and Budget 1995/96', February.

Solnik, B., 1991. 'International Investments', Addison-Wesley, Reading, Massachusetts.

Appendix

BENCHMARKS METHODOLOGY

SETTLEMENT BENCHMARK

The purpose of the Settlement Benchmark is to provide a means of comparing the settlement efficiency of different markets and track the evolution of settlement performance in individual markets over time. The Benchmark incorporates four components which, combined together, reflect the overall cost to market participants of failed trades. These include average trade size, local market interest rates, the proportion of trades that fail, and the length of time for which they fail. By converting information back into a base currency, comparisons between markets become possible.

The Benchmarks are expressed as a score out of a maximum of 100. The lower the score the higher the effective operational costs of failed transactions in any given market. While the level of failed trades is naturally the principal influence on the Benchmark for each market, it is not the only one.

SAFEKEEPING BENCHMARK

The purpose of the Safekeeping Benchmark is to allow readers to compare the efficiency of different markets in terms of the collection of dividends and interest, reclamation of withheld taxes, and protection of rights in the event of a corporate action.

In the case of income collection, there is both a financial and an administrative cost associated with timely and effective collection. There are also risks to be borne in the area of corporate actions. The Benchmark seeks to assess all of these aspects through use of a five-factor model. The factors include typical market yields on equities and fixed income securities, rates of withholding tax and reclaim potential, average time between payable date and receipt of payment, local market interest rates, and the number and type of corporate actions that occur.

By assigning weights to each of these factors, it is possible to calculate the Benchmark expressed as a score out of a maximum of 100. The lower the score the higher the effective operational cost and greater the administrative effort involved in a given market. While the time taken to collect dividends or interest due is the most important factor in scoring, it is not the only one that can impact on individual country Benchmarks.

OPERATIONAL RISK BENCHMARK

The Operation Risk Benchmark is designed to allow comparison of the overall operational risk associated with individual markets. The Benchmark takes into consideration the Settlement and Safekeeping Benchmarks. However, it assigns them a different weight depending on the relative complexity of each in the different markets. The Benchmark also takes into account other operational factors, such as the level of compliance with the recommendations of the Group of Thirty (G30). It also accounts for the complexity and effectiveness of the legal and regulatory structure of the market, such as constraints on capital flows, foreign investment restrictions and market supervision. Finally, it seeks to incorporate two factors which may not be the direct responsibility of the custodians but cannot be ignored by them, namely counterparty risk and 'force majeure' risk. The Benchmark is expressed as a score out of 100. The lower the score, the higher the risk.

Appendix Table 1. Settlement Benchmark, 1994

Country	Q1	Q2	Q3	Q4	1993 average	1994 average	Outlook	% change
Australia	92.2	96.3	94.4	96.2	92.1	94.8	0	3.0
Austria	94.3	83.5	81.6	90.1	91.1	87.4	0	-4.1
Belgium	86.5	84.2	89.2	92.1	88.6	88.0	+ve	-0.7
Canada	93.7	95.1	90.0	91.5	89.4	92.6	-ve	3.6
Denmark	94.9	94.9	94.1	93.2	91.9	94.3	0	2.6
Finland	61.3	86.8	77.0	82.7	62.4	77.0	+ve	23.4
France	87.8	94.3	94.8	94.2	91.5	92.8	0	1.4
Germany	89.2	89.3	93.0	92.9	82.4	91.1	+ve	10.6
Hong Kong	87.0	93.6	92.2	93.9	82.4	91.7	0	11.2
Italy	91.4	91.2	97.0	92.1	92.9	92.9	+ve	0.0
Japan	92.2	96.8	93.6	92.4	78.5	93.8	0	19.4
Netherlands	86.5	87.9	91.5	91.6	84.5	89.4	+ve	5.8
New Zealand	89.2	82.5	94.3	94.6	80.5	90.2	+ve	12.0
Norway	63.5	82.1	84.5	80.2	70.2	77.6	0	10.5
Singapore	84.3	91.6	88.9	89.0	79.3	88.5	0	11.5
Spain	77.5	70.8	77.2	85.6	67.3	77.8	+ve	15.7
Sweden	82.9	85.1	89.4	88.5	76.9	86.5	+ve	12.5
Switzerland	80.7	88.4	85.2	89.4	81.1	85.9	0	6.0
UK	88.5	90.1	80.2	86.8	85.4	86.4	-ve	1.1
USA	96.6	97.4	96.2	96.5	94.7	96.7	0	2.1

Source: GSCS (1995).

Appendix Table 2. Safekeeping Benchmark, 1994

Country	Q1	Q2	Q3	Q4	1993 average	1994 average	% change
Australia	94.4	91.6	93.6	94.9	93.7	93.6	0.0
Austria	92.5	91.9	91.7	92.0	92.3	92.0	-0.3
Belgium	81.9	89.6	92.3	94.2	84.9	89.5	5.4
Canada	96.0	94.1	92.6	92.3	94.9	93.8	-1.2
Denmark	94.7	97.1	94.5	95.2	92.9	95.4	2.7
Finland	88.5	99.1	94.6	96.7	98.3	94.7	-3.6
France	88.9	90.9	89.9	90.7	85.7	90.1	5.2
Germany	94.0	90.2	89.9	91.3	87.1	91.4	4.9
Hong Kong	96.3	93.3	96.4	93.0	93.1	94.8	1.8
Italy	50.5	93.2	77.1	90.4	78.9	77.8	-1.4
Japan	94.6	97.8	93.2	92.2	95.0	94.5	-0.6
Netherlands	92.6	95.8	95.8	91.0	88.2	93.8	6.4
New Zealand	92.4	88.6	92.6	94.2	91.0	92.0	1.1
Norway	82.7	90.8	96.5	94.2	98.0	91.1	-7.1
Singapore	92.4	95.5	89.3	90.5	93.4	91.9	1.5
Spain	87.5	86.3	91.2	90.7	86.8	88.9	2.5
Sweden	N/A	97.9	88.3	92.8	88.8	93.0	4.7
Switzerland	92.7	92.6	87.3	91.9	90.9	91.1	0.3
UK	93.9	95.4	95.5	95.6	93.3	95.1	1.9
USA	95.9	95.3	95.7	95.0	95.2	95.5	0.3

Source: GSCS (1995).

Appendix Table 3. Operational Risk Benchmark, 1994

Country	Q1	Q2	Q3	Q4	1993 average	1994 average	% change
Australia	81.9	82.8	82.7	84.0	81.5	82.9	1.7
Austria	80.8	76.3	75.5	78.9	79.4	77.9	-1.9
Belgium	73.9	76.7	80.0	82.1	76.2	78.2	2.6
Canada	83.7	83.4	80.5	81.1	81.2	82.2	1.2
Denmark	80.4	81.5	80.0	80.0	78.3	80.5	2.8
Finland	59.6	74.0	68.3	71.4	63.5	68.3	7.6
France	79.6	83.1	83.3	83.0	79.3	82.3	3.8
Germany	83.6	81.9	83.3	84.0	77.0	83.2	8.1
Hong Kong	76.0	77.9	78.5	78.0	72.3	77.6	7.3
Italy	59.8	78.7	73.9	77.8	73.1	72.6	-0.7
Japan	80.5	84.1	80.8	79.9	72.5	81.3	12.1
Netherlands	78.1	80.0	81.8	79.7	75.4	80.0	6.1
New Zealand	76.5	72.0	78.7	79.5	71.7	76.7	7.0
Norway	61.5	72.7	76.1	73.3	70.7	70.9	0.3
Singapore	71.0	75.2	71.6	72.1	68.9	72.5	5.2
Spain	65.3	61.9	66.5	70.0	60.6	65.9	8.8
Sweden	78.2	78.9	76.8	78.2	71.4	78.0	9.2
Switzerland	75.4	78.6	74.8	78.6	74.3	76.9	3.5
UK	79.6	80.9	76.9	79.7	77.6	79.3	2.2
USA	86.7	86.7	86.3	86.2	85.1	86.5	1.7

Source: GSCS (1995).

Appendix Table 4. Changes in Equities Volumes Against Changes in Settlement Benchmark, 1993/4

Country	Year-on-year % changes in volumes	Year-on-year % change in average settlement benchmark
Australia	75.0	3.0
Austria	78.9	-4.1
Belgium	42.4	-0.7
Canada	48.5	3.6
Denmark	55.0	2.6
Finland	90.8	23.4
France	36.6	1.4
Germany	31.3	10.6
Hong Kong	58.2	11.2
Italy	70.1	0.0
Japan	41.6	19.4
Netherlands	41.3	5.8
New Zealand	40.8	12.0
Norway	51.3	10.5
Singapore	24.2	11.5
Spain	-9.6	15.7
Sweden	89.7	12.5
Switzerland	24.6	6.0
UK	42.0	1.1
USA	22.9	2.1

Source: GSCS (1995).

Chapter 10

EXCHANGE RATES AND THE SINGLE CURRENCY

This chapter examines the role that exchange rate variability plays in impeding the integration of equity markets, and in particular the role that Economic and Monetary Union (EMU), or at least stabilization of European exchange rates, could play in advancing the integration of European equity markets. Two kinds of integration are of interest: cross-border trading and holding of equities; and the consolidation of financial centres that are currently dispersed across countries into one or more major ones. The currency question is relevant for both.

1. IS REGIONAL INTEGRATION OF EQUITY MARKETS TO BE DESIRED?

International economic integration is, in general, a trend that is well worth promoting. The clearest and most familiar case is the one in favour of international trade in goods and services, which promotes welfare both for buyers, who can buy imported goods more cheaply than at home, and sellers, who can sell exports for higher prices abroad than at home. There is an analogous case to be made in favour of international capital flows. Internationally liberalized financial markets allow corporations and other borrowers to raise capital more cheaply than when they are restricted to raising funds at home, and investors earn higher expected returns for a given level of risk by diversifying abroad.

The case for capital mobility requires a few more nuances than does the case for trade in goods and services. Some believe that there are possible market failures in financial markets – arising, for example, from the presence of speculative overshooting and from the absence of an international debtors' bankruptcy court – and that these have contributed to recent difficulties in emerging markets and in foreign-exchange markets among industrialized countries. But overall, the advantages of open financial markets dominate. Equities are a particularly attractive mode for international capital flows. In the event of adverse economic outcomes, equity prices automatically fall, eliminating the need for lengthy and costly negotiations between borrower and creditor countries, such as occurred over the terms of bank loans in 1982, or over the terms of bonds in other crises.[1]

The case in favour of the integration of equity markets on a *regional* basis requires yet more nuances. Integration on a worldwide basis is better from the standpoint of economic welfare than regional integration alone. Interesting questions arise when one takes the degree of worldwide integration as given, constrained by political considerations. If the first-best is not attainable, what is the second-best? The net welfare effects of regional trade integration depend on weighing costs and benefits, often phrased as trade diversion versus trade creation. Breaking down some barriers within regional groupings can raise economic welfare on net, even when it gets a bit ahead of worldwide liberalization.[2] A particular advantage of regional integration is that it can allow the exploitation of economies of scale, which are not taken into account in classical models of trade under perfect competition. Furthermore, regional economic integration helps foster regional political integration, which can be an important goal in its own right.

Regional integration of equity markets has two distinct facets. First, issuers and investors expand their activities more widely across the region. Here the point is that the abolition of barriers to cross-border equity holdings allows borrowers to raise capital more cheaply and allows investors to earn better returns. Such integration of capital markets also helps promote integration along other lines as well, such as integration of money markets and of markets in goods and services.

Second, equities are increasingly traded on exchanges outside the home-country. Trading in equities is a financial service. Much like other goods and services, comparative advantage may dictate that it is more efficient to undertake the trading in a foreign financial centre than in the home market. The point made above about economies of scale is particularly relevant for financial centres. In the absence of barriers, there is a powerful tendency for certain types of financial transactions to be geographically concentrated. The exact reasons for this are not entirely known, given that, unlike goods-producing industries, the financial industry in the age of telecommunications and computer technology is not affected by shipping costs. One force behind the powerful tendency towards regional ag-

[1] Caves, Frankel and Jones (1996: 517-18).

[2] The argument is essentially that at the early stages of regional integration, trade creation outweighs trade diversion. There is a rapidly growing literature on the regionalization of the world economy. Frankel and Wei (1995) review the literature, develop the notion of an optimal degree of regionalization that can be justified by natural factors, and consider some dynamic political-economy connections between regional integration and multilateral integration.

glomeration appears to be the necessity of face-to-face contact in deal-making, although this is becoming decreasingly relevant for equity trading.[3]

It seems likely that the current structure in Europe, where each country has its own financial centre (or centres), is inefficient. Steil (1993: 7) notes, 'Compared with the US securities markets, European markets remain highly fragmented. The US has eight stock exchanges and seven futures and options exchanges, as compared with 32 stock exchanges and 23 futures and options exchanges in the EC. In the increasingly competitive environment which is developing at present, some consolidation would appear inevitable, although national exchanges will not face the direct threat of extinction until European monetary union becomes a reality.'[4] Integration would put downward pressure on transactions costs, both through competitive pressure on existing national stock markets and through economies of scale in the event of consolidation on a continental level.

One view is that the world is heading towards a system of three big financial centres, one in the western hemisphere time zone, one in the East Asia time zone, and one in the European time zone. The first two are clearly New York and Tokyo. Currently the leading financial centre in the European time zone is obviously London. In the event that EMU is successfully accomplished, but with the United Kingdom on the outside, then it is certainly conceivable that an alternative centre on the continent would begin to develop. Since London-based dealers already quote European equities in local currency, the mere fact of a change of currencies should not directly affect the geographic concentration of dealers, although it could do so indirectly by first attracting other banking activities onto the continent. One advantage which London will retain is the English language.[5] Another is that the residents of the continent simply have not developed the habit

[3] Gerd Häusler, of the Bundesbank Directorate, believes that the tendency towards concentration in Europe will be much greater if a new European Central Bank adopts binding minimum requirements for (non-interest-paying) reserves. His argument is that in this case, reserves and interest rates vary little over time. As in Germany currently, monetary policy can take place in 'slow motion'. The central bank is seldom in a hurry to smooth interest rate fluctuations, and so can conduct open market operations by dealing with hundreds of banks throughout the country in an auction over a period of 24 hours. When banks are not subject to binding reserve requirements, on the other hand, they are always optimizing, in a highly competitive market environment. Every shock to reserves impacts interest rates. As in the UK currently, the central bank must move very quickly. To do so, it must transact with a handful of primary dealers. The conclusion is that if a European Central Bank switches away from a system of binding reserve requirements, there would be a tendency towards financial concentration in a single European financial centre. This would presumably be Frankfurt, if that were where the central bank was.

[4] Goldstein and Folkerts-Landau (1993: 42-43) note that there is a 'tradeoff between the advantages of competition between different market centers ... – which tends to drive down the costs of transacting and to encourage innovative trading methods – and the beneficial effects of concentration on market liquidity.'

[5] Grilli (1989: 391).

of holding or trading equities to the same extent as the Anglo-Saxons. One advantage that Frankfurt has is the site of the European Monetary Institute, and almost certainly of the future European Central Bank. But there are reasons to believe that Paris is more likely than Frankfurt to compete directly and aggressively with London.

The central question for this paper is whether monetary union, or perhaps some lesser form of currency integration, is a prerequisite for effective integration of equities trading. One might also ask the reciprocal question of how integration of equities markets in Europe affects the desirability or feasibility of currency integration. The *optimum currency area* literature offers a possible analogy regarding integration of goods markets or labour markets. Floating exchange rates have both advantages (especially the ability to pursue an independent monetary policy) and disadvantages (the absence of a nominal anchor, and the negative effects of exchange rate uncertainty and misalignments on international trade and investment). The theory of optimum currency areas suggests that if countries or regions belonging to a certain grouping are highly open with respect to one another economically, they are likely to be better off by pegging their currencies to one another. Openness can be defined as a high proportion of internationally traded goods (in the McKinnon version of the optimum currency area criterion) or as a high degree of labour mobility (in the Mundell version).[6]

An analogous optimum currency area argument for financial markets would say that if a group of countries or regions already engage in a lot of financial transactions, they are likely to be better off pegging their currencies to each other. But it is not clear that the parallel argument really holds. A high degree of financial openness is known to make stabilizing the exchange rate more difficult. This is true in particular if countries are not prepared to give up all monetary independence. Hence the famous Impossible Trinity of open financial markets, fixed exchange rates, and monetary independence.[7] A common view of the 1992 crises in the European Exchange Rate Mechanism (ERM) – common, at least, among American economists – is that the EU tried to achieve the Impossible Trinity, and once again found it to be impossible. In any case, this chapter will concentrate on the implications of the exchange rate regime for equity markets, not on the reverse direction of causality. In the penultimate section, we will return to the theory of optimum currency areas in an attempt at a broad perspective on the desirability of European monetary integration.

[6] To the extent that the stabilization of exchange rates is thought to promote trade bilaterally, a currency union is more likely to meet the optimum currency area criterion after it has been in place awhile than *ex ante*. (In other words, the criterion has a *status quo* bias.)

[7] For example, Rose (1994) or Caves, Frankel and Jones (1996: 564-66).

2. WHAT MIGHT BE THE ROLE OF CURRENCY INTEGRATION?

The subject of this chapter is the role, if any, of currency integration in fostering the integration of equity markets in Europe. The words 'if any' are necessary, because economic theory offers a number of reasons to believe that exchange rates are less relevant to the question of equity market integration than one might think. This is in particular true of such 'macro' aspects as the determination of cross-border capital flows and the determination of equity prices and rates of return. Most econometric studies find that exchange rate variability, even when it is large, as it was among most countries in the 1970s and 1980s, has little effect on, for example, the volume or prices of international trade.[8] The usual explanation is that importers and exporters are able to hedge their exchange risk. Why should the same not also be true of borrowers and investors? Indeed, it should be even easier for those who already reside in the financial markets to hedge their foreign currency risk, as compared with some of the smaller importers or exporters, who may not be sophisticated enough to use such financial instruments as forwards and options.

The possible irrelevance of foreign-exchange variability holds less for 'micro' aspects, such as how many financial centres are supported in equilibrium, where they are located, and the volume of trade or profitability of each one. It should be conceded immediately that transactions costs arising from foreign-exchange variability, even if relatively small, could easily make a difference in location, by analogy with other transactions costs or turnover taxes.[9] Given the near-indeterminacy of the location of trading (i.e. there is no strong reason for trading to take place in one location rather than another), even relatively small costs can have a big effect on the possible consolidation of many small trading centres into a few large ones, and in determining which location wins the battle to become the premier financial centre of Europe.

The location of trading is irrelevant, in theory, to such questions as the determination of the price of equity or its rate of return. The location is admittedly important to those who do the trading. It may have implications for the magnitude of bid-ask spreads or other transactions costs, if, for example, regional integration of equity trading results in greater efficiency. But transactions costs are already small enough so that arbitrage closely equalizes the price of equity in a given company across markets.

[8] Frankel and Wei (1995) find that the effects of bilateral exchange rate variability on bilateral trade were statistically significant in the 1970s, but disappeared after 1980, perhaps owing to the spread of hedging techniques. The literature is surveyed in Edison and Melvin (1990).

[9] Campbell and Froot (1994) and Hakkio (1994) show that these make a difference to the location and amount of trading.

3. THE NEUTRALITY VIEW

It is probably fair to characterize the conventional wisdom in finance theory with an expression of neutrality: the exchange rate regime has no important implications for equity markets. The extreme form of this neutrality proposition is that currencies have no important implications for *anything* real, because all nominal magnitudes adjust instantly and proportionately to movements in nominal exchange rates (which in turn move only in proportion to changes in money supply conditions). A much more reasonable form of the proposition is that – even though the level of the exchange rate has implications for variables such as real goods prices, real output, real interest rates, and real equity prices – exchange rate *variability* does not have significant real consequences because exchange risk is diversifiable or hedgeable. We consider each argument in turn.

Many highly abstract theoretical finance models assume that all wages and prices are perfectly flexible, and thereby conclude that movements in nominal exchange rates have no real effects.[10] This may sound absurd on the face of it: a currency depreciation is clearly likely to raise the price of equity in a company that produces for export, for example, relative to the price of another company.[11] These theories, sometimes known as the *equilibrium view*, acknowledge that not all fluctuations in nominal exchange rates are matched by corresponding fluctuations in prices, whether of goods or equities. In other words, they acknowledge that, of course, fluctuations in real exchange rates and relative equity prices occur across countries. But they argue that such fluctuations are due to exogenous causes. This means that they are caused by fundamental shifts in productivity or in consumer demand patterns, and will occur regardless of the exchange rate regime. Under a regime of floating exchange rates, an increase in productivity will cause a real currency appreciation that shows up as an increase in the value of the currency. Under a regime of fixed exchange rates, an increase in productivity causes the same real currency appreciation, but it shows up as an increase in the price level.

These models rely on the proposition that prices of goods and services adjust instantly to exchange rate fluctuations. The reply to the equilibrium view begins by noting that there is abundant evidence that prices of goods and services are sticky in the currency of the country of production. One convincing kind of evidence is that real exchange rates are always more variable under

[10] Examples include Helpman (1981), Helpman and Razin (1979), and Stockman (1983).

[11] The empirical evidence is surprisingly weak on this. Examples include Amihud (1993), Bartov and Bodnar (1994) and Bodnar and Gentry (1993).

regimes of variable nominal exchange rates than under regimes of stable nominal exchange rates.[12]

Proponents of the equilibrium view, even when conceding that the price-flexibility proposition is only an approximation, might adopt as a fallback position the point that prices in *financial* markets *are* completely flexible and free to adjust. This point is correct, so far as it goes. But it certainly does not then follow that exchange rate fluctuations do not have real effects on equity prices. On the contrary, it follows from price stickiness that exchange rate fluctuations, even if purely monetary in origin, have effects on real exchange rates and real interest rates. It also follows that there are in turn effects on real equity prices. A mechanism operating via the real interest rate, if nothing else, will bring this about: a monetary contraction that causes an increase in the real interest rate and in the real value of the currency will reduce the price of equity (the present discounted value of future dividends) in terms of domestic currency or goods, even while raising it in terms of foreign currency or goods. Other effects follow more directly from the fluctuation in the real exchange rate itself. A currency depreciation will raise the equity value of companies in domestic terms when their products gain competitiveness on world markets in terms of price or unit labour costs.

The proponents of the equilibrium view repeat that, even so, if the government suppresses fluctuations in the exchange rate, then the fluctuations will simply show up elsewhere. For example, if the central bank responds to fluctuations in the demand for money by buying and selling unwanted currency, rather than by letting the exchange rate respond to clear the market, then the fluctuations will show up in the money supply and the interest rate. The rebuttal admits that this is often true to a certain degree, but points out that there is no reason to expect complete invariance in real equity prices. In particular, there is some evidence that floating exchange rates are sometimes characterized by 'excess volatility' in the form of speculative bubbles.[13] Perhaps the excess volatility could be reduced or the speculative bubbles suppressed under a regime of target zones or fixed exchange rates.[14] In that case, the eliminated volatility need not show up anywhere else.

Later in the chapter, we consider some new evidence on the proposition that relative equity prices are neutral with respect to exogenous exchange rate

[12] The evidence is reviewed in Part II of Frankel and Rose (1995). An important example is the paper by Mussa (1990) that is described in section 6 below.

[13] Examples include Dornbusch (1982), Frankel (1993b), Goodhart (1988), and Meese (1986).

[14] For example, Rose (1994), Krugman and Miller (1993) and Williamson (1985). A contrary argument is that speculators can generate movements that are excessive (in the sense of being unrelated to economic fundamentals), not only under floating rates, but under pegged exchange rates as well, as in the speculative attack model of Obstfeld (1986).

movements. We will find some evidence that this proposition is wrong; that relative equity price movements are affected by the degree of variability in the exchange rate.

The more reasonable form of the neutrality proposition recognizes that the *level* of the exchange rate has implications for real variables, but argues that exchange rate *variability* does not have major consequences for the degree of market integration, because exchange risk is diversifiable or hedgeable. That it can be hedged, at relatively low transaction cost, is clear. Anyone holding French assets, for example, can easily sell French francs forward to hedge against the risk that the franc will depreciate. The question is whether one must pay a substantial *exchange risk premium* for the privilege of eliminating the risk, defined as a forward price of francs that lies below the expected future spot rate. Those who wish to protect their homes from the risk of an earthquake by taking out earthquake insurance, or to protect their portfolios from the riskiness of equities themselves by holding bonds instead, must give up quite a bit of money in expected value terms in return for laying off the risk on someone else. Should not the same principle apply to the forward exchange market? If so, the exchange risk premium should be smaller under a regime of fixed rates or target zones than under floating, because exchange rate uncertainty is smaller. It would then follow that variable exchange rates can discourage cross-border equity investing, and exchange rate stability can promote it.[15]

There has been a lot more research on exchange risk in the context of markets in bonds, bills, and deposits than in the context of equity markets. Many of the conclusions are ambiguous, but the general point is that exchange rate uncertainty can prevent perfect arbitrage. An exchange risk premium can separate one country's interest rate from another's. The analogous result could carry over to equity markets in two ways. First, there could be an analogous exchange risk premium in equity returns, because equity prices are tied to local currencies, in the way that bonds are, even though to a much smaller extent. Secondly, the existence of extra frictions in international equity markets (e.g. regulatory barriers and information costs that do not apply to highly rated bonds) could mean that the most effective means of arbitrage across equity markets is via the fixed-income market: arbitrage by domestic investors equates the expected rate of return on domestic equity with the domestic interest rate (plus an equity premium);

[15] The possibility has been suggested that exchange rate volatility might actually constitute an *inducement* to greater volumes of cross-border capital flows on the part of speculators who thrive on volatility. This is too cynical a view, even for a sceptic of market efficiency. Exchange rate volatility is very likely an inducement to higher turnover in the foreign-exchange market, but not in general to greater volume of flows of securities. Bank trading rooms may like volatility, but corporate treasurers do not.

arbitrage by international investors equates the domestic interest rate with the foreign interest rate (plus an exchange risk premium); and arbitrage by foreign investors in turn equates the foreign interest rate with the expected rate of return on foreign equity (again, plus an equity premium). The middle step on this route of arbitrage would then be impeded by exchange rate risk.

There is good reason to believe that the exchange risk premium is considerably smaller than the earthquake insurance premium or the equity market premium (the average rate of return on equities minus the treasury bill rate). The reason is that much of exchange risk is diversifiable. For every Englishman who wishes to lay off the exchange risk he incurs from holding French assets, by selling francs in the forward market for pounds, there is likely to be a Frenchwoman who wishes to lay off the exchange risk she incurs from holding British assets, by selling pounds in the forward market for francs. There is no reason why the rate that clears the forward market need lie above or below the expected future spot rate. In other words, there is no reason why the exchange risk premium need be positive or negative. It is in theory possible that all exchange risk is diversifiable, in which case the exchange risk premium is zero, and exchange rate uncertainty need not discourage cross-border holding of securities.[16]

It is more likely that the balance of buyers and sellers will go in one direction or the other than that the forward market will clear at an exchange risk premium of exactly zero. The logic of diversifiability still argues that the premium is likely to be relatively small. The logic also suggests that to hedge equities held in a foreign country, international investors need not even incur the bother or transactions costs of dealing with the futures market. (It should be noted that as yet forward contracts tend not to go out to horizons much beyond one year, and the theoretically correct strategy of rolling over short-term forward contracts can be expensive.) If investors reduce their holdings of bonds in that foreign country, relative to what they would otherwise hold, it will have the same effect as selling a like amount of foreign currency forward. Of course, this works only if the investor was otherwise planning on holding foreign bonds.

Nevertheless, to say that exchange risk is largely diversifiable or that the exchange risk premium is relatively small is not to say that risk does not matter at all. Even a relatively small premium could discourage cross-border equity holdings. Some research argues that the exchange risk premium is substantial, despite

[16] Frankel (1979, 1982). Perold and Schulman (1988), on similar logic, offer currency-hedging to international equity holders as a 'free lunch'. (While Perold and Schulman advise investors to hedge their exchange risk, Froot (1993) comes to a somewhat different conclusion, for the case of investors who have long horizons.)

the arguments above.[17] In that case it would follow that exchange risk creates obstacles to capital market integration.

4. THE HOME-COUNTRY BIAS PUZZLE, AND OTHER EVIDENCE OF CURRENCY MYOPIA

In practice, there are reasons to believe that exchange rate fluctuations, even if purely monetary in origin, have effects on relative equity prices and return differentials. Most of the remainder of this chapter is dedicated to demonstrating this proposition empirically. Prices of plant and equipment are sticky in home-currency price, much like real estate prices. Part of the explanation is probably that the prices of the goods that the plant produces are sticky, and the value of the plant is related to the value of the goods it produces, since capital is not easily substitutable among different uses once it has been embodied in the form of a factory.

There are also reasons to believe that the risk and expense of dealing in foreign currencies, although not large enough to deter an investor who believes that substantially higher returns are to be had abroad, may nevertheless be large enough to have some deterrent effect for the typical investor. Institutional investors such as pension funds and life insurance companies may be prohibited by law or by their own guidelines from holding foreign-currency assets altogether, or from holding more than a certain proportion of their portfolios in that form. Fear of derivatives, based on lack of knowledge and the publicity surrounding recent scandals, may currently inhibit some funds from legitimate hedging of currency risk, and thereby inhibit them from holding foreign-currency assets in the first place. Foreign-currency assets are still much harder for the small investor to obtain from a broker than domestic assets. Mutual funds are clearly the easiest way for individual investors to diversify abroad. But international mutual funds have expense ratios that are considerably higher than those for domestic mutual funds. The funds themselves cite the risk and expense of dealing in foreign currencies as one of the major reasons for their high expense ratios.

Furthermore, investors appear in some ways to exhibit a sort of currency myopia; a reluctance to hold equities that are transacted in foreign currencies. Given the ability to hedge exchange risk, this reluctance seems to exceed what can be justified under the standard hypothesis that markets are efficient.[18] Such a

[17] E.g. Hodrick (1988) and Frankel and Chinn (1993).

[18] On efficiency in the context of international capital markets, see Steil (1992) or the contributions in Frankel (1994).

failure of market efficiency does not necessarily mean that people are irrational. There are a number of institutional peculiarities and frictions that can explain the phenomenon.

Most well-documented is the famous puzzle of 'home-country bias' in equity investing. Investors who reside in different countries are thought to exhibit a bias towards holding home assets. French and Poterba (1994), Golub (1991), and Tesar and Werner (1992) find that there is such a bias in portfolios actually held, notwithstanding the widely noted progress already made in recent years toward the globalization of equity markets. In 1989, US investors reportedly held 94 percent of their stock-market wealth in domestic stocks, Japanese investors held 98 percent, and UK investors held 82 percent. In 1990, pension funds in G-7 countries continued to hold more than 90 percent of their assets domestically. Why do they not all hold more of one anothers' equities?[19]

One can readily explain a substantial home-country bias in investors' holdings of short-term bonds, as opposed to equities. The explanation is rational preferences for local currency habitats. Assume a simple model of investors' portfolio allocations based on one-period mean-variance optimization – which is the Capital Asset Pricing Model (CAPM). Assume further that goods prices are predetermined in the currency of the country where the good is produced, over a horizon as long as the maturity of the bond. Calculating the optimal portfolio for a given investor, even approximately, is very difficult because of sensitivity to expected rates of return, which are difficult to measure precisely. Calculating the *difference* between optimal portfolios held by domestic and foreign residents is much easier, however, assuming that both share the same expectations (and, for simplicity, the same coefficient of risk-aversion). The reason is that the expectations component of the optimal portfolio share drops out of the difference.

Let x_A be the share of their portfolio that Americans allocate to US assets and x_G the share of their portfolios that Germans allocate to US assets. Then it can be shown that

$$x_A - x_G = [a_A - a_G][1 - 1/\rho],$$

where a_A and a_G are the shares of their consumption that optimally diversified American and German residents, respectively, allocate to US goods, and ρ is the coefficient of relative risk-aversion.[20] Intuitively, to the extent that investors are

[19] Frankel (1994). Recent surveys by Dumas (1993) and Obstfeld (1994) each devote sections to this observed bias and its possible explanations.

[20] One of many possible citations for the derivation of this equation is Frankel (1983), equations (1) and (3).

relatively risk-averse ($\rho>1$), they differ in their portfolio preferences in simple proportion to how they differ in their consumption preferences. The more they consume of their own country's goods, the more they view their own currency as safe in real terms, and the foreign currency as risky. In short, a home-country bias in consumption preferences implies a home-country bias in portfolio preferences.

The term representing the home-country bias in consumption, $a_A - a_G$, is certainly large in practice. Assume for simplicity that it takes its maximum value of 1-0 = 1. (In other words, Americans consume only US goods and Germans only German goods.) Let us try a value for the coefficient of risk-aversion that emerges from Engel's (1994) CAPM estimates: 4. It follows that the measure of home-country bias is relatively large: $x_A - x_G = .75$. If residents of each country in fact hold a mere 10 or 15 percent of their portfolios in foreign bonds (.85-.15 = .70 < .75), that is fully consistent with optimal diversification! At first glance, home-country bias poses no puzzle.

The puzzle arises in a portfolio that includes equities. We will see below that the return on equities in the currency of the home-country has a surprisingly low correlation with the exchange rate. The key point is that exchange rate risk is not an impediment to holding foreign equities in the way that it is an impediment to holding foreign bonds. Once investors have given vent to the home-country bias that optimally follows from differences in consumption patterns, in the form of bond portfolios that are relatively undiversified, there is little reason for their equity portfolios to exhibit the same home-country bias. Rather, in theory, American investors should take advantage of the opportunity to diversify by holding approximately the same amount of German equities as German residents hold. They can easily eliminate the gratuitous exchange risk by reducing their holdings of German bonds correspondingly or, equivalently, by selling marks on the forward market. (As already noted, the prescription to hold foreign equities but hedge the exchange risk has been offered to portfolio-managers as a 'free lunch'.)

Clearly, investors' equity portfolios are in fact less diversified than this. In a framework that allows investors of each country to diversify among countries' stocks and bonds as they will, rejection of the CAPM constraint might be attributed to its implication that investors should exhibit home-country bias only in their bonds, not in their stocks. Tesar and Werner (1994) infer that there is a significant home-country bias puzzle – which cannot be explained by transactions costs – from their evidence that investors trade a lot on the small fraction of the portfolio that they dedicate to foreign assets. They find that gross transactions volumes are very large by comparison with the magnitude of the corresponding net transactions volume.

The existence of a home-country bias need not necessarily be due to currency myopia, of course. One alternative hypothesis is that investors in each country feel that they have better information on domestic equities than foreign equities. But there is evidence that currency myopia does play a role. We discuss the cases of FASB 8 and country-funds, before turning to a statistical analysis of the exchange rate data and equity price data in subsequent sections.

If corporate managers do not have confidence that their shareholders can see through all the complexities of modern finance and accounting, they may be reluctant to make an investment that does not 'look good on the books' even if they believe it is in the true interest of the company. To take an example, in 1976 the US Financial Accounting Standards Board adopted a rule, FASB 8, requiring companies to translate their overseas earnings into dollars at the current exchange rate. Many companies reacted by suddenly altering their behaviour so as to reduce exposure in foreign currency. They knew that such exposure would show up on their annual reports as earnings that were highly variable in terms of dollars. They sought to hedge their foreign earnings – for example, by selling foreign-exchange on the forward market.[21] While some hedging may always be prudent for a company with large overseas operations, in this case the change in corporate behaviour in response to FASB 8 was a sign that managers did not think that shareholders would see through the accounting rule change. Such managers may err in the direction of the simple rule that the domestic currency is safe and the foreign currency is risky.

The second case, which is especially difficult to reconcile with standard notions of market efficiency, arises from closed-end country-funds. It is always difficult to test whether the market price of a stock is equal to its fundamental value, because of the uncertainty regarding what is the correct model of the fundamental value. There is little doubt, however, that the market price of a fixed portfolio of equities ought to be equal to the net asset value of the portfolio; that is, the aggregate of the market prices of the individual stocks. Closed-end country-funds are just such fixed portfolios, and yet their prices when traded in New York or London are observed to differ substantially from their net asset values (the aggregate value of the basket of equities at local market prices) expressed in dollars or pounds.

A number of authors have observed the discrepancy between the price of country-funds and their respective net asset values.[22] Hardouvelis, La Porta, and Wizman (1994) study how it moves through time. To summarize briefly the outcome of a systematic and thorough analysis, the New York prices of country-funds are observed in the short run to behave far more like the New York prices

[21] Revey (1981). Incidentally, the rule has since been abolished.

[22] For example, Bosner-Neal, Brauer, Neal, and Wheatley (1990) and Diwan, Senbet, and Errunza (1993).

of other US securities than like the aggregated net asset value of the individual foreign securities that constitute the portfolio. Specifically, when there is a fluctuation in the exchange rate between the dollar and the currency of the local country in question, the country-fund price tends in the short run to follow the dollar, not the local currency. When there is a fluctuation in the price of the world stock market, or in US stocks, again the country-fund price tends in the short run to follow the world portfolio or the US stocks, not its respective local national stock market. Only slowly over time does the price converge to the net asset value, as it should right away. (The weekly autoregressive coefficient is estimated at .89, for a half-life of five weeks.) It is difficult to reconcile this behaviour with the hypothesis of an efficient and frictionless world capital market. It seems to be clear evidence of currency myopia on the part of investors.

5. CORRELATIONS OF STOCK MARKETS ACROSS COUNTRIES

The correlation of countries' stock markets is rather low on an absolute scale. This fact, which has been widely documented, is the basis for the long-standing advice from international economists that great gains await the investor who decides to diversify his or her portfolio internationally. Standard asset-pricing theory – in the form, for example, of the famous CAPM – tells us that an investor can minimize the risk to his or her overall portfolio, for a given expected return, by diversifying among assets that have a low correlation. This is why a low correlation among international equities implies gains to diversification.[23]

Countries' stock markets have over time become more highly correlated. The tendency for markets to fall sharply on the same day, such as the crash of 19 October 1987, has been widely noted.[24] Co-movements as a phenomenon occur more generally than just the occasional spectacular crashes, however.

Of stock markets in 16 industrialized countries, 13 experienced an increase in correlation with the aggregate world portfolio between the period January 1959–December 1970 and the period January 1971–December 1978. Only Canada and the United States experienced declines in their correlation with the world portfolio.[25] Of the 16, a total of 12 experienced an increase in their correlation with

[23] Early contributors to this literature were Levy and Sarnat (1970) and Solnik (1974). Adler and Dumas (1983) surveyed the early literature. More recently, Grauer and Hakansson (1987) and Jorion (1989b) have updated the estimates.

[24] E.g. Eun and Shim (1989), King and Wadwhani (1990), von Furstenberg and Jeon (1989), and Ito and Lin (1994).

[25] This may be because Canada and the United States themselves constituted a large fraction of the world portfolio in the 1960s, and less in the 1970s. Italy experienced no change, to two digits. These figures are derived from statistics in Jorion (1989), Tables 2-4.

Germany's stock market in particular. European countries such as Belgium, Denmark, France, the Netherlands, and Spain became far more correlated with Germany. Again, Canada, the United States, and Italy are the only exceptions.

Of 18 national stock markets, 12 experienced a further increase in correlation with the world portfolio in the period January 1979-December 1986.[26] The correlation was somewhat concentrated in Europe. During the period January 1971-December 1978, the correlation among 66 pairs of European countries averaged .419, and among 28 pairs of EC countries the average was as high as .433, as compared with only .346 for 87 other pairs of countries. During the period January 1979-December 1986, the intra-European correlations averaged .417 and the inter-EC correlations .439, while the correlations among other pairs of countries on average actually fell to .320.[27]

The salience of the intra-European links has been amplified more recently. During the period April 1988-March 1991, correlations among 91 pairs of European countries averaged .488 and among 36 pairs of EC members as high as .541, while correlations among 185 other pairs of countries averaged as low as .228.[28] Steil (1993: 7-8) notes continued convergence of European equity market returns during the period 1987-91, despite a setback in 1992 that was presumably temporary.[29]

The interesting questions are (1) why have the correlations within Europe been higher than in the rest of the world; and (2) why have the correlations increased over time? There are (at least) three leading categories of explanation, all of which probably play a role in explaining correlations worldwide, as well as within Europe.

First, the existence of capital controls, transactions costs, and other barriers to the free movement of capital across national boundaries could explain the low correlation initially, and a reduction of these barriers since 1971 could explain the increase in the correlation.[30] Investors are now more free to arbitrage

[26] Five countries experienced declines in correlation – Australia, Belgium, Hong Kong, Norway, and Singapore – and the United States experienced no change. Between the 1971-8 period and the 1979-86 period, eight countries became more highly correlated with Germany and nine less so. The split is even among the European countries.

[27] These calculations are based on numbers reported in Jorion (1989a), Tables 26-3 and 26-4.

[28] These calculations are based on numbers reported in Roll (1992), Table 7.

[29] Those returns are expressed in local currency. Steil also notes earlier econometric research on European excess returns that shows a strong correlation with US excess returns.

[30] Among the many references on the nature of barriers to international capital movements, and the progress made at removing them, is Frankel (1991). Tests of short-term arbitrage suggest that the most rapid rates of liberalization in the 1980s were recorded (in order) by Portugal, Spain, France, Denmark, Italy, Germany, Switzerland, and the Netherlands. Austria, Belgium and the United Kingdom already had low barriers at the beginning of the sample period (1982). Frankel (1994), and the accompanying papers, investigates similar trends for equity markets.

across national boundaries when they see expected returns in one market higher than those in another. By responding to such return differentials, they increase the demand for securities in the high-return countries, thereby driving down the required rate of return there, and decrease the demand for securities in low-return countries, thereby driving up the required rate of return there. In this way, they act to bring rates of return across countries more nearly in line with one another.

Second, industry composition is different in different countries. If there are fluctuations in the price of oil and natural gas, for example, a stock market index for Norway will fluctuate relative to Germany. This explains a low correlation across countries, but does not explain an increase in the correlation over time. Indeed, in the case of energy prices, they have certainly been more volatile since 1971 than previously. But an increase in the international integration of goods markets – in the form of reductions in tariffs, non-tariff barriers, and transportation costs – might be able to explain it. An increase in correlation might be explained by arbitrage on the part of consumers, who are now better able to substitute among products of different countries. This is particularly true if one thinks in terms of industries disaggregated into individual commodities, and of the commodities disaggregated into individual brand names. If consumers are better able to substitute between Mercedes and Lexus, then equity holdings in Daimler-Benz and Honda become closer substitutes as a result.

Third, an industry within a given country shares some features with other industries in that country which it does not share with firms in the same industry in other countries. They share the same macroeconomy, and particularly the same currency. Since the Bretton Woods system of exchange rates ended in 1971, exchange rates have become more variable worldwide. Within Europe, however, the pattern is different, as the statistics show.

Table 1 shows that exchange rate variability among pairs of countries worldwide rose sharply in the mid-1970s, and rose further in the 1980s. Of 1,770 pairs of countries, the standard deviation of monthly exchange rate changes was 1.9 percent during 1969-70. (This means that monthly changes as large as 3.8 percent occurred, assuming a log normal distribution of exchange rates, five percent of the time). This measure of variability almost doubled during the period 1974-5, and then doubled again during the period 1989-90. There was a similar variability pattern for the *real* exchange rate (i.e. adjusted for price levels).

Among 11 members of the European Community, on the other hand, bilateral exchange rate variability (that is, *vis-à-vis* each other) *fell* during the 1980s, as Table 1 shows. The standard deviation was 1.8 percent in 1974-5, after the end of the Bretton Woods regime but before the founding of the European Monetary System. It declined to 1.0 percent in 1989-90. Regression estimates can determine the implicit weights placed on major currencies, particularly for

Table 1. Mean Volatility of Monthly Real and Nominal Exchange Rates (Bilateral)

'Entire World' (63 countries)

Year	Real rate	Nominal rate
1965	0.042075	0.028132
1970	0.029120	0.019186
1975	0.044608	0.036175
1980	0.032227	0.031364
1985	0.080961	0.072245
1990	0.069847	0.077298
No. of observations	1081	1770

European Economic Community

	Among members		With the rest-of-the-world	
Year	Real rate	Nominal rate	Real rate	Nominal rate
1965	0.017975	0.0013808	0.033617	0.018203
1970	0.013521	0.0077273	0.023547	0.014857
1975	0.023947	0.0181820	0.039339	0.032903
1980	0.020350	0.0178340	0.032199	0.031967
1985	0.019171	0.0165860	0.064494	0.058641
1990	0.012036	0.0097418	0.055230	0.059050
No. of observations	45	55	370	539

Notes:
1. Volatility is defined as the standard deviation of the first difference of the logs of the monthly exchange rate over the current and preceding years (24 months).
2. To ensure comparability over time, all computations are performed over country pairs that have non-missing values throughout the period 1965-90.

countries such as Sweden and Thailand that have in the past measured their currency values in relation to a basket (whether through loose, informal relationships or by tighter formal pegs). Such tests confirm that the Deutschmark is dominant for European countries, while the dollar is dominant for Pacific countries.[31] The increase in the correlation of equity prices across European countries might be associated with the stronger links among their currencies.

The problem is that the other factors mentioned above are also particularly relevant within Europe. There has been a fairly steady process of reduction

[31] Frankel and Wei (1995).

in barriers to financial integration among European countries since 1973.[32] Trade liberalization has also progressed more rapidly among European countries than between them and the rest of the world.[33] The macroeconomic factors have changed over time as well.

In an important recent paper, Heston and Rouwenhorst (1994) investigated the reasons for differing movements in equity prices across 12 European countries between 1978 and 1992. They tested the role of industrial structure, using disaggregated data on the actual equity returns of individual sectors,[34] and found that industrial structure explains very little of the cross-sectional difference in country return volatility. Low correlation between country indices is, rather, due almost completely to country-specific sources of return variation. This paper is important because it seems to eliminate the second of the three hypotheses listed above.

Macroeconomic disturbances, shared by all the firms within a country but shared much less completely across countries, are the natural explanation for the Heston-Rouwenhorst finding. Currency fluctuations are a major example of such macroeconomic disturbances. Heston and Rouwenhorst conclude that currency fluctuations can explain only a small component of the variation in country-specific return variation – between 1 percent for Sweden and 25 percent for the United Kingdom. But these estimates seem large enough to be interesting. Furthermore in most cases the authors cannot reject the hypothesis that the country effects measured in *local* currency are uncorrelated with the exchange rate movements. This null hypothesis is the same as the proposition that currency-adjusted equity returns vary one-for-one with exchange rate fluctuations.[35]

The greatest difficulty in evaluating whether or not exchange rate volatility causes variation in equity return differentials is the usual difficulty in inferring causality from observed correlation. A great many causal connections are

[32] There are many references documenting this process for Europe. They include: Artis and Taylor (1990), Eijffinger and Lemmen (1994, 1995), Frankel, Phillips, and Chinn (1993), Giavazzi and Spaventa (1990), Grilli (1989), and Wyplosz (1986).

[33] The high level of intra-European trade is not in itself necessarily evidence of the effect of the formation of the European Community or other preferential trade policies; much of this trade can be explained by such natural factors as the proximity and size of the European economies. However a careful gravity-model analysis does show that intra-European trade increased rapidly in the 1980s even after holding constant for these other factors (Frankel and Wei, 1995).

[34] Roll (1992), by contrast, tried to address this problem with aggregate stock market indices, relying on data on the weights of different sectors in various economies.

[35] Given the high levels of volatility in both the equity and foreign-exchange markets, one should not be surprised if the power of tests is low, and one should not conclude too much from the failure to find an effect. But if one finds an effect of exchange rate movements on currency-adjusted returns (even if a small one), and none on local-currency returns, that seems to suggest that exchange rate variability may play an important role in determining international return differentials.

possible, some of which would lead one to expect positive correlations between exchange rates and equity prices, and some negative.[36] It is easy to show that exchange rates and international differentials in stock prices are related. Table 2 shows the results of regressing currency-adjusted movements in relative equity prices against exchange rate changes. If exchange rates were utterly irrelevant to the determination of relative stock prices, there would be no statistical relationship. As it is, the coefficient is always negative, and usually significant at the 99 percent level. But what is the reason for this relationship? One possibility is that the exogenous disturbances involve generalized portfolio shifts among countries' assets. If investors lose confidence in a country's assets, for example, in response to poor prospects for economic growth, this should result in a simultaneous decline in the value of the currency and in the value of its equities, even when expressed in domestic currency.[37] This explanation is consistent with those cases – e.g. Spain in Table 2 – where the coefficient is not only greater than zero in absolute value, but is also greater than one.

The best case in favour of stabilizing exchange rates within Europe would be if floating exchange rates regularly exhibited 'speculative movements' that (1) were unrelated to fundamentals; (2) had real consequences; and (3) were thought likely to disappear under fixed exchange rates or a target zone.[38] The sort of real consequence that an exogenous speculative drop in a currency value might have would be to raise the price competitiveness of the country's firms on world markets, and thereby increase the domestic currency value of the firm's equity, by an amount that is not fully proportionate to the change in the exchange rate. (The case where the change is fully proportionate is where there are no real effects.) The results in Table 2 are not inconsistent with this hypothesis. The trouble, as noted, is that the results are also consistent with a great many other hypotheses.

[36] Roll (1991: 27-28, 38), for example, claims that causality may lead from equity prices to exchange rates as follows: a shock adversely affecting a country's producers causes the monetary authorities to vary the exchange rate in response.

[37] If the exogenous disturbance is a change in the real interest rate, on the other hand, the effect on the value of the domestic currency should be the *opposite* of the effect on equity prices in domestic currency. Another possibility is that exogenous disturbances involve changes in expected inflation, though the effect on nominal equity prices is in this case unclear (depending on various tax and accounting issues, for example).

[38] Williamson (1985) asserts that speculative bubbles would be less likely to develop under target zones. Until recently there has been little basis for such an assertion, other than intuition, but Krugman and Miller (1993) now offer some theoretical support and Rose (1994) some empirical support.

Table 2. The Effects of Exchange Rates on Currency-Adjusted Equity Price Differentials

Country	Partner Country	Constant	Coefficient	D-W	N. Obs.	R^2	Adj. R^2
France	US	.00011	-.8628†	2.25	407	.09	.09
		(.00314)	(.1350)				
France	Germany	.00290	-1.282†	2.27	407	.56	.53
		(.00333)	(0.263)				
Netherlands	US	.00044	-.6144†	1.66	417	.15	.15
		(.00163)	(.0720)				
Netherlands	Germany	.00066	-.8580†	1.83	415	.02	.02
		(.00172)	(.2643)				
Belgium	US	.00234	-.7948†	2.09	420	.15	.15
		(.00210)	(.0924)				
Belgium	Germany	-.00046	-1.024†	2.01	418	.03	.03
		(.00234)	(0.278)				
Denmark	US	.00095	-.8544†	1.92	419	.12	.12
		(.00254)	(.1135)				
Denmark	Germany	.00272	.9430†	1.86	418	.02	.02
		(.00284)	(.2968)				
Luxembourg	US	-.00371	-.8402†	2.21	172	.15	.14
		(.00458)	(.1538)				
Luxembourg	Germany	-.00091	-.8547	2.39	170	.01	.003
		(.00482)	(.6822)				
Italy	US	-.00265	-.84729†	1.54	419	.08	.08
		(.00303)	(.14096)				
Italy	Germany	-.00030	-.9969†	1.71	418	.06	.06
		(.00313)	(.1923)				
Portugal	US	-.00929	-1.062†	1.63	84	.13	.12
		(.00842)	(.3002)				
Portugal	Germany	-.00914	-.4117	1.43	82	.004	-.01
		(.00844)	(.6661)				
Spain	US	.00078	-1.101†	1.88	408	.17	.17
		(.00280)	(.1208)				
Spain	Germany	.00484	-1.255†	1.84	406	.15	.15
		(.00302)	(.1466)				
UK	US	.00143	-0.9766†	1.72	419	.22	.22
		(.00210)	(0.0903)				
UK	Germany	.00397	-1.1330†	1.52	418	.16	.16
		(.00265)	(0.1273)				

Notes:
Regressions are over entire period (1960-95, or where available).
(Standard errors in parentheses.)
Equation 1: parity index = constant + coefficient*(change in log exchange rate).
†denotes significance at the 99% level.
Parity index defined as: $\ln(S_t/S_{t-1}) - \ln(S^*_t/S^*_{t-1}) - \ln(e_t/e_{t-1})$
where: S is the local share price index in local currency
S^* is the US (or German) share price index in dollars (or DM)
e is the local currency per dollar (or DM)
and the time period is monthly.

(Continued)

Change in log exchange rate defined as $\ln(e_t/e_{t-1})$ where data is monthly and e is local currency units per dollar (or DM).
All data from IFS (both CD and print versions) and all series from January 1960 to January 1995 except where noted. Data are monthly averages of local share index.
Netherlands: Missing observations for April and May 1993.
Denmark: 'Break in homogeneity' at January 1973 and January 1983. Series from OECD data.
Portugal: Series begins January 1988.
France: Series ends December 1993.
Luxembourg: Series begins January 1980. Observations for April-October 1993 missing.
Germany: Series ends November 1994.
Italy: Series ends December 1994.
UK: Series ends December 1994.
Spain: Series begins January 1961.

6. HOW CAN WE TELL IF THE CORRELATION BETWEEN CURRENCY VARIABILITY AND EQUITY PRICE VARIABILITY IS CAUSAL?

We noted earlier that equity prices have become more highly correlated among European countries, over the same period of time that policy-makers have sought to stabilize the value of European currencies against one another through the Exchange Rate Mechanism and other measures. But the case of European integration is clearly an instance of the causality problem. A high degree of economic integration between two countries is likely to show up both in the form of links between their equity prices and links between their currencies. How are we to know that the greater degree of intra-European exchange rate stability under the European Monetary System, by comparison with the years 1971-9, contributed to a higher correlation among equity prices in a causal sense? Could it not be that a higher degree of political and economic integration overall (e.g. integration of goods markets through removal of trade restrictions) raised both the currency correlation and the equity price correlation?

The evolution of European monetary arrangements over the past few decades offers some natural experiments for getting a handle on the question of a causal relationship between exchange rate variability and equity markets. There is an analogy here with some very interesting tests of the causal relationship between nominal exchange rate variability and real exchange rate variability. Many economists have observed that nominal and real exchange rate movements tend to be highly correlated. The usual interpretation is that goods prices are 'sticky' in domestic currency, so that nominal exchange rate changes cause real exchange rate changes. It might follow that if nominal exchange rate variability could be suppressed under a fixed-rate regime, real variability could be suppressed as well. Sceptics, however, have argued that real exchange rate variability is caused by real shocks (e.g. changes in productivity or in consumer demand patterns), and that these shocks will show up either under a regime of fixed exchange rates (as fluctuations in price levels) or under a regime of floating rates (as fluctuations in the exchange rate). Statistical analyses such as those undertaken by Mussa (1990), comparing across regimes, convincingly refute the sceptics.

Mussa demonstrated that nominal and real exchange rate volatility are both substantially lower during regimes of fixed rates and higher during regimes of flexible exchange rates. Persuasive examples include the Canadian experiment with floating in the 1950s, and changes in Ireland's exchange rate regime from a pound to a Deutschmark peg. Eichengreen (1988) provides similar evidence from the interwar period. In every case, exogenous exchange rate variation appears to have effects on variation in currency-adjusted relative goods prices.

Here we propose an analogous experiment for equity prices. To be sure, equity prices are determined in markets that come far closer to satisfying the classical market paradigm than do the prices of most goods and services. Equities in a given company are homogeneous, non-perishable, and traded in relatively competitive markets with freely determined prices. Nevertheless, we are willing to consider a number of hypotheses under which equity prices might appear to be slightly sticky in their home-country currency, in the sense that exogenous exchange rate fluctuations might have an effect on currency-adjusted changes in relative equity prices. In the first place, if goods prices are sticky in domestic currency, it is reasonable to suppose that the prices of capital equipment dedicated to producing these same goods might behave similarly. In the second place, institutional details of accounting and taxes might work to tie equity prices to the domestic currency. Third, as noted in section 4, there may be an investor-clientele effect (equities are known to be held disproportionately by domestic residents) that ties their prices to prices of other same-country assets.

7. A NATURAL EXPERIMENT: THE CASE OF IRELAND

The cleanest experiment is offered by the case of Ireland, because it has experienced a number of clear-cut changes in regime *vis-à-vis* major currencies, the effects of which are not likely to be confused with the effects of gradually increasing economic integration. Table 3 reports the statistics.

The first regime change occurred in 1971 with the break-up of the Bretton Woods system, when the link between the Irish pound and the dollar was broken (along with other currencies, of course). The first line of Table 3(c) reports how much the variance of the Irish exchange rate against the dollar went up subsequently, and Table 3(d) shows the same thing in terms of the variance of the *change* in the exchange rate. (Our discussion will henceforth focus on the variability of first differences, rather than levels, in part because of non-stationarity concerns.) If

Table 3. The Case of Ireland: Currency Links and Equity Links to Major Partners under Various Currency Regimes

(a) Correlation of Log Irish Share Price with Log Foreign Share Price

Country	Jan. 1960- Dec. 1970	March 1973- Feb. 1979	April 1979- Oct. 1990	Nov. 1990- August 1992	Sept. 1992- Jan. 1995
US	.90	.50	.96	.61	.85
UK	.84	.87	.94	.80	.90
Germany	.17	.68	.92	.74	.91

Notes:
Equation: correlation In(Irish share price) & ln(foreign share price).
Each country's share price measured in domestic currency. Monthly average observations.

(b) Correlation of Changes in Log Irish Share Price with Changes in Log Foreign Share Price

Country	Jan. 1960- Dec. 1970	March 1973- Feb. 1979	April 1979- Oct. 1990	Nov. 1990- August 1992	Sept. 1992- Jan. 1995
US	.07	.34	.32	.20	.08
UK	.26	.61	.47	.54	.14
Germany	.07	.29	.44	.38	.27

Notes:
Equation: correlation [ln(Irish share price)$_t$-ln(Irish share price)$_{t-1}$] & [ln(foreign share price)$_t$-ln(foreign share price)$_{t-1}$].
Each country's share price measured in domestic currency. Monthly average observations.

(c) Variance of Log Irish Punt per Foreign Currency

Exchange Rate	Jan. 1960- Dec. 1970	March 1973- Feb. 1979	April 1979- Oct. 1990	Nov. 1990- August 1992	Sept. 1992- Jan. 1995
Punts/$	.005	.019	.042	.003844	.004764
Punts/£	.000	.000	.004	.000159	.001681
Punts/DM	.008	.041	.017	.000005	.001376

Notes:
Equation: variance ln(punts/foreign currency).
Monthly average observations (IFS series rf or rh).

(d) Variance of Change in Log Irish Punts per Foreign Currency

Exchange Rate	Jan. 1960- Dec. 1970	March 1973- Feb. 1979	April 1979- Oct. 1990	Nov. 1990- August 1992	Sept. 1992- Jan. 1995
Punts/$	.00018	.00043	.00079	.00104	.000843
Punts/£	.00000	.00000	.00044	.000008	.000496
Punts/DM	.00026	.00064	.00012	.000004	.000353

Notes:
Equation: variance [ln(punts/foreign currency)$_t$-ln(punts/foreign currency)$_{t-1}$].
Monthly average observations (IFS series rf or rh).

(e) Variance of Change in Log Share Parity Condition (variances multiplied by 1000)

Partner Country	Jan. 1960- Dec. 1970	March 1973- Feb. 1979	April 1979- Oct. 1990	Nov. 1990- August 1992	Sept. 1992- Jan. 1995
US	1.86	5.44	4.32	4.58	3.500
UK	1.49	4.20	4.10	3.54	2.486
Germany	3.46	5.38	4.05	4.45	3.511

Notes:
Equation: variance [ln(Irish share price$_t$/Irish share price$_{t-1}$)-ln(partner share price$_t$/partner share price$_{t-1}$)-(ln(punts/foreign currency)$_t$-ln(punts/foreign currency)$_{t-1}$)].
Monthly average observations.

(f) Correlation of Change in Log Share Prices (accounting for exchange rate effects)

Partner Country	Jan. 1960- Dec. 1970	March 1973- Feb. 1979	April 1979- Oct. 1990	Nov. 1990- August 1992	Sept. 1992- Jan. 1995
US	.03	.34	.30	.18	.05
UK	.26	.61	.42	.49	.29
Germany	.04	.32	.43	.38	.21

Notes:
Equation: correlation [ln(Irish share price$_t$/Irish share price$_{t-1}$)-(ln(punts/foreign currency)$_t$-ln(punts/foreign currency)$_{t-1}$)] & ln(partner share price$_t$/partner share price$_{t-1}$).
Monthly average observations.

Key dates:
January 1960 - Beginning of OECD data
March 1979 - Beginning of EMS

Sources: All data are from IFS (both print and CD-ROM versions) except Irish share prices which come from OECD Main Economic Indicators (both monthly and historical statistics supplement).

exchange rate variability were irrelevant, then there should be no effect on the variation in Irish equity prices (currency-adjusted) relative to US equity prices. Yet the first line of Table 3(e) shows that the variance of the price differential (Irish equities relative to US, exchange rate adjusted) increased after 1970 as well.

One must remember that the world became a more volatile place in the 1970s (e.g. as a result of oil price shocks). Other measures of real variability went up as well, including share price *vis-à-vis* the United Kingdom despite the fact that Ireland remained pegged to the pound in the 1970s. So this first experiment is not a particularly convincing one.

The second columns of Tables 3(c) and 3(d) show that Irish pound exchange rate variability *vis-à-vis* the British pound remained at zero during the 1970s, while the variability *vis-à-vis* the dollar and mark were sharply higher. The corresponding second column of Table 3(e) shows that the variance of the Irish equity price differential *vis-à-vis* UK equities remained lower than the equivalent variabilities *vis-à-vis* US and German equities. The second column of Table 3(f) shows the same thing with a different statistic: the correlation of Irish equity prices with UK equity prices in the 1970s remained higher than the correlations with German equity prices. These statistics are consistent with the hypothesis that the Irish currency link with Britain fostered a link between the Dublin and London equity markets. The statistics, however, are also consistent with the hypothesis that the Irish economy is integrated more closely with the British economy than with the US or German economies.

The evidence starts to become convincing with the second regime change, at the time of the formation of the European Exchange Rate Mechanism in 1979. Ireland jumped ship, abandoning its peg to the United Kingdom and instead tying its currency (now called the punt) to the ERM. Table 3(d) shows, as one would expect, that the variability of the punt/pound exchange rate rose sharply in the 1980s (from zero previously), while the variability of the punt/DM rate fell sharply (not to zero, under the terms of the ERM, but to a level much lower than the variance of the punt/pound rate). The third columns of Tables 3(e) and 3(f) show that *Irish equity prices in the 1980s became more highly correlated with German equity prices than with British equity prices.* This experiment is fairly convincing, because of the sharp contrast with the 1970s: the switch in equity market links neatly follows the switch in currency links. Ireland may have experienced a bit of financial market opening during this period.[39] But this would not explain closer finan-

[39] Ireland was one of several countries that was given an extension on the 1990 deadline for full capital market liberalization agreed to by most members of the European Community. Tests of interest parity conditions in the money market show some possible signs of liberalization in Ireland during the 1980s, but much less than most other European countries: Eijffinger and Lemmen (1994, 1995), Frankel (1991), and Frankel, Phillips, and Chinn (1993).

cial integration to Germany than to Britain. The same applies to any consequences of goods market integration under the European Community. We thus have one piece of evidence that currency links may help foster equity market links.

The next regime change occurred in October 1990, when Britain joined the ERM as well (albeit with wide bands, at +/- 6 percent). This regime lasted until the ERM crisis of September 1992, when Britain was forced to drop out of the arrangement. During the period November 1990-August 1992, variability in the punt/pound exchange rate was sharply lower than during the period April 1979-October 1990, as a comparison of columns 3 and 4 in Table 3(d) shows. What pattern do the equity prices show? Comparing the analogous entries in Table 3(e), the variability of the equity price differential *vis-à-vis* Britain fell (relative to the 1980s, and also relative to the differentials *vis-à-vis* the United States and Germany, presumably reflecting the fact that the Irish economy is indeed more closely linked to the British economy). Comparing the analogous entries in Table 3(f) gives the same answer: Irish equity prices became more highly correlated with British equity prices while the pound was in the ERM. This constitutes a second clear data point in support of the hypothesis that currency links are causally related to equity market links.[40]

Another way of stating the hypothesis that exchange rate variability affects relative equity prices (currency-adjusted) is that relative *nominal* equity prices do not adjust to offset exchange rate fluctuations fully. We have used the word 'sticky' to describe this hypothesis. An extreme form of the hypothesis would be that relative nominal equity prices do not adjust to offset exchange rate fluctuations *at all*. It would be quite surprising if this extreme proposition were true. Even in a 'sticky-price' view of the world, an exogenous depreciation increases a firm's nominal value by raising the domestic-currency value of its overseas earnings and by increasing the price competitiveness of its domestic output on world markets. Nevertheless, simple regressions in Table 4 of European local-currency equity prices against the prices of foreign currency show coefficients that are seldom positive, and sometimes negative for some countries. This probably reflects the common effect that adverse economic news has on a country's equities and currency at the same time, rather than the exogenous effect of an exchange rate change. It is worth testing the form of the hypothesis in the context of clear-cut regime changes.

[40] The final regime one might wish to consider is September 1992-January 1995, when the pound had dropped out of the ERM, and the punt/pound exchange rate became more variable, as in the 1970s. The second row of Table 3(f) shows that the UK equity prices became more correlated with Irish prices (currency-adjusted) during this period, which tends to support the hypothesis. The variance criterion in Table 3(e), however, shows the reverse.

Table 4. The Effects of Exchange Rates on Local Equity Prices

Country	Partner Country	Constant	Coefficient	D-W	N. Obs.	R^2	Adj. R^2
France	US	.00543†	.0956	2.15	407	.001	-.001
		(.00323)	(.1388)				
France	Germany	.00620†	-.2782	2.16	407	.003	.0004
		(.00330)	(.2602)				
Netherlands	US	.00475*	-.3595**	1.32	417	.04	.04
		(.00192)	(.0846)				
Netherlands	Germany	.00394*	.2554	1.34	417	.002	-.001
		(.00196)	(.3009)				
Belgium	US	.00282	-.1813†	1.91	420	.01	.01
		(.00211)	(.0930)				
Belgium	Germany	-.00252	.0873	1.92	420	.0003	-.002
		(.00214)	(.2551)				
Denmark	US	.00610**	-.1178	1.76	419	.004	.001
		(.00213)	(.0953)				
Denmark	Germany	.00595**	.0585	1.74	419	.0002	-.002
		(.00219)	(.2284)				
Luxembourg	US	-.00472	-.2169	2.01	172	.01	.01
		(.00442)	(.1482)				
Luxembourg	Germany	-.00450	.2430	1.99	172	.001	-.01
		(.00451)	(.6471)				
Italy	US	.00260	.1137	1.49	419	.002	-.001
		(.00301)	(.1401)				
Italy	Germany	.00342	-.1189	1.49	419	.001	-.001
		(.00312)	(.1921)				
Portugal	US	-.00185	.0933	1.41	84	.001	-.01
		(.00817)	(.2913)				
Portugal	Germany	-.00173	.0173	1.40	84	.0001	-.01
		(.00837)	(.6673)				
Spain	US	.00601*	-.0605	1.68	408	.001	-.002
		(.00271)	(.1169)				
Spain	Germany	.00696	-.2413*	1.70	408	.01	.01
		(.00276)	(.1339)				
UK	US	.00659**	.0244	1.35	419	.0001	-.002
		(.00238)	(.1022)				
UK	Germany	.00750	-.2331*	1.34	419	.01	.01
		(.00240)	(.1154)				

Notes:

Equation 2: change in log share price = constant + coefficient*(change in log exchange rate).

† (*) [**] denotes significance at the 90% (95%) [99%] level.

R-squared is quite low. In only one of the regressions is it above .02, and then it is .04.

Change in log share price defined as $\ln((\text{share price country a})_t/(\text{share price country a})_{t-1})$ where share price is measured in local currency.

Change in log exchange rate defined as $\ln(e_t/e_{t-1})$ where data is monthly and e is local currency units per dollar (or DM).

All data from IFS (both CD and print versions) and all series from January 1960 to January 1995 except where noted. Data are monthly averages of local share index.

Netherlands: Missing observations for April and May 1993.

Denmark: 'Break in homogeneity' at January 1973 and January 1983. Series from OECD data. (Continued)

Portugal: Series begins January 1988.
France: Series ends December 1993.
Luxembourg: Series begins January 1980. Observations for April-October 1993 missing.
Germany: Series ends November 1994.
Italy: Series ends December 1994.
UK: Series ends December 1994.
Spain: Series begins January 1961.

Table 3(b) reports statistics on the correlations of Irish nominal equity prices with those in the three major foreign countries. In the case of each of the five experiments described above, the sign of the comparison of nominal equity price correlations is the same as the sign of the currency-adjusted equity correlations discussed above. When the United Kingdom joined the ERM in 1990, for example, local Irish equity prices (in punts) once again became more highly correlated with local UK equity prices than with US or German equity prices: there is no longer a major exchange rate barrier intervening between Ireland and Britain. Thus the extreme form of the hypothesis does not hold. (Table 5 computes the correlations of nominal equity prices for the cases of other Euorpean Community members. The conclusions are similar to the Irish case.) Table 3(b) is no reason to discount the earlier evidence that the exchange rate regime has real implications for equity markets. It suggests that the equity markets have some ability to pierce the currency veil, not that they see through the veil as if it were not there.

8. THE EXPERIMENT FOR OTHER EUROPEAN COMMUNITY MEMBERS

The Irish case offers some persuasive bits of evidence. But in the absence of any formal hypothesis-testing, one would like to have more evidence. We now consider regime changes for a broader set of European countries.

With the break-up of the Bretton Woods system, the currencies of France, the Netherlands, Belgium, and Denmark all experienced an increase in exchange rate variability *vis-à-vis* the dollar. Variability *vis-à-vis* the dollar rose above the level of variability *vis-à-vis* the DM, to which they were tied (intermittently in some cases) under the Snake arrangement that lasted until 1979. (The same was true of Luxembourg and Portugal, but we lack the equity market data for the 1960s to conduct the experiment for them.) The variances are reported in Table 6. Variances of changes in the exchange rates are reported in Table 7. In the cases of each of these four north European countries, the variability of their stock prices (currency-adjusted) *vis-à-vis* the United States also increased, while the variabil-

Table 5. Correlation of Changes in Log Share Price

	Before formation of the ERM				During existence of ERM (with narrow margins)										After crisis of ERM	
	Jan. 1960 to Dec. 1970		Mar. 1973 to Mar. 1979		Mar. 1979 to Mar. 1986		Mar. 1979 to Dec. 1986		Jan. 1987 to Aug.1992		Before country joined ERM[1]		After country joined ERM[2]		Sept. 1992 to Jan. 1995	
Country	US	Germany	US	Germany	US	Germany	US	Germany	US	Germany	US	Germany	US	Germany	US	Germany
France	.29	.34	.21	.23	.39	.19	.34	.19	.69	.75					.19	.15
Netherlands	.65	.55	.55	.74	.49	.63	.50	.56	.74	.83					.08	.71
Belgium	.38	.29	.49	.37	.31	.31	.29	.30	.65	.72					.003	.67
Denmark	-.04	.02	.11	.20	.19	.09	.20	.17	.38	.37					.02	.22
Luxembourg					.09	.36	.12	.41	.44	.18					.26	.60
Italy	.17	.38	.32	.24									.34	.43	.17	.37
Portugal											.34	.30	.09	.61	-.02	.31
Spain	.06	.08	.26	.25							.33	.22	.58	.34	.22	.47
UK	.42	.23	.61	.41							.58	.45	.62	.68	.13	.30

Notes:

[1] Dates are: Portugal: January 1988 to April 1992; Spain: March 1979 to June 1989; UK: March 1979 to October 1990.

[2] Dates are: Italy: March 1979 to August 1992; Portugal: April 1992 to August 1992; Spain: June 1989 to August 1992; UK: October 1990 to August 1992.

Equation is: correlation [ln((share price country a)$_t$/(share price country a)$_{t-1}$)] & [ln((share price country b)$_t$/(share price country b)$_{t-1}$)].

All data from IFS (both CD and print versions) and all series date from January 1960 to January 1995 except where noted. Data are monthly averages of local share index.

Germany, France, Netherlands, Belgium, Denmark, Luxembourg, Italy, and Ireland were members of the ERM from its inception to at least its *de facto* collapse in 1992.

Netherlands: Missing observations for April and May 1993.
Portugal: Series begins January 1988.
Germany: Series ends November 1994.
UK: Series ends December 1994.
Denmark: 'Break in homogeneity' at January 1973 and January 1983. Series from OECD data.
France: Series ends December 1993.
Italy: Series ends December 1994.
Spain: Series begins January 1961.
Luxembourg: Series begins January 1980. Observations for April-October 1993 missing.

Table 6. Variation of Log Level Exchange Rate*

	Before formation of the ERM				During existence of ERM (with narrow margins)										After crisis of ERM	
	Jan. 1960 to Dec. 1970		Mar. 1973 to Mar. 1979		Mar. 1979 to Mar. 1986		Mar. 1979 to Dec. 1986		Jan. 1987 to Aug.1992		Before country joined ERM[1]		After country joined ERM[2]		Sept. 1992 to Jan. 1995	
Country	US	Germany	US	Germany	US	Germany	US	Germany	US	Germany	US	Germany	US	Germany	US	Germany
France	1.57	4.75	3.95	12.3	87.2	14.8	79.3	16.3	5.69	.056					2.42	.117
Netherlands	.225	.754	9.56	4.08	37.4	.189	34.8	.191	5.85	.003					2.22	.003
Belgium	.000	1.08	8.60	.661	77.4	11.0	70.1	11.2	6.62	.065					2.94	.238
Denmark	1.38	3.82	3.06	5.07	66.3	6.99	60.1	7.39	5.95	.085					2.80	.300
Luxembourg	.000	1.08	8.60	.661	77.4	11.0	70.1	11.2	6.62	.065					2.94	.238
Italy	.001	1.10	25.4	56.9									51.7	29.9	6.71	3.48
Portugal	.000	1.08	59.3	115							187	212	2.39	.256	.738	3.41
Spain	4.91	8.54	18.0	48.5							88.5	48.0	6.44	.175	8.93	4.87
UK	4.83	8.47	18.5	41.0							33.3	24.8	3.22	.199	2.26	.729

Notes:

*All variances multiplied by 1000 for readability.

[1] Dates are: Portugal: January 1988 to April 1992; Spain: March 1979 to June 1989; UK: March 1979 to October 1990.

[2] Dates are: Italy: March 1979 to August 1992; Portugal: April 1992 to August 1992; Spain: June 1989 to August 1992; UK: October 1990 to August 1992.

Equation: variance [ln(national currency/$ or DM)].

All data from IFS (both CD and print versions) and all series date from January 1960 to January 1995. Data are monthly averages (IFS series rf or rh).

Table 7. Variance of Changes in Log Exchange Rates*

	Before formation of the ERM				During existence of ERM (with narrow margins)										After crisis of ERM	
	Jan. 1960 to Dec. 1970		Mar. 1973 to Mar. 1979		Mar. 1979 to Mar. 1986		Mar. 1979 to Dec. 1986		Jan. 1987 to Aug.1992		Before country joined ERM[1]		After country joined ERM[2]		Sept. 1992 to Jan. 1995	
Country	US	Germany	US	Germany	US	Germany	US	Germany	US	Germany	US	Germany	US	Germany	US	Germany
France	.106	.182	.643	.339	.959	.075	.914	.077	.777	.017					.612	.054
Netherlands	.018	.061	.638	.104	.904	.016	.870	.014	.876	.001					.634	.002
Belgium	.000	.078	.629	.075	.944	.082	.900	.076	.863	.004					.656	.097
Denmark	.052	.128	.600	.103	.867	.061	.832	.056	.853	.013					.634	.140
Luxembourg	.000	.078	.629	.075	.944	.082	.900	.076	.863	.004					.656	.097
Italy	.000	.078	.488	.729									.731	.064	1.12	.663
Portugal	.000	.078	.930	.552							.740	.221	.201	.352	.881	.268
Spain	.181	.257	.621	1.10							.626	.276	.836	.089	1.12	.351
UK	.181	.257	.434	.640							.834	.499	.839	.104	1.14	.613

Notes:

*All variances multiplied by 1000 for readability.

[1] Dates are: Portugal: March 1979 to April 1992; Spain: March 1979 to June 1989; UK: March 1979 to October 1990.

[2] Dates are: Italy: March 1979 to August 1992; Portugal: April 1992 to August 1992; Spain: June 1989 to August 1992; UK: October 1990 to August 1992.

All data from IFS (both print and CD versions).

One data point is the average exchange rate over one month (IFS series rf or rh).

Germany, France, Netherlands, Belgium, Denmark, Luxembourg, Italy, and Ireland were members of the ERM from its inception to at least its *de facto* collapse in 1992.

Equation: variance $[\ln(\text{national currency}/\$(\text{or DM}))_t - \ln(\text{national currency}/\$(\text{or DM}))_{t-1})$.

ity *vis-à-vis* Germany either fell or, in the case of France, rose by less than *vis-à-vis* the United States. The variances of the currency-adjusted equity prices are reported in Table 8. Here is another data point in favour of the hypothesis that currency regimes matter.[41]

The second regime change was the shift from the Snake to the Exchange Rate Mechanism. Tables 6 and 7 show that for each of the four northern European countries, exchange rate variability *vis-à-vis* the dollar rose after 1979, relative to variability *vis-à-vis* the mark. In the cases of the Netherlands and Belgium, the variance of equity price differentials increased more *vis-à-vis* the United States than *vis-à-vis* Germany, which tends to support the hypothesis. In the cases of France and Denmark, the results are less supportive.

The third regime change, after 1986, was not a formal one. But it has been widely noted that there were far fewer realignments from 1986 to 1992 than during the first seven years of the ERM's existence. Giavazzi and Spaventa (1990) called this period a 'new' EMS. Tables 6 and 7 show that exchange rate variability for the four north European countries fell further *vis-à-vis* the mark; variability in three cases also fell *vis-à-vis* the dollar during this period, but by to a smaller degree. Table 9 reports another measure of the equity market links to the United States and Germany: the correlation coefficient (currency-adjusted). If we use the correlation criterion, we see that in each of the four countries, the link with German equity markets increased from the first period to the second, to levels higher than the links with American equity markets, again supporting the hypothesis. If we use the variance criterion of Table 8, the results are more ambiguous. (The variability in the differential *vis-à-vis* Germany is down in three out of four cases, but only in the case of France is it down by more than the variability *vis-à-vis* the United States.)

Another experiment is offered by three countries that joined the ERM late: the United Kingdom, Portugal, and Spain. The British case clearly supports the hypothesis: the variance in the equity price differential *vis-à-vis* Germany fell during the period October 1990- August 1992, relative to the period March 1979-October 1990, and it fell by more than the variance *vis-à-vis* the United States. The correlation criterion shows the same thing: British stocks became more highly correlated with German stocks (and less correlated with US stocks). Portugal shows the same strengthened link with the German equity market.[42] The case of

[41] Bartov, Bodnar, and Kaul (1994) find that the switch to variable exchange rates after the breakdown of the Bretton Woods system raised the monthly variability of equity returns on US multinational companies.

[42] In the case of Portugal, there are only five months between the date it joined the ERM and the September 1992 crisis. During this short period, changes in the escudo/mark rate actually became more variable, though the *level* of the escudo/mark rate became less variable, as expected. We should probably ignore the Portuguese case, owing to the small sample size.

Table 8. Variance of Changes in Bilateral Share Parity*

Country	Before formation of the ERM				During existence of ERM (with narrow margins)										After crisis of ERM	
	Jan. 1960 to Dec. 1970		Mar. 1973 to Mar. 1979		Mar. 1979 to Mar. 1986		Mar. 1979 to Dec. 1986		Jan. 1987 to Aug.1992		Before country joined ERM[1]		After country joined ERM[2]		Sept. 1992 to Jan. 1995	
	US	Germany	US	Germany	US	Germany	US	Germany	US	Germany	US	Germany	US	Germany	US	Germany
France	2.17	3.22	7.81	7.31	5.44	5.48	5.50	5.42	1.85	1.56					15.7	16.7
Netherlands	.928	1.99	1.96	.801	4.71	.893	1.37	1.08	.882	.987					2.06	.665
Belgium	1.12	2.63	2.55	2.56	3.48	2.74	3.61	2.85	1.78	1.64					3.02	1.08
Denmark	2.32	3.82	3.28	2.36	3.68	3.64	3.57	3.53	3.57	3.17					3.19	2.38
Luxembourg					4.84	3.01	4.61	2.79	4.00	5.81					3.70	1.65
Italy	2.92	3.27	5.59	5.48									4.65	4.12	5.49	4.56
Portugal											4.63	4.55	.925	.392	10.6	7.23
Spain	1.98	3.09	4.88	4.79							5.47	5.79	3.54	3.96	2.42	1.16
UK	1.64	3.38	4.97	5.99							2.07	3.16	1.35	1.27	13.6	14.1

Notes:

*All variances multiplied by 1000 for readability.

[1] Dates are: Portugal: January 1988 to April 1992; Spain: March 1979 to June 1989; UK: March 1979 to October 1990.

[2] Dates are: Italy: March 1979 to August 1992; Portugal: April 1992 to August 1992; Spain: June 1989 to August 1992; UK: October 1990 to August 1992.

Equation: variance [ln((share price local)$_t$/(share price local)$_{t-1}$) - ln((share price US(or Germany))$_t$/(share price US(or Germany))$_{t-1}$) - (ln(national currency/\$(or DM))$_t$- ln(national currency/\$(or DM))$_{t-1}$)]

All data from IFS (both CD and print versions) and all series date from January 1960 to January 1995 except where noted. Data are monthly averages of local share index.

Netherlands: Missing observations for April and May 1993.
Portugal: Series begins January 1988.
Germany: Series ends November 1994.
UK: Series ends December 1994.
Luxembourg: Series begins January 1980. Observations for April-October 1993 missing.

Denmark: 'Break in homogeneity' at January 1973 and January 1983. Series from OECD data.
France: Series ends December 1993.
Italy: Series ends December 1994.
Spain: Series begins January 1961.

Table 9. Correlation of Changes in Log Share Indices (Measured in Common Currency)

	Before formation of the ERM				During existence of ERM (with narrow margins)										After crisis of ERM	
	Jan. 1960 to Dec. 1970		Mar. 1973 to Mar. 1979		Mar. 1979 to Mar. 1986		Mar. 1979 to Dec. 1986		Jan. 1987 to Aug.1992		Before country joined ERM[1]		After country joined ERM[2]		Sept. 1992 to Jan. 1995	
Country	US	Germany	US	Germany	US	Germany	US	Germany	US	Germany	US	Germany	US	Germany	US	Germany
France	.29	.32	.26	.22	.40	.18	.37	.18	.61	.76					.17	.14
Netherlands	.65	.54	.56	.75	.54	.61	.53	.55	.73	.82					.01	.71
Belgium	.38	.28	.53	.38	.37	.30	.32	.30	.55	.72					-.15	.60
Denmark	-.06	.004	.22	.20	.27	.11	.26	.19	.19	.38					-.08	.18
Luxembourg					.17	.36	.18	.41	.33	.19					.12	.60
Italy	.17	.36	.33	.21									.33	.44	.10	.40
Portugal											.27	.31	.13	.88	-.08	.33
Spain	.10	.001	.21	.20							.29	.21	.49	.48	.13	.55
UK	.36	.20	.58	.42							.52	.37	.50	.65	-.01	.51

Notes: see Table 8.

Equation: correlation [ln((share price local)$_t$/(share price local)$_{t-1}$) - (ln(national currency/\$(or DM))$_t$- ln(national currency/\$(or DM))$_{t-1}$] & ln[(share price US(or Germany))$_t$/(share price US(or Germany))$_{t-1}$].

Spain is ambiguous in that the two variances are both down by about the same amount. The correlation criterion is more supportive: the correlation with German equity prices more than doubled after Spain joined the ERM in June 1989.

Other comparisons are possible, and not all of them support the hypothesis. In particular, the post-1992 period of increased exchange rate variability features a mixed pattern of equity market variances. It bears repeating, moreover, that none of these statistics constitutes a formal hypothesis test. Nevertheless, the weight of this evidence seems to support the proposition that exchange rate variability has real implications for equity markets, even when the changes in exchange rate variability are the exogenous result of regime shifts.

9. SUMMARY OF FINDINGS REGARDING THE INTEGRATION OF EQUITY MARKETS

We have seen that the existence of fluctuating currencies need not be as large an obstacle to integration of equity markets within a region as might at first appear. Investors can hedge exchange risk on the forward exchange market, at a relatively small cost.

Nevertheless the extreme neutrality view held by some finance theorists, that the exchange rate regime is irrelevant to equity markets, does not accord with the facts. Evidence of currency myopia or related institutional rigidities was offered in section 4, in the form of such examples as the home-country bias puzzle in portfolio holdings, the reaction to FASB 8 by US corporations in 1976, and the effect of exchange rate changes on country-fund discounts and premiums. Section 5 documented the evidence that return differentials between countries' equity markets appear to be correlated with bilateral exchange rate variability. This result could easily be attributable to the fact that foreign-exchange prices are endogenous as much as equity prices; that is, that both markets are affected by third factors. For this reason, it is important that a statistical test try to isolate an exogenous component of exchange rate variability. Sections 6-8 did so by examining statistically the patterns of international equity market correlations under different exchange rate regimes. When Ireland switched from a pound peg to the ERM, the increase in punt/pound variability and decrease in punt/DM variability were exogenous. Yet Irish equity prices became more closely linked with German equity prices. In short, currency regimes do matter.

What does all this mean for the European Union? If the goal is to integrate European equity markets, stabilizing bilateral exchange rates would help, and going to a common currency would help still more. In the absence of such steps, the volume and pattern of cross-border equity investment in Europe may be further from the optimum than they need be.

It is obviously very difficult to quantify the likely effects of currency union on equity markets. Steil (1993:9) says, 'A single European currency is essential for a truly unified [equity] market', while admitting that the political support for European Monetary Union may not be strong enough to bring it off in the near future. The obstacles to EMU are great, as the principle of the Impossible Trinity and the experience of the 1992 crisis show. The pros and cons involved go far into weighty issues of macroeconomics, politics, and history. Few would claim that the desirability of integrating equity markets in itself constitutes a good reason for undertaking a monetary union that would not otherwise be attempted.

Clearly, further integration of equity markets is possible even under current conditions. It would help if forward and futures markets were more highly developed; that is, going out to longer horizons, and dealing more widely in direct European cross-rates, rather than using the dollar as a vehicle currency. It would also help to eliminate needless restrictions in some countries that prohibit some institutional investors, such as life insurance companies, from holding foreign-currency assets despite the gains that diversification would bring to their portfolios (see Chapter 5).

10. IS EUROPE READY FOR MONETARY UNION?

The plans for eventual European Monetary Union agreed upon at Maastricht in 1991 ran into serious difficulty in the crises of 1992 and 1993. Since then, the membership of the European Community has expanded into an even larger European Union, with the accession of Austria, Finland, and Sweden. Is this too large or diverse a collection of countries to constitute an optimum currency area?

The theory of optimum currency areas indicates a number of economic criteria, generally falling under the rubric of the degree of economic integration. Regional units are more likely to benefit, on balance, from joining together to form a monetary union if: (1) they trade a lot with each other; (2) there is a high degree of labour mobility among them; (3) the economic shocks they face are highly correlated; and (4) there exists a federal fiscal system to transfer funds to regions that suffer adverse shocks.[43]

[43] A fifth criterion is more political than economic: that there be enough political congruence across the area for residents of different countries to put similar weights on reducing inflation versus unemployment, or to be willing to sacrifice their optimum macroeconomic choice for the sake of area-wide solidarity.

Each of these economic criteria can be quantified, but it is very difficult to know what is the critical level of integration at which the advantages of belonging to a currency area outweigh the disadvantages. The states of the USA constitute a possible standard of comparison. It seems quite clear that the degree of openness of the states, and the degree of economic integration among them, are sufficiently high to justify their use of a common currency. How do the members of the European Union compare with the states in this regard? US states are more open than European countries, by both the trade and labour mobility criteria. It appears that when an adverse shock hits a particular region of the US, such as New England or the oil states of the South, out-migration of workers is the most important mechanism whereby unemployment rates and wages are eventually re-equilibrated across regions.[44] Labour mobility among (and even within) European countries is much lower than in the United States.

The other two criteria are also better satisfied within the United States than within Europe. Disturbances across US regions have a relatively high correlation, by comparison with that among members of the European Union.[45] When disparities in income do arise in the United States, federal fiscal policy helps to narrow them. Estimates suggest that when a region's per capita income falls by one dollar, the final reduction in its disposable income is only 60 cents. The difference consists of an automatic decrease in federal tax receipts of 34 cents plus an automatic increase in unemployment compensation and other transfers of 6 cents. Neither the fiscal transfer mechanisms that are already in place within the European Union nor those that are contemplated under EMU (so-called 'cohesion funds') are as large as those in the US federal fiscal system.[46] It should be emphasized, however, that the benefits of further centralizing redistributional powers in Europe cannot be assumed to outweigh the costs. Large-scale transfers to less well performing regions will tend to reinforce maladaptive economic policies, rather than encouraging timely and effective change.[47] This is especially true of the costly and distortionary Common Agricultural Policy.

By standard optimum currency area criteria, then, the European Union is not as good a candidate for a monetary union as the United States. This helps account for the troubles that the Maastricht plan has encountered.

[44] Blanchard and Katz (1992).

[45] Bayoumi and Eichengreen (1993). An analysis of which countries would stand to gain or lose the most from subordinating their economies to a single European monetary policy, in light of such correlations, is offered by Alesina and Grilli (1992).

[46] Sala-i-Martin and Sachs (1992).

[47] See Migué (1993).

All is not lost however. In the first place, some north European countries probably do meet the criteria. These are economies that are relatively small and open, and that are linked to the German economy sufficiently closely to be willing in essence to subordinate their monetary policies to the Bundesbank: the Netherlands, Luxembourg, Austria, and probably Belgium and Denmark.

Under the terms of the Maastricht Treaty, the countries that will be admitted to EMU by the end of the decade will be only those that meet four tests. The candidate's currency must have succeeded in remaining within the EMS band for two years; its inflation rate must be close to that of the three best-performing EU countries; the same must hold for its interest rates; and its budget deficit and debt should not exceed specified fractions of GDP. The signatories to the agreement hoped in this way to assure convergence of macroeconomic policies. While the four Maastricht tests do not coincide completely with the optimum currency area criteria, European leaders are likely to judge most of the north European countries named above as meriting admission.

The second point is that European countries are gradually becoming more highly integrated with one another economically, and more willing to think of themselves as being permanently embedded in a common European space, so that they are a bit more likely to meet the optimum currency area criteria with each decade that passes. A case in point is France. Each time the French franc bumped up sharply against the limit in the Snake band, the French government would drop out of the agreement, rather than alter its policies. The EMS, founded in 1979, constituted a more serious attempt at stabilization of European exchange rates and was more successful in the 1980s than the Snake had been. Its first important test arose when François Mitterrand first came to power in France in 1981, and tried to expand the French economy at a time when other European countries were not expanding theirs. The consequent balance-of-payments deficit and downward pressure on the French franc forced Mitterrand to choose between abandoning the expansionary policies and abandoning the exchange rate constraint. Partly for the sake of the EMS and the cause of European integration, he chose the former. Thereafter the French monetary authorities were determined to maintain sufficiently anti-inflationary policies to keep the franc as strong in value as the mark.[48] The speculative attack against the French franc that succeeded in August 1993, requiring a subsequent widening of the band to +/-15 percent, cannot readily be attributed to any effort of the French to exercise monetary independence.

European integration continues to increase, partly as a result of such measures as the removal of (many, if not all) barriers to trade and labour mobility

[48] Sachs and Wyplosz (1986).

in 1992. Even if France, Italy, and other EU members do not satisfy the criteria for joining the optimum currency area in the 1990s, perhaps they will subsequently.

11. MARKET STRUCTURE EFFECTS OF EMU

What are the implications of different EMU scenarios for financial centres? By now it is clear to almost all that EMU will not happen until 1999 at the very earliest, and that if it is to happen in the foreseeable future, it will have to be on a two-speed basis. For well-known political and historical reasons, EMU will not be allowed to go ahead without France. Yet if a Franco-German monetary union goes ahead prematurely, or if a new shock hits during a delicate transition, we could see a replay of the currency instability of 1992–3. In that case, both monetary union and the integration of equity markets would be set back another five or ten years.

If, on the other hand, monetary union does succeed, then the structure of European equity trading may be altered considerably as a consequence. The primary continental trading systems are basically variations on the same theme: continuous electronic auctions. With currency costs and risks removed, and government-imposed currency matching requirements on pension funds rendered meaningless, the positive network externalities and economies of scale in trading service provision should swamp any remaining benefits to, or barriers supporting, trading fragmentation along national lines. Thus, the forces for concentrating trading – at least within different market architectures (e.g. continuous auction, call auction, and dealer market) – will be very strong. Some exchanges can be expected to merge, while others will simply disband. Monetary union may therefore act as a far more powerful force for liberalizing European market structure than any directive ever could.

References

Adler, Michael and Bernard Dumas, 1983. 'International Portfolio Choice and Corporation Finance: A Synthesis', *Journal of Finance*, 38: 925–84.

Alesina, Alberto and Vittorio Grilli, 1992. 'The European Central Bank: Reshaping Monetary Policies in Europe', in M. Canzoneri, V. Grilli and P. Masson, eds, *Establishing a Central Bank: Issues in Europe and Lessons from the US*, Cambridge University Press, Cambridge, 49–77.

Amihud, Y., 1993. 'Exchange Rates and the Valuation of Equity Shares', in Y. Amihud and R. Levich, eds, *Exchange Rates and Corporate Performance*, Business One, Irwin, Homewood, IL.

Artis, Michael and Mark Taylor, 1990. 'Abolishing Exchange Control: The UK Experience', in A.S. Courakis and M.P. Taylor, eds, *Private Behaviour and Government Policy in Interdependent Economies*, Clarendon Press, Oxford, Chapter 5, 129–58.

Bartov, Eli and Gordon Bodnar, 1994. 'Firm Valuation, Earnings Expectations and the Exchange Rate Exposure Effect', *Journal of Finance*, 49, 5: 1755–86.

Bartov, Eli, Gordon Bodnar and Aditya Kaul, 1994. 'Exchange Rate Variability and the Riskiness of US Multinational Firms: Evidence from the Breakdown of the Bretton Woods System', Weiss Centre for International Financial Research Working Paper No. 94–6, Wharton School, University of Pennsylvania.

Bayoumi, Tamim and Barry Eichengreen, 1993. 'Shocking Aspects of European Monetary Unification', in F. Giavazzi and F. Torres, eds, *The Transition to Economic and Monetary Union in Europe*, Cambridge University Press, New York.

Beckers, Stan, Richard Grinold, Andrew Rudd and Dan Stefek, 1992. 'The Relative Importance of Common Factors Across the European Equity Markets', *Journal of Banking and Finance*, 16, 75–95.

Blanchard, Olivier and Lawrence Katz, 1992. 'Regional Evolutions', *Brookings Papers on Economic Activity*, No. 1, 1–61.

Bodnar, G. and W. Gentry, 1993. 'Exchange Rate Exposure and Industry Characteristics: Evidence from Canada, Japan and the US', *Journal of International Money and Finance*, 12: 29–45.

Bosner-Neal, Catherine, Greggory Brauer, Robert Neal and Simon Wheatley, 1990. 'International Investment Restrictions and Closed-end Country-fund Prices', *Journal of Finance*, 45: 523–47.

Buiter, Willem, Giancarlo Corsetti and Nouriel Roubini, 1993. '"Excessive Deficits": Sense and Nonsense in the Treaty of Maastricht', Centre for Economic Policy Research, London; *Economic Policy*, 16, Cambridge University Press, Cambridge and Editions de la Maison des Sciences de l'Homme, Paris, April.

Campbell, Jonathan and Kenneth Froot, 1994. 'International Experiences with Securities Transactions Taxes', in J. Frankel (ed.), *The Internationalization of Equity Markets*, University of Chicago Press, Chicago.

Caves, Richard, Jeffrey Frankel and Ronald Jones, 1996. 'World Trade and Payments', Seventh Edition, HarperCollins, New York.

Directorate-General for Economic and Financial Affairs, Commission of the European Communities, 1990. 'One Market, One Money: An Evaluation of the Potential Benefits and Costs of Forming an Economic and Monetary Union', *European Economy*, No. 44, October.

Diwan, Ishac, Lemma Senbet and Vihang Errunza, 1993. 'The Pricing of Country-funds and their Role in Capital Mobilization for Emerging Economies', PRE Working Paper No. 1058, The World Bank, Washington, DC.

Dornbusch, Rudiger, 1982. 'Equilibrium and Disequilibrium Exchange Rates', *Zeitschrift für Wirtschafts-und Sozialwissenschaften*, 102, 6: 573–99. (Reprinted in Dornbusch, R., *Dollars, Debts, and Deficits*, MIT Press, Cambridge, MA.)

Drummen, Martin and Heinz Zimmerman, 1992. 'The Structure of European Stock Returns, *Financial Analyst Journal*, 48: 15–26.

Dumas, Bernard, 1993. 'Partial-Equilibrium vs. General-Equilibrium Models of International Capital Market Equilibrium', Groupe H.E.C. (Hautes Etudes Commerciales), France. Forthcoming in Frederick van der Ploeg (ed.), *Handbook of International Macroeconomics*, Basil Blackwell, Oxford.

Edison, Hali and Michael Melvin, 1990. 'The Determinants and Implications of the Choice of an Exchange Rate System', in William Haraf and Thomas Willett (eds), *Monetary Policy for a Volatile Global Economy*, AEI Press, Washington, DC.

Eichengreen, Barry, 1988. 'Real Exchange Rate Behaviour Under Alternative International Monetary Regimes: Interwar Evidence', *European Economic Review*, 32: 363–71.

Eijffinger, Sylvester and Jan Lemmen, 1994. 'The Catching up of European Money Markets: The Degree vs. the Speed of Integration', Centre for Economic Research, Tilburg University, The Netherlands, May.

Eijffinger, Sylvester and Jan Lemmen, 1995. 'Money Markets Integration in Europe', *Swiss Journal of Economics and Statistics*, 131, 1: 3–37.

Engel, Charles, 1994. 'Tests of CAPM on an International Portfolio of Bonds and Stocks', in J. Frankel (ed.), *The Internationalization of Equity Markets*, University of Chicago Press, Chicago.

Eun, C. and S. Shim, 1989. 'International Transmission of Stock Market Movements', *Journal of Financial and Quantitative Analysis*, 24: 241–56.

Frankel, Jeffrey, 1979. 'The Diversifiability of Exchange Risk', *Journal of International Economics*, 9, North-Holland Press, Amsterdam, August: 379–93.

Frankel, Jeffrey, 1982. 'In Search of the Exchange Risk Premium: A Six-Currency Test Assuming Mean-Variance Optimization', *Journal of International Money and Finance* 1 December: 255–74. (Reprinted in R. MacDonald and M. Taylor (eds), 'Exchange Rate Economics', Vol. II, *International Library of Critical Writings in Economics*, Edward Elgar Publishing, Cheltenham, Glos., 1992.)

Frankel, Jeffrey, 1983. 'Estimation of Portfolio: Balance Functions that are Mean-Variance Optimizing: The Mark and the Dollar', *European Economic Review*, 23: 315–27.

Frankel, Jeffrey, 1991. 'Quantifying International Capital Mobility in the 1980's', in D. Bernheim and J. Shoven (eds), *National Saving and Economic Performance*, University of Chicago Press, Chicago, 227–60. (Reprinted in Dilip Das (ed.), *International Finance: Contemporary Issues*, Routledge, London, 1993.)

Frankel, Jeffrey, 1993a. '"Excessive Deficits": Sense and Nonsense in the Treaty of Maastricht; Comments on Buiter, Corsetti and Roubini', *Economic Policy*, 16, Cambridge University Press, Cambridge, and Editions de la Maison des Sciences de l'Homme, Paris, April, 92–7.

Frankel, Jeffrey, 1993b. *On Exchange Rates*, MIT Press, Cambridge, MA.

Frankel, Jeffrey, 1994. 'Introduction', in J. Frankel (ed.), *The Internationalization of Equity Markets*, University of Chicago Press, Chicago.

Frankel, Jeffrey and Menzie Chinn, 1993. 'Exchange Rate Expectations and the Risk Premium: Tests for a Cross-Section of 17 Currencies', *Review of International Economics*, 1, 2 (June), 136–44.

Frankel, Jeffrey and Steve Phillips, 1992. 'The European Monetary System: Credible at Last?', *Oxford Economic Papers*, 44: 791–816.

Frankel, Jeffrey, Steve Phillips and Menzie Chinn, 1993. 'Financial and Currency Integration in the European Monetary System: The Statistical Record', Centre for German and European Studies, U.C. Berkeley, in Francisco Torres and Francesco Giavazzi (eds), *Adjustment and Growth in the European Monetary Union*, Cambridge University Press, Cambridge: 270–306.

Frankel, Jeffrey and Andrew Rose, 1995. 'A Survey of Empirical Research on Nominal Exchange Rates', NBER Working Paper No. 4865, September 1994, in Gene Grossman and Kenneth Rogoff (eds), *Handbook of International Economics*, 3, North-Holland Press, Amsterdam.

Frankel, Jeffrey, and Shang-Jin Wei, 1995. 'European Integration and the Regionalization of World Trade and Currencies: The Economics and the Politics', in Barry Eichengreen, Jeffry Frieden, and Jurgen von Hagen (eds), *Monetary and Fiscal Policy in an Integrated Europe*, Springer-Verlag, Heidelberg, forthcoming.

French, Kenneth and James Poterba, 1991. 'Investor Diversification and International Equity Markets', *American Economic Review*, 81 (May): 222–6.

Froot, Kenneth, 1993. 'Currency Hedging Over Long Horizons: Empirical Evidence', National Bureau of Economic Research, No. 4355, May.

Giavazzi, Francesco and Luigi Spaventa, 1990. 'The "New" EMS', Centre for Economic Policy Research Paper No. 369, in P. De Grauwe and L. Papademos (eds), *The European Monetary System in the 1990s,* Longman, London.

Goldstein, Morris and David Folkerts-Landau, 1993. 'The Single European Financial Market', Chapter V in *International Capital Markets: Part II, Systemic Issues in*

International Finance, International Monetary Fund, Washington, DC, August.

Golub, Stephen, 1994. 'International Diversification of Social and Private Risk: The US and Japan', *Japan and the World Economy*, 6.

Goodhart, Charles, 1988. 'The Foreign-exchange Market: A Random Walk with a Dragging Anchor', *Economica*, 55: 437–60.

Grauer, R.R. and Nils H. Hakansson, 1987, 'Gains from International Diversification: 1968–85 Returns on Portfolios of Stocks and Bonds', *Journal of Finance*, 42: 721–39.

Grilli, Vittorio, 1989. 'Europe 1992: Issues and Prospects for the Financial Markets', *Economic Policy*, 9, October, 388–421.

Hakkio, Craig, 1994, 'Should We Throw Sand in the Gears of Financial Markets?', Federal Reserve Bank of Kansas City, *Economic Review*, 2, 17–30.

Hardouvelis, Gikas, Rafael La Porta and Thierry Wizman, 1994. 'What Moves the Discount on Country Equity Funds?', in J. Frankel (ed.), *The Internationalization of Equity Markets*, University of Chicago Press, Chicago.

Helpman, Elhanan, 1981. 'An Exploration into the Theory of Exchange Rate Regimes', *Journal of Political Economy*, 89: 865–90.

Helpman, E. and A. Razin, 1979. 'A Consistent Comparison of Alternative Exchange Rate Regimes', *Canadian Journal of Economics*, 12: 394–409.

Heston, Steven and K. Geert Rouwenhorst, 1994. 'Does Industrial Structure Explain the Benefits of International Diversification?', *Journal of Financial Economics*, 36, North-Holland Press, Amsterdam, August: 3–27.

Hodrick, Robert, 1978. 'An Empirical Analysis of the Monetary Approach to the Determination of the Exchange Rate', in J. Frenkel and H.G. Johnson (eds), *The Economics of Exchange Rates*, Addison-Wesley, Reading, MA, 97–116.

Hodrick, Robert, 1988. *The Empirical Evidence on the Efficiency of Forward and Futures Foreign Exchange Markets*, Harwood Academic Publishers, Chur, Switzerland.

Ito, Takatoshi and Weng-Ling Lin, 1994. 'Price Volatility and Volume Spillovers Between the Tokyo and New York Stock Markets', in Jeffrey Frankel (ed.), *The Internationalization of Equity Markets*, University of Chicago Press, Chicago.

Jorion, Philippe. 1989a. 'The Linkages Between National Stock Markets', in Robert Aliber (ed.), *The Handbook of International Financial Management*, Dow-Jones-Irwin, Homewood, IL.

Jorion, Philippe. 1989b. 'Asset Allocation with Hedged and Unhedged Foreign Stocks and Bonds', *Journal of Portfolio Management*, Summer.

King, Mervyn and Sushil Wadwhani, 1990. 'Transmission of Volatility Between Stock Markets', *Review of Financial Studies*, 3: 5–33.

Kouri, Pentti and Jorge de Macedo, 1978. 'Exchange Rates and the International Adjustment Process', *Brookings Papers on Economic Activity*, 1: 111–50.

Krugman, Paul and Marcus Miller, 1993. 'Why Have a Target Zone?', CEPR Discussion Paper No. 718, *Carnegie-Rochester Conference Series*, 38: 279–314, North Holland Press, Amsterdam.

Levy, Haim and Marshall Sarnat, 1970. 'International Diversification of Investment Portfolios', *American Economic Review*, 60, 4 (September): 668–75.

McKinnon, Ronald, 1963. 'Optimum Currency Areas', *American Economic Review*, 53 (September): 717–24.

Meese, Richard A., 1986. 'Testing for Bubbles in Exchange Markets', *Journal of Political Economy*, 94, 345–73.

Migué, Jean-Luc, 1993. 'Federalism and Free Trade', Hobart Paper No. 122, Institute of Economic Affairs, London.

Mundell, Robert, 1961. 'The Theory of Optimal Currency Areas', *American Economic Review*, 51 (November), 509–17.

Mussa, Michael, 1990. 'Exchange Rates in Theory and in Reality', *Essays in International Finance*, 179, Princeton University, Princeton, NJ.

Obstfeld, Maurice, 1986. 'Balance of Payments Crises and Devaluation', *American Economic Review*, 76, 1: 72–81.

Obstfeld, Maurice, 1994. 'International Capital Mobility in the 1990s', in Peter Kenen (ed.), *Understanding Interdependence: The Macroeconomics of the Open Economy*, Princeton University Press, Princeton, NJ.

Perold, André and Evan Schulman, 1988. 'The Free Lunch in Currency Hedging: Implications for Investment Policy and Performance Standards', *Financial Analysts Journal*, May, 45–50.

Revey, Patricia, 1981. 'Evolution and Growth of the United States Foreign Exchange Market', *Federal Reserve Bank of New York Quarterly Review*, 6, Autumn: 32–44.

Roll, Richard, 1992. 'Industrial Structure and the Comparative Behaviour of International Stock Market Indices', *Journal of Finance* 47: 3–42.

Rose, Andrew, 1994. 'Exchange Rate Volatility, Monetary Policy, and Capital Mobility: Empirical Evidence on the Holy Trinity', NBER Working Paper No. 4630, January.

Sachs, Jeffrey and Charles Wyplosz, 198., 'The Economic Consequences of François Mitterrand', *Economic Policy*, 2: 261–313.

Sala-i-Martin, Xavier and Jeffrey Sachs, 1992. 'Fiscal Federalism and Optimum Currency Areas', in M. Canzoneri, V. Grilli and P. Masson (eds), *Establishing a Central Bank: Issues in Europe and Lessons from the US*, Cambridge University Press, Cambridge, 195–219.

Solnik, Bruno, 1974. 'Why Not Diversify Internationally Rather than Domestically?', *Financial Analyst Journal*, 30: 48–54.

Steil, Benn, 1992. 'Regulatory Foundations for Global Capital Markets', *Finance and the International Economy, The AMEX Bank Review Prize Essays*, Vol. 6, Oxford University Press, Oxford.

Steil, Benn, 1993. *Competition, Integration and Regulation in EC Capital Markets*, Royal Institute of International Affairs, London.

Stockman, Alan, 1983. 'Real Exchange Rates under Alternative Nominal Exchange Rate Systems', *Journal of International Money and Finance*, 2, 2: 147–66.

Stulz, René, 1981. 'A Model of International Asset Pricing', *Journal of Financial Economics*, 9, December, 383–406.

Tesar, Linda and Ingrid Werner, 1992. 'Home Bias and the Globalization of Securities

Markets', NBER Working Paper No. 4218.

Tesar, Linda and Ingrid Werner, 1994. 'International Equity Transactions and US Portfolio Choice', in J. Frankel (ed.), *The Internationalization of Equity Markets*, University of Chicago Press, Chicago.

von Furstenberg, George and B.N. Jeon, 1989. 'International Stock Price Movements: Links and Messages', *Brookings Papers on Economic Activity*, 1: 125–67.

Williamson, John, 1985. *The Exchange rate System*, Policy Analyses in International Economics No. 5, Institute for International Economics, Washington, DC, September 1983. Revised 1985.

Wyplosz, Charles, 1986. 'Capital Flows Liberalization and the EMS: A French Perspective', INSEAD Working Paper No. 86/40, Fontainebleau, France; also in *European Economy*, European Economic Community, June 1988.

INDEX